Exploring Intertextuality

Exploring Intertextuality

Diverse Strategies for
New Testament Interpretation of Texts

Edited by
B. J. Oropeza
Steve Moyise

 CASCADE *Books* · Eugene, Oregon

EXPLORING INTERTEXTUALITY
Diverse Strategies for New Testament Interpretation of Texts

Cascade Books
An Imprint of Wipf and Stock Publishers
199 W. 8th Ave., Suite 3
Eugene, OR 97401

www.wipfandstock.com

PAPERBACK ISBN: 978-1-4982-2311-9
HARDCOVER ISBN: 978-1-4982-2313-3
EBOOK ISBN: 978-1-4982-2312-6

Cataloguing-in-Publication data:

Names: Oropeza, B. J. | Moyise, Steve

Title: Exploring Intertextuality : Diverse Strategies for New Testament Interpretation of Texts / B. J. Oropeza and Steve Moyise.

Description: Eugene, OR: Cascade Books, 2016 | Includes bibliographical references and indices.

Identifiers: ISBN 978-1-4982-2311-9 (paperback) | ISBN 978-1-4982-2313-3 (hardcover) | ISBN 978-1-4982-2312-6 (ebook)

Subjects: LCSH: Bible. New Testament—Relation to the Old Testament. | Intertextuality. | Bible—Criticism, interpretation, etc.

Classification: BS511.2 E8 2016 (print) | BS511.2 (ebook)

Manufactured in the U.S.A.   OCTOBER 3, 2016

Contents

Contributors | vii

Abbreviations | x

Introduction: Diverse Strategies for Intertextual Interpretation | xiii

Part I: Established Strategies

1 Dialogical Intertextuality | 3
   Steve Moyise

2 Hypertextuality | 16
   Gil Rosenberg

3 Metalepsis | 29
   Jeannine K. Brown

4 Rhetoric of Quotations | 42
   Christopher D. Stanley

5 Midrash | 63
   Lori Baron and B. J. Oropeza

6 Shadows and Realities | 81
   Kenneth L. Schenck

7 Mimesis | 93
   Dennis R. MacDonald

8 Poststructural Intertextuality | 106
   Gary A. Phillips

9 Intertextuality Based on Categorical Semiotics | 128
   Stefan Alkier

Part II: Eclectic and Novel Strategies

10   Sociorhetorical Intertexture | 151
Roy R. Jeal

11   Narrative Transformation | 165
J. R. Daniel Kirk

12   Orality and Intertextuality | 176
James F. McGrath

13   Enunciation, Personification, and Intertextuality | 187
Alain Gignac

14   Relevance Theory and Intertextuality | 207
Peter S. Perry

15   Multidimensional Intertextuality | 222
Erik Waaler

16   Reference-Text-Oriented Allusions | 242
Korinna Zamfir and Joseph Verheyden

17   Probability of Intertextual Borrowing | 254
Elizabeth A. Myers

Bibliography | 273

Author Index | 301

Biblical and Ancient Literature Index | 307

Subject Index | 321

Contributors

Stefan Alkier is Prof. Dr. for New Testament and History of the Early Church at Fachbereich Evangelische Theologie, Johann Wolfgang Goethe-Universität, Frankfurt am Main, Germany. He is author of the book, *The Reality of the Resurrection: The New Testament Witness* (2013), and co-author of *Reading the Bible Intertextually* (2009).

Lori Baron holds a PhD in New Testament from Duke University. Her book, *The Shema in the Gospel of John* (Mohr-Siebeck, forthcoming), explores how the Fourth Gospel uses the Shema (Deut 6:4–5) in order to include Jesus within the divine unity and to portray believers in Jesus as unified, restored, eschatological Israel. She is currently teaching Biblical Greek at Duke Divinity School.

Jeannine K. Brown is Professor of New Testament at Bethel Seminary, San Diego. She is the author of *Scripture as Communication* (2007), *Matthew* in the Teach the Text series (2015). She is co-editor of *Dictionary of Jesus and the Gospels* (with Green and Perrin; 2013). Brown is a standing member of the Committee on Bible Translation (NIV).

Alain Gignac is Professor of New Testament and Hermeneutics at Université de Montréal, Canada. He published a Commentary on *Romans* for Éditions du Cerf, France. He is an active member of the French speaking international research network, Réseau de recherche Narratologie et Bible (RRENAB).

Roy R. Jeal is Professor of Religion at Booth University College. His research and writing centers on literary, rhetorical, and sociorhetorical interpretations of New Testament texts. He is the author of *Exploring Philemon: Freedom, Brotherhood, and Partnership in the New Society* (Rhetoric of Religious Antiquity, Society of Biblical Literature, 2015).

J. R. Daniel Kirk, PhD Duke University, has been a New Testament professor at Fuller Theological Seminary and Biblical Theological Seminary. His books include *A Man Attested by God: the Human Jesus of the Synoptic Gospels* and *Unlocking Romans: Resurrection and the Justification of God* (2008).

Dennis R. MacDonald is a Research Professor at the Claremont School of Theology. His is the author of a dozen books, most recently *The Gospels and Homer: Imitations of Greek Epic in Mark and Luke-Acts* (2014), *Luke and Vergil: Imitations of Classical Greek Literature* (2014), and *Mythologizing Jesus: From Jewish Teacher to Epic Hero* (2015).

James F. McGrath, PhD University of Durham, is the Clarence L. Goodwin Chair in New Testament Language and Literature at Butler University. He is author of many publications such as *The Only True God: Early Christian Monotheism in Its Jewish Context* (2009) and *John's Apologetic Christology* (2004). He blogs at Exploring Our Matrix on the Patheos web site.

Elizabeth Myers is an independent New Testament scholar with education and experience in the engineering profession and biblical and scientific fields of study. She holds academic degrees in multiple disciplines, including a PhD in Biblical Studies, ThM, MDiv, MS in Management of Technology, and BS in Electrical Engineering and Computer Science.

Peter S. Perry is pastor of St. John's Lutheran Church in Glendale, AZ and Adjunct Faculty at Fuller Theological Seminary-Arizona. He is the author of *The Rhetoric of Digressions: Ancient Communication and Revelation 7:1–17 and 10:1—11:13* (2009), and articles such as "Relevance Theory in the Performance of Revelation 17–19," *The Bible Translator* 66 (2015).

Gary A. Phillips is the Edgar H. Evans Professor of Religion and former dean at Wabash College. He is co-author of *The Postmodern Bible (1995)*, and co-editor of *Intertextuality and Reading the Bible (1995)*, and *Representing the Irreparable: The Shoah, the Bible, and the Art of Samuel Bak (2008)*. His interests focus on poststructural hermeneutics of the Bible.

Gil Rosenberg is a PhD candidate in Religious and Theological Studies at Iliff School of Theology and the University of Denver. He has published in the journals *Biblical Interpretation* and *The Bible & Critical Theory*, and is interested in reading the Hebrew Bible in conversation with political theory, philosophy and literary theory, and gender and sexuality studies.

Kenneth Schenck is Professor of New Testament and Ancient Languages in Indiana Wesleyan University's School of Theology and Ministry, and served as dean of Wesley Seminary (Indiana). He is author of numerous publications including, *Cosmology and Eschatology in Hebrews: The Setting of the Sacrifice* (2007) and *A Brief Guide to Philo* (2005).

Christopher D. Stanley is Professor of Theology at St. Bonaventure University in New York. He is the author of *Paul and the Language of Scripture* (1992) and *Arguing With Scripture: The Rhetoric of Quotations in the Letters of Paul* (2004) along with numerous articles and two edited books on Paul's use of Scripture.

Joseph Verheyden, DTheol, is currently Professor of New Testament Studies in the Faculty of Theology and Religious Studies at the University of Leuven, Belgium. He recently co-edited *The Elijah-Elisha Narrative in the Composition of Luke* (2014), *Studies in the Gospel of John and Its Christology* (2014), and *Christ and the Emperor: The Gospel Evidence* (2014).

Erik Waaler, DTheol, is Associate Professor and Rector of the New Testament at NLA University College in Bergen, Norway. He is the author of the book, *The Shema and the First Commandment in First Corinthians: An Intertextual Approach to Paul's Re-reading of Deuteronomy* (2008) and several articles related to the use of Old Testament texts found in Ketef Hinnom, Jerusalem.

Korinna Zamfir, Prof. Dr., is Faculty of Roman Catholic Theology at Babes-Bolyai University, Romania, and is author of *Men and Women in the Household of God: A Contextual Approach to Roles and Ministries in the Pastoral Epistles* (2013).

Abbreviations

AB	Anchor Bible
ABD	*Anchor Bible Dictionary* (David Noel Freedman, ed.; 6 vols., 1992)
BECNT	Baker Exegetical Commentary on the New Testament
BETL	Bibliotheca Ephemeridum Theologicarum Lovaniensium
BNTC	Black's New Testament Commentaries
BZNW	Beihefte zur Zeitschrift für die neutestamentliche Wissenschaft
CSEL	Corpus Scriptorum Ecclesiasticorum Latinorum
EKK	Evangelisches–katholischer Kommentar zum Neuen Testament
FRLANT	Forschungen zur Religion und Literatur des Alten and Neuen Testaments
HUCA	*Hebrew Union College Annual*
HUT	Hermeneutische Untersuchungen zur Theologie
ICC	International Critical Commentary
JAJSup	Journal of Ancient Judaism Supplements
JBL	*Journal of Biblical Literature*
JSJSup	Journal for the Study of Judaism, Supplement
JSNTSup	Journal for the Study of the New Testament, Supplement Series
JSOT	*Journal for the Study of the Old Testament*

LXX	Septuagint
MT	Masoretic Text
NCBC	New Century Bible Commentary
NIGTC	New International Greek Testament Commentary
NovT	*Novum Testamentum*
NTD	Das Neue Testament Deutsch
NTL	New Testament Library
NTM	New Testament Message
NTOA	Novum Testamentum et Orbis Antiquus
NRSV	New Revised Standard Version
NTS	*New Testament Studies*
PG	*Patrologia graeca* (J.-P. Migne, ed.)
RRA	Rhetoric of Religious Antiquity
RNT	Regensburger Neues Testament
RRENAB	Réseau de la Narratologie et Bible
SNT	Studien zum Neuen Testament
SNTSMS	Society for New Testament Studies Monograph Series
SPhA	Studies in Philo of Alexandria
SPhilo	*Studia Philonica*
TANZ	Texte und Arbeiten zum neuntestamentlichen Zeitalter
TDNT	*Theological Dictionary of the New Testament* (Kittel and Bromiley, eds.)
VoxR	*Vox Reformata*
VTSup	Vetus Testamentum Supplement
WBC	Word Biblical Commentary
WUNT	Wissenschaftliche Untersuchungen zum Neuen Testament

INTRODUCTION

Diverse Strategies for
New Testament Intertextuality

This volume aims to provide both advanced students and academics with an introduction to various approaches to the intertextual interpretation of the New Testament. By intertextuality we mean the study of how a given text is connected with other texts (broadly understood) outside of itself and how those texts affect the interpretation of the given text.[1] This definition moves beyond what is often referred to as the "Use of the Old Testament in the New." It opens up texts to fresh interpretations by engaging with contexts, themes, traditions, and ideologies extending well beyond a specific quotation. As such, intertextual studies can provide rewarding insights for those who engage in it. In each chapter the reader will be introduced to the respective intertextual approach or strategy and see how it can be used with a specific New Testament text. The authors bring the selected reading into sharper relief with their respective approaches, and they provide recommended resources that will invite readers to pursue other studies related to the strategies.

This book is divided into two parts. In part I, the authors describe approaches that have been around for some time and are now part of the landscape of what is sometimes called "literary approaches to the Bible." Most were part of a cultural shift away from an exclusively historical study of the Bible and can be found in numerous books and articles over the last few decades. In part II, we present a selection of more recent approaches that might be described as eclectic or novel, or both. Most of the chapters

---

1. On the definition of "intertextuality" and a survey of its use among major scholars, see Oropeza, "Intertextuality," 1.453–63.

in part II were presented by the respective scholars at the Society of Biblical Literature's "Intertextuality in the New Testament" sessions between the years of 2008–2013.[2] They have been adapted to a more user-friendly style and format for this volume.

Although text references and allusions are clearly evident in ancient texts, the term "intertextuality" is relatively new, penned by literary critic and philosopher Julia Kristeva when involved with the *Tel Quel* editorial team in Paris during the late 1960s.[3] For Kristeva, any text becomes "a mosaic of quotations" that can transform and be transformed by other texts.[4] Biblical scholars have always tried to understand how the New Testament authors arrived at their interpretations of scripture, especially after the discovery of the Dead Sea Scrolls. They even acknowledged that sometimes a text can support multiple interpretations, as in the use of Gen 15:6 ("Abraham believed God, and it was reckoned to him as righteousness") in Rom 4:3 and James 2:23. However, the assumption was that texts usually have a single meaning (what the author intended), even if it is sometimes difficult from this distance to discover what that was. Kristeva argues that given the complex interactions between texts, readers are inevitably involved in the production of meaning, and so multiple interpretations are not so much the exception as the rule. One of the simplest examples of this draws on Mikhail Bakhtin's notion of dialogism, where the "voice" of one of the characters in a novel is contrary to the voice of the author. In our first chapter, Steve Moyise draws on this to show that the juxtaposition of Lion and Lamb in Revelation 5 not only causes a reinterpretation of the Lion (victory is through self-sacrifice), it also causes a reinterpretation of the Lamb (he conquers as "Lord of lords and King of kings").

Given the perspective that the meaning of texts is continually being altered when transposed to new contexts and locations, it is not surprising that intertextuality itself might be reconfigured during the immediate decades that followed the term's origin. Thus it has been used to apply structural models to interpret texts, despite its origins in poststructuralism.[5] In

2. This section of the SBL was chaired by B. J. Oropeza, founder of the section. As of this publication, it is now chaired by Erik Waaler and Max Lee (co-chair). Special thanks to Erik, Max, and the steering committee members who have served (past and present): Lori Baron, Roy Jeal, James McGrath, Rodrigo Morales, Steve Moyise, H. Junia Pokrifka, Love Sechrest, Alice Yafeh-Deigh.

3. Kristeva, *Desire in Language*, 64–67; Moi, *Kristeva Reader*, 3–9; McAfee, *Julia Kristeva*, 4–8.

4. Moi, *Kristeva Reader*, 37.

5. E.g., Riffaterre, *Semiotics in Poetry*; Genette, *Palimpsests*; the latter especially maintains a growing influence on biblical scholars (e.g., Larsson, "Intertextual Density," 309–31). Movement away from intertextuality's origins has been criticized by some

chapter 2, Gil Rosenberg provides an example of this through his use of hypertextuality, which belongs to an interpretative system popularized by literary theorist Gérard Genette. Among other texts, he compares the genealogy in Matthew 1 with Ruth 4 and 1 Chronicles 1–3.

Many scholars have come to adopt an intertextual approach through reading Richard Hays's highly influential book, *Echoes of Scripture in the Letters of Paul* (1989). Hays emphasized the term metalepsis for when the reader is invited to go beyond the actual words of a quotation or allusion and draw on its wider context to interpret the New Testament text. Jeaninne Brown in chapter 3 exemplifies this in her reading of Psalm 34 [33LXX] in 1 Pet 3:10–12 and Genesis 4 in relation to the parable of forgiveness (Matt 18). Such approaches have led to many insights, but it should be noted that they have also been subject to criticism, notably that they might be assuming a level of literary sophistication that is simply anachronistic.[6] In chapter 4 Christopher Stanley draws our attention to this, assessing the capabilities of ancient audiences and the importance of Paul's rhetoric for overcoming it. His case study is on the use of Isa 28:7–13 in 1 Cor 14:20–25.

In 1990 Daniel Boyarin wrote a significant book on Jewish interpretation, *Intertextuality and the Reading of Midrash*, which among other things, suggested a parallel between Kristeva's idea of a "mosaic of texts" and the way that the Torah functions in Midrash. In chapter 5, Lori Baron and B. J. Oropeza explore how some of Hillel's traditional principles of interpretation provides insights into Paul's exegesis in 1 Cor 10:1–11. Somewhat differently, in chapter 6, Ken Schenck looks at Philo's interpretation of Scripture as an example of "foreshadowing" and the light this sheds on the letter to the Hebrews; and in chapter 7, Dennis MacDonald works with the ancient idea of mimesis (imitation), as he compares the order of events and sometimes specific words and phrases in Mark's Gospel with portions of Homer's *Iliad* and *Odyssey*.

Also in the 1990s scholars such as Timothy Beal, Gary Phillips, and George Aichele returned to a poststructural basis for biblical intertextuality (as in Kristeva's original idea).[7] Phillips in chapter 8 contributes to our

---

(e.g., Meek, "Intertextuality, Inner-Biblical Exegesis," 280–91; Hatina, "Intertextuality and Historical Criticism," 28–43; Van Wolde, "Trendy Intertextuality?" 43–49) and encouraged by others (e.g., Carr, "Many Uses of Intertextuality,"515–16; Cook, "Intertextual Readings," 119–34; Litwak, *Echoes of Scripture*, 49–51; cf. Culler, *Pursuit of Signs*, 105–111; Friedman, "Weavings," 154).

6. E.g., Evans and Sanders, *Paul and the Scriptures of Israel*; Porter, "Use of the Old Testament," 79–96; "Further Comments," 98–110; Hübner, "Intertextualität," 881–98. For rejoinders, see Hays, "On the Rebound," 70–96; Lucas, "Assessing Stanley E. Porter's Objections," 93–111.

7. Beal, "Ideology and Intertextuality," 27–39; "Intertextuality"; Aichele and Phillips,

volume with a poststructural reading of the slaughter of the innocents in Matthew 1, which finds parallels in a number of texts, past and present, and highlights Samuel Bak's artistic work, *Collective,* as he stresses the ideas of textual instability and responsible reading. In chapter 9 Stefan Alkier ends the strategies we explore in Part I by presenting his approach of intertextuality through semiotics, which attempts to forge a way between the classical impasse of synchronic and diachronic text reading. His approach, which invites a conversation with both structural and poststructural interpretations, is exhibited through his reading of Matthew 1 with texts from Isaiah and Genesis.

Part II, which includes eclectic and novel strategies, begins with the sociorhetorical analytic in chapter 10. This approach that originates from Vernon Robbins combines inner texture, intertexture, social and cultural texture, ideological texture, and sacred texture.[8] This analytic has flourished and evolved to the present day with the Rhetoric of Religious Antiquity commentary series.[9] In Robbins's view, intertexture is not limited to scriptural referencing but may include an eclectic blend of oral, social, cultural, and historical elements. Roy Jeal adopts this approach as he interprets Col 2:11–15 in light of Jewish Scripture, Second Temple literature, and Plutarch. In chapter 11 J. R. Daniel Kirk presents his recent model of narrative transformation, a strategy based on mapping of the story sequencing developed by A. J. Greimas, to interpret the intertext of Jesus's temple cleansing in Mark 11:15–17 with Isaiah 56 and Jeremiah 7, as well as Rom 10:6–12 with Deuteronomy 30, and Acts 13:16–41 with Psalm 2.

James McGrath in chapter 12 combines orality and intertextuality as he explores the hymnic passage of Philippians 2:6–11 in conversation with Genesis and Isaiah 45. In chapter 13, Alain Gignac combines intertextuality and enunciation, a concept developed from Émile Benveniste, to examine Rom 9:25–29; 10:5–13; and 15:7–9 in the light of texts from Hosea, Leviticus, Deuteronomy, and Psalms. Peter Perry addresses the relationship between intertextuality and relevance theory, which claims that when people communicate they naturally maximize the impact of their communication while minimizing the processing effort required of the hearer/reader. In chapter 14, he applies this strategy to Jude's Epistle in comparison with *1 Enoch* and other Jewish literature, as well as the Beatle's famous song, *Hey Jude.* Erik Waaler presents us with a multi-dimensional recontextualization of intertexts in chapter 15. A total of twenty-eight change and continuity

---

Intertextuality and the Bible.

8. Robbins, *Tapestry of Discourse;* Robbins, *Exploring the Texture of Text.*

9. The series is published through Atlanta: SBL Press.

aspects are applied to Matt 23:31–46 in concert with various passages from Jewish Scripture and Second Temple literature.

Our final two contributions look at the relationship between particular New Testament documents. In chapter 16 Korinna Zamfir and Joseph Verheyden, adopting a strategy from Annette Merz, examine what they call reference-text-oriented allusions. Proposing the Pastoral letters as fictitious letters, they compare 2 Tim 4:1–8 with some of Paul's words in Philippians 1–2. Finally in chapter 17, Elizabeth Myers employs probability formulae to determine literary dependence and textual borrowing between James and Philippians and Jude and 2 Peter. This method may have far-reaching ramifications for other studies extending beyond mere NT borrowing.

It will be clear from these lucid contributions that the term intertextuality has become an umbrella term for a diverse range of reading strategies.[10] It is also true that scholars use the terms quotation, allusion, and echo in different ways.[11] Some would like to reserve the term quotation (or citation) for when a particular set of words are introduced by an introductory formula such as "It is written" or "Isaiah says." Others would call this a "marked" quotation and acknowledge that there are also "unmarked" quotations, which can be identified by either syntactical changes or simply close verbal agreement with another text. Allusion is even more slippery. There is general agreement that the parallel is less precise and may involve only a person, place, event, or a few words (perhaps only one if it is distinctive). However, there are major debates as to whether one can have an "unconscious" allusion (how could a reader tell?) and whether their function or role is substantially different from that of a quotation. Hays popularized the use of the term "echo" for a whisper-like parallel to another text or texts (drawing on John Hollander's *Figure of Echo*) but added that sometimes this can be "so loud that only the dullest or most ignorant reader could miss it."[12] Put another way, an echo can be quite loud if you are standing between two mountains and so "volume" (one of the seven criteria listed by Hays to verify an echo) is not necessarily a guide to its significance. The fact that each of these terms resists precise definition is one of the reasons why many have turned to intertextuality, a word that suggests complexity.

---

10. Moyise, "Intertextuality."

11. For various positions and nuances of these and related terms, see e.g., Hays, *Echoes*, 18–21, 29–32; Ben-Porat, "Poetics of Literary Allusion," 105–28; Fewell, *Reading between Texts*, 21; Porter, "Further Comments," 107–09; "Allusions and Echoes," 29–40; Gillmayr-Bucher, "Intertextuality," 18–20; Edenburg, "Intertextuality, Literary Competence," 144.

12. Hays, *Echoes*, 29.

It is also worth noting that a variety of terms, such as "Hebrew Bible," "Jewish Scripture" or simply "Scripture" is used for what Christians have traditionally termed "Old Testament." The point, of course, is that the term, "Old Testament" is anachronistic before the formation of the "New Testament" (though see 2 Pet 3:15–16). However, since it is generally recognized that the quotations and allusions in the New Testament are generally from a Greek translation (primarily Septuagint/LXX), the term "Hebrew Bible" is also misleading and it is unclear if "Jewish Scripture" or simply "Scripture" includes or excludes those books in the LXX that have no parallel in the Hebrew Bible. Thus some of our contributors continue to use "Old Testament" on the basis that the body of literature to which it refers is clearly understood. It should also be noted that some of our studies are interested in parallels outside of this body of literature.

It is our hope that both students and scholars might appreciate, learn, and put into practice some of the many strategies for intertextual interperetation presented in this volume.

Recommended Reading

Aichele, George, and Gary A. Phillips, eds. *Intertextuality and the Bible. Semeia* 69/70 (1995).

Allen, Graham. *Intertextuality.* 2nd ed. New Critical Idiom. London: Routledge, 2011.

Bauks, Michaela, Wayne Horowitz, and Armin Lange, eds. *Between Text and Text: The Hermeneutics of Intertextuality in Ancient Cultures and Their Afterlife in Medieval and Modern Times.* Journal of Ancient Judaism Supplements 6. Göttingen: Vandenhoeck & Ruprecht, 2013.

Bazerman, Charles. "Intertextuality: How Texts Rely on Other Texts." In *What Writing Does and How It Does It: An Introduction to Analyzing Texts and Textual Practices,* edited by Charles Bazerman and Paul A. Prior, 83–96. Mahwah: Lawrence Erlbaum, 2003.

Brodie, Thomas L., Dennis R. MacDonald, and Stanley E. Porter, eds. *The Intertextuality of the Epistles: Explorations of Theory and Practice.* New Testament Monographs 16. Sheffield: Sheffield Phoenix, 2007.

Broich, Ulrich and Manfred Pfister, eds. *Intertextualität: Formen, Funktionen, anglistische Fallstudien.* Tübingen: Niemeyer, 1985.

Clayton, Jay, and Eric Rothstein, eds. *Influence and Intertextuality in Literary History.* Madison, WI: University of Wisconsin, 1991.

Draisma, Sipke, ed. *Intertextuality in Biblical Writings: Essays in Honour of Bas van Iersel.* Kampen: Kok, 1989.

Emadl, Samuel. S. "Intertextuality in New Testament Scholarship: Significance, Criteria and the Art of Interpretation." *CBR* 14 (2015) 8–23.

Evans, Craig, and James A. Sanders, eds. *Early Christian Interpretation of Israel: Investigations and Proposals.* JSNTSS 148. Studies in Scripture in Early Judaism and Christianity 5. Sheffield: Sheffield Academic, 1997.

Evans, Craig A., and Jeremiah J. Johnston, eds. *Searching the Scriptures: Studies in Context and Intertextuality.* Studies in Scripture in Early Judaism and Christianity 19; LNTS. London: T. & T. Clark, 2015.

Evans, Craig A., and Shemaryahu Talmon, eds. *The Quest for Context and Meaning: Studies in Biblical Intertextuality in Honor of James A. Sanders.* Leiden: Brill, 1997.

Fewell, Danna Nolan, ed. *Reading Between Texts: Intertextuality and the Hebrew Bible.* Literary Currents in Biblical Interpretation. Louiseville, KY: Westminster John Knox, 1992.

Fishbane, Michael. "Types of Intertextuality." In *Congress Volume: Oslo 1998,* edited by André Lemaire and Magne Saebø, 39–44. VTSup 80. Leiden: Brill, 2000.

Hays, Richard B., Stefan Alkier, Leroy A. Huizenga, eds. *Reading the Bible Intertextually.* Waco: Baylor University Press, 2009.

Hebel, Udo J. *Intertextuality, Allusion, and Quotation: An International Bibliography of Critical Studies.* New York: Greenwood Press, 1989.

Huizenga, Leroy A. "The Old Testament in the New, Intertextuality and Allegory." *JSNT* 38 (2015) 17–35.

Marguerat, Daniel, and Adrian Curtis, eds. *Intertextualités: La Bible en échos.* Le Monde de la Bible 40. Geneva: Labor et Fides, 2000.

McKay, Niall. "Status Update: The Many Faces of Intertextuality in New Testament Study." *Religion & Theology* 20 (2013) 84–106.

Moi, Toril, ed. *The Kristeva Reader.* New York: Columbia University Press, 1986.

Morgan, Thaïs E. "Is There an Intertext in this Text? Literary and Interdisciplinary Approaches to Intertextuality." *American Journal of Semiotics* 3.4 (1985) 1–40.

Moyise, Steve. "Intertextuality and Biblical Studies: A Review." *Verbum et Ecclesia* 23 (2002) 418–31.

Oropeza, B. J. "Intertextuality." In *The Oxford Encyclopedia of Biblical Interpretation.* Edited by Steven L. McKenzie, 1.453–63. Oxford: Oxford University, 2013.

Orr, Mary. *Intertextuality: Debates and Contexts.* Cambridge: Polity, 2003.

Plett, Heinrich F, ed. *Intertextuality.* Research in Text Theory 15. Berlin: Walter de Gruyter, 1991.

Porter, Stanley E., and Christopher D. Stanley, eds. *As it is Written: Studying Paul's Use of Scripture.* SBLSS 50. Atlanta, GA: Scholars, 2008.

Shuart-Faris, Nora, and David Bloome, eds. *Uses of Intertextuality in Classroom and Educational Research.* Greenwich: Information Age, 2004.

Part I

Established Strategies

1

Dialogical Intertextuality

Steve Moyise

Though the study of how texts affect one another is as old as literature itself, Julia Kristeva is generally credited as the first to introduce the term *intertextualité* into literary discussion in 1969. Drawing on the work of Mikhail Bakhtin, Kristeva suggests a dialogical relationship between "texts," broadly understood as a system of codes or signs. Moving away from traditional notions of agency and influence, she suggests that such relationships are more like an "*intersection of textual surfaces* rather than a *point* (a fixed meaning)."[1] As Bakhtin says, "The word lives, as it were, on the boundary between its own context and another, alien context."[2] No text is an island and contrary to structuralist theory, it cannot be understood in isolation. It can only be understood as part of a web or matrix of other texts, themselves only to be understood in the light of other texts. Each new text disturbs the fabric of existing texts as it jostles for a place in the canon of literature. Intertextuality suggests that the meaning of a text is not fixed but open to revision as new texts come along and reposition it.[3] As the name suggests, "dialogical intertextuality" is interested in the interaction that takes place between such "textual surfaces." As Harriet Davidson says of T. S. Eliot's, *The Waste Land*, "The work alluded to reflects upon the present context even as

---

1. Conveniently found in Moi, *Kristeva Reader*, 36.

2. Conveniently found in Holquist, *Dialogic Imagination*, 284.

3. Critics have often discussed whether a text should be seen as primarily a window, painting, or mirror. Geoff Webb suggests that in the light of Bakhtin's work, perhaps the image of the "interactive website" affords a better model, where visitors effectively "update" the site by their interaction with it. See Webb, *Mark at the Threshold*, 9–10.

the present context absorbs and changes the allusion."[4] The point is that if an author points the reader to a particular source (whether that is a specific text, a trope, or other cultural phenomenon), it becomes another "voice" in the process of interpretation. The author may have a specific reason for doing this,[5] but once the reader has made the connection, the author cannot control the interactions that may result. Traditional biblical categories, like allegory, typology, and midrash often assume that the source text is entirely malleable to what is being done with it. When the interpretation has been made, there is no further role for the "voice" of the source text. Dialogical intertextuality operates with a more dynamic understanding of meaning, where the particular "voices" (intertexts) are not silenced but continue to affect one another. As Raj Nadella says:

> Dialogism is about a lively and constant exchange of ideas among the many, disparate voices. It seeks intersection—rather than integration—of divergent viewpoints, and it provides a platform for them to encounter each other on equal footing without necessarily coming into agreement.... Dialogism conceives of truth as that which requires more than one perspective.[6]

In his analysis of imitation in Renaissance poetry, one of Thomas Greene's categories is "dialectical imitation." He defines this as when a source text is allowed a subversive influence on the alluding text. Thus the alluding text "makes a kind of implicit criticism of its subtexts, its authenticating models, but it also leaves itself open to criticism from [the text]... it had begun by invoking."[7] The result, Greene says, is that the alluding text is "the locus of a struggle between two rhetorical or semiotic systems that are vulnerable to another and whose conflict cannot easily be resolved."[8] This is in contrast to "heuristic imitations," which come to us "advertising their derivation from the subtexts they carry with them, but having done

---

4. Davidson, *T. S. Eliot and Hermeneutics*, 117.

5. The question of whether one can make an unconscious allusion depends on definitions. People frequently use proverbial expressions ("where angels fear to tread") without intending a biblical reference. However, for those with a good knowledge of the Bible, they will function as an allusion whether intended or not. Thus Gaskin says that we should view "unconscious allusion" in the same way we view "unconscious desire" or "unconscious motive." It might not have been part of our thinking process, but it is demonstrated by our actions (in this case writing). See Gaskin, *Language, Truth, and Literature*, 237.

6. Nadella, *Dialogue Not Dogma*, 112. For an overview of recent scholarship, see Green, *Mikhail Bakhtin and Biblical Scholarship*.

7. Greene, *Light in Troy*, 45.

8. Ibid., 46.

that, they proceed to *distance themselves* from the subtexts and force us to recognize the poetic distance traversed."[9] It is the openness to mutual influence that is the essence of dialogical intertextuality.

Richard Hays draws on Greene (and John Hollander) in his analysis of the relationship between Paul and Moses in 2 Corinthians 3. On the surface, it appears that Paul is simply offering Moses as a "foil against which to commend the candor and boldness of his own ministry."[10] The generation of Moses was unable to see clearly, but those who respond to Paul's preaching have the "veil" removed (2 Cor 3:16). The reader is led to expect a completely negative verdict of religion under the old covenant, but the mention of "veil" reminds Paul that Moses did in fact remove his veil when he entered God's presence (Exod 34:34). Thus, Paul is able to "appropriate some of the mythical grandeur associated with the Sinai covenant—particularly the images of glory and transformation—even while he repudiates the linkage of his ministry to that covenant."[11] Hays calls this a "dissimile" and states:

> The rhetorical effect of this ambiguous presentation is an unsettling one, because it simultaneously posits and undercuts the glory of Moses' ministry. . . . Since Paul is arguing that the ministry of the new covenant outshines the ministry of the old in glory, it serves his purpose to exalt the glory of Moses; at the same time, the grand claims that he wants to make for his own ministry require that the old be denigrated.[12]

A similar example is found in Heb 12:18–25, where the author compares Christian experience with that of the Sinai generation. An initial denial ("You have not come . . .") is followed by a positive affirmation ("But you have come . . ."):

> You have not come to something that can be touched, a blazing fire, and darkness, and gloom, and a tempest, and the sound of a trumpet, and a voice whose words made the hearers beg that not another word be spoken to them. (Heb 12:18–19)

> . . . But you have come to Mount Zion and to the city of the living God, the heavenly Jerusalem, and to innumerable angels in festal gathering, and to the assembly of the firstborn who are

9. Ibid., 40. Thus "heuristic imitation involves a passage from one semiotic universe to another . . . dialectical imitation, when it truly engages two eras or two civilizations at a profound level, involves a conflict between two *mundi significantes*" (46).

10. Hays, *Echoes*, 147.

11. Ibid., 142.

12. Ibid., 132–33.

enrolled in heaven, and to God the judge of all, and to the spirits
of the righteous made perfect, and to Jesus, the mediator of a
new covenant, and to the sprinkled blood that speaks a better
word than the blood of Abel. (Heb 12:22–24)

However, it turns out that the denial also has a positive function, for
the warning "not to refuse the one who is speaking" is supported by the argument that "if they did not escape when they refused the one who warned
them on earth, how much less will we escape if we reject the one who warns
from heaven!" (Heb 12:25). Thus, even when an allusion attempts to deny
certain aspects of its source text, it is still able to add a "voice" (however
muted) to the interpretative process. Hays notes that this phenomenon has
also been observed of Milton, who "repeatedly denies the beauty of countless pagan paradises in comparison with Eden, while tacitly employing their
strong legendary associations to enhance and embellish its incomparable
perfections."[13]

A third example can be found in John's denial in Rev 21:22 that there is
a temple in the New Jerusalem, for "its temple is the Lord God the Almighty
and the Lamb." This comes as no surprise for those who know the story
recorded in John 2, where Jesus says, "Destroy this temple, and in three
days I will raise it up" (2:19), which the author of the Gospel interprets as a
reference to the "temple of his body" (2:21). However, what is surprising for
the reader of the book of Revelation is that John has been following fairly
precisely the sequence of events in the book of Ezekiel, which ends with a
detailed description of a new temple:

Ezekiel		*Revelation*	
37:10	Revival of dry bones	20:4	Saints come to life
37:21	Israel reunited under Da-vidic king	20:4	Saints rule with Christ for 1000 years
38:2–16	Gog of Magog roused for battle	20:8	Gog and Magog* roused for battle
38:22	Gog of Magog destroyed by fire	20:9	Gog and Magog destroyed by fire
39:4	Birds invited to gorge on corpses	19:21	Birds invited to gorge on corpses**
40:2	Transported in spirit to high mountain	21:10	Transported in spirit to high mountain

13. Ibid., 142. The quotation is from Lord, *Classical Presences*, 40–41.

40:5	Angel measures the temple	21:15	Angel measures the *city*
43:2	Temple full of the glory of God	21:23	*City* full of the glory of God
47:12	River of life, leaves for healing	22:1–2	River of life, leaves for healing
48:30–34	Three gates on each side of city, bearing the names of the 12 tribes	21:12–13	Three gates on each side of city, bearing the names of the 12 tribes.

*The LXX rendering is indicative of a tendency found as early as 4Q523 and developed in later rabbinic works (e.g. Aqiba in b. Ber. 7b) and the *targumim* (Exod 40:11; Num 11:26; Deut 32:39) to treat these as the names of two heathen leaders.

**It is possible that the change in order here was prompted by variations in the manuscript tradition, since in ms 967 and the Würzburg Codex of the Old Latin, Ezek 37 follows Ezek 38–39. See Lust, "Ezekiel 36–40," 517–33.

Up until Revelation 21:22, readers have been led to expect a description of a new temple, for that is what Ezekiel 40–48 is all about. They are probably expecting the description to have symbolic significance, as with so much in Revelation, but they are not expecting a complete denial. In part, John prepares them for this by saying that the city is measured (Rev 21:23) rather than the temple (Ezek 40:5), and God's glory fills the city (Rev 21:23) rather than the temple (Ezek 43:2). Nevertheless, the preceding allusions are so strong that we may adapt the quotation from Hays above and say that John "appropriates some of the mythical grandeur associated with Ezekiel's new temple—particularly the images of glory and transformation—even while he denies the very existence of a temple in the New Jerusalem."[14]

The Lion and the Lamb of Revelation 5

The three examples above demonstrate that even when a source is negated, its "voice" is not completely silenced and can bring associations and connotations that contribute to the interpretation of the text. How much more might this be true when the source is not denied but affirmed? The example that I explored in my dissertation was the juxtaposition of Lion and Lamb in Rev 5:5–6:[15]

> Then one of the elders said to me, "Do not weep. See, the Lion of the tribe of Judah, the Root of David, has conquered, so that

14. Hays, *Echoes*, 142.

15. Moyise, *Old Testament in the Book of Revelation*, 108–38.

he can open the scroll and its seven seals." Then I saw between the throne and the four living creatures and among the elders a Lamb standing as if it had been slaughtered, having seven horns and seven eyes, which are the seven spirits of God sent out into all the earth.

In this example, there is no denial of the source texts but a juxtaposition of contrasting images—John *hears* of the "Lion of the tribe of Judah" and *sees* a "Lamb standing as if it had been slaughtered." If connotations from denied images can continue to "speak" to the reader, then how much more is that true for positive assertions? However, that is not how the juxtaposition has been understood by most commentators. George Caird suggests that John wished to replace the violent imagery associated with a lion with that of a lamb and went on to assert that this is how Christians should read the whole of the Old Testament: "Wherever the Old Testament says 'Lion,' read 'Lamb.' Wherever the Old Testament speaks of the victory of the Messiah or the overthrow of the enemies of God, we are to remember that the gospel recognizes no other way of achieving these ends than the way of the Cross."[16]

John Sweet agrees, claiming that the "Lion of Judah, the traditional messianic expectation, is reinterpreted by the slain Lamb: God's power and victory lie in self-sacrifice."[17] Eugene Boring draws on the synagogue practice of replacing a word in the text with another word and then quotes Caird to the effect that:

It is as though John had adopted the familiar synagogue practice of "perpetual Kethib/Qere," whereby a word or phrase that appears in the traditional text is read as another word or phrase: "wherever the tradition says 'lion', reads 'Lamb'." . . . Every event of apocalyptic violence in chapters 6–19 must be seen as derived from the scene of chapters 4–5.[18]

However, it has to be said that in the chapters that follow, the Lamb appears to have gained some of the war-like characteristics of the Lion rather than the other way around. For example, in Rev 6, John offers a picture of a terrified humanity calling to the mountains and rocks: "Fall on us and hide us from the face of the one seated on the throne and from the *wrath of the Lamb*" (Rev 6:16). In Revelation 14, those who worship the beast will "drink the wine of God's wrath, poured unmixed into the cup of his anger, and they

16. Caird, *Revelation of St John*, 75.

17. Sweet, *Revelation*, 125.

18. Boring, *Revelation*, 110, 118.

will be tormented with fire and sulphur in the presence of the holy angels *and in the presence of the Lamb*" (Rev 14:10). And in Revelation 17, the kings will "make war on the Lamb, and the Lamb will conquer them, for he is Lord of lords and King of kings" (Rev 17:14). As David Aune notes, while the "irony of kingship through crucifixion" is prominent in Revelation 5, it is a "marginal conception elsewhere in the book."[19] Indeed, Ron Farmer says that "if chapters 6–20 stood alone, it would be hard to see them as anything other than a cry for vengeance arising from anger, hatred, and envy."[20]

Nevertheless, commentators continue to assert that John's *intention* in using the Lion/Lamb juxtaposition is to replace the violent imagery associated with a Lion for that of a Lamb. Mark Bredin puts it like this:

> The juxtaposition of "Lamb" and "wrath" may, at first sight, appear incomprehensible, as was the combination of Lion and Lamb in Revelation 5.5–6. John reinterprets 'wrath' by placing it alongside the most non-militaristic image, Lamb. Wrath no longer depicts a military, conquering God on the battlefield; God is not one who slays with a sword. Suffering love is the essence of wrath, and therefore suffering love is that which brings about God's judgement and kingdom.[21]

James Resseguie seeks to support such an interpretation with his literary analysis of the book. He thinks that in John's visions, "hearing brings out the inner reality, the spirit and the essence of what he sees."[22] He begins by noting the importance of hearing in the seven messages, with its repetition of the command to "*listen* to what the Spirit is saying to the churches" (Rev 2:7, 11, 17 etc.). He then highlights a number of examples. Thus in Revelation 7, John *sees* a countless multitude but *hears* about its meaning in the symbolic number of 144,000. In Revelation 9, John *sees* a vision of horses with lions' heads and *hears* their number, 200 million. Resseguie comments: "The number is the inner reality that says something about the nature of evil."[23] In Revelation 12, John *sees* a heavenly battle between Michael and Satan but does not understand its meaning until he *hears* the heavenly voice. In Revelation 14, John *sees* the 144,000 and *hears* a multitude singing. In Revelation 15, John *sees* those who have conquered the beast and *hears* the song of Moses and the Lamb. In Revelation 21, John *sees* a new heaven and

19. Aune, *Revelation 1–5*, 352.
20. Farmer, *Beyond the Impasse*, 156.
21. Bredin, *Jesus, Revolutionary of Peace*, 195.
22. Resseguie, *Revelation Unsealed*, 33.
23. Ibid., 34.

earth and *hears* about its meaning (that God will wipe away their tears and dwell with them).

Clearly this juxtaposition of hearing and seeing is an important feature of Revelation, but there are two problems with his conclusion. First, it is by no means clear that *hearing* always interprets *seeing*. Thus, the meaning of Revelation 7 could just as easily be that John was perplexed that only 144,000 are to be saved, but was given the meaning when he *saw* a countless multitude afterward. The fact that John *hears* of the 144,000 in Revelation 7 but *sees* the 144,000 in Revelation 14 should have alerted Resseguie to this ambiguity. Second, even if it is agreed that John used a principle of *hearing* interprets *seeing*, it would not lead to the conclusion that "Lamb" interprets "Lion," because in Revelation 5, John hears about a "Lion" and sees a "Lamb." If Resseguie was consistent, it should mean that "Lion" is the "inner reality, the spirit and the essence" of "Lamb." Since this is not the conclusion that he wants, he is forced to introduce a caveat into his principle:

> The Lion of the tribe of Judah interprets what John sees. Death on the cross (the Lamb) is not defeat but is the way to power and victory (the Lion). *In this instance, seeing also reinterprets the hearing.* The traditional expectation of messianic conquest by military deliverance (the Lion of Judah) is reinterpreted so that messianic conquest occurs through sacrificial death (the Lamb).[24]

The only justification for doing this is that he does not like the conclusion that would result if he applied his principle consistently. In fact, by introducing this caveat, Resseguie is agreeing with the principle of dialogical intertextuality that there is a *mutual* influence between the juxtaposed images. From a purely literary point of view, there is no reason why the "lamb" imagery should dominate the "lion" imagery. Indeed, all things being equal, it is more likely to be the other way around, for a lion is a universal symbol of power and strength. It is used over 150 times in the Old Testament, sometimes for the actual animal,[25] but mostly as a metaphor for devouring enemies. Numbers 23:24 is typical: "The people rise like a lioness; they rouse themselves like a lion that does not rest till he devours his prey and drinks the blood of his victims." Thus, when 1 Peter wishes to portray the activity of the devil against Christians, he says, "Like a roaring lion your adversary the devil prowls around, looking for someone to devour" (1 Pet 5:8). And when John wishes to portray the terrifying activity of the locusts ("their torture was like the torture of a scorpion when it stings someone"),

24. Ibid., 34. Emphasis added.

25. Judg 14:5; 1 Sam 17:34; 1 Kgs 13:24.

he says their teeth were like lion's teeth (Rev 9:8). The same image is used of the devouring beast, which has "a mouth like that of a lion" (Rev 13:2). There can hardly be any doubt that John knows what sort of connotations will be unleashed when he identifies his lead figure with a lion.[26]

Indeed God is occasionally likened to a lion in the Old Testament. Job 10:6 speaks of God stalking him like a lion and displaying his awesome power against him. Isaiah 31:4 records an oracle where God speaks of himself as a lion coming to do battle, and Jer 50:44 has a similar oracle where God will deal with Babylon as a lion. The most graphic reference is Hosea 5:14, where God will attack Ephraim and Judah as a lion: "I will tear them to pieces and go away; I will carry them off, with no one to rescue them." Since John goes out of his way to identify Jesus with various divine characteristics (Rev 1:12–18), there seems no reason to assume that he would be averse to also identifying him with lion imagery.

Furthermore, the specific phrase, "Lion of the tribe of Judah," points the reader to Gen 49:9, a text that receives a messianic interpretation in the *targumim* (Tg. Neof.; Tg. Ps.-J.), *midrashim* (Tanh. *Gen* 12:12; Gen. Rab. 97) and at Qumran (1QSb 5:29). On his deathbed, Jacob tells each of his sons what will happen to them in the future. To Judah, he says:

> Judah, your brothers will praise you; your hand will be on the neck of your enemies; your father's sons will bow down to you. You are a lion's cub, O Judah; you return from the prey, my son. Like a lion he crouches and lies down, like a lioness—who dares to rouse him? The scepter will not depart from Judah, nor the ruler's staff from between his feet, until he comes to whom it belongs and the obedience of the nations is his. He will tether his donkey to a vine, his colt to the choicest branch; he will wash his garments in wine, his robes in the blood of grapes (Gen 49:8–11).

That John was aware of this passage is confirmed by Revelation 19:13–16, where the violent imagery is applied to the rider of the white horse. The epithet "King of kings and Lord of lords" (Rev 19:16) identifies the rider with the Lamb of Rev 17:14. There can hardly be a more blood-thirsty description:

> He is clothed in a *robe dipped in blood*,[27] and his name is called The Word of God. And the armies of heaven, wearing fine linen,

---

26. Jesus is referred to as a Lamb (*arnion*) on twenty-eight occasions. There is one other reference, when the beast is said to have two horns like a lamb (Rev 13:11).

27. Caird, *Revelation*, 244, interprets the blood as that of the martyrs: "His blood has made their robes white, and theirs has made his red," but the clear allusion to Isaiah

white and pure, were following him on white horses. From his mouth comes a sharp sword with which to *strike down the nations*, and he will rule them with a rod of iron; *he will tread the wine press* of the fury of the wrath of God the Almighty. On his robe and on his thigh he has a name inscribed, *"King of kings and Lord of lords."* (Rev 19:13–16)

Commenting on the juxtaposition in Revelation 5, Frederick Murphy notes that the "central issue is whether the warlike traits of a lion are replaced by the meekness of the Lamb or whether the messiah retains warlike qualities?"[28] His conclusion is that neither is replaced: "Christ won his victory over Satan and made possible the victory of Christians through his suffering and death. This is non-violent. But he will also exercise force against the partisans of evil (chapter 19) and will punish them as they deserve."[29] Greg Beale is similar, stating that "Christ's past defeat of the enemy as a 'lion' has begun in an ironic manner through death and suffering as a 'lamb.'" However, at his second coming, he will "judge decisively and openly both his earthly and cosmic enemies, including Satan himself."[30]

Thus, one way of doing justice to the Lion/Lamb juxtaposition is to apply the images to the first and second comings of Jesus. However, David Barr has two problems with this. First, he does not think the vision of military victory in Revelation 19 is describing a *future* battle, for the scene does not occur on earth. He also notes that it unlikely to be evoking the "second coming" tradition, since the figure comes on a horse, not the traditional "clouds of heaven" (Rev 1:7). He thus asserts that "John's divine warrior is not some evil twin of the savior Jesus who conquered by his own death. He is the same person, and the battle has already been won. We have all the paraphernalia of Holy War, but no war."[31] Here he agrees with Richard Bauckham, who thinks that the "distinctive feature of Revelation seems to be, not its repudiation of apocalyptic militarism, but its lavish use of militaristic *language* in a non-militaristic *sense*. In the eschatological destruction of evil in Revelation there is no place for real armed violence, but there is ample space of the imagery of armed violence."[32]

Second, Barr has an ethical problem with Beale and Murphy's solution. He asks, "if violence is not acceptable now how can it be acceptable at

63:1–3 makes this unlikely.

28. Murphy, *Fallen is Babylon*, 193.

29. Ibid.

30. Beale, *John's Use of the Old Testament*, 46.

31. Barr, "Lamb Looks Like a Dragon," 215. Emphasis added.

32. Bauckham, *Climax of Prophecy*, 233.

the Parousia?"[33] Although often unstated, it is this objection that underlies the attempts of Caird, Sweet, and Boring to "silence" the aggressive connotations of the lion imagery. They think that associating such characteristics with Jesus is contrary to Christian doctrine and must therefore be an incorrect interpretation. However, dialogical intertextuality acts as a reminder that the text itself does not compel readers to make this move. If interpreters *choose* to "silence" the lion imagery because it is incompatible with their understanding of Christianity, then that needs to be acknowledged (as in liberation and feminist readings of the book). And here we see the post-structuralist roots of intertextuality. Readers always have a role in configuring the various "voices" in the text. They might believe with Resseguie that a reader should aim to do this "the way the author intended those gaps should be filled in,"[34] but the latter is itself a construct of the text. Farmer provides a good example of the problem. He recognizes that in terms of sheer quantity, violent imagery would appear to dominate, but he considers this to be outweighed by the powerful "undercurrent" of the replacement imagery in Revelation 4–5 (and 21–22): "Although the dominant 'surface' imagery portrays God's power as coercive, all-controlling, and unilateral, the analysis revealed a strong 'undercurrent' working against the dominant imagery by means of basal lures suggesting that divine power be understood as persuasive, all-influencing, and relational."[35]

Two things can be said of this. First, even if it is true that the "undercurrent" suggests that the violent imagery faces opposition, it does not eliminate it (or there would be no point to the analogy). Second, and more fundamentally, on what basis is the violent imagery aligned with what lies on the surface of the waters? Could not the analogy just as equally be reversed, so that John's attempt to portray the Lamb as self-sacrificing love (mainly confined to Rev 5) is constantly being thwarted by the "undercurrent" of the violent language? That is certainly how the book is read by most readers and why commentators such as Caird, Sweet, and Boring have to go to such great lengths to persuade them to read it differently.

As a slight aside, during the writing of this chapter I attended a conference on Paul's opposition to empire. Several speakers tried to show that his seemingly passive stance in Romans 13 is just the opposite when one considers the "undercurrent" of what Paul says about the lordship of Christ. Although most of the audience were in sympathy with such a view, they found it difficult to see this "undercurrent" in Romans 13, even when highlighted

33. Barr, "Lamb Looks Like a Dragon," 220.

34. Resseguie, *Revelation Unsealed*, 30.

35. Farmer, *Beyond the Impasse*, 160.

by the various speakers.[36] I spent my time reflecting on how one group of scholars have a book full of violent imagery and try to persuade us that it makes "lavish use of militaristic *language* in a non-militaristic *sense*," while another group have an exceptionally passive text and try to persuade us that it is really about resisting empire. Would it not be more true to say that there are multiple voices in both books which *could* lead to the views just discussed if readers *choose* to amplify one of the voices. Bauckham, Bredin, and Barr are correct to point out that God's enemies are not slain by a literal sword and no physical battle actually takes place, but the distinction might be lost on those whose bodies are said to be gorged by the birds (Rev 19:21) and end up in the lake of fire (Rev 20:15). That we are talking symbolically rather than literally is an important point, but it does not take away the horror that such images evoke. Paul could talk about the "kindness and the severity of God" (Rom 11:22), and we should acknowledge that John talks about Christ as both lion and lamb.

Conclusion

The idea of dialogical intertextuality is that the alluded text adds a "voice" to the alluding text, so that the reader is forced to configure multiple "voices." As the name suggests, it points to openness and mutuality rather than closure and singularity. It does not imply that all "voices" are equally loud, and it is possible for an author to steer readers towards particular interpretations.[37] But as we saw in the introduction, even negation does not necessarily silence an allusion, and the task of the reader is to decide what role the associations and connotations continue to exert in the alluding text. Given that the lion imagery is both affirmed in Revelation 5 and its violent associations reappear throughout Revelation 6–20, I suggest that dialogical intertextuality makes it very difficult to accept that this imagery is simply replaced by lamb imagery. Theologically and pastorally, this might be a desirable reading strategy, but let us not turn John into a first-century Jürgen Moltmann writing about a "Crucified God."[38]

36. One of the speakers was Lloyd Pietersen. See his *Reading the Bible after Christendom*.

37. It should be noted that Bakhtin did not consider all texts to be dialogic. He thought this was an appropriate description of Dostoyevsky's novels because the author allowed the characters in the story a "voice" different from his own. Even on this definition, Revelation would appear to fit the genre, but as we have seen, Bakhtin's idea has been extended by more recent writers, so that even denied images continue to have a "voice," however muted.

38. Recently republished: Moltmann, *Crucified God—40th Anniversary Edition*. For

Recommended Reading

Bakhtin, Mikhail. *The Dialogic Imagination. Four Essays.* Edited by Michael Holquist. Austin: University of Texas, 1981.

Green, Barbara. *Mikhail Bakhtin and Biblical Scholarship.* Atlanta: Society of Biblical Literature, 2001.

Webb, G. R. *Mark at the Threshold: Applying Bakhtinian Categories to Markan Characterisation.* Leiden: Brill, 2008.

---

its influence on Bauckham's thought, see Bauckham, *God Crucified*.

2

Hypertextuality

Gil Rosenberg

Gérard Genette and Hypertextuality

Gérard Genette's theory of intertextuality, which he presents in his well-known book, *Palimpsests,* is taxonomical.[1] That is, Genette offers a system that organizes and classifies types of relationships between two texts. Because of this, the first and primary step in understanding Genette's intertextuality is to learn the terminology.

Genette uses the term *transtextuality* to refer to the whole set of relationships texts have with one another. Note that already, with just this one definition, we can understand one of the critiques of Genette's theory—his terminology does not always fit with that of other theorists, and without due attention the differences between his definitions and those of other theorists can cause confusion.[2] For example, I began this chapter by introducing Genette's theory of "intertextuality," using that term in a way that would be roughly familiar from the title of this volume and from its other chapters. But in Genette's terms, his is a theory of "transtextuality," not

---

1. A palimpsest is a text which is literally written over another text, often from the ancient world where writing materials were scarce and had to be reused.

2. Genette recognizes the terminological difficulties: "The point will surely be made, 'Why don't you talk like everybody else?' Alas, that would only make matters worse, because common usage is paved with words so familiar, so deceptively transparent, one often tends to use them in long theoretical volumes or at symposia without even stopping to question the meaning of what one is saying" (*Palimpsests,* 430).

"intertextuality" (from this point forward I will employ Genette's terms and definitions). Making things more confusing, he uses "intertextuality" in a more restrictive sense. It is the first of his five broad categories of transtextuality, and it refers only to "the actual presence of one text within another."[3] Quotations and plagiarism are typical examples of intertextuality.

The four remaining categories are as follows. (1) *Paratextuality* is the relationship between the main text and everything that surrounds it including titles, prefaces, indices, page numbers, and so on.[4] When New Testament scholars use the marginal notes and comments written by ancient scribes to help them interpret a text, they are attending to paratextuality. (2) *Metatextuality* refers to the relationship of commentary. Commentary is, of course, an important focus of biblical studies. However, it is not always recognized that this is a transtextual relationship. (3) *Hypertextuality* exists when one text is integrally based on and transforms another text.[5] Hypertextuality is Genette's primary interest in *Palimpsests*, and the bulk of that book consists of describing types of hypertextuality. As such, it will also be my primary focus. To the extent that the gospel of Matthew constructs itself as a continuation and fulfillment of Israel's Scriptures, it is creating a hypertextual relationship. (4) Finally, *architextuality* is the relationship between a text and other texts through their participation in shared genres, types, and modes. The fact that a book is a gospel is a feature of its architextuality, as is the fact that it is narrative and reported in the third person.

It should be noted that these categories are not absolute or mutually exclusive. For example, both metatextuality and hypertextuality often use intertextuality (a commentary will cite the text it interprets, and frequent allusions help establish that one text is hypertextually based on another).

Most scholarship on the relationship between the Old and New Testaments focuses on intertextual relationships: quotations and allusions. Once those quotations or allusions are established, scholars explain the significance of the intertextuality for the meaning of the New Testament text. Why did the authors include these Old Testament references? What were they trying to communicate to the reader by linking their text to the Old Testament? These questions begin to move toward questions of hypertextuality, which concerns the relationships between entire texts rather than isolated phrases or passages. Genette's taxonomy of hypertextuality is useful for identifying and describing these larger relationships.

---

3. Genette, *Palimpsests*, 2.

4. See Genette, *Paratexts*.

5. Genette used the term "hypertextuality" before it became widely used to refer to links between pages on the internet.

Hypertextuality concerns the relationship between two texts—an earlier text and a later text, which is based on or transforms the earlier text. He calls the later text the *hypertext*, and the earlier text its *hypotext*. In the context of New Testament studies, the Old Testament is frequently (but of course not exclusively) the hypotext of the New Testament hypertext.

Genette's classification of hypertextuality begins with a distinction between *transformations* and *imitations*. Transformations rely on the content of their hypotext: plot, characters, and so forth. For example, the account of Jesus' transfiguration on the mountain in Matthew 17 is a transformation of Moses' revelation on Sinai in Exodus 24.[6] The basic elements remain the same—a trip up the mountain, God speaking from a cloud, seven days, changes in appearance, etc. But these elements have been transferred to a new context. Imitations, on the other hand, connect to their hypotexts by copying their style. For example, when scholars point out the ways that New Testament Greek sometimes uses words or phrases that are unknown in ancient Greek outside of the Greek translation of the Old Testament, they are asserting that the relevant New Testament passages are imitative hypertexts of the Greek OT.[7]

Genette places these two basic types of hypertextuality along one axis, and across a second axis he proposes three hypertextual moods—*playful* (intended for amusement and entertainment), *satirical* (intended to mock, critique, or attack), and *serious* (intended as literature in its own right). The result is the following chart.[8]

	playful	satirical	serious
transformation	PARODY	TRAVESTY	TRANSPOSITION
imitation	PASTICHE	CARICATURE	FORGERY

The rest of the hypertextual relationships that Genette introduces and analyzes throughout *Palimpsests* fit into one of these six categories, though they are always with potential overlap and blurred lines, as the dotted lines in the table suggest.

The most useful categories for the study of hypertextuality in the New Testament are the serious categories of *forgery* and *transposition*.[9] Contrary

---

6. See Allison, *New Moses*, 243–48.

7. See Fitzmyer, *Luke*, 113–27.

8. See Genette, *Palimpsests*, 28–29.

9. I do not mean to exclude the possibility of playful or satirical hypertextuality. In fact, it is likely that we only assume New Testament hypertextuality is serious because the NT is usually assumed (but rarely demonstrated) to be serious. Two useful exercises would be to attempt to interpret NT hypertextuality as playful or satirical rather

to common usage, Genette's forgery does not necessitate an attempt to deceive. It is simply a serious imitation. Categories of forgery that apply to the New Testament include *continuation* and *sequel:* a continuation completes an unfinished hypotext, while a sequel offers new episodes following a complete hypotext. The New Testament, at least at times, presents itself as a continuation of the Old Testament, while the Deutero-Pauline epistles can be understood as a sequel to the undisputed letters of Paul. Indeed, all of the Pauline epistles can be read as a series of sequels to his first extant letter, 1 Thessalonians.

Some of the types of transposition (serious transformation) that are useful to New Testament scholars are *translation* (in the usual sense), varieties of *reduction* and *augmentation* (different ways of shortening or lengthening a text, as in the differences between parallel gospel passages), *transdiegetization* (a change in the time or place of the action, as with the transfiguration connections to Moses),[10] and *transvaluation* (differences in what the texts consider to be important; this is also present in the transfiguration story, in that Matthew values Jesus where Exodus values Moses).

Hypertextuality and the New Testament

There are a number of ways that Genette's theory of hypertextuality can be useful for New Testament studies. A straightforward application is simply to use some of Genette's terminology to describe a perceived hypertextual relationship. Selecting just the right term of the relationship helps the scholar achieve precision and clarity.

Another use of Genette's list of possible relationships is as a tool for gaining creative insight into NT texts. For example, we can begin with a category such as *pastiche* and search for possible examples of pastiche among NT texts. Alternatively, we can begin with a particular text, and try to imagine how that text could be interpreted as different types of hypotexts. Could the given text be read as an augmentation of another text, a transvaluation, or a sequel? Either exercise might allow the interpreter to recognize and describe a relationship that would otherwise have been difficult to see. According to Genette, one of the benefits of his taxonomy is that it creates categories of relationships even before examples of such a relationship have

---

than serious, and to attempt to justify the assumption that NT hypertextuality is indeed serious.

10. Genette redefines *transfiguration* as a change in literary figures, refuting any connection to the more traditional meaning of the term, which I employ here.

been identified, and we are more likely to find examples once we have a name for the relationship.[11]

A third way to use Genette's categories is as a springboard for creating more categories. As Genette admits, his categories and analysis, while detailed and thorough, are not exhaustive.[12] Especially because Genette used primarily modern European literature for his examples, biblical literature offers additional types of hypertextual, and more broadly transtextual, relationships. Nevertheless, Genette's categories serve as models that can guide an extension of his hypertextual taxonomy. For example, are transformation and imitation a sufficient dichotomy for the first level of the taxonomy, or does biblical literature show evidence of a relationship that is not quite either, or a sufficient blend of each to warrant a new term? Might *fulfillment* be a third alternative? Or is it better subsumed under one of Genette's categories? Note how, even if "fulfillment" is a term that is already widely used in NT studies, the attempt to place it in Genette's dichotomy can help us to understand better that particular hypertextual relationship.[13]

Adaptations for Biblical Studies

This last method of application suggests that Genette's theory is not perfectly suited for biblical literature, and that some adaptations might be necessary. In addition to possessing hypertextual relationships that Genette did not discuss, there are several other features of the New Testament that complicate the use of "hypertextuality."

Genette's ideal model of hypertextuality involves two texts, one early and one late. But biblical literature complicates this both numerically and temporally. Numerically, NT hypertextuality often involves more than two texts. A single gospel passage might have a relationship with Genesis, Exodus, one or more of the prophets, a psalm, two other gospels, and one of Paul's letters. While Genette's hypertextuality can help us analyze the relationships on a pairwise basis, it does not tell us about more complicated

---

11. Genette puts it this way: "It seems to me, however, that the taxonomic principle that has guided our inquiry will have served to avoid most serious gaps (those most damaging from a theoretical viewpoint), thanks to what I should like to call the heuristic virtue of the empty square. I am referring not only to the six squares of the initial tables but to a few other more localized combinations; some of their virtualities may well appear to be devoid of any actuality, but they are an incitement to inquisitiveness. This inquisitiveness will eventually come across some attested practice that would otherwise have escaped it . . ." (*Palimpsests*, 394).

12. Ibid.

13. See Kirk, "Conceptualising Fulfillment."

networks of relationships. On occasion he recognizes that hypertexts often have more than one hypotext, naming this *contamination*, but he defers an extended analysis of such cases.[14]

Temporally, questions about the dating of biblical texts suggest that we relax Genette's rather strict requirements for hypertextuality. Genette restricts himself in *Palimpsests* to "the sunnier side of hypertextuality: that in which the shift from hypotext to hypertexts is both massive (an entire work B deriving from an entire work A) and more or less officially stated."[15] At the same time, however, he admits that hypertextuality, as the relationship between two texts, is much more general than that, and can even apply to hypertexts that are earlier than their hypotexts. That is, one can analyze the relationship between texts on a purely formal level, without reference to the intention of the authors. Even if there may be little interest in "reverse" hypertextuality, such as reading Exodus as a hypertext with Matthew as hypotext, the focus on formal relationships between texts allows the scholar to sidestep, as desired, tricky questions of dating and intention. This can be useful when dealing with texts for which so little is known about their composition. In fact, by beginning with formal relationships that ignore theories of dating, it may be possible to support arguments about dating and dependency—a convincing argument that text A is a hypertext of text B can contribute positive evidence that text A is later than text B.

Genette's requirement that hypertextuality concern entire works also leads to difficulties in biblical literature, where it is not always clear what the appropriate unit of analysis is. On the one hand, it seems appropriate to take either a single book or the New Testament as a whole as the "entire work." But collections of books (the Gospels, Paul's epistles, Luke-Acts) might also be appropriate. Nor does it seem unreasonable to treat certain passages or chapters as a work, as with the transfiguration example. While the hypertextual relationships involved may be different from those at the level of the book or the New Testament, the results may nevertheless be useful or interesting. Finally, note that we see here a blending of the intertextual with the hypertextual. If the unit of analysis becomes small enough, then we will have intertextual quotations and allusions rather than the systematic relationships of hypertextuality. Many of the relationships between the NT and other texts seem to exist in this border area between inter- and hypertextuality.

14. Genette, *Palimpsests*, 46, 207, 258.
15. Ibid., 9.

Hypertextuality in Matthew 1

One genre that did not come up in Genette's work on hypertextuality is the list—more specifically, the genealogy. But it turns out that Genette's approach to hypertextuality offers new insights into Jesus' genealogy in Matthew 1. It is immediately clear that there is a relationship between Matthew's genealogy and the genealogies in the Old Testament. That is, Matthew 1 is a hypertext of Ruth 4 and 1 Chronicles 2. These relationships will not be the only ones I examine, but they are a natural place to begin.

Ruth 4

There are ten names in the genealogy in Ruth 4:18–22. The genealogy is linear, meaning that it lists only one member of each generation, avoiding branches. There are no extra details, simply the introductory "This, then, is the family line of Perez," (Ruth 4:18) and the list of who fathered who: "Perez was the father of Hezron, Hezron the father of Ram, Ram the father of Amminadab . . . and Jesse the father of David" (vv. 18–22).[16] One function of linear genealogies is to connect and emphasize the first and last figures, in this case Perez and David.

The same ten figures appear in the genealogy in Matthew 1 (vv. 3–6). But there are several changes. Most notable is the fact that the genealogy is embedded in a much longer genealogy, now over forty generations instead of ten. Thus, Matthew 1 is an *extension* or "augmentation by massive addition."[17] It is also a transvaluation, because Matthew's genealogy emphasizes Abraham and Jesus and their connection rather than Perez and David.[18] Another aspect of this transvaluation is the change in how these ten names in Ruth, this particular list, is to be understood. In Ruth, this list is an end in itself. But when Matthew extends it on both ends, it loses some importance by merging with the rest of the names. The idea of the Ruth genealogy as a self-contained unit is lost completely in Matthew.

A final notable change is the inclusion of several notes that break up the otherwise sparse list of fathers and sons. Almost all of the notes add extra family members, either brothers or women who are identified as mothers.[19]

16. All biblical citations are from the New International Version.

17. Genette, *Palimpsests*, 254.

18. See Wilson, *Genealogy and History*, 137–205. Note that some attention to David is preserved in Matthew. He is the only one named as "king" (Matt 1:6), despite the fact that many of the names were indeed kings. Moreover, David's name sits at one of the transition points identified in Matt 1:17.

19. The additions are Judah's brothers (Matt 1:2), Perez's twin Zerah (v. 3), Tamar

We might describe these notes as an example of minimal *amplification*, in which such things as additional details, examples, or explanations are provided.[20] The purpose of this amplification, and especially the presence of the women in the genealogy, is a source of uncertainty and debate. As I will show, one result of careful attention to hypertextual relationships will be a possible explanation for the additional notes in the Matthew 1 genealogy.

1 Chronicles 1–3

The entirety of 1 Chronicles 1–8 is a massive genealogy, the largest single genealogy in the Bible by far. It begins with Adam and extends down many generations through complicated branches, organized roughly by tribe of the sons of Israel. Thus, 1 Chronicles 1–8 is a branched (or segmented) genealogy, in contrast to the linear genealogies of Ruth 4 and Matthew 1. The part of the Chronicles list that corresponds with Matthew 1 extends from the first mention of Abraham in 1:27 until the mention of Zerubbabel in 3:17. Genette offers many varieties of *reduction*, which is clearly at stake in the move from 1 Chronicles to Matthew. Perhaps *excision*, "suppression pure and simple," is the best fit for the elimination of multitudes of names and branches.[21] Something like *digest* might also be appropriate since the author of Matthew shortens the genealogy in Chronicles by presenting only the most important pieces from his perspective.[22] We might also coin the term *linearization*, specific to genealogies, to describe the change from a branched genealogy to a linear one. (The inverse, which describes the relationship between 1 Chronicles and Ruth, would be *branchification*.) Finally, despite its shorter length, the genealogy in Matthew is not simply a shortened version of 1 Chron 1:27—3:17. The last section, Matt 1:13–17, contains names that are not recorded in Chronicles. So the author of Matthew does not just eliminate parts of Chronicles; he also introduces some new material.[23] Genette uses *substitution* to name this combination of *addition* and *suppression*.

---

the mother of Perez and Zerah (v. 3), Rahab the mother of Boaz (v. 5), Ruth the mother of Obed (v. 5), Uriah's wife the mother of Solomon (v. 6), and the brothers of Jeconiah (v. 11). There are also changes at the transition points identified in Matt 1:17: "King" is added to David's name in v. 6 and the exile is noted in vv. 11–12. The information about Jesus and his family also differs from the standard formula (v. 16),

20. Genette, *Palimpsests*, 262.

21. Ibid., 229.

22. Ibid., 246.

23. We do not know the gender of the author of Matthew. Given gender relations in the ancient world, it is likely the author was male. My use of "he" reflects this probability,

All of these changes result in a dramatic *transfocalization,* a change of focus and perspective. Because of its length, branching, and frequent digressions, the focus of the genealogy in 1 Chronicles is purposefully broad. While everything starts with Adam, there is no clear ending, so no single individual is emphasized. In contrast, Matthew's primary focus is on Jesus and his connection to Abraham. Chronicles presents the genealogy of a nation, while Matthew presents the genealogy of an individual.

Just as the changes from Ruth to Matthew resulted in a transvaluation, so do the changes from 1 Chronicles to Matthew result in a change of values. If we consider the genealogy in Chronicles as a whole, it clearly values the nation of Israel and especially its cult, military, and possession of land.[24] The Matthew genealogy clearly values Jesus and his descent through this particular line. Note also the effect on the particular generations that appear in both 1 Chronicles and Matthew. In the former, these generations are interspersed throughout the chapters with many other branches. A reader (like Matthew's author?) must work hard to connect these figures and to see the line that becomes so transparent in Matthew. This has the opposite effect of what we saw between Ruth and Matthew. There, the list in Ruth is devalued because it becomes a small part of the much greater list in Matthew. But when Matthew selects one particular line from the multitudes in 1 Chronicles, the importance of those names and that line is heightened.

Recall that when we compared Ruth and Matthew we noted the inclusion in Matthew's genealogy of several notes that were absent from Ruth's. Do those notes bear on the hypertextual relationship between 1 Chronicles and Matthew as well? It turns out that most of the notes in Matthew's genealogy can be understood in terms of the hypertextual relationship between Matthew and 1 Chronicles.

The first note is Judah's brothers (Matt 1:2). Because the genealogy in 1 Chronicles is branched, all brothers of a son are normally listed, while in Matthew's linear genealogy (Matt 1:11) only the brothers of Judah and Jeconiah are included (with the phrase "and his brothers," not addressed by name). In both cases, there are hypertextual reasons that Matthew chose to mention these brothers. In the case of Judah, his brothers are key figures in the organization of the Chronicles genealogy. Once they are introduced, the rest of the genealogies are comprised of Judah's brothers' respective lineages with more or less detail depending on the Chronicler's assessment of that tribe's importance. Matthew's reference to Judah's brothers acknowledges

---

and is not intended to exclude the possibility of female authorship.

24. Sparks, *Chronicler's Genealogies.*

their importance in 1 Chronicles, even as it constitutes a radical *abridgement* of their respective genealogies.

Jeconiah's brothers do not hold the same importance in the genealogy in 1 Chronicles as do Judah's brothers. But they are nonetheless noteworthy. For 14 generations, from Solomon to Josiah, the Chronicles genealogy narrows and becomes linear (1 Chron 3:10–14). Then, at Jeconiah's generation, the genealogy branches again and lists his brothers. Matthew's inclusion of Jeconiah's brothers may reflect this feature of Chronicles. Moreover, it serves to further emphasize Matthew's own organization of his genealogy in that Jeconiah's generation stands at the exile, one of Matthew's two explicit transition points.

In addition to these references to the brothers, two more of Matthew's notes can be explained through the hypertextual relationship with 1 Chronicles. These are the inclusion of Tamar and Bathsheba. Chronicles sometimes includes women as wives and mothers in its genealogies. Among the parts of the list that 1 Chronicles and Matthew share, Tamar and Bathsheba are the only women that 1 Chronicles includes. That is, wherever Chronicles includes a woman, so does Matthew. As with Matthew's notes about brothers, the inclusion of these women suggests the faithfulness of Matthew's genealogy to its hypotext.

But if this explains some notes, it does not explain them all. In particular, it does not explain the presence of the other two women in the genealogy, Ruth and Rahab. Attention to additional hypertextual relationships suggests a possible explanation for Ruth's presence. As we will see, an explanation for Rahab's presence must remain more speculative.

Ruth Again

To understand why the author of Matthew might have deemed it appropriate to include Ruth in his genealogy, I return to the genealogy in Ruth 4. But instead of treating Ruth's genealogy purely as hypotext to Matthew's hypertext, I attend to a more complex network of hypertextuality. In particular, Ruth's genealogy is closely related to Ruth's narrative, for which it serves as a conclusion (Genette's *epilogue* is appropriate here), and it is related with the story of Tamar in Genesis 38.

Ruth's story concludes with the birth of her son, Obed. This sign of fertility and continuity resolves the problem of famine and death that set Ruth and Naomi's narrative in motion. The genealogy, then, situates Obed's climactic birth in the larger biblical narrative, connecting him both to those who came before (back to Perez) and those who would come after (King

David). While Ruth does not explicitly appear in the genealogy, the placement of the genealogy at the end of her story creates a close association
between Ruth and the genealogy. This is an "intratextual" relationship between the narrative and genealogical portions of the book. The genealogy is
Ruth's genealogy, whether she is named in it or not, because of its placement
in her book and its role as an epilogue to her narrative. By including Ruth
in his genealogy, the author of Matthew was simply making explicit what
was already implicit in the book of Ruth—Ruth's presence in the genealogy.

In addition, there is a close connection between Ruth and Tamar who,
as we have already seen, is already a part of the genealogical tradition. Elle
van Wolde has traced the many connections between the stories of Ruth
and Tamar, including key words, plot, the role of the narrator, and the roles
of the characters.[25] Van Wolde does not use Genettes' terminology, but she
describes what Genette calls a *heterodiegetic transformation*.[26] That is, basic
structures of the story remain the same, while the setting and certain features of the characters change. Also, van Wolde's identification of several
humorous sexual *double entendres* in Ruth suggest that the tone of Ruth's
hypertextuality in relationship to Genesis 38 is not wholly serious, and contains an element of parody.

Enhancing the connection between Ruth and Tamar, Tamar is invoked explicitly at the very end of Ruth's narrative. As part of their speech
in honor of Obed's birth, the elders declare to Boaz, "Through the offspring
the LORD gives you by this young woman [Ruth], may your family be like
that of Perez, whom Tamar bore to Judah" (Ruth 4:12). Shortly thereafter
comes the genealogy which begins with Perez. Taken all together, there is
a web of hypertextual (and intratextual) relationships that serve to connect
both Tamar and Ruth with the genealogical list. This connection continues
and is made manifest in Matthew's genealogy.

Rahab?

If the presence of Tamar, Ruth, and Bathsheba in Matthew's genealogy can
be explained, at least in part, through hypertextuality, how can we explain
Rahab's presence? Rahab occurs nowhere in the Hebrew Bible outside of the
Jericho narrative in Joshua 2 and 6, and none of her relatives are named in
those chapters. The New Testament references outside of Matthew's genealogy do not contain any genealogical information. Other Second Temple
literature is similarly silent. So where does Matthew get the idea that Rahab

25. Van Wolde, "Texts in Dialogue."
26. Genette, *Palimpsests*, 296–312.

is part of this particular genealogical line? There are two possibilities: (1) the author of Matthew made up Rahab's genealogical connections, or (2) he had a source unknown to us that associated Rahab with Salmon. Given the strong hypertextual relationships that I have demonstrated so far, it appears that Matthew valued connections to his sources. It therefore seems unlikely that Matthew would have created this genealogical relationship on his own. Other scholars agree, searching rabbinic materials for traditions that would explain Rahab's connection to the genealogy.[27] However, my argument requires only the very minimal assumption that Matthew knew of a source that connected Rahab with this genealogy. He then included that source in his hypertextual network.

Conclusion

Scholars have offered a variety of explanations for the presence of the four women (five including Mary) in the otherwise male genealogy in Matthew 1—the women were Gentiles, they had unusual marriages, they took initiative, or they represented one point of view about the lineage of the expected Messiah.[28] While I do not dismiss these explanations, the hypertextual relationships that I identify suggest that they are at the very least incomplete. The women, I argue, are included because the author of Matthew recognized that they were an important part of the literary tradition that he had inherited, and to which he wanted to connect Jesus. The purpose of the genealogy is not just to show that Jesus came through a particular line, but also to relate Jesus to that tradition. The author of Matthew created a relationship between Jesus and sacred history by creating a hypertextual relationship between his genealogy and the genealogical literature which preceded him.

The difference between my conclusions and other scholars results from two differences in method. First, while other interpreters look to the women's narratives to explain their presence in Matthew's genealogy, I look to their genealogies. That is, I pursue a different set of hypotexts. Second, I employ Genette's taxonomy to investigate and describe the relationship between texts. Genette's classifications help to describe precisely the variety of relationships that exist between the biblical texts. But just as important, if not more so, his taxonomy can help us see those relationships in the first place. Given a suspicion that a relationship exists between two texts,

27. Bauckham, "Tamar's Ancestry"; Johnson, *Biblical Genealogies*, 162–65.

28. Brown, *Birth of the Messiah*, 57–95, 497–99; Johnson, *Biblical Genealogies*, 139–228.

Genette's taxonomy leads the interpreter to ask a series of questions: Does the text involve transformation or imitation? What is the mood or function of the hypertext? Is there an addition or reduction? What precisely is transformed, and what remains the same? In the case of Matthew's genealogy, this last question led me to recognize the stable presence of Ruth, Tamar, and Bathsheba in a network of genealogies and their associated narratives. This in turn led to new insights into the question of Matthew's motivation for including those women in his genealogy. Genette's theory of hypertextuality has not often been used in biblical studies, but it has great potential to add to the conversation. His terminology offers precision in describing hypertextuality, and the organization of his taxonomy offers a set of useful and interesting questions, some of which will lead to unexpected interpretations.

Recommended Reading

Brooke, George J. "Hypertextuality and the 'Parabiblical' Dead Sea Scrolls." In *In the Second Degree: Parabiblical Literature in Ancient Near Eastern and Ancient Mediterranean Culture and its Reflections in Medieval Literature*, edited by Philip S. Alexander, Armin Lange, and Renate J. Pillinger, 43–64. Leiden: Brill, 2010.

Genette, Gérard. *Palimpsests: Literature in the Second Degree.* Translated by Channa Newman and Claude Doubinsky. Lincoln, NE: University of Nebraska Press, 1982.

Phillips, Peter. "Biblical Studies and Intertextuality: Should the Work of Genette and Eco Broaden Our Horizons?" In *The Intertextuality of the Epistles: Explorations of Theory and Practice,* edited by Thomas L. Brodie, Dennis R. MacDonald, and Stanley E. Porter, 36–45. NTM 16. Sheffield: Sheffield Phoenix, 2006.

Stahlberg, Lesleigh Cushing. "Naming the Animals." In *Sustaining Fictions: Intertextuality, Midrash, Translation, and the Literary Afterlife of the Bible,* 59–91. New York: T. & T. Clark, 2008.

3

Metalepsis

Jeannine K. Brown

Interpreters of the New Testament can explore intertextuality from a variety of angles and assumptions. A key assumption of this essay is that when NT authors cite or allude to "a brief part of another text . . . [they] may be evoking the entire context, message, or story of that other text."[1] This assumption has a name in literary circles—*metalepsis*. I suggest that metalepsis is an important feature of intertextuality and that it has a basic storied quality.

Before commencing further discussion of metalepsis and examples from the use of the Old Testament in the New, I share a contemporary example of this discursive feature to illustrate the commonplace nature of importing context and story by means of verbal and conceptual references to another (precursor) text. Gospels scholar Rikki Watts shares this story:

> As an Australian student studying in the United States I was fascinated by my lecturers' occasional references to "four score and seven years ago" and the uniformly "knowing" response of my American fellow-students. Only on learning that the phrase was the first line of Abraham Lincoln's famous Gettysburg address did its significance [become] apparent. By evoking the Founding Fathers' ideology these few words functioned as a hermeneutical indicator, pointing not so much to the text of Lincoln's address *per se* . . . but to the larger interpretation of American history which Lincoln's speech assumed and with which it interacted.[2]

1. Brown, *Scripture as Communication*, 110.
2. Watts, *Isaiah's New Exodus*, 3.

If just a few (well-known) words can evoke not only another text—an intertext—but also the story that sits behind and within the intertext, then careful attention to precursor texts and their contexts in the interpretation of a work is a valuable enterprise.

Description of Metalepsis

The term metalepsis has been connected in the history of rhetoric to metonymy, a figure of speech often described as a part standing in for the whole.[3] Using this association, we can understand metalepsis as an author's reference to the larger literary context when offering a citation or allusion from an earlier text. In this sense, *metalepsis* is the use of a part of a precursor text to evoke the whole of it. As Litwak defines it, metalepsis is "the way in which one text is taken up and changed by another text through an echo of the former."[4] For example, Isa 57:9 is alluded to in Eph 2:17:

> Isa 57:19a: " . . . peace and peace to those who are far away and to those that are near. And the Lord said, 'I will heal them.'" (LXX).

> Eph 2:17: "And he came and preached peace to you who were far away and peace to those who were near."

In this case, it is telling that "those who are far away" in Isaiah are those from Israel still in exile. So the announcement of peace evokes the promise of God's restoration of Israel from exile (e.g., 57:14). Exile and restoration are storied features of the Isaiah text. The allusion in Ephesians then plays on this language of "near" and "far" (and its associated story), not to reference Israelites in the land and those in exile but now Jews and Gentiles, respectively. "Those who are far away" is expanded to refer to the Gentiles who are most remote from Israel's God (2:12). In this way, the Isaiah text "is taken up and changed by" the Ephesians text "through an echo of the former."[5]

Those who highlight the importance of metalepsis for New Testament studies often point to the seminal work of John Hollander, *The Figure of an Echo* (1981). Hollander introduces the concept of an "echo" from one text to another via "transumption" or "metalepsis."[6] For Hollander,

---

3. See the discussion in Hollander, *Figure of Echo*, 133–49.

4. Litwak, *Echoes of Scripture in Luke-Acts*, 52.

5. Quotation adapted from Litwak, 52.

6. "Transumption" comes from the Latin *transumptio* and "metalepsis" from the Greek *metalambanō*. See Hollander, *Figure of Echo*, 133–34.

"[I]nterpretation of metalepsis entails the recovery of transumed material."[7] In other words, reading texts well includes attention not only to the parts of precursor texts that are referenced (e.g., citations, allusions, or echoes) but also focuses on the context and (back)story of the former text.

Richard Hays takes up Hollander's insights to explore intertextuality in the New Testament in *Echoes of Scripture in the Letters of Paul* (1989) and later in *The Conversion of the Imagination* (2005).[8] Hays defines metalepsis and its significance in Pauline interpretation as "a rhetorical and poetic device in which one text alludes to an earlier text in a way that evokes resonances of the earlier text *beyond those explicitly cited*. The result is that interpretation of a metalepsis requires the reader to recover unstated or suppressed correspondences between the two texts."[9] As Hays indicates more recently, a metalepsis "beckons readers to recover more of the original subtext in order to grasp the full force of the intertextual link."[10]

Understandings of metalepsis have frequently accented its storied nature, since NT authors often draw upon and "transume" the storied features of Old Testament texts. Some of the facets of the meta-story of the OT include creation, covenant, slavery, sojourning, and return from exile. Viewing OT references in this broader storied context helps us to avoid the rather commonplace assumption that the NT authors treat the Scriptures more atomistically. Hays argues for such a storied reading: "[W]e do not simply scour the OT for isolated prooftexts and predictions; rather, we must perceive how the whole story of God's covenant promise unfolds and leads toward the events of Jesus' death and resurrection."[11]

Some brief examples will help us see these storied features of metalepsis more clearly. Since narratives are built on the basics of *setting, plot,* and *characters*, we will look at an example of storied metalepsis from each of these categories.

New Testament writers often exploit *settings* to highlight associations with an Old Testament story or text. For example, a crucial setting for Jesus' passion, burial, and resurrection in the Gospel of John is "a garden" (18:1, 26; 19:41; 20:15). This setting very likely echoes the setting of the creation accounts (e.g., Gen 2:8–10), especially given other significant points of resonance between John 18–20 and Genesis 1–2.[12] The author of John uses this

---

7. Ibid., 115.

8. Hays later applies his method to the Gospels in *Reading Backwards*.

9. Hays, *Conversion of the Imagination*, 2 (author's emphasis).

10. Hays, *Reading Backwards*, 42.

11. Ibid., 15–16.

12. See Brown, "Creation's Renewal," 275–90.

association to accent Jesus' role in inaugurating the renewal of creation in his death and resurrection. Yet this storied feature from Genesis into John's Gospel is easily overlooked if we only focus on pronounced verbal connections between the two texts and ignore storied ones.[13]

New Testament writers often draw on *events* portrayed in Old Testament texts to inform their reflections on the advent of Messiah Jesus. In his cataloging of how the NT authors draw on the OT text, Peter Mallen includes what he calls "narrative patterns" in addition to quotations and allusions (both verbal and conceptual). Mallen defines narrative pattern as "a series of events or interactions between characters whose similarity to those in an earlier text is apparent although the specific details and the language of expression may vary."[14] One example of a narrative pattern occurs in Matthew's Gospel when the identity formation of Jesus is compared to (and contrasted with) that of Israel. "Jesus goes through the waters [of baptism] (cf. Exod 14:21–22), is pronounced 'God's son' (cf. Exod 4:22–23), and is then led into the wilderness to be tested in the same way Israel was (cf. Exod 14–32)."[15]

In addition to settings and narrative patterns or events, we can also note the "peopled" nature of NT references to the OT. References to OT *characters* abound in the Gospels and Epistles and provide further examples of what we are calling storied metalepsis. For example, when Matthew mentions a figure like Abraham (1:1, 2), he potentially raises a number of associations about Abraham for his reader. Part of the interpretive task is determining what parts of the Abraham "backstory" are relevant in these initial verses of Matthew. In other words, how has Matthew transumed the Abraham character for his specific purposes as he narrates Jesus' story?[16] Is Matthew signaling covenantal associations via Abraham or his role as the ancestor of many nations (e.g., Gen 17:4–5) or both?[17] What is important to note is that the reader experiences the reference to Abraham as a storied reference not necessarily tied or limited to a specific OT text.[18]

---

13. John uses κῆπος rather than παράδεισος, potentially muting the intertextual connection. Yet there is good reason for John to avoid παράδεισος, since that term in the NT refers to the final state (Suggit, "Jesus the Gardener," 166). See discussion in Brown, "Creation's Renewal," 279–81.

14. Mallen, *Reading and Transformation*, 24.

15. Piotrowski, "After the Deportation," 190.

16. Abraham is also mentioned at 1:17; 3:9; 8:11; and 22:32.

17. See my discussion in "Genesis in Matthew's Gospel," 54–55.

18. On the idea of a character evoking a "composite figure" residing in the collective memory of author/audience, see Thatcher, "Cain and Abel," 749–50.

A central methodological question regarding metalepsis revolves around how to recognize allusions and echoes the author intends, especially as echoes may have fewer linguistic connections to a precursor text (and more storied and conceptual links). Any NT author steeped in Scripture, "was bound to express himself in ways that subconsciously echoed Scriptural texts on a regular basis without any metaleptic intentions."[19] So what are the signals that an echo is part of the author's communicative intention?[20] Powell suggests three basic criteria to start the conversation.[21]

1. *Availability* of alluded text to author and readers of text being analyzed.

2. *Degree of repetition* of alluded text in text being analyzed.[22]

3. *Thematic coherence* between the texts.[23]

To these, we can add three additional discreet criteria from Hays:[24]

4. *Historical plausibility*: could the author have intended the echo and the original readers understood it?

5. *History of interpretation*: have other contemporary or historical interpreters noticed the echo?

6. *Satisfaction*: Does "the proposed reading make sense?" Is it coherent?[25]

If a potential echo or allusion (not to mention a citation) is determined to have the support of these varied criteria, what do we do next? How do we apply a *storied metaleptical approach* to a specific NT author and text?

---

19. Lucas, "Assessing Stanley E. Porter's Objections," 95.

20. On the possibility of *unattended meanings* still being a part of communicative intention, see Brown, *Scripture as Communication*, 108–10.

21. Powell, *Following the Eastern Star*, 101–2.

22. The seven criteria of Hays, *Echoes*, 30, expand on the idea of repetition to explore *volume* (repetitions in the specific verse/text at hand) and *recurrence* (the same precursor text used at more than one place in the entire work).

23. Hays, ibid., also indicates the importance of *thematic coherence*, which we might define as "the alignment of a possible echo within the author's rhetorical emphases" (Brown, "Creation's Renewal," 289; I reshape Hays's language originally developed for epistles to allow for a narrative focus for this criterion).

24. Ibid., 29–32.

25. Lucas, "Assessing Stanley E. Porter's Objections," 99–100, addresses Porter's critique of Hays's criteria by noting that the latter actually both provide ways for determining potential allusions and act as guides to the meaning of allusions.

Examples of Storied Metalepsis in 1 Peter and in Matthew

To illustrate further the concept of metalepsis and its storied features, as well as exploring how to take account of these when interpreting the Bible, we will look at two extended examples from 1 Peter and Matthew, both of which are filled with citations, allusions, and echoes from the OT. We will first attend to the use of Psalm 34 in 1 Peter. The author of 1 Peter draws upon this Psalm more than once and in significant ways; and some have argued that it is foundational for his reflection upon the situation of his audience. The second example is a more subtle evocation—Gen 4:24 in Jesus' saying about forgiving another "seventy-seven times" in Matt 18:22. Yet "Matthew tells a story that demands a very high level of intertextual awareness."[26] So we do well to listen closely for storied connections at the intersection of these two passages.

Psalm 34 in 1 Peter

Psalm 34 (33 LXX) pictures a righteous person suffering and in trouble, but with the hope of the Lord's redemption and deliverance on the horizon. The psalm's attribution to David when pursued by Abimelek connects to the individual voice in the psalm reflecting on former troubles and present deliverance. The psalm is a thanksgiving hymn with some wisdom elements, such as the contrast between the righteous and evildoers (34:15–16, 21) and the "fear of Yahweh" motif (34:7, 9, 11).

The author of 1 Peter seems to find Psalm 34 fertile ground for reflection upon the situation of his audience.[27] He draws upon it paradigmatically to parallel their situation and to suggest a way forward for them.[28] We might put it this way—the psalmist's story and the story of the Petrine audience align in enough ways to invite a metaleptical reading of the psalm into 1 Peter.[29] Peter marshals the psalm's theological vision to draw his audience into reflection on their own situation and behavior and to provide a rationale for their exemplary behavior even in the midst of suffering. He does this with

26. Piotrowski, "After the Deportation," 189.

27. Without wading into authorial questions, I will use "Peter" to designate the author of the letter; similarly, "Matthew" will be used below.

28. Moyise, *Later New Testament Writings*, 43–44, notes that Psalm 34 is only quoted here in all of the NT; it "appears to be the author's own discovery."

29. The connection between the stories is heightened in the Septuagint (33:5), where the Hebrew noun for "fears" (34:5) is rendered with the language of "sojourns" (παροικία), a word that occurs in 1 Peter 1:17 as part of a Petrine exilic motif (1:1, 17; 2:11). See Jobes, *1 Peter*, 220.

a lengthy citation from Psalm 34 in 1 Pet 3:10–12, as well as with a clear allusion in 2:3.

Peter writes to believers in Jesus in Asia Minor (1:1) who are experiencing slanderous accusations from their neighbors and even members of their household (e.g., 2:18; 3:1) because they have withdrawn from various socio-religious activities of their former pre-Christian way of life (1:18; 2:12; 3:16; 4:3–4, 14). As Elliott notes, this withdrawal was perceived as "antisocial" and resulted in "social tensions deriving from the social, cultural, religious differences demarcating believers from their neighbors."[30] In the face of this situation, Christians were susceptible "to charges of wrongdoing and conduct injurious to the well-being of the commonwealth and the favor of the gods."[31] Into this difficult situation, Peter commends a way of living characterized by "soft difference," that is, a stance toward society that is distinctive when necessary and accommodating whenever possible.[32]

There are two clear references to Psalm 34 in 1 Peter—an extended citation at 3:10–12 (Ps 34:12–16 [33:13–17aLXX]) and an obvious allusion at 2:3 (Ps 34:8 [33:9 LXX]). Peter uses the extended citation to conclude a household code begun at 2:11 (2:11—3:12).

Ps 33:13–17 (LXX; Eng: 34:12–16)	1 Pet 3:10–12
13 Who is the person who desires to love life and to see good days?	10 For whoever desires to loves life and to see good days
14 Stop your tongue from evil and your lips from speaking deceit.	must stop their tongue from evil and their lips from speaking deceit;
15 Turn away from evil and do good; seek peace, and pursue it.	11 That one must turn from evil and do good, they must seek peace and pursue it.
16 The eyes of the Lord are on the righteous and his ears are attentive to their prayer,	12 For the eyes of the Lord are on the righteous and his ears are attentive to their prayer,
17a But the face of the Lord is set against those who do evil.	But the face of the Lord is set against those who do evil.

The gist of the quotation is an exhortation to honorable speech and peaceable living through doing good; these are actions that Peter has already commended in his letter (cf. 1:15; 2:1, 12). They aptly sum up the sense of the household code, which focuses on how those with little power in the

---

30. Elliott, 1 Peter, 103.

31. Ibid., 94.

32. This language comes from Volf, "Soft Difference," 15–30.

household might mitigate hostilities toward their faith within that sphere (e.g., 2:18; 3:1).[33] By living peaceably, within cultural constraints, these slaves and wives, along with the other believers, will "silence the ignorant talk of foolish people" (2:15).[34]

The allusion to Ps 34:8 in 1 Peter consists in the words "taste[d] that the Lord is good" (1 Pet 2:3: "ἐγεύσασθε ὅτι χρηστὸς ὁ κύριος"). In the psalm it is paired with a blessing: "Taste and see that the Lord is good; Blessed is the person who hopes in him" (Ps 33:9; LXX).

In 1 Peter, the allusion provides (part of) the basis for the encouragement to "grow up into your salvation" (2:2). Additionally, a referent has shifted between the psalm and its use in 1 Peter. While "Lord" (κύριος) in the Psalm refers to Yahweh, Israel's God, in 1 Peter it has a Christological focus. The subsequent verse clearly identifies the "Lord" (κύριος) of 2:3 with Christ, who is described as the living stone, chosen by God (2:4). In a move not uncommon in the New Testament, Jesus the Messiah is identified with Yahweh in such a way that texts about the latter can be applied to the former.[35] In this way, Psalm 34 is transumed into the fabric of meaning of 1 Peter.

Just a verse prior, Peter very likely alludes to Psalm 34:13 (LXX: 33:14) as well, given verbal repetition and thematic resonance: "Stop your tongue from evil [κακός] and your lips from speaking deceit [δόλος]. . ." (Ps 33:14; LXX). "So rid yourselves of all evil [κακία] and all deceit [δόλος]. . ." (1 Pet 2:1).[36]

Given the aligning of the stories of these texts—a beleaguered person who has experienced rescue and a group of Christians who hope for the same—along with these two or three citations/allusions to the psalm in 1 Peter, we are justified in continuing with this metaleptical reading to notice some of the psalm's motifs that make their way into 1 Peter. The "fear of the Lord" is an important theme in Psalm 34 (34:7, 9, 11 [Eng]), and in 1 Peter fearing God (1:17; 2:18) displaces fear of those who seek to harm Christians (3:14; also 2:18; cf. Ps 34:4 [Eng]). The psalm also indicates that the shame that would naturally attend trouble and affliction (e.g., 34:17–18 [Eng]) melts away as the righteous look to Yahweh their God (34:5 [Eng])— "Come to him and be enlightened; and your faces will never be covered with

---

33. See Brown, "Silent Wives," 395–403.

34. Moyise, *Later New Testament Writings*, 43, suggests that Peter uses the Psalm's references to "those who use their 'tongues' and 'lips' to do evil" to refer (obliquely) to those who are maligning the Petrine Christians with their malicious speech.

35. On this identification, see e.g., Bauckham, *God Crucified*.

36. Woan, "Psalms in 1 Peter," 222, refers to this connection as a strong or significant allusion (vs. a weak one), with shared language of κακός/κακία ("evil") and δόλος ("deceit") as well as thematic resonance.

shame" (33:6 LXX). Similarly, Peter affirms that those who trust in Christ "will never be put to shame" (1 Pet 2:6; citing Isa 28:16). The Petrine audience is later exhorted to be unashamed if they are suffering as a Christian (one who bears the name of Christ; 4:16). Rather, Peter indicates that those who slander them might themselves be put to shame if believers respond "with gentleness and respect" (3:15–16).[37]

By following this trail of citations, allusions, and themes, we have mapped the context and backstory of the psalm onto 1 Peter.[38] For a group of Jesus followers who are experiencing verbal slander from those around them as well as the fear and shame that would naturally accompany this social persecution, Peter evokes the story of Psalm 34. It is the story of a troubled person (David, by psalm attribution) who remains faithful and true in spite of persecution and is restored by his God. Peter uses this story of God's faithfulness and salvation to encourage his audience to persevere in doing good, "commit[ting] themselves to their faithful Creator" (4:19) and redeemer. As Jobes notes,

> [Peter's] logic appears to be just as God delivered David from his sojourn among the Philistines, God will deliver the Asian Christians from the afflictions caused by their faith in Christ, because they are no less God's covenant people than was David.[39]

Genesis 4 in Matthew 18

A more allusive connection to the Old Testament occurs at Matt 18:22 in Jesus' reference to the "seventy-seven times" a follower of Jesus should be ready to forgive a brother or sister (18:21–22). While only consisting of three words in Greek (ἑπτάκις and ἑβδομηκοντάκις ἑπτά), this allusion to the Septuagint is strong given the thematic and storied connections between the two texts.[40]

---

37. For a summary of these connections, see Christensen, "Solidarity in Suffering," 346.

38. We have also seen how the psalm is transformed at points to meet the needs and eschatological time frame of the Petrine audience.

39. Jobes, 1 Peter, 223. As Christensen, "Solidarity in Suffering," 351, notes: "The psalm thus functions well to bring the Christian reader into solidarity with the experience of Israel through the lens of David."

40. Woan, "Psalms in 1 Peter," 215, defines a strong allusion as well replicated and the only textual contender for the reference.

> Seven times (ἑπτάκις) vengeance has been taken by Cain, but by Lamech seventy-seven times (ἑβδομηκοντάκις ἑπτά). (Gen 4:24 LXX)

> Then Peter approached [Jesus] and said, "Lord, how many times will my brother or sister sin against me and I forgive them? Up to seven times (ἑπτάκις)?" Jesus replied, "I tell you, not up to seven times (ἑπτάκις) but seventy-seven times (ἑβδομηκοντάκις ἑπτά)." (Matt 18:21–22)

If we apply Powell's criteria to this potential allusion, we can affirm that Genesis, the precursor text, was available when Matthew's Gospel was written (criterion of availability) and that there is a three-word repetition between the texts (criterion of repetition). Remembering that Hays includes *recurrence* as a criterion that expands upon repetition (Hays's *volume*),[41] we can note that Genesis is frequently referenced in Matthew,[42] and the specific precursor text of Genesis 4 (the Cain and Abel story with its aftermath) is alluded to at Matt 23:35 and likely also at 5:21–24.[43]

Quite importantly, this allusion fulfills the criterion of thematic coherence and is best seen through a storied (metaleptical) lens. The story of Genesis 4 follows the entry of sin into the human condition (Gen 3:1–19) and illustrates the escalation of sin's effects on subsequent human generations (4:1–8). The story that is picked up metaleptically in Matthew focuses on one of Cain's descendants, Lamech (4:17–18). Lamech makes the claim that the vengeance God declared would be visited upon anyone killing Cain ("seven times," ἑπτάκις; 4:15–16) will now be visited upon anyone who kills Lamech, and it will be applied *seventy-seven fold* (ἑβδομηκοντάκις ἑπτά; 4:23–24 [LXX]).[44] With the number seven functioning as an expression of fullness, seventy-seven implies an unlimited figure.[45] Thus, a theme of this story is the multiplication of revenge—from God's word to protect

---

41. Lucas, "Assessing Stanley E. Porter's Objections," 96, helpfully points to Hays's own subsequent clarification of *volume* to note that it focuses not only on the degree of verbal and syntactical repetition, but also on the prominence of the precursor text and the rhetorical stress the repeated language receives in both literary contexts. In this regard, Genesis is arguably a prominent OT text for NT authors and audiences.

42. See Brown, "Genesis in Matthew's Gospel," 42–59.

43. See Allison, *Studies in Matthew*, 65–78.

44. While the number in Greek is ambiguous and could refer either to the equation 70 times 7 or the number 77, the Hebrew behind the rendering clearly denotes the number: cf. Hultgren, *Parables of Jesus*, 22.

45. Davies and Allison, *Gospel According to Saint Matthew*, 2:793.

Cain the murderer, to Lamech's self-pronouncement that he will be avenged exponentially.[46]

This Genesis story is echoed in Matthew 18, providing a compelling vision of competing stories. The first story centers on archetypal revenge as it spirals out of control. This story is contrasted with the unlimited forgiveness that should characterize believers in Jesus. The Community Discourse, as Matthew 18 is called, focuses on Jesus' teachings to his followers about the ways they are to live with one another in community. If we think of the storied elements of the chapter—the vision of the church that is projected by it, we see a community that rejects the hierarchical status categories ("greatness") imposed on it by society, where stratification of honor, resources, and privilege creates a differential system of valuing people (18:1, 10). Instead, Jesus points to a child—representative of those with little or no status—to be the model for those who gather in his presence (18:2–5). Renunciation of status and its privilege corresponds to the care for "little ones" (itself a status category)—those who are most vulnerable and at the margins (18:6–9).[47]

In fact, because God cares so deeply for "little ones" (18:10), care for these "little ones" extends to searching them out like a shepherd leaving the flock to seek out the single straying sheep (18:12–14). Care for the whole church works itself out in recognition of the seriousness of sin within and against the community (18:15–20; already in vv. 6–9). Addressing sin has as its goal full restoration of the offending person (18:15). Yet the accused person is also protected by the biblical requirement of adequate testimony about the identification of sin (18:16). The church as a whole is responsible for communal restoration and health (18:17–18).

This thematic pairing and potential tension between care for all, especially the most vulnerable, and the potentially serious communal effects of sin segues well to the topic of forgiveness. A community that is called to deep care for one another and taught to watch out especially for those who have little value in the eyes of society (18:10) may be tempted to overlook sin. Alternately, a community that is focused on purity and the seriousness of sin as an obstacle to communal wholeness or *shalom* may be tempted to see certain people as expendable. Into this tension, Matthew highlights and concludes with the theme of extravagant forgiveness (18:21–35). Forgiveness as Matthew envisions it here does not minimize sin's seriousness. The huge debt of the parable of the unforgiving slave emphasizes that forgiveness

46. Narrative-critical methodology raises the question of point of view in stories such as this one. What Lamech (a character in the narrative) claims should not be read as expressing the narrator's point of view, or the divine point of view for that matter. See Brown, *Matthew*, 37.

47. See Brown, "Matthew's 'Least of These' Theology," 294.

is not simply an overlooking of sin (18:23–24).[48] Yet the use of Genesis suggests that forgiveness in the Jesus community is to be without limit (i.e., "seventy-seven times;" 18:21–22); it is to be extravagant, even excessive. As Lamech claims unlimited revenge, Matthew's Jesus announces unlimited forgiveness.

Conclusion

In this chapter, we have explored the intertextual category of metalepsis as an important feature of NT texts. Metalepsis refers to the NT authors' frequent practice of drawing upon the surrounding material—and, often more importantly, the contextual story—of their specific citations, allusions, or echoes of OT texts. Even fairly allusive references, if recognized, can conjure up significant textual backstory. In this way, intertextuality moves beyond allusion and quotation to include "a common nexus of images and themes informing a whole passage."[49]

So it is important to determine the legitimacy of any particular allusion or echo (in addition to clear citations and allusions). To do this, I have suggested following the criteria discussed above and provided by Hays and Powell. Once these are delineated, the full import of the metalepsis can be explored. In our discussion, I have provided two extended examples, one from a psalm in 1 Peter and the other a Genesis allusion in Matthew. In both cases, we have seen that the expressed or implied stories of the OT precursor text have been important for a fuller understanding of its NT use. Given the conviction of the writers of the New Testament that Jesus the Messiah completes the story of the Old Testament, their liberal and evocative use of not only Scriptural texts but also the Scriptural stories surrounding those texts should come as no surprise.

---

48. "Some interpreters have complained that if God is the king in this analogy, then even God does not live out Jesus' exhortation to unlimited forgiveness (18:22). Presumably, the king in this parable does not even forgive the servant up to seven times, much less seventy-seven, so the logic goes. However, the purpose of the parable is to provide the basis for forgiveness—God's forgiveness of the greatest of debts—not to provide an example of unlimited forgiveness. This basic analogy between the parable and the kingdom stands without requiring all details to be analogous." (Brown, *Matthew*, 217).

49. Litwak, *Echoes of Scripture*, 52–53.

Recommended Reading

Brown, Jeannine K. "Creation's Renewal in the Gospel of John." *Catholic Biblical Quarterly* 72 (2010) 275–90.

———. "Genesis in Matthew's Gospel." In *Genesis in the New Testament*, edited by Maarten J. J. Menken and Steve Moyise, 42–59. New York: T. & T. Clark, 2012.

Hays, Richard. *The Conversion of the Imagination: Paul as Interpreter of Israel's Scripture.* Grand Rapids: Eerdmans, 2005.

———. *Echoes of Scripture in the Letters of Paul.* New Haven: Yale University Press, 1989.

———. *Reading Backwards: Figural Christology and the Fourfold Gospel Witness.* Waco: Baylor University Press, 2014.

Mallen, Peter. *The Reading and Transformation of Isaiah in Luke-Acts.* New York: T. & T. Clark, 2008.

Thatcher, Tom. "Cain and Abel in Early Christian Memory: A Case Study in 'The Use of the Old Testament in the New.'" *Catholic Biblical Quarterly* 72 (2010) 749–50.

Woan, Sue. "The Psalms in 1 Peter." In *The Psalms in the New Testament.* Edited by Steve Moyise and Maarten J. J. Menken, 213–29. London: T. & T. Clark, 2004.

4

Rhetoric of Quotations

Christopher D. Stanley

Until recently, virtually all scholarly studies of Paul's use of Scripture have focused on the literary, hermeneutical, or theological dimensions of his engagement with the biblical text. The central aim of these studies has been to develop a deeper and richer understanding of the varied ways in which Paul read and interpreted his ancestral Scriptures. Most follow a similar methodology. They identify a text from Paul's letters where he seems to be referring directly or indirectly to the text of Scripture, then investigate the similarities and differences between the two texts and their contexts in an effort to uncover the deeper thought-patterns and interpretive strategies that lie behind Paul's application of the text. Some focus primarily on explicating the meaning of particular passages while others strive to comprehend Paul's overall approach to Scripture and/or the role and influence of Scripture in his theology. The goal, however, is the same—to understand how Paul viewed and interpreted his ancestral Scriptures in the light of his Christ-centered faith.

One of the little-noticed side effects of this preoccupation with Paul's interpretive activity is that the real-world social and rhetorical setting of Paul's letters tends to fall by the wayside. For most interpreters the task is not to explain how Paul used biblical references to shape the thinking and behavior of a particular audience but rather to reconstruct how Paul engaged with the biblical text prior to the composition of his letters. Now and then a scholar will talk about how a particular quotation, allusion, or echo might relate to the concerns and interests of Paul's original audience.[1] Such

1. As used here, the term "quotation" refers to "any series of several words that

42

observations, however, are generally limited to passages where Paul uses Scripture to battle opposing viewpoints, as in his references to Abraham in Galatians 3 or his discussions of "wisdom" in 1 Corinthians 1–3.

This approach is undoubtedly helpful as far as it goes. Paul's letters are saturated with biblical language, and it makes sense to look for patterns that might indicate how his thinking was shaped by his ancestral Scriptures both before and after he became a Christ-follower. The problem with such investigations is that they say little about why Paul referred to the Jewish Scriptures at all when writing to predominately Gentile congregations or what he was trying to accomplish when he did so. In short, they overlook the rhetorical dimension of Paul's appeals to Scripture.

As used here, the term "rhetorical" refers to the conscious and skillful use of language to persuade an audience to embrace or reject a particular set of ideas or actions. The study of rhetoric was a vital element of the elite educational system in the Greco-Roman world, and virtually all ancient writings bear the marks of the author's rhetorical training. Whether Paul himself received a formal rhetorical education is unclear, but all scholars agree that his letters are rhetorical compositions designed to motivate specific groups of Christ-followers to believe and/or act in particular ways. Direct appeals to Scripture play an important role in the persuasive strategies of several of his letters.[2] This is especially evident in the case of quotations and allusions, both of which are clearly marked for recognition by the audience.[3]

reproduces with a reasonable degree of faithfulness the general word order and at least some of the actual language of an identifiable passage from an outside text" (Stanley, *Paul and the Language of Scripture*, 36). An "allusion" is a more general reference to material that the author presumes is familiar to the audience, such as Paul's references to the Elijah story in Rom 11:2–4 or the Exodus story in 1 Cor 10:1–11.

2 The importance of *explicit* biblical quotations for Paul's argumentation is sometimes overestimated. Paul quotes directly from Scripture in only four of his assured letters (Galatians, 1 and 2 Corinthians, and Romans), and he addresses many weighty issues without adducing specific verses in support of his views (e.g., Gal 3:19–4:7; 1 Cor 7:1–8:13; 2 Cor 5:1–21; Rom 5:1–8:30; cf. Phil 3:1–21). Conversely, many of his quotations appear in contexts that bear little relation to those "central issues of the faith" that are said to have motivated Paul's studies in the Jewish Scriptures (e.g., 1 Cor 9:9; 14:21; 2 Cor 4:13, 9:9; Rom 14:11).

3. As used here, the term "quotation" refers to "any series of several words that reproduces with a reasonable degree of faithfulness the general word order and at least some of the actual language of an identifiable passage from an outside text" (Stanley, *Paul and the Language of Scripture*, 36). To have a rhetorical effect, a quotation must be marked for recognition by the original audience, whether by an explicit quotation formula ("as it is written," etc.), an interpretive comment, or an obvious grammatical tension with the surrounding passage; see Stanley, *Paul and the Language of Scripture*, 31–39.

The present chapter outlines a rhetorical approach to Paul's biblical quotations. A rhetorical approach examines how quotations work to enhance the persuasiveness of Paul's arguments, not how Paul himself read and interpreted the biblical text. It raises questions about why Paul inserted a verse of Scripture at a particular point in his argument, how the quotation relates to his broader rhetorical purposes, and how audiences from diverse social and religious backgrounds might have responded to this sudden intrusion of material from a Jewish religious text. Attention is given to both the emotional and intellectual effects of these encounters with the Scriptures of Israel. The central question is not, "What does Paul's use of this text tell us about his theology?" but "How well does this quotation cohere with the rhetorical purposes of the letter and the needs and capabilities of his intended audience?" In short, a rhetorical study examines what quotations *do* as part of a developing argument, not just what they *say*.

Quotations as Rhetorical Devices

Speakers and writers have used quotations to enhance the rhetorical quality of their works since ancient times, but the technique has been largely neglected in both ancient rhetorical treatises and modern studies of rhetoric and speech communication. The subject is ordinarily treated rather briefly (if at all) in a section dealing with the use of outside evidence or testimony to lend credibility to an argument.[4] According to Chaim Perelman, such an "argument from authority" is used to anticipate and/or close off debate regarding a statement made by the speaker/author in direct speech: "One resorts to it when agreement on the question is in danger of being debated."[5] Arguments from authority are especially common in contexts where power is unevenly distributed between speaker and audience. Such imbalances can affect the way the speaker interprets the source text: "The superior participant will often choose to mask his or her own position by exploiting the ambiguities available in the language" of the source.[6] The effectiveness of appeals to authority (including quotations) depends heavily on the audience's

---

4. Aristotle (*Rhetoric* 1.15, 2.21, 2.2.3) and Quintilian (*Inst. Orat.* 5.36-44) comment briefly on the practice, but other ancient rhetoricians are silent. Among modern studies, the classic work of Chaim Perelman and L. Olbrechts-Tyteca, *New Rhetoric*, contains only four references (in 514 pages!) to the subject of "quotations," all of them quite brief.

5. Ibid., 308.

6. Leith and Myerson, *Power of Address*, 124.

perception of the authority and relevance of the source text and the credibility of the speaker/author who uses them.

Not all quotations are used to lend authority to an argument. Sometimes they serve to illustrate or exemplify a point made by a speaker using
ordinary language. As one popular rhetorical textbook puts it, "The value
and power of any literary material quoted in a speech depends upon its
relevance to the point of the message and upon its strength in saying something—with grace, felicity, and a sense of the poetic or the dramatic—that
could not be said as aptly in the speaker's own words."[7] Here we see a
recognition of the poetic effects of the quotation process: a quotation can
have "value and power" due to the attractiveness with which the thought is
expressed, regardless of what authority is attributed to the source text.

Quotations are also used to create or reinforce a sense of communion
between the speaker and the audience. In cases where the speaker is already
viewed favorably by the audience, quotations from a source that is familiar
to both parties can serve to highlight the bond between them and make
the audience more receptive to the speaker's message. In cases where the
audience is uncertain or hostile toward the speaker, a well-chosen quotation
can increase the audience's confidence in the speaker by revealing values
that are shared by the two parties. In both cases the quotation appeals to the
emotions of the audience by recalling positive memories and/or reinforcing
community pride.

In short, contemporary studies of rhetoric tell us that a quotation from
a respected text can serve to increase an audience's receptivity to a speaker's
message and arguments. But they have little to say about how to analyze the
effectiveness of a particular act of quotation. Rhetorical analysis involves
more than just describing what a speaker or author was trying to accomplish through the use of arguments; it includes evaluating how well those
arguments were tailored to the needs and capabilities of the intended audience. With regard to Paul's letters, this means that we must ask not only why
Paul inserted a quotation from Scripture at a particular point in his letters
but also whether his audiences were capable of understanding and responding to his biblical arguments. Paul's letters provide ample evidence that he
did not always speak in a way that his audiences could comprehend or accept (e.g., 1 Cor 5:9–11; 2 Cor 10:8–11; Gal 3:1–3). We should not therefore
presume that the people whom he addresses understood all of his biblical
references or approved his interpretations when they did understand them.
Instead, we must investigate whether quoting from the text of Scripture was
an effective strategy for influencing particular congregations. Our answers

7. Hance, Ralph, and Wiksell, *Principles of Speaking*, 88.

to such questions will invariably be tentative due to our lack of evidence regarding how Paul's letters were received in his churches. But that does not mean that the task is hopeless. Contemporary rhetorical critics have formulated a variety of techniques for evaluating the likely effectiveness of a piece of argumentation. A brief review of what they have to say on the subject will give us a theoretical foundation for assessing the likely effects of Paul's rhetorical appeals to Scripture.

A Model of Rhetorical Communication

Most of the work that is done these days in the area of rhetorical criticism is rooted in the "New Rhetoric" developed by Chaim Perelman and Lucie Olbrechts-Tyteca in the 1950s and 1960s. One of their successors, Eugene E. White, has formulated a theory of rhetorical communication that has proved useful for analyzing the effectiveness of rhetorical works.

According to White, all rhetorical speech is rooted in what he calls a "provoking rhetorical urgency." This term refers to the perception by a speaker or author that (a) something is wrong in the situation of a potential audience, and (b) language can be used to influence the audience to effect a change in the situation. The nature of the "rhetorical urgency" depends entirely on the perceptions of the communicator. As White puts it, "Rhetorical urgencies are not really 'out there' as sequences of objective events; they are patterns of thought and feeling in people's heads."[8] Ordinarily these perceptions have some basis in social reality, but they should not be taken as accurate representations of the audience's situation; rhetorical communication is often elicited by inadequate information or misunderstanding of a real-world situation. By addressing a group of people in terms meant to win their adherence, the communicator hopes to induce them to think or act in such a way as to remove the rhetorical urgency that evoked the address. Rhetorical speech is therefore audience-centered speech; its purpose is to stimulate action on the part of an audience, not simply to communicate the ideas of the speaker/author.

The central criterion by which the effectiveness of a rhetorical act should be judged, according to White, is the degree of congruence between the communicator's language and various circumstantial forces that influence the rhetorical process. Put differently, the arguments used by the speaker must be relevant to the real-world situation of the audience and expressed in ways that they can comprehend and approve. White lists six factors that influence the effectiveness of a rhetorical communication:

8. White, *Context of Human Discourse*, 105.

1. The potential for modification of the urgency (i.e., whether the situation can in fact be changed);

2. The capacity of the audience to alter the urgency (i.e., whether they have the power to make the desired change);

3. The readiness of the readers/listeners to be influenced (including whether they are favorably or unfavorably disposed toward the speaker/author);

4. The occasion of the rhetorical work (i.e., the nexus of circumstances in which the communication takes place);

5. Relevant aspects of the persuader's self-system (personal history, beliefs, values, self-image, attitudes toward the audience, etc.); and

6. The persuader's real and apparent purposes in communicating (insofar as those can be determined from the communication).

The most important of these rhetorical constraints, in White's view, is the audience. The success of a rhetorical communication depends heavily on the audience's willingness to allow themselves to be influenced by the words and ideas of the speaker/author. To induce a positive response, the communicator must be able to create a sense of coherence between the beliefs and values commended in the message and the prior convictions of the audience. The audience's opinion of the character of the communicator and their perception of the degree of "fit" between the message and their situation also influence their response to the message.

In some cases the audience may be either unable or unwilling to provide the response that the communicator desires. They might harbor negative views of the character and/or the beliefs and values of the person who is addressing them; they might regard the situation in a different light than the speaker/author; they might be incapable of comprehending the ideas and/or language used by the author; they might be divided among themselves over the issue at hand; or they might simply be disinterested in the subject. If the speaker/author fails to recognize and counteract these potentially damaging influences, the effectiveness of the rhetorical act will be hindered. The effective communicator is one who takes full account of the capabilities and likely responses of the intended audience within a particular rhetorical context.

Quotations in Paul's Rhetoric

So what did Paul's predominately Gentile audiences think of his practice of quoting from the Jewish Scriptures? Did they find his biblical argumentation persuasive, or did they ignore it as obscure or irrelevant or both? Did they share his high regard for the authority of Scripture, including his drive to ground his beliefs and practices in its words? Or did they view his biblical quotations as a distraction, a means of obscuring the real issues at hand?

Questions such as these highlight how little we really know about the way Paul's letters were received by his first-century audiences. The fact that the letters were preserved indicates that at least some of the recipients found them valuable. Those who already agreed with Paul's positions would of course have been predisposed to embrace his arguments as valid. Those whom we commonly style his "opponents" would have had an opposite response. Some of them may have offered new arguments to counter those raised in Paul's letters, including arguments from Scripture.

For the rest of Paul's audience members we have no direct information. But careful historical research can lead us toward a reasonable approximation of their response. Using White's model as a guide, we can (a) investigate how Paul used biblical quotations as part of his broader strategy of persuasion, then (b) compare his approach with what we know about ancient audiences to assess the likelihood that his congregations were capable of responding in the manner that he expected. In this way we can formulate credible historical judgments regarding the likely effects of Paul's rhetorical use of biblical quotations.

A careful examination of the various ways in which Paul used biblical quotations to advance the arguments of his letters is beyond the scope of this chapter. We can, however, present the results of one such study.[9]

1. In Eugene White's terms, Paul faced a different "provoking rhetorical urgency" when writing to each of his churches. The identification of each situation as a "rhetorical urgency" requiring a written response reflects Paul's own perception of the circumstances, which may or may not have coincided with the perceptions of others in the audience (or the "real" situation). In each case Paul crafted a response that he believed would persuade the audience to see things as he did and follow his advice about removing the "rhetorical urgency."

2. In a few of these letters—Galatians, 1 and 2 Corinthians, and Romans—Paul used explicit quotations from the Jewish Scriptures as part of his rhetorical strategy. It is probably no accident that these four letters were

---

9. Adapted from Stanley, *Arguing with Scripture*, 171–75.

addressed to churches where his integrity or apostolic authority had been called into question. In this setting, his repeated appeals to Scripture would have served to reinforce his standing with the audience by highlighting the bond that united them all, Jew and Gentile alike, under the sway of the God of Israel. He may also have hoped that his skill in handling the community's holy text would enhance his reputation with the audience and thus secure a more favorable hearing for his message.

3. From Paul's quotations we can see that he, like other Jews, regarded the Jewish Scriptures as the final authority on any subject that they addressed. He also expected his non-Jewish audience to share this opinion, which they would have learned by participating in one of his house-churches. By citing the words of Scripture, Paul sought to bring the recipients of his letters face-to-face with the God of Israel whose power and truthfulness they could not deny without undermining their own faith. This subtle appeal to the audience's prior beliefs and emotions would have carried significant weight with those who shared Paul's lofty view of Scripture.

4. Though he wrote to predominately Gentile churches, Paul expected his audiences to know the background of at least some of his biblical references and fill in material that he left unexpressed. He also assumed that they were familiar with major elements of the belief-system embedded in the Scriptures, allowing him to use words like "God," "covenant," and "law" without stopping to explain their meaning. These subtle appeals to a shared belief-system served to reinforce the ideological and social bond that united Paul and his audiences while also allowing him to frame his response to the "provoking rhetorical urgency" in a way that built on these common beliefs and values.

5. Even in passages where quotations play an important role, Paul rarely grounds his arguments on the authority of Scripture alone. His usual practice is to embed his quotations in a carefully structured argument that he believes will speak to the needs and capacities of his audience. Occasionally he frames an argument around a specific text of Scripture (e.g., Rom 4:1–25; 2 Cor 3:7–18), but more often he develops his position using the normal canons of rhetorical speech, appealing to Scripture as part of a broader argument. Now and then he quotes a verse of Scripture not to trade on its authority, but for other reasons: to illustrate or exemplify a point, to say something in a particularly apt manner, to establish the premise of an argument, to remind the audience of a biblical character or event, etc. In these cases the rhetorical purpose of the quotation cannot always be determined with confidence.

6. To increase the chances that his audience would understand and respond to these "words of God" in the way that he intended, Paul frequently

revised or adapted the wording of his quotations so as to highlight the link between the biblical text and his own argument.[10] He also made a practice of surrounding his quotations with introductory and/or exegetical comments that explained how he meant for the quotation to be understood. In these cases we have a reasonably clear indication of the rhetorical strategy that informed Paul's handling of the biblical text, though we cannot always be sure about ancillary aspects of the quotation.

7. Sometimes Paul fails to clarify how a particular quotation relates to his broader argument. In some cases the ambiguity is only temporary, i.e., the audience is left to puzzle over the quotation until its significance becomes clear from the ensuing discussion. In other cases the quotation takes the place of a direct argument, whether because the wording of the text was deemed particularly fitting or because it conveyed a point that Paul was hesitant to express in his own words. In still other cases the link remains obscure. While it is possible that these remaining ambiguities are intentional, most rhetorical critics would regard them as missteps in a developing argumentative strategy.

8. Paul did not quote Scripture in a vacuum. When writing to the Galatians and Corinthians, he assumes that they will remember at least some of his biblical teachings (e.g., the stories of Abraham and Moses) from his earlier visits to their communities. Others also taught from the Scriptures in these churches, some of them in ways that Paul believed to be wrongheaded and dangerous. At least some of Paul's biblical quotations were inserted in an effort to counter such "false teachings" and to present other ways of understanding the authoritative text. How much Paul knew about these opposing viewpoints, and whether his "opponents" subsequently cited Scripture to counter the arguments that Paul raised in his letters, is unfortunately lost to us. But we can be sure that Paul's letters represent only one stage in a developing rhetorical situation.

Assessing the Capabilities of Paul's Audiences

Clearly Paul believed that direct quotations from the Jewish Scriptures could be an effective tool for motivating his audiences to think and act as he believed they should and to remove any obstacles that hindered them from following his recommendations. But was he correct in this view? For a piece of rhetoric to be effective, careful argumentation alone is not sufficient; the work must also be appropriate to the intended audience. This means that the audience must be capable of following the argument sufficiently

10. For evidence, see Stanley, *Paul and the Language of Scripture*.

to comprehend the speaker's points, and willing to consider seriously the course of action proposed by the speaker. If problems are expected in either of these areas, an effective rhetor will take this into account and craft the speech accordingly.

But how do we determine what Paul's audiences were capable of understanding and accepting? The letters are our only direct source of information, and scholars disagree over what we can infer from them about the biblical knowledge and literary capabilities of Paul's audiences. But we do have outside evidence regarding literacy levels in general and biblical literacy in particular in Greco-Roman antiquity, and we can use these materials to formulate a historically responsible estimate of what Paul's audience were capable of doing. Studies of the social composition of Paul's churches have shown that the vast majority of his followers came from non-elite and non-Jewish backgrounds. We should therefore focus the bulk of our attention on what can be known about the literary capabilities of people from these social strata. Yet we cannot ignore the fact that a small percentage of Paul's audiences might have been Jews or attended a Jewish synagogue prior to joining the community. Thus, we need also to ask whether the knowledge and skills of these people might have differed from those who possessed no prior experience with ancient Judaism.

So what do we learn when we pose these kinds of questions? On the general subject of literacy in the ancient world, the evidence is fairly clear. In his acclaimed study of ancient literacy, William Harris concludes that not more than 10–20 percent of the population would have been able to read or write at any level throughout the classical, Hellenistic, and Roman imperial periods.[11] Virtually all elite males would have been literate, but their numbers were too small in relation to the broader society to have much influence on the overall literacy figures. The percentage of women who could read was even smaller. In a subsequent investigation of books and literacy in early Christianity, Harry Gamble concludes that even if the early church had a disproportionate number of semi-literate craftspeople and small business workers among its numbers, the percentage of Christians who could read and write during the first few centuries CE would not have exceeded the upper end of the range specified by Harris.[12]

But what about the Jewish members of Paul's congregations? Biblical scholars have long presumed that literacy rates were high among Jews in antiquity, since written texts played a vital role in Jewish worship and Jews relied heavily on written texts to guide their daily conduct. Josephus claims

11. Harris, *Ancient Literacy*, 272, 284, 328–30.
12. Gamble, *Books and Readers*, 2–11.

that Jews throughout the Mediterranean world were trained to read and discuss their sacred texts (*Contra Apion* 2:18, 2:25, 2:178). The Mishnah and Talmud also refer often to schools where apparently literate boys were trained to study the Torah.

In recent years, however, a number of studies have demonstrated that literacy levels were not as high among the Jews of antiquity as scholars had supposed. After an exhaustive review of the literary and inscriptional evidence for literacy in Roman Palestine, Catherine Hezser concludes that less than 10 percent of the Jewish population would have been able to read simple texts and sign their names during the imperial era. Hezser describes Jewish literacy using the image of concentric circles.

> At the center one has to imagine a very small number of highly literate people who could read literary texts in both Hebrew/ Aramaic and Greek. Then there was another, slightly broader circle of those who could read literary texts in either Hebrew/ Aramaic or Greek only. They were surrounded by people who could not read literary texts but only short letters, lists, and accounts. A broader proportion of the population may have been able merely to identify individual letters, names, and labels. They as well as the vast majority of their entirely illiterate contemporaries had access to texts through intermediaries only.[13]

Thus, while it is reasonable to think that the Jewish members of Paul's churches would have been familiar with common biblical stories and key texts from a lifetime of participation in Jewish synagogue services, there is little reason to think that they were capable of reading Scripture on their own. In other words, the presence of Jews in the early Christian congregations tells us little about literacy levels in the churches to whom Paul's letters were addressed.

Occasionally, scholars have suggested that Paul expected the literate members of his churches to teach their illiterate brothers and sisters the content of Scripture so that they, too, could recognize the broader literary contexts of the biblical verses that he cites. While this idea sounds reasonable, it overlooks the many barriers that stood in the way of such a practice. At the most basic level, it is anachronistic to think that the uneducated masses who labored from sunup to sundown would have had either the time or the intellectual inclination to listen to their social superiors expounding the meaning of biblical texts. It is even less likely that the early house-churches, which as far as we know met only once a week, developed

---

13. Hezser, *Jewish Literacy*, 473.

any system for training illiterate people to memorize vast portions of Scripture, especially when there is no mention of such a practice anywhere in the New Testament.[14]

As for the small number of literate elites in Paul's churches, it seems equally unlikely that many of them would have made a habit of studying the Jewish Scriptures on their own. Only the local synagogue would have owned a significant number of biblical scrolls, and the tensions that often prevailed between synagogue authorities and the followers of Jesus would have made it difficult for members of the latter group (especially non-Jews) to gain access to them. The sheer cost of having a biblical scroll copied by hand would likewise have limited their availability, though it is certainly possible that some of the wealthier Christ-followers might have owned a few scrolls for personal or congregational use. More likely, however, they would have followed the common practice of copying verses onto wax tablets, papyrus scrolls, or parchment notebooks during times when they had access to biblical scrolls, in addition to relying on their memories.[15] Some of these people may have read their notes aloud or quoted from memory during their weekly gatherings, but there is little reason to think that the physical scrolls were consulted on such occasions.[16]

Even when the few literate members of Paul's congregations had access to biblical scrolls, other factors would have limited their ability to engage thoughtfully with specific texts. Ancient scrolls had no chapter or verse divisions to aid the reader in locating passages, and readers had no concordances or other tools to assist them. As a result, only those who possessed a thorough knowledge of the Scriptures (invariably Jews) would have been able to chase down a particular verse in a biblical scroll. Those who came from non-Jewish backgrounds—the vast majority by the time the New Testament texts were written—would have had no idea how to locate the biblical verses that were cited by Paul and other early Christian writers. Even if they had attended Jewish synagogues before joining the Christian movement, the bulk of their biblical knowledge would have come from sermons delivered orally by synagogue leaders. Literate Gentiles who had studied biblical scrolls for themselves while attending the synagogue would have been rare to non-existent.

14. The Jewish synagogue is not an analogous situation, since even illiterate Jews were trained to know the content of their Scriptures from childhood.

15. See further, Stanley, *Paul and the Language of Scripture*, 73–78.

16. Interestingly, there is no mention of public Scripture-reading in the few passages where Paul himself speaks about corporate worship (1 Cor 11:17–34; 14:1–40; cf. Eph 5:19–20).

In short, the evidence suggests that not more than a few people in any given church, i.e., those recruited from the educated Jewish or non-Jewish elites, would have been capable of reading and studying written texts on their own, and even they would have found it difficult to engage regularly with the Jewish Scriptures. Jewish Christians and non-Jews who had attended synagogues as "God-fearers" might have recognized some of the biblical references in Paul's letters that escaped those from non-Jewish backgrounds, but there is no reason to suppose that more than a handful would have been capable of recalling the literary context of less common passages or looking up biblical verses for themselves.

Paul's Biblical Rhetoric in Context

So how might this information concerning the literary capacities of ancient audiences affect our understanding of Paul's biblical rhetoric? On the one hand, it cautions us against the common assumption that Paul quoted from the Jewish Scriptures as a means of inviting his audiences to reflect on the broader literary contexts of the verses that he cites. Not only is it is unlikely that many of the recipients of his letters could read, but the few who were able to do so would have faced difficulties in accessing and using biblical scrolls. On top of this, a careful comparison of Paul's quotations with their original contexts reveals numerous places where a reader who was familiar with the original context could have raised serious objections to his inter-pretations along with others where the link between his interpretation and the original text is so obscure as to leave a knowledgeable reader fumbling to comprehend his reasoning.[17] Scholars who believe that Paul expected his audiences to reflect on the relation between his interpretations and the original contexts of his quotations typically minimize or ignore these prob-lems. If this was indeed what Paul expected, he was an ineffectual rhetor in many of his appeals to Scripture.

On the other hand, there is ample reason to suppose that Paul did not expect his audiences to possess a deep or broad knowledge of Scrip-ture. Most of his quotations can be understood without reference to the original context, since he routinely surrounds them with interpretive comments that indicate how he means for the text to be understood and applied. In cases where he mentions only part of a story or passage and leaves the audience to fill in the gaps, the level of biblical knowledge that he presumes is consistent with what we might expect from an illiterate audience that had encountered Christian interpretations of Scripture in

17. For more on these points, see Stanley, *Arguing with Scripture*, 75–170.

a local house-church. Examples include 1 Cor 10:1–12 and 2 Cor 3:7–18, where he assumes that the Corinthians are familiar with some of the central episodes of the Exodus story; Gal 3:6–8, 16, 28; and 4:21–31, where he alludes to certain elements of the Abraham narrative; and Romans 5:12–21, where he presupposes at least a general awareness of the story of Adam's fall in Genesis 3. But the amount of prior knowledge that the audience is expected to supply in these passages is quite limited.[18] We cannot conclude from these scattered references that he expected them to know the entire story-line of the narratives to which he refers any more than we can presume from his few Torah quotations that he expected them to know the entire Torah. Paul knew better than this, since he had lived and worked among the Christ-followers in Galatia and Corinth and had many contacts in the church at Rome (Rom 16:3–16) who could have told him if conditions were different there.

As it turns out, the types and amount of biblical knowledge that Paul presupposes in his letters is similar to what we find in other early Christian materials. The Christian gospel was accompanied by biblical proof-texts from its earliest days, and Christian moral teachings were likewise grounded in part on biblical injunctions. Certain biblical characters (Abraham, Moses, etc.) appear regularly in early Christian literature, suggesting that stories about them circulated broadly among the communities of Christ-followers. The same was probably true for verses that could assist believers in defending their faith before a hostile world. None of this is beyond the capability of a functionally illiterate Gentile audience that had received a modest amount of oral biblical instruction in a Christian setting.

Taken as a whole, these observations suggest that Paul was aware of the limited biblical knowledge of his intended audiences and crafted his biblical arguments to suit their capabilities. Rather than expecting his audiences to recall and reflect on the original context of his biblical references, Paul seems to have made a serious effort to indicate to his audiences how he meant for his references to be understood. The success of this effort did not depend on anyone being able to reconstruct Paul's interpretive methods or approve his handling of the biblical text. All that was required was that they follow his arguments (no easy feat!) and accept his interpretations of Scripture as valid.

Why then did Paul quote at all from the Jewish Scriptures when writing to largely illiterate Gentile audiences? Sometimes he was compelled to do so by his subject matter, as when he was dealing with belief or practices that were already deeply rooted in the biblical text (faith, righteousness,

18. For more information, see ibid., 75–78, 116–18, 139–42.

atonement, etc.). This was especially true in cases where people were quoting Scripture in support of ideas that Paul believed were wrong-headed. Another factor was his own deep familiarity with the language and ideas of Scripture, which no doubt brought biblical references unbidden to his mind.

The primary reason for his appeals to Scripture, however, seems to have been the rhetorical effectiveness of biblical quotations within early Christian communities. Paul knew that his audiences revered the words of Scripture, even if most of them were unable to read it. Biblical quotations carried weight with them regardless of whether they knew the exact source of the reference, since the quotation showed the God of Israel standing firmly on Paul's side. The ability to quote and interpret Scripture can be a powerful tool within a religious community, especially when the skill is limited to a handful of practitioners, and Paul did not hesitate to use this tool to advance his arguments. Neither literacy nor familiarity with the original context is required for people to be persuaded by an argument that is backed by a text that they regard as authoritative. As long as Paul's audiences acknowledged the authority of Scripture, quotations from the holy text would be greeted with respect and (Paul hoped) submission. Who would dare to argue with the bearer of God's word?

Taking the Audience Seriously

A brief example will illustrate how different constructions of Paul's audiences can affect the way we evaluate the rhetorical effectiveness of his explicit quotations. The text to be examined here is one of his lesser-known quotations, that of Isa 28:11–12 in 1 Cor 14:21. Following a brief overview of Paul's arguments in the verses leading up to the quotation, we will analyze the potential rhetorical effectiveness of the quotation for two hypothetical audiences, one that is familiar with the original context of the quotation and one that knows only as much biblical content as Paul presupposes in his letters to the Corinthians.[19]

The provoking rhetorical urgency that motivated Paul to write the letter that we know as 1 Corinthians was his perception of a dangerously high level of disunity within the church. A woman from Corinth named Chloe whom Paul apparently knew and respected had sent a message to Paul (1:11) describing how factions were disrupting the community (cf. 5:1, 11:18). The community's leaders had also sent him a letter asking his advice on some of the issues over which they were divided (7:1; cf. 8:1; 12:1;

19. For a more detailed treatment, see ibid., 90–96.

16:1). Chapters 12–14 present Paul's answer to one of the questions over which the community was divided: the proper exercise and relative importance of what he calls the *charismata*, in particular the value of "speaking in tongues." The problem, as he sees it, is not "speaking in tongues" itself—he actually encourages the practice with proper regulation (15:5, 13, 15, 18, 26–27)—but rather its unrestrained use in the gathered congregation. His solution is clear: the public exercise of "tongues" should be limited because other members of the congregation cannot understand what the speaker is saying (15:2, 7–9, 11, 16, 23) and thus cannot benefit from the experience (15:5, 6, 12–13, 17, 19).

From the amount of rhetorical energy that he expends on the issue, we can infer that (a) Paul viewed the current Corinthian practice as highly problematic; (b) he expected at least some of the Corinthians to disagree with his assessment of the situation; and (c) he did not think that a simple assertion of his own authority would be effective in this situation. To overcome these problems, he laid out a variety of arguments that appealed to the reason and experience of the Corinthians, including formal instruction (12:4–11, 27–28; 14:6–12), analogies from ordinary experience (12:12–26; 14:7–8), personification (12:15–16, 21), rhetorical questions (12:17, 29–30; 14:7–8), personal examples (14:6, 11, 15, 18–19), poetic exposition (13:1–13), hypothetical situations (13:1–3; 14:6), and authoritative pronouncements (14:5, 13).

By 14:20, however, Paul has had enough of this line of reasoning. He moves therefore to seal the argument with the rhetorical strategy that seems to come most naturally to him, the argument from authority. First he belittles the Corinthians as "children" in their thinking by comparison with his own "mature" view (14:20). Then he appeals to the authoritative Scriptures, whose force he underlines by identifying the verse as a statement from "the Law" (Torah) (14:21a). In reality, it comes from Isa 28:11–12. Paul quotes from the Greek translation known as the Septuagint (LXX), which diverges markedly from the Hebrew here.

> *Isa 28:7–13* (LXX; author's translation)
>
> 7. For these have gone astray by wine; they were led astray because of liquor. Priest and prophet have lost their wits; they were shaken up because of wine, they were led astray by the drunkenness of liquor. This is an omen.
>
> 8. A curse will devour their advice, for it is advice rooted in greed.
>
> 9. To whom did we announce evil things? To whom did we announce a report? Those who have been weaned from milk, those who have been torn away from the breast.

10. Expect trouble upon trouble, hope upon hope, a little more, a little more,

11. because of (the) contempt of lips, through another language. For they speak to this people, *saying to them,*

12. *"This is the place of rest for the one who hungers, and this is the affliction,"* and they did not want to listen.

13. And the oracle of the Lord God to them will be, "Trouble upon trouble, hope upon hope, a little more, a little more," that they may keep on going and fall backward. And they will be endangered and crushed, and they will perish.

1 Cor 14:20–25 (author's translation)

20. Brothers, do not be children in your thinking; instead, be infants in evil, but be mature in your thinking.

21. In the law it is written, "By people of other tongues and by the lips of others I will speak to this people, and not even then will they listen to me," says the Lord.

22. Therefore tongues are a sign not for believers but for unbelievers, while prophecy is not for unbelievers but for believers.

23. If then the whole assembly comes together and everyone is speaking in tongues and some ignorant or unbelieving people come in, will they not say that you are out of your minds?

24. But if everyone is prophesying and unbelievers or ignorant people should come in, they will be tested and examined by everyone.

25. The secrets of their hearts will be revealed so that they will fall on their faces and worship God, declaring, "Surely God is among you."

The importance of this quotation to Paul's argument can be seen from the fact that he spends vv. 22–25 expounding its relevance to the Corinthians' situation. How might the Corinthians have responded to this sudden intrusion of a biblical citation into an argument that had relied to this point on appeals to reason?

Those who revered the Jewish Scriptures, and especially those who respected Paul as an interpreter of the sacred text, would have been eager to hear how this verse applied to the issue under discussion. The language of the quotation, with its references to "people of other tongues" and a people who "will not listen" to them, would have sounded pertinent to Paul's argument, since it echoes language that he himself had used in the preceding verses. But the precise significance of the quotation is by no means clear. Who is the "I" who speaks in this verse? Who are the people who "will not listen" to the "other tongues" that are mentioned in the quotation? How does the verse relate to the situation of the Corinthians? The comments that Paul appends to the citation (vv. 22–25) answer some of these questions, but the audience would have been left to fill in the gaps at other points.

An audience that was familiar with the original context of Isa 28:11–12 would have noticed immediately that Paul has altered the wording of the quotation to make it fit better with his argument.[20] This in itself would have posed no problem for an ancient audience, since the practice of incorporating interpretive elements into the wording of a quotation was an accepted literary convention in antiquity.[21] But when they saw how far the language and sense of Paul's quotation-plus-interpretation diverged from the original, even a sympathetic audience might have been dismayed. Two differences are especially noteworthy. The most obvious is the omission of the first half of verse 12, which contains the words that someone identified as "they" will say to "this people." Paul's application of this verse in 1 Cor 14:23 indicates that the most important part of the quotation from his standpoint was the negative reaction of "this people" when they encountered the incomprehensible speech of the "people of other tongues." If he had included the irrelevant and obscure message that the prophet said would be spoken to "this people," it would have undercut his entire argument.

The other notable change concerns the overall sense of the verse. Unlike the Hebrew text, where God is the one who speaks "with stammering tongue and with alien lip" to "this people" (i.e., Judah), the Greek text appears to attribute the speech in 28:12a (and v. 11?) to the drunken priests and prophets who appear first in 28:7. The meaning of vv. 10–11 is also obscure, though they appear to be pronouncing judgment against someone (the priests and prophets?) for speaking in a contemptuous manner. These verses were problematic for Paul not only because they portrayed "prophets" in negative terms (cf. 1 Cor 14:1–5, 18–19), but also because the "lips" and "language" mentioned in 28:11 are those of the people who are going to be judged, not those whose prophetic speech convicts others as in 1 Cor 14:24–25. By extracting these verses from their original context and altering their wording, Paul was able to suppress these problematic elements of the text in favor of a version that was better suited to his argument. In other words, Paul had to ignore both the original sense and the original language of Isa 28:11–12 in order to make the passage relevant to the Corinthians' situation. This would have been obvious to anyone who consulted the original

20. The exact nature of the changes that Paul has made in the wording of his quotation is difficult to determine due to the complex textual history of the Greek text of Isaiah on this point. See Stanley, *Paul and the Language of Scripture*, 197–205.

21. For more on the common ancient practice of incorporating interpretive cues into the wording of quotations, see ibid., 267–337.

text. In this case, then, a familiarity with the original context would have raised serious questions about the validity of Paul's biblical argumentation and his reputation as a reliable interpreter.

An audience that was unfamiliar with the original text, by contrast, would have seen none of this. Their understanding of the quotation would have been mediated through the interpretive comments that Paul offers in 14:22–25. From these comments they would have learned that Paul meant to highlight certain portions of the quotation and ignore others. The parts that he uses are given an allegorical interpretation—the phrases "people of strange tongues" and "lips of others" are applied to Corinthians who "speak in tongues" during their worship gatherings, while the phrase "this people" is taken as a reference to outsiders ("ignorant or unbelieving people," v. 23b) who enter the room while the Corinthians are speaking and, judging them to be insane, refuse to "listen" to the Christian message. The identity of the "I" who speaks in the quotation is clarified by Paul's addition of the words "says the Lord" at the end of the verse, though the resultant image of "speaking in tongues" as the voice of God speaking to the congregation stands in tension with other verses that regard it as originating in the mind of the individual and being directed to God (14:2, 4, 9, 15, 18–19, 27–28). Nevertheless, the assertion that these words were spoken by "the Lord" would have significantly enhanced the weight of Paul's argument in the eyes of his audience. As long as they remained ignorant of how he had reshaped the quotation to serve his rhetorical purpose, they might well have viewed this as the most effective of Paul's arguments on the subject. The structure of Paul's argument suggests that this was his intention, since he shifts the argument to a higher level once he is done with the quotation.

Thus in this case it appears that audience members who knew nothing of the original context of Isaiah 28 would have found it easier to understand and accept his biblical argumentation than those who were familiar with that context. This sounds counterintuitive until we remember that there were few if any individuals in Paul's churches who possessed the level of biblical literacy and/or access to biblical scrolls that would have been needed to check his references and critique his handling of Scripture. Had he anticipated that people would be doing this, he might have been more careful to explain or change what he was doing. It seems that he counted on the fact that no one in his audience would know the biblical text well enough to question his interpretation.

Here as elsewhere Paul's aim in quoting Scripture was not to engage in debates about the meaning of the biblical text but to induce his audience to grant to his own arguments some of the respect that they accorded to the words of Scripture. The audience did not have to know the original text for this strategy to be successful; all that was required was a general respect for the authority of Scripture and recognition of Paul's status as a literate and reliable interpreter. The ability to read and interpret texts, especially sacred texts, imbued people with authority in the ancient world. Thus even when he did not appeal explicitly to his own authority as an apostle, Paul's rhetorical appeals to Scripture reminded his audiences of his superior abilities and so enhanced the credibility of his pronouncements.

Conclusion

From what we know about first-century audiences, it seems highly unlikely that many of the people in Paul's house-churches would have known enough of the Jewish Scriptures to check his citations against their original contexts. In view of the time that he had spent among them prior to writing his letters, it is even less likely that Paul overlooked this fact. When we look carefully at the way biblical quotations actually work as rhetorical devices in his letters, we see that Paul made a practice of framing his biblical arguments so that audience members with only a rudimentary knowledge of the biblical text could follow and approve his arguments.

It is vitally important that we keep these facts in mind when analyzing the rhetoric of Paul's biblical quotations. Whether the same is true for other early Christian authors must be examined on a case-by-case basis. For example, it seems clear that the authors of Matthew's gospel and the letter to the Hebrews presumed a much higher level of biblical knowledge than we see in Paul's letters, a finding that is in keeping with the general opinion that these documents were addressed to predominately Jewish audiences. If that is so, an analysis of the rhetorical effects of quotations in these documents might well include an examination of unstated resonances between the author's use of the quotation and its original context. Even here, however, a rhetorical approach will remain focused on the role that biblical references play in the surface structure of the author's argument. This is what sets rhetorical analysis apart from other modes of intertextual study.

Recommended Reading

Fisk, Bruce N. "Synagogue Influence and Scriptural Knowledge among the Christians of Rome." In *As It Is Written: Studying Paul's Use of Scripture*, edited by Stanley E. Porter and Christopher D. Stanley, 157–85. SBLSymp 50. Atlanta: Society of Biblical Literature, 2008.

Gamble, Harry Y. *Books and Readers in the Early Church: A History of Early Christian Texts*. New Haven: Yale University Press, 1995.

Hezser, Catherine. *Jewish Literacy in Roman Palestine*. Tübingen: Mohr Siebeck, 2001.

Harris, William V. *Ancient Literacy*. Cambridge: Harvard University Press, 1989.

Moyise, Steve. "Does Paul Respect the Context of His Quotations?" In *Paul and Scripture: Extending the Conversation*, edited by Christopher D. Stanley, 97–114. Atlanta: Society of Biblical Literature, 2012.

———. *Evoking Scripture: Seeing the Old Testament in the New*. London and New York: T. & T. Clark, 2008.

Porter, Stanley E. "Paul and His Bible: His Education and Access to the Scriptures of Israel." In *As It Is Written*, edited by Stanley E. Porter and Christopher D. Stanley 97–124. Atlanta: Society of Biblical Literature, 2008.

Stamps Dennis L. "The Use of the Old Testament in the New as a Rhetorical Device." In *Hearing the Old Testament in the New Testament*, edited by Stanley E. Porter, 9–27. Grand Rapids: Eerdmans, 2006.

Stanley, Christopher D. *Arguing with Scripture: The Rhetoric of Quotations in the Letters of Paul*. New York: T. & T. Clark, 2004.

———. "Paul's 'Use' of Scripture: Why the Audience Matters." In *As It Is Written*, edited by Stanley E. Porter and Christopher D. Stanley, 125–55.

———. "The Rhetoric of Quotations: An Essay on Method." In *Early Christian Interpretation of the Scriptures of Israel: Investigations and Proposals*, edited by Craig A. Evans and James A. Sanders, 44–58. Sheffield: Sheffield Academic, 1997.

5

Midrash

Lori Baron and B. J. Oropeza

Many if not most of the writers of the various documents contained within the New Testament were Jewish, and therefore it is not surprising that they use typically Jewish ways of expressing the message that Jesus is the promised Messiah. These writers frequently cite or allude to the Jewish Scriptures in order to demonstrate that faith in Jesus is compatible with, and indeed, foreshadowed within the Jewish Bible. Their use of the Jewish Scriptures is often puzzling to modern readers, whose contemporary context is far removed from that of the original authors. An understanding of ancient Jewish hermeneutical methods is helpful in discerning the function of many of these citations and allusions in their New Testament contexts.

Jewish interpretive practices are often called "midrash," a Hebrew word which means "to search after" or "to inquire." The term refers to the ways in which rabbis studied and interpreted Scripture; it also refers to the collections of literary anthologies containing their interpretations. Examples of these collections include the *Mekhilta de Rabbi Ishmael* (a commentary on Exodus), *Sifra* on Leviticus, *Sifre* on Numbers and Deuteronomy, and *Midrash Rabbah* (a collection of ten midrashim on the five books of the Torah and the five scrolls—i.e., Song of Songs, Ruth, Lamentations, Ecclesiastes, and Esther). To summarize, the term "midrash" signifies both an approach to scriptural interpretation and the anthologies in which these interpretations were published.

There are two major categories of midrash: *halakhic*/legal discussions and *aggadic*/non-legal commentaries consisting of narrative, legend, lore, and homiletical material. Both categories of midrash deal with a wide variety of issues; for example, the sages attempt to clarify how and when various legal stipulations are to be fulfilled, to harmonize verses that conflict with or contradict one another, to explain instances in which biblical characters seem to behave inappropriately, or to reapply a biblical image or story to a new historical context.[1]

This discussion of the use of Jewish exegetical practices in the New Testament introduces three key points central to the present study. First, New Testament writers were steeped not only in the Jewish Scriptures, but also in Jewish methods of reading and interpreting Scripture. As Geza Vermes observes:

> Since the Christian *kerygma* was first formulated by Jews for Jews, using Jewish arguments and methods of exposition, it goes without saying that a thorough knowledge of contemporary Jewish exegesis is essential to the understanding (and not just a better understanding) of the message of the New Testament and, even more, of Jesus.[2]

It is, therefore, incumbent upon readers of the New Testament to gain an understanding of Jewish methods of biblical interpretation at the time of Jesus in order to grasp how NT writers deployed the Jewish Scriptures to communicate the gospel message.

The second key point is that for the New Testament writers and their audiences, the use of Jewish interpretive methods in the NT underscores the continuity between the Jewish Scriptures and the gospel of Jesus Christ. Early followers of Christ understood themselves to be God's people, part of a long trajectory that began with God's covenant with Israel and was manifest in their own day through the death and resurrection of Jesus the Messiah. The retelling of Israel's Scripture as part of the Christian narrative was therefore crucial to early Christian identity, which was rooted and grounded in the story of Israel.

The third point relating Jewish exegetical practices to the New Testament is that like the community at Qumran, earliest Christians had a sectarian view of the Scriptures; they believed that these Scriptures were being fulfilled in the events of their own time.[3] Both groups believed that

---

1. For a more detailed explanation of *midrash* with examples, see Stemberger, *Introduction to the Talmud and Midrash*, 233–359, esp. 233–40; Kasher, "Interpretation of Scripture in Rabbinic Literature," 547–94, esp. 560–84; Stern, "Midrash and Jewish Interpretation," 1863–75.

2. Vermes, "Bible and Midrash," 1.229. See also Brettler, "New Testament Between the Hebrew Bible, 504, and Barrera, *Jewish Bible and the Christian Bible*, 490.

3. For more on biblical interpretation at Qumran and its use of an exegetical method known as *pesher*, see Barrett, "Interpretation of the Old Testament in the New,"

they lived in the eschatological moment when God's purposes were being fulfilled in their midst and that they therefore understood the true meaning of the Scriptures, while those who remained outside of their communities did not. To summarize, the writers of the New Testament had much in common with various strands of formative Judaism that thrived toward the end of the first century—they shared the developing interpretive methodology of Jewish scholars, a strong sense of continuity with the story of Israel, and the belief that the true meaning of Scripture was being fulfilled in their own time. Commitment to achieving a deeper understanding of these points will prove invaluable for interpreting the New Testament, and the resources at the end of this chapter provide a good starting point for such an endeavor.

This chapter will focus on two elements of ancient Jewish exegesis: *gezerah shavah* and the importance of contextual reading. The first section of the chapter will discuss each of these features and provide examples. The second section will show how Paul uses these exegetical techniques in a specific New Testament passage.

Gezerah Shavah

Gezerah shavah is the second principle of interpretation in the list of the seven *middot* (rules or norms) of Hillel (first century CE) and the thirteen *middot* of Rabbi Ishmael (first to second century CE). Hillel's seven points are: (1) *kal waᵈomer* (from the lesser to the greater); (2) *gezerah shavah* (argument by analogy); (3) *binyan av mikatuv eᵈad* (law deduced from common feature in one Scripture); (4) *binyan av mishenei ketuvim* (law deduced from common feature in two Scriptures); (5) *kelal uferat* (from the general to the particular); (6) *kayotse bo mi-makom aher* (same interpretation applies to another place); (7) *davar ha-lamed meinyano* (meaning of a statement may be deduced from its context).[4]

386–94; Fishbane, "Use, Authority and Interpretation," 339–77; Maier, "Early Jewish Biblical Interpretation," 108–29; Barrera, *Jewish Bible and the Christian Bible*, 452–59; Brooke, "Pesharim," 778–82.

4. These rules are found in Tosefta *Sanhedrin* 7.11, *Avot de Rabbi Natan* A 37, and *Sifra* 3a. Although there are differences in the early lists, R. Ishmael's first two rules are identical to Hillel's. For a description of these norms of interpretation and of ancient Jewish hermeneutical principles in general, see Stemberger, *Introduction to the Talmud and Midrash*, 15–30; Kasher, "Interpretation of Scripture in Rabbinic Literature," 584–88; Barrera, *Jewish Bible and the Christian Bible*, 479–81; Elman, "Classical Rabbinic Interpretation," 1844–63; Doeve, *Jewish Hermeneutics*, 61–71; Kern-Ulmer, "Hermeneutics, Techniques of Rabbinic Exegesis," 1.268–92.

These lists of rules of biblical interpretation expanded and developed over time, and although rabbinic texts were compiled and edited after 200 CE, Hillel's rules are likely to have originated before the first century when he collected and compiled them.[5] *Gezerah shavah*, which means something like "comparison with an equal" or "similar decree," is a type of word comparison; it is an analogy drawn between two verses in the Torah based upon a word they have in common. This kind of comparison generally occurs when a legal ruling is clear in the case of one verse, but is unclear in the other; the legal ruling in the former case is then applied to the latter, based strictly on the use of a common word.

The following is frequently cited as a classic example of *gezerah shavah*: the question arises in the Talmud (b. *Pes.* 66a) whether or not the Passover lamb should be sacrificed when Passover falls on the eve of the Sabbath, which would involve work normally prohibited on the Sabbath. The command to offer the Passover lamb merely states: "Let the children of Israel offer the Passover sacrifice *at its appointed time* (*b'moado*; בְּמוֹעֲדוֹ). On the fourteenth day of this month at twilight, you shall offer it at its appointed time (*b'moado*); according to all of its laws and all of its ordinances you shall offer it" (Num 9:2–3). The word *b'moado* is also used of the *tamid* or daily sacrifice: "Command the children of Israel and say to them: 'My offering, my food made by fire, my soothing odor, you shall observe to offer to me *at its appointed time* (*b'moado*; בְּמוֹעֲדוֹ)'" (Num 28:2). In the case of the daily offering, however, the Torah is unquestionably clear that it is to take place on the Sabbath: "This is the burnt offering for every Sabbath, in addition to the regular burnt offering and its drink offering" (Num 28:10). Hillel makes an analogy inferring that because the command for both the Passover and the *tamid* or daily offerings contain the word *b'moado* ("in its appointed time"), the Passover lamb is, indeed, to be offered even on the Sabbath. In other words, just as the daily offering takes place *at its appointed time*, even on the Sabbath, so also the Passover lamb is to be offered *at its appointed time*, which means it, too, is offered on the Sabbath.

This kind of reasoning highlights a central assumption underlying ancient Jewish biblical exegesis, something that James Kugel calls "omnipresence": "The basic assumption underlying all rabbinic exegesis [is] that the slightest details of the biblical text have a meaning that is both comprehensible and significant. Nothing in the Bible . . . ought to be explained as the product of chance. . . . Every detail is put there to teach something new

---

5. So Lieberman, "Hellenism in Jewish Palestine," 54; Stemberger, *Introduction to the Talmud and Midrash*, 17.

and important, and it is capable of being discovered by careful analysis."[6] Each word in the text is there for a purpose, creating a unified and divinely-inspired whole. Any perceived gaps or incongruities in the text are not mere accidents, but meaningful truths awaiting proper exegesis. This kind of intertextual, or more properly, inner-biblical reading focuses on the linguistic level, which includes historical matters, but also transcends them, allowing the interpreter to read and apply the text afresh, in his or her own day.[7]

The example of the *gezerah shavah* discussed above demonstrates that ancient Jewish exegesis relies upon a notion of intertextuality which Daniel Boyarin describes as

> A radical intertextual reading of the canon, in which potentially every part refers to and is interpretable by every other part. The Torah, owing to its own intertextuality, is a severely gapped text, and the gaps are there to be filled by strong readers, which in this case does not mean readers fighting for originality, but readers fighting to find what they must in the holy text.[8]

The gap, in the example of *gezerah shavah* discussed above, is whether or not the Passover lamb should be offered on the Sabbath. Some scholars believe that by means of this analogy, Hillel and his contemporaries found a way to justify the present practice of offering the Passover lamb on the Sabbath. In other words, the *gezerah shavah* did not answer the question of what to do, but rather explained why things were traditionally done as they were.[9] This was not always the reason for constructing such analogies; as noted above, there were various features within the Scriptures that inspired the sages to seek out the underlying meaning of a text, and these are collected in the Talmud and the various anthologies of midrashim.

The Jewish sages were concerned that the *gezerah shavah* needed controls in order to prevent its misuse, so restrictions were placed on its application to *halakhic* or legal matters. For example, it was not permitted for a *gezerah shavah* to be a matter of private interpretation, but rather, the

---

6. Kugel, *Idea of Biblical Poetry*, 103–4.

7. For the idea that the methods of ancient Jewish exegesis originate in the Jewish Scriptures themselves, see Fishbane, *Biblical Interpretation in Ancient Israel*; for an example of the use of *gezerah shavah* in the Scriptures, see p. 159 n. 36. For further discussion and examples of *gezerah shavah* in both *halakha* and *aggadah*, see Kasher, "Interpretation of Scripture in Rabbinic Literature," 576–7.

8. Boyarin, *Intertextuality and the Meaning of Midrash*, 16.

9. As Vermes, "Bible and Midrash," notes, "The point of departure for exegesis was no longer the Torah itself, but contemporary customs and beliefs which the interpreter attempted to connect with scripture and to justify," 1.221; cf. Kasher, "Interpretation of Scripture," 578–79.

interpretation must be handed down from one's teacher (b. *Pes.* 66a; b. *Nid.* 19b); new laws could not be deduced apart from the authority of tradition. Furthermore, both passages in the analogy must be taken only from the Torah, and as is the case in the example cited above, the catchword must be unique to the two passages used in the comparison. Finally, the catchwords must be syntactically or logically superfluous; that is, not essential to the meaning of the passage. Rather, the catchwords (such as *b'moado* above) are understood to stand in the text in order to create a *gezerah shavah*, a word comparison that fills in the gap in a text or provides an explanation or clarification of a specific issue (e.g. b. *Shab.* 13a; b. *Nid.* 22b).[10] It is important to note that the Jewish sages continued to find word connections in the text of Scripture, even when the above conditions were not met. They did not always consider these analogies to be true examples of *gezerah shavah*, even though the word connections performed in many of the same ways as those that were labeled as such. To what extent restrictions were consistently applied to *gezerah shavah* in first-century settings is not clear. Midrashic principles continued to develop as exemplified by the expansion of the original seven principles to thirteen and even more in later centuries.[11] This suggests that when New Testament writers used midrashic interpretive methods, they probably used them in a flexible way.

The primary goal for constructing a *gezerah shavah*—or for the task of midrash in general—was to appropriate Scripture to make it relevant to the current context of the interpreters. The rabbis believed that the Torah addressed itself to them in their cultural and historical situation, and that through midrashic creativity, the divine word made its claim upon them and upon their generation. Through midrashic exegetical methods such as *gezerah shavah*, New Testament writers also were able to interpret the divine *logos*, which had made a radically new claim upon them through the life, ministry, and death of Jesus the Messiah.

Midrash and the Context of Scripture

For our purposes, the traditional sixth and seventh principles compiled by Hillel—"the same interpretation applies to another place" and "the meaning of a statement may be determined from its context"—give evidence that early midrash encouraged interpreters to recognize the importance of context

10. Kasher, "Interpretation of Scripture," 578.

11. Similarly, *heqesh* ("comparison") was sometimes used interchangeably or as a variant of *gezerah shavah*, which beyond word and phrase links, could connect common subjects (Instone-Brewer, "Hermeneutics," 1.294).

for interpretation.[12] In keeping with the importance of scriptural context for interpretation, Eugene Mihaly, when studying *Sifre* Deuteronomy 32, draws our attention to this feature:[13]

> It is very helpful, in probing the meaning of a Midrash, to consider the total context, the "magnetic field," of the biblical text, especially in the earlier, Tannaitic Midrashim. The Rabbis, it is true, often disregard context. They derive their lesson not infrequently by treating each verse and, at times, each phrase or even each word as an isolated entity. This is most typical of the pleonastic exegesis of the Midrash Aggadah. Yet, often, the Rabbis will cite the first half of a verse when the "proof" is contained in the latter part of the text or even in the following or preceding verse. On occasion, however, the total biblical passage is implicit in the subtlety of the exegesis.

William Stegner observes this feature from Romans 9 when noticing the catchword "son" (υἱός) from Gen 18:10 (Rom 9:9) also appears in the "proof-texts" of Hos 1:10 (Rom 9:26) and Isa 10:22–23 (Rom 9:27). In Rom 9:7, referencing Gen 21:12, the key word σπέρμα ("seed"/ "descendent") draws in Isa 1:9 (Rom 9:29), and κληθήσεταί ("shall be called/"named") draws in Hos 2:23 and 1:10 (Rom 9:25–26) to form an *inclusio* with Rom 9:29.[14] Stegner then observes from Romans 9:

> If we examine the contexts in the LXX of the proof-texts that do not seem to be linked by the key words "call," "seed," and "son," we find that all of the proof-texts in Romans 9.6–29 are linked by key words, although Paul, like the rabbis, did not always include the "proof" in his composition. In the proof-text found in Romans 9.12, which quotes Genesis 25.23, no key word is found. Nevertheless, the key word "son" is located in Genesis 25.25. Romans 9.13 quotes Malachi 1.2–3 and the key word "call" is located in Malachi 1.4. Romans 9.15 quotes Exodus 33.19 and the key word 'call' is located within the same verse. Romans 9.17 quotes Exodus 9.16 and here the key word "sons" (of Israel) is located within the same passage in 9.26.[15]

---

12. See terminology and examples in Kern-Ulmer, "Hermeneutics, Techniques of Rabbinic Exegesis," 1.283–85; Doeve, *Jewish Hermeneutics*, 70–71.

13. Mihaly, "Rabbinic Defense," 104. Stahlberg, *Sustaining Fictions*, 144 (cf. 156), similarly suggests that *gezerah shavah* works not with verses as such but "the narrative as a whole. Here a passage is expounded by inference to a similar passage."

14. Stegner, "Romans 9,6–29," 40.

15. Ibid., 41.

This aspect of ancient Jewish interpretation in which one draws from the larger context of the actual quote or allusion and derives "catchwords" for the context seems to have influenced the way Paul interprets Scripture. We find here ancient authors doing something similar to modern metalepsis.[16] It is unlikely, though, that an early confessor of Christ like Paul followed an established set of criteria for discerning "echoes" when quoting or alluding to other texts. Paul's own approach probably included a healthy dose of subjectivity. His choice of key words and citations was motivated at least in part by how the Spirit was prompting him to read or recall certain texts (cf. 1 Cor 2:12–13).

Even so, it is quite plausible to suggest that Paul worked with midrashic interpretative principles. As a former Pharisee zealous for Jewish tradition (Phil 3:5; Gal 1:14), he would have been schooled in ancient Jewish interpretation of Scripture and may have even been familiar with Hillel's interpretative approach or one similar to it.[17] If so, he would have been familiar with principles such as *gezerah shavah* and interpreting words from a scriptural passage's context. At the same time, it is unlikely that he held to a rigorous set of rules that characterized some midrash centuries later. First, midrashic interpretation at his time was still developing, as is evident for example, by expansion of interpretative principles from Hillel's original seven to Rabbi Ishmael's thirteen to even later expansions. Second, after Paul became a follower of Christ, he was no longer accountable to a Pharisaic school of interpretation but to the earliest form of kerygma about Christ handed to him orally by the earliest apostles. Third, as a Spirit-filled believer, and perhaps even at times despite the methods he previously learned, he depended on what he perceived as Spirit-led wisdom and guidance when interpreting and communicating scripture. Finally, if a comparison with his use of ancient rhetoric is of help here, we do not find rigid conformity to the rhetorical handbooks in Paul's letters even though many examples of rhetorical use are quite evident in them.[18] The same might be said for his use of midrash. Although his interpretative and communicative approaches to Scripture were flexible and dynamic, certain principles of midrash including *gezerah shavah* are still evident in his messages, as a number of scholars have recognized.[19]

16. On the term, see Brown, ch. 4 above.

17. In Acts, Paul was a student of Gamaliel (Acts 22:3), who was said to be the grandson of Hillel (Schechter, Bacher, "Gamaliel I").

18. On rhetoric, see the respective chapters in this book by Stanley and Jeal.

19. On the use of *gezerah shavah* in various Pauline passages, see e.g., Stockhausen, *Moses' Veil,* 56–59; Plag, "Paulus und die *Gezera Shawa,*" 135–40; Collins, *First Corinthians,* 165; Keener, *1–2 Corinthians,* 127. Even Hays, *Echoes,* admits its use in Paul though not emphasizing it and is critical of scholars' assumptions about Paul's

Could we expect Paul's predominantly Gentile audiences as a whole, even if informed about the Scriptures, to understand Paul's apparent use of midrashic interpretation with all or most of its links to various words, phrases, and themes from the larger contexts? Probably not. Then again, would the majority of his audience's lack of scriptural knowledge have prevented Paul from constructing his message using such an approach? The answer again is probably not! Although his education and Jewish upbringing conditioned him to interpret Scripture this way, his transformation through Christ added the element of rereading and retelling these texts in light of his new experience. This helped him re-contextualize the texts for a new era in which messianic prophecies were being fulfilled, God's Spirit was being poured out upon the faithful, and Gentiles were coming to know about this Messiah and the God he worshipped. Moreover, God's Spirit, he believed, was shared among this community in Christ, and the Spirit bestowed both him and his converts with special gifts and spiritual wisdom to understand and be transformed by teachings and proclamations related to Scripture (e.g., 1 Cor 2:9–13; 12:8, 28–29). It is reasonable to affirm that Paul thought himself to be spiritually illuminated and equipped to connect and emphasize certain words, phrases, and contexts together from Scripture. Thus when composing his messages, he probably blended such insights with midrash and rhetorical principles he had previously learned. And if such is the case, then he would have presented his messages both with overt and subtle scriptural references regardless of how many or few of them each of his auditors might be able to comprehend.[20] If the Spirit was behind his message, he could be confident that his message was authoritative and would accomplish the purpose for which he had communicated it.[21]

Midrash and 1 Corinthians 10:1–11

Various scholars have suggested that Paul works with midrash in 1 Cor 10:1–11 when retelling certain episodes of the children of Israel in the

---

use of midrash (e.g., 165–66; cf. 10–14). See Jervis, "Paul's Midrashic Intertextual Response," 232–34, for a reply.

20. This is perhaps true of most artists, composers, and preachers, past or present. Film-makers, for example, compose children's films in a way in which children "get" the main message and scenes of the movie. Yet certain subtleties and double-entendres go completely over the children's heads which are appreciated by adults and film critics.

21. An ironic twist is that, if 2 Corinthians is any indication of this, Paul's message did not turn out to be as persuasive as he had anticipated! But, from his perspective, this shows that his auditors might decide to reject his message regardless of its power.

wilderness.[22] This does not mean, however, that Paul has to adopt an *already existing* midrash on the wilderness generation and insert it here in his letter.[23] The repertoire of scriptures in this passage clearly addresses the situation of his Corinthian auditors, which suggests that Paul selected and compiled these scriptures together himself. In this context, Paul attempts to persuade certain congregation members, who think they know better, against the idea that it is harmless for them to eat meat sacrificed to idols (cf. 1 Cor 8–10). Also relevant to this passage, certain members were having sex with prostitutes (6:9–20), and the congregation was plagued by factions that promoted elitism, arrogance, rivalry, and quarreling (1 Cor 1–4).[24] The inclusion of Christ in the wilderness travels of Israel appears to be Paul's own invention (10:4, 9). In this text, Paul creates his *own* midrashic discourse by working with certain midrashic principles available to him as he reinterprets Jewish Scriptures and re-contextualizes them, making them applicable for his predominantly Gentile audience.

Paul's starting point appears to be in Numbers 20. Beginning in 1 Cor 10:1, our apostle seems to adopt the phrase "our fathers" from Num 20:15.[25] Through this designation, he makes the bold move of prompting his Gentile audience to consider themselves as part of the same family with the wilderness generation. Paul characteristically adds his Gentile converts to the people of God so that they, too, inherit blessings given to Abraham through Christ (Gal 3:6–9, 27–29). Although the Corinthians probably know about the exodus-wilderness episodes (e.g., 1 Cor 5:7–8; 2 Cor 3:7–18), they may not have known how divine judgment on their "fathers" in the wilderness pertained to *them* also.

But before unfolding the tragic events, Paul claims the wilderness generation was "baptized" through the "cloud" of God's presence and through the "sea," and fed with spiritual sustenance (10:1–3). These words, minus baptism, allude to Israel's deliverance from Egypt at the Red Sea and being fed miraculously with manna, quail, and water in Exodus 14–17. Barrera adds that Paul's passage "has to be read in the light of the rabbinic passages of the Babylonian Gemara (Yebamot 46a and Keritot 9a), which justify the

---

22. E.g., Meeks, "And Rose Up to Play," 64–78; Collier, "That We Might Not Crave," 55–75; McEwen, "Paul's Use of the Old Testament," 3–10; Stegner, "Romans 9,6–29," 44; Davies, *Paul and Rabbinic Judaism*, 105; Doeve, *Jewish Hermeneutics*, 109–11.

23. Against the idea that Paul uses an already existing midrash (as e.g., Meeks, "And Rose up to Play," proposes), see, Oropeza, "Laying to Rest the Midrash," 57–68.

24. See Oropeza, *First Corinthians*.

25. Another close parallel includes Psalm 77[78]:3–5. On possible allusions to the wilderness Psalms, see Oropeza, *Paul and Apostasy*, 120, 136–37, 150.

baptism of proselytes by assuming that the Exodus supposes a baptism."[26] Although the Gemara, a component of the Talmud, was written much later than Paul's letters, it is quite possible that he learned during his Pharisaic education a similar tradition connecting the Red Sea, baptism, and Gentile converts. Even so, the phrase "baptized into Moses" is almost certainly the apostle's own play on Corinthian conversion as being "baptized into Christ" (1:13; 12:13; cf. Acts 2:38; 19:5). Likewise, by describing the sustenance as "spiritual," he goes beyond the miraculous and divine origin described in Exodus. By choosing this word, he deliberately wants to highlight the wilderness generation's connection with the Corinthians, who considered themselves to be excelling in spiritual gifts and partaking of the Lord's Supper.

Gezerah Shavah and the Lord on the Rock That Followed Them

Paul goes on to say that Israel was sustained by water that came from the spiritual rock that "followed" them in the wilderness, and that the "rock was Christ" (10:4). The imperfect "was" (ἦν) implies Christ's preexistence—Paul claims that Christ was actually present with the wilderness generation during their travels. Richard Hays suggests that Christ is being associated with God as the metaphoric "rock" from the Song of Moses (Deut 32:4, 15, 18, 30–31).[27] This reading finds some contextual support through the allusions of God's faithfulness (10:13/Deut 32:3), sacrificing to demons (10:20/Deut 32:17), and possibly provoking the Lord to jealousy (10:22/Deut 32:21 [but see Num 25:10–12 below]).[28] Moreover, the content of Moses's song addresses Israel's apostasy, a theme that seems to foreshadow Paul's warning against the Corinthians committing apostasy in 10:1–22.[29] Doubtless, Paul is informed by the Deuteronomic text, but it is not so clear that he associates Christ with the "rock" only in a metaphorical sense. God is described as the "rock" (צוּר) only in the Hebrew text of Deuteronomy, not in the Septuagint. As a Hellenistic Jew communicating to Greek speaking audiences, however, Paul's scriptural references normally resemble the Greek more than Hebrew text. Hays explains that Paul was familiar with a Hebrew version even though his readers would not be able to trace the reference back to

---

26. Barrera, *Jewish Bible and Christian Bible,* 499.

27. Hays, *Echoes,* 94.

28. Interestingly, the Samaritan Midrash, *Memar Marqah* (4th c. CE), explicates the Song of Moses cross-referencing Exodus and Numbers episodes, esp. 4.4, 8 (cf. Meeks, "And Rose Up to Play," 66, 76).

29. See further, Oropeza, *Paul and Apostasy,* 215–18.

Deuteronomy 32.[30] This is certainly possible, but this explanation still does not fully explain Paul's use of this imagery. Why is Christ associated with God/rock? How is it that this rock "followed" the wilderness generation? If the imagery of a rock providing "drink" in the wilderness clearly reflects the events in Exod 17:1–7 and Num 20:1–13, might not these texts provide us with clues here?[31] At the very least, Deuteronomy 32 does not exhaust the subtexts that inform Paul in 10:4.

We suspect that Paul used *gezerah shavah* with the association of events in Exod 17:1–7 and Num 20:1–13—both narrate a thirsty, grumbling people who are provided with water that emerges from a rock in the wilderness. God shows Moses the rock he is to strike with his rod in order that water may come forth: "The Lord (κύριος) said to Moses . . . I have taken my stand before you there on the rock at Horeb" (Exod 17:5–6 LXX).[32] The Lord promises to be present on this rock. This incident takes place near the beginning of the wilderness travels. Towards the end of their travels, about 40 years later, in the wilderness of Sin in Kadesh (Num 20:1, 7–11), the people thirst and complain again, and so the Lord (κύριος) tells Moses to speak to the rock before them and it will bring forth water.[33] Whether Paul or one of the Jewish traditions that informed him first made this connection,[34] someone interpreted the latter rock in light of the former rock and concluded that the *same rock* in both incidents provided water for the murmuring people. From this it was inferred that since one incident happened at the beginning of the wilderness travels and the other at the end of them, this rock must have *followed* the people throughout their journeys so that they would not die of thirst. If Paul was not the originator of this inference, he nonetheless employs what is surely his own use of *gezerah shavah* by inferring that if this is the same rock in both episodes, then the Lord's presence which was on the rock of Horeb must also have been present on the rock at Kadesh. It now becomes evident how Paul could equate Christ with this rock. His typical designation for Christ is "Lord" (κύριος), and given that the Divine

30. Hays, *Echoes*, 94.

31. These texts are certainly reflected better in this regard than the poetic "oil" and "honey" that come from the rock of Deuteronomy 32:13.

32. Exactly how Horeb is associated with the locations of Rephidim, Massah and Meribah (17:1, 7) will not detain us. It will have to suffice to say that Paul did not read Exodus and Numbers in light of source and redaction criticism.

33. Various scholars suggest Num 20 is at or near the 40th year (cf. 20:1, 22–29 with 33:37–39). Budd, *Numbers*, 217, considers it priestly material (P).

34. The latter is more likely; we can adduce from other near contemporaries to Paul that the following rock or well (cf. Num 21:16–18) tradition was known since at least in the first century CE (Ps.-Philo *L.A.B.* 10.7; Tg.Onq Num 21:16–20). See further rock traditions in Ellis, *Prophecy and Hermeneutic*, 209–12; Enns, "Moveable Well," 23–38.

Tetragrammaton in Hebrew (יהוה) was replaced by κύριος in the Greek text Paul used, he read Christ as that same κύριος who appeared to Moses and the wilderness generation.[35] Since the Lord (κύριος) stood on this rock, Paul could say that Christ was present with this rock that followed the people, so that "the rock was Christ."[36]

Judgment and Contextual Midrash in the Wilderness

In our text, 10:5 provides the transitory bridge to descriptions of negative behavior and judgments that follow. Beginning with verse 6, the text forms a chiasm with parallel wording and verb use, which reinforces that these verses are structurally linked as a unit, emphasizing the importance of these examples in the wilderness for the Corinthian auditors:[37]

10:5 But God was not pleased with the majority of them,
for they were strewn out in the wilderness.

A. 10:6 Now these things happened as types for us
that we might not crave evil things
as they also craved.

B. 10:7 And do not become idolaters
as some of them did;
As it is written: "The people sat down to eat and drink and rose up to play."

C. 10:8 And let us not commit fornication
as some of them committed fornication
and 23,000 fell in one day.

C¹. 10:9 And let us not test Christ
as some of them tested
and were destroyed by serpents.

B¹. 10:10 And do not grumble
as some of them grumbled
and were destroyed by the Destroyer.

A¹. 10:11 Now these things happened to them as types
and were written for our admonition,
upon whom the ends of the ages have come.

35. For other examples of Paul's use of κύριος in Jewish Scripture for Christ, see e.g., Rom 10:10–13/Joel 2:32[3:5LXX]; Phil 2:9–11/Isa 45:23–26, and further Capes, *Old Testament Yahweh Texts*; Hurtado, *Lord Jesus Christ*, 108–18.

36. We refrain, however, from saying with Thiessen that "God might reside in or take up the body of the rock" ("Rock was Christ," 118). In Exod 17:6, ἐπί properly means "on" not "in."

37. See further, Oropeza, *Paul and Apostasy*, 128–30.

Paul, knowing well the context of Numbers 20, links words and ideas from this text to other texts and strings them together so that the scriptural allusions we find in 10:5–10 are interrelated via catchwords.

First, it seems that Paul combined the phrase "in the wilderness" in Num 20:1–5 with the people's complaint and revilement of Moses toward the end of their wilderness travels in Kadesh, with a similar complaint "in the wilderness" in Kadesh toward the beginning of their travels in Numbers 14 (cf. 13:26; 32:8–13). In Numbers 14 and 20 the people complain, want to die, and they regret leaving Egypt (20:3–5) and want to return to it (14:1–5). As a result of their rebellion, God determines the people must spend 40 years in the desert until the older generation dies before the new generation enters the land of promise (14:29–33). Hence, in 10:5, Paul alludes to Numbers 14:16 (cf. vv. 29, 32) and writes that the judgment of the people being "strewn out in the wilderness" was due to divine displeasure. Paul transforms this life-long trek of the wilderness generation into a metaphor signifying the lifelong journey the Corinthians must take until Christ returns, and their own potential to displease God and be judged. Thus, Paul links the Corinthians with the Israelites, not only as wanderers "in the wilderness," but also in danger of incurring divine judgment.

Second, Paul seems to compare the prior contexts of Numbers 14 and 20 and finds a new context, stringing together themes related to the people's desire for food in the wilderness (20:1–5), wanting to go back to Egypt (14:1–5), and incurring divine judgment (14:16). These aspects are combined in Numbers 11 with the people now craving the foods of Egypt and longing to go back there (11:4–9). Paul's words, "that we should not crave after evil things" (10:6; cf. Num 11:34) references the "graves of craving" episode in which many people died of a plague after eating quail in the wilderness.[38] Perhaps Paul's choice of this text may have also been influenced by the people in this Numbers episode lusting for "meat" (χρέας: 11:4), which was entirely relevant for the problem of meat sacrificed to idols in Corinth, which is explained further below (1 Cor 8:13).

Third, it is not coincidental that in Numbers 11 the people "sat down" (καθίζειν: 11:4) crying for "meat" to "eat," and then "rose up" (ἀναστῆναι 11:32) to collect quail. These words inform Paul's choice of the next text in Exod 32:6 that he cites explicitly in 1 Cor 10:7. Collier rightly affirms that Exod 32:6 is "midrashically derived from Numbers 11 by way of *gezerah shavah* on καθίζειν and ἀναστῆναι."[39] Paul's reading by means of *gezerah sha-*

---

38. Exod 16:13 also mentions quail, but without divine judgment ensuing after the people ate them.

39. Collier, "That We Might Not Crave," 72.

vah links elements from Numbers 11 and Exodus 32, so that God's people provoke divine displeasure by sitting, rising, eating meat, and performing sacrifices before an idol, the golden calf of Exodus 32. He thus attaches his prior discussion of idol meat with the experience of the wilderness generation. The text doubtless evokes Paul's earlier mention of his auditors reclining to eat meat in an idol's temple (1 Cor 8:10).

Fourth, the notion of the people rising up to "play" (παίζω: 1 Cor 10:7/ Exod 32:6), may connote here cultic dancing and sexual play (cf. Jdg 21:21; Gen 26:8; Philo *Mos.* 1.302).[40] By use of this catchword, Paul draws upon another wilderness episode involving cultic eating, idolatry, and more explicit sexual misconduct—the Baal-Peor incident in Num 25:1–18.[41] The men of Israel committed sexual sin with Moabite women and "ate of their sacrifices and bowed down in worship of their idols" (Num 25:2). Paul appeals to the Corinthians to avoid committing fornication and so incur divine judgment (1 Cor 10:8). Perhaps Paul's notion of divine judgment was first elicited by the three thousand deaths that took place in the context of the passage he last quoted (Exod 32:26–28; cf. 34–35).[42] This number of deaths seems to have prompted him to mention the number of deaths from Num 25:9, though possibly confusing or blending the two incidents, he mentions 23,000 rather than 24,000.[43]

Fifth, Paul seems to be contextually informed by the notion of the Lord being provoked to jealousy (Num 25:10–12), which prompts our apostle to find another wilderness episode with a similar idea of the people provoking the Lord. Their railing against God and Moses on account of their lack of food and water in Num 21:4–6 turns out to be Paul's choice for the background text that informs his words in 1 Cor 10:9a: "let us not test Christ.[44] Perhaps he equates *speaking against the Lord* with *testing the Lord*, as does Psalm 77[78]:18–19, when the psalmist interprets the same passage in Numbers 21. As a result, the Lord sends poisonous snakes to bite and kill the troublemakers (Num 21:6; cf. 1 Cor 10:9b). Paul will continue in 1 Cor

40. Meeks, "And Rose Up to Play," 70, extends the meaning of this term further to include "testing" and "grumbling" (10:9–10), which is improbable in our view.

41. Collier, "That We Might Not Crave," 70, notices a similar connection based on *gezerah shavah* in Midrash *Tanhuma* 2.21 [Gen 9.18 and following]. The way Paul connects these texts in the light of the Corinthian situation, however, seems to suggest his own invention.

42. Although a mass destruction also took place in Num 11:33, the amount is not numbered.

43. For several possible explanations for this discrepancy, see Mody, "Case of the Missing Thousand," 61–79.

44. Other possibilities are Exod 17:1–7; Num 14:22; Deut 9:7–8, 22; 32:19–21.

10:22–23 to say that the Corinthians are those who are provoking the Lord to jealousy by eating idol meats and claiming all things are permissible.[45]

Finally, Paul's command not to grumble in 1 Cor 10:10 may be informed by Korah's rebellion, which involves grumbling (Num 16:11, 41) and provoking the Lord (16:30), and which links this story with Paul's previous allusion to divine provocation and testing (Num 21:4–6; cf. 25:10–12). Later rabbinic sources also viewed Korah's rebellion against Moses and Aaron's leadership as a prime example of grumbling and rebellion.[46] Paul claims the rebels' destruction is brought on by "the Destroyer," presumably an angelic being that is not designated as such in Numbers 16. It seems that Paul, informed by the earlier context of Numbers 20, recalls the people's complaint in 20:3 that includes a wish that they had died earlier in the destruction (ἀπώλεια) of their "kinsmen before the presence of the Lord." This earlier event refers to Korah's rebellion.[47] The notion of the "Destroyer" causing this destruction may be an assumption Paul learned from an earlier midrash tradition, perhaps related to the destructive angel that strikes a plague on the Passover night in Exod 12:23 (cf. 4 Macc 7:11; Heb 11:28).[48] Wisdom 18:20–25 retells Korah's destruction and likewise connects it with a destroying angel, and so the association probably pre-dates and may have influenced Paul. Part of this rebellion included frustration over food and drink, of not being able to enjoy vineyards, milk, and honey of the promised land (Num 16:11–14).

Paul relates that what happened to Israel in the wilderness are "types" (10:6, 11), more specifically, prefigurations of what has happened to the Corinthians (10:1–4) and hypothetical prefigurations of what might happen to them (10:5–11), unless they change their beliefs and practices regarding idol meats, fornication, and divisive behavior. All the same, Christ appears to be present with both the wilderness generation in the past and Corinthians in the present.[49] It becomes evident throughout 1 Cor 10:1–11 that Paul links his scriptural allusions together through *gezerah shavah* and contextual catchwords so as to make the wilderness texts relevant to his

---

45. His perception may have been that divine provocation results from testing the Lord; cf. Phua, *Idolatry and Authority*, 159.

46. See sources in Perrot, "Les examples du désert," 440.

47. Cf. Budd, *Numbers*, 218.

48. Later Jewish writers also use *mašḥit*(Exod 12:23/מַשְׁחִית) as one of their designations for a destroying angel: "It was an outgrowth of the rabbinic concept that God's mercy and wrath is put into effect by opposing groups of angels. A specific angel is supported by the presence of the definite article" (Watson, "Destroyer," 2.160).

49. Cf. Oropeza, *Paul and Apostasy*, 128–32.

auditors' situation.[50] His midrash *aggadah* is tailor-made for warning congregation members that their present standing in grace and salvation might be jeopardized because of their vices and presumptuous attitude regarding idol meats (10:12).

Conclusion

Paul has drawn upon texts from the wilderness episodes that capitalize on food, drink, and rebellion leading to divine judgment, even though all of these aspects are not always evident through the allusions that appear on the surface of his text. This is because the contexts of the Scriptures he quotes and alludes to have important things to say that sometimes go beyond the mere words Paul writes. As we have observed from 1 Cor 10:1–11, his allusions to the Scriptures are intricately linked together through catchwords found in the referenced text, or the context of the referenced text. Our exploration of this passage has uncovered how, through midrash, Christ could be the rock in the wilderness and follow the people in their journeys. The apostle's midrashic exegesis turns out to be a finely orchestrated retelling of the exodus-wilderness episodes that accomplishes the task of warning his auditors against repeating the rebellions of their spiritual predecessors in the wilderness.

To be sure, midrash may not be able to explain sufficiently every Pauline reference to earlier texts, but it surely helps explain *some*. *Gezerah shavah*, for example, may be a viable exegetical device worth recognizing when interpreting Paul and other NT authors if: (1) we have good reason to suspect the author might know ancient midrashic traditions; and (2) the author refers to two or more passages (through quotes or allusions) that enable a three-way conversation between the passages and the way the author is interpreting them. These are the starting points for such an interpretation.

Recommended Reading

Barrera, Julio Trebolle. *The Jewish Bible and the Christian Bible: An Introduction to the History of the Bible*. Translated by Wilfred G. E. Watson. Leiden: Brill, 1998.

Barrett, C. K. "The Interpretation of the Old Testament in the New." In *The Cambridge History of the Bible, Vol. 1: From the Beginnings to Jerome*, edited by Peter R. Ackroyd and Craig F. Evans, 377–411. Cambridge: Cambridge University Press, 1980.

---

50. This procedure of chain quotations/allusions might also be relevant for discussions with Talmudic *haraz* (Ellis, *Paul's Use of the Old Testament*, 49–51) and Christian *testimonia* (Albl, *Testimonia Collections*, 41–42).

Boyarin, Daniel. *Intertextuality and the Reading of Midrash*. Bloomington: Indiana University Press, 1990.

Ellis, E. Earle. *Paul's Use of the Old Testament*. Reprint. Eugene: Wipf & Stock, 2003 (esp. 38–84).

Lieberman, Saul. *Hellenism in Jewish Palestine: Studies in the Literary Transmission, Beliefs, and Manners of Palestine in the I Century BCE—IV Century CE*. New York: The Jewish Theological Seminary of America, 1950.

Vermes, Geza. "Bible and Midrash: Early Old Testament Exegesis." In *The Cambridge History of the Bible, Vol. 1: From the Beginnings to Jerome*, edited by Peter R. Ackroyd and Craig F. Evans, 199–231. Cambridge: Cambridge University Press, 1980.

6

Shadows and Realities

Kenneth L. Schenck

The New Testament book of Hebrews interacts with the Jewish Scriptures perhaps more than any other book in the New Testament. The methods it uses in its interactions have long been a matter of great interest to scholars.[1] In some circles, there is strong motivation to demonstrate continuity between the way Hebrews (or any New Testament text) interprets passages from the Jewish Scriptures and the original, historical meanings of those texts.[2] However, in the end, the author of Hebrews had no problem with making what we might call "figural" interpretations—interpretations of the Scriptures that were not bound to the "literal" sense of those texts or their originally intended meanings. For example, the interpretation of the wilderness tabernacle of Exodus in Heb 9:9–10 takes the wilderness tabernacle as an allegory for two periods in salvation history and may even have overtones of the distinction between the creation and heaven.[3]

There is a richness to this polyvalence within biblical texts, the multiplicity of potential meanings a text can assume. On the one hand, it is understandable that some would resist the notion of multiple meanings. It is inevitable that varying interpretations of the biblical texts to some extent undermine the stability of a community of Bible readers. If the Bible is

---

1. For two recent treatments, see Guthrie, "Hebrews" 919–95; Cockerill, *Hebrews,* 41–59. Both emphasize continuity of meaning between the Jewish Scriptures and Hebrews' interpretations more than I would.

2. For a quick sense of how significant an issue this is in some circles, see Kaiser, Bock, Enns, *Three Views*; Guthrie, "Hebrews."

3. Kaiser, "Single Meaning," 45–89, is of this sort.

understood to be the basis for life and belief, then unstable meanings strike at the heart of community stability. So some would deny that the text has varying meanings or that New Testament authors ever take passages from the Jewish Scriptures in any way other than their originally intended meanings.[4] Similarly, some would deny that we should read the texts in any way other than their originally intended meanings, even if other meanings are possible.[5]

By contrast, we side with those who see in this polyvalence of texts both a potential richness and a revelation that all interpreters inevitably rely on criteria *outside* the biblical texts in order to appropriate them.[6] We should accept the legitimacy of "figural intertextuality," the interplay of a reader of multiple texts in dialog with one another that is not limited to what those texts might have meant originally in context. We should accept it because it exists in the Bible whether we accept it or not. We should also accept it because of the incredible depth and richness of meaning it offers, especially when our interpretive sensibilities are guided by the values of an interpretive community to which we belong.

It would perhaps be helpful at this point to pause and specify how terms like "literal" and "figural" are used in this chapter. By "literal," I refer to words taken by an interpreter in what he or she considers to be their everyday or "ordinary" sense.[7] This definition is not without complications, but it will suffice for our purposes. There are of course dead metaphors, whose ordinary sense was originally metaphorical (e.g., a "wild goose chase") but that have been used long enough that their metaphorical origins are largely forgotten. In such instances, a little reflection usually suffices to show that we are looking at an expression that was originally metaphorical.[8]

---

4. So Vanhoozer, *Is There a Meaning in this Text?*, e.g., 32, argues for a "Golden Rule" in hermeneutics, an ethics of interpretation that treats texts with love and respect by listening to what they actually meant. Longenecker, *Biblical Exegesis*, 197, once argued that while NT authors sometimes read the Jewish Scriptures in non-contextual ways, this practice was a cultural dynamic of the time that we should not practice today.

5. E.g., Longenecker, *Biblical Exegesis*, 219, critiqued by Hays, *Echoes*, 180–81, 228.

6. See Schenck, "Allegory of the Tent."

7. In common English use, the word *literal* has wandered from the strict sense we are taking it here. People often use the word *literally* to mean something like "truly" or "in truth." We do not use the word in that way in this chapter. An added complication is that a reader may *think* he or she is taking a word in its literal or originally intended sense and yet be mistaken.

8. Lakoff and Johnson, *Metaphors We Live By*, would argue that all language was originally metaphorical and thus that all "literal" language ultimately consists of layer after layer of dead metaphor.

To consider Christ's death a sacrifice, for example, was originally to think of his death metaphorically, for someone living in the Mediterranean world would not normally have thought of a crucifixion as a sacrifice in the manner of a temple altar. Rather, it was an event of capital punishment meant to shame the person being crucified, as well as any group to which the person might belong. In time, a metaphorical sense can become the everyday sense of a word or expression, even if its originally metaphorical nature is evident.

A metaphor, then, is the creation of a new semantic pertinence by the comparison of two unlike things.[9] "No one is an island" compares a person to an island—even though a person is not an island—and in the process creates a new meaning that neither of those words had by themselves. It is important to recognize that metaphors are often part of someone's intended meaning. That is to say, the intended meaning of a person is not always literal. We might thus distinguish between the "plain" meaning of words, which can be literal or metaphorical, and the literal use of words. So what has sometimes been called the "plain sense" of a sentence may involve metaphors whose figurative meaning is intended. In the sentence, "He worked like a dog on this project," there is a non-literal use of language that is intended as the plain sense of the sentence.[10]

By "figural" interpretation, then, I refer to an intentionally metaphorical interpretation on the part of a *reader* or "receiver" of a text that is seen as *unintended* by the author or "sender" of that text.[11] This definition differs slightly from the way Erich Auerbach first expressed this interpretive practice in 1938: "Figural interpretation establishes a connection between two events or persons in such a way that the first signifies not only itself but also the second, while the second involves or fulfills the first."[12] From a hermeneutical standpoint, this description is ambiguous, because Auerbach does not identify the vantage point of the person establishing this connection. His approach tended to see such connections more in terms of the texts themselves than in terms of the individuals reading or writing those texts.

9. Ricoeur, *Time and Narrative*, 1.ix; *Interpretation Theory*, 45–70; *Rule of Metaphor*, 65–100.

10. Note that I am using the word *metaphor* here in a broader sense than it sometimes has in the context of literary analysis. As Ricoeur did, I am including similes and other non–literal speech as subcategories of metaphor as a general semantic category.

11. By "receiver," I allude to basic communication theory of Jakobson, "Closing Statement," 350. We are thus not assuming that the communication in view is limited to authors and readers of *written* texts but to creators and receivers of all sorts of "texts" in general—visible, audible, and so forth.

12. This quasi-definition of sorts first appeared in 1938 in "Figura," reprinted in *Scenes from the Drama*, 53. It is referenced also by Auerbach, *Mimesis*, 73. Hays, *Reading Backwards*, also draws on this definition.

By contrast, any actualization of a text's meaning is a function of some *receiver* of that text.[13] Auerbach only speaks of two texts, the second of which evokes a figural meaning in relation to the first. However, unless we reference specific contexts of interpretation, the meaning of both texts remains somewhat ambiguous. There was a first meaning, a function of the context in which the text was first uttered, and there can be metaphorical readings of that text by later receivers of that text. Such latter appropriations are figural readings, as I am defining the term, readings that do not take the words in their plain sense but in extended senses created by later receivers of that text.

Figural interpretations can be more or less extensive. The reader of a text can take a single word in a text as a metaphor for some other single entity extraneous to the original meaning of the text. On the other end of the spectrum is a full blown allegory, where multiple features of the plain meaning of a text are systematically taken to represent some other set of truths.[14] The most familiar example of such allegorical interpretations is Augustine's fifth century interpretation of the Parable of the Good Samaritan. In his allegorical interpretation, each character and element of the parable is taken to represent an element of the Christian metanarrative, the overall story of salvation played out in history.[15]

In our case, we are interested both in the way the author of Hebrews heard figural meanings in the texts of the Jewish Scriptures and in the way the first century Jewish thinker Philo heard figural meetings in those texts. Do their methods of figural interpretation coincide in any significant ways, ways that were somewhat distinctive among the exegetical techniques of the time? We would suggest that there are indeed some significant parallels. In particular, the way in which Philo used quasi-Platonic language in reference to more and less substantial interpretations of the biblical texts is suggestive of some of Hebrews' own interpretations of biblical texts. Philo speaks of literal and figural interpretations of biblical texts as analogous

13. See especially Fish, *Is There a Text*. Also, in a much broader sense, see Gadamer, *Truth and Method*.

14. It should be clear from my lumping of allegory and metaphor together—and therefore implicitly types—that I substantially disagree with the distinction Goppelt, *Typos*, tried to make in 1939 between typological interpretation and allegorical interpretation. As Young has demonstrated in "Typology," 29–48 and in *Biblical Exegesis*, this distinction was unknown in both biblical and patristic times. It is rather a creation of a modern era for whom interpretation in historical context became a key criterion of value.

15. The mugged man represents Adam. The Samaritan is Christ. The priest and Levite represent the Law and the Prophets. The inn represents the church, and a number of other elements are allegorized as well.

to the difference between the "shadows" of things and the "bodies" of the things themselves. So also Hebrews seems to consider some elements of the Jewish Scriptures as "shadows" and "antitypes" that point to the true realities themselves.

Philo

Philo was a philosophically-minded Jew who lived in the Egyptian city of Alexandria around the same time as Jesus.[16] Philo was somewhat unusual among his contemporaries in that, in most cases, he accepted both the validity of the literal meaning of biblical texts in addition to figural and allegorical meanings.[17] Most of his Jewish contemporaries only accepted one or the other.[18] So there were many Jews in his day who only interpreted and practiced the instructions of the biblical texts in a straightforwardly literal way (e.g., *Somn.* 1.39).[19] Similarly, Philo mentions allegorists in his day who only considered symbolic and figural interpretations of the biblical texts to be valid (e.g., *Mig.* 89).[20] Unusually, Philo accepted both modes of interpretation, although he clearly considered the figural meanings of the biblical texts to be far more significant than their literal ones.

In his analysis of the practices of the Jewish law, Philo considers the relationship between the literal practices and their symbolic meanings to be analogous to the difference between the body and the soul. "We should look on all these outward observances as resembling the body, and their inner meanings as resembling the soul" (*Mig.* 93).[21] Further, "if we keep and observe these, we shall gain a clearer conception of those things of which

16. Philo specialists prefer to categorize Philo primarily as an exegete or interpreter of the Jewish Scriptures rather than as a philosopher. See Borgen, *Philo of Alexandria*. We now have several good introductions to Philo, including Schenck, *Brief Guide to Philo*; Kamesar, *Cambridge Companion to Philo*; and Seland, *Reading Philo*.

17. Most discussions of Philo at this point blur the distinction I have made above between the literal meaning of a text and the plain sense of a text. By "literal interpretation" of the Torah here, we mean passages in the Torah that were originally intended to be taken literally. Of course when we say Philo accepted certain literal interpretations, we mean the literal meaning as he understood it.

18. For general treatments of Philo's interpretation of Scripture, see Kamesar, "Biblical Interpretation in Philo," 65–91; Borgen, "Philo—An Interpreter," 75–101.

19. For Philo's mention of literalists, see Shroyer, "Alexandrian Jewish Literalists," 261–84.

20. For Philo's mentions of those who only interpreted the Torah allegorically, see Hay, "Philo's References to Other Allegorists," 41–75.

21. All translations of Philo in this chapter are taken from the Loeb translation by Colson and Whitaker, *Philo*.

these are the symbols." In this passage, Philo refers to Jewish practices of the law like circumcision and Sabbath observance. For Philo, these practices had important figural meanings. Circumcision symbolizes that we are to excise our pursuit of pleasures and passions (*Mig.* 92). The Sabbath reminds us that our labors are ineffective in comparison to the activity of God (*Mig.* 91). Nevertheless, despite Philo's sense that the figural meanings of these practices are far more significant, they do not abrogate the need for Jews to practice literal circumcision and to observe the literal seventh day of the week.

In another key passage, Philo encourages readers of the Torah not to stop at a literal interpretation "but to press on to allegorical interpretations and to recognize that the letter is to the oracle but as the shadow [σκιά] to the substance [σῶμα] and that the higher values therein revealed are what really and truly exist" (*Conf.* 190). The passage he is interpreting here is Genesis 11:1–9, the confusion of languages at the Tower of Babel. While Philo accepts that this event happened in history, there is a much more important allegorical meaning he does not want the interpreter to miss. On a literal level, the story is about how humans came to speak in differing languages, but much more significant is the figural truth that God scatters impiety and wickedness. The skilled reader does not merely stop at the literal story but goes on to see the deeper truth. These truths do not contradict or negate the surface meaning of the text. They simply take the reader to a more profound meaning hidden in the text by way of a figural interpretation.

Philo found many truths in the biblical texts by way of figural interpretations. One of the primary ones is what has been called the "allegory of the soul" (e.g., *Opif.* 165). In this allegory, the story of Adam and Eve in the Garden of Eden (Genesis 3) represent the struggle of the mind (Adam) against the pleasures (the serpent) that work on the senses (Eve). This allegorical interpretation of the Adam and Eve story was far more significant for Philo than the literal story itself. For him, it illustrated the need for our minds to prevail over our senses as a source of truth and to eliminate any role that passion or pleasure might assert. To apply his language elsewhere to this interpretation, the literal story of Adam and Eve was like a shadow of the more substantial truth about the relationship between the mind, the senses, and pleasure.

We can see in Philo's imagery the influence of the philosophical traditions of his environment. They provided him with the tools and categories by which he interpreted the biblical texts. The chief influence on him in this regard was clearly Plato, especially as Plato had come to be understood by others in Philo's day.[22] This version of Plato was mixed with other Greek

22. This version of Platonism is sometimes called "Middle Platonism." For an

schools of thought, especially Stoicism. We can see some stereotypical Platonic imagery in the passages in Philo we mentioned above. First there is the distinction between the body and the soul. Second, there is the sense that the visible world around us is a shadow of a more real world of ideas. The literal relates to the body in which the more important soul is housed. The literal interpretation is the shadow cast by the more important underlying figural truth.

In his figural interpretations, Philo made connections between elements of the biblical texts and elements of his own philosophy/theology. In his mind, he was seeing the deep meaning of the text itself on a symbolic level. He considered his philosophy to be the real meaning, the deeper and more substantial meaning, the "soul" meaning. By contrast, the literal meaning for him became the shadow meaning or, alternatively, the "body" that carried the hidden soul meaning. However, from our perspective, these were not connections inherent in the text at all but creative, metaphorical meanings of his own making. In some cases, he likely inherited these allegorical interpretations from other interpreters from Alexandria.

Hebrews

The book called Hebrews in the New Testament was quite possibly a sermon that its author sent ahead of himself to a destination to which he hoped soon to travel, possibly Rome.[23] Like Philo, the author of Hebrews believed that the literal practice of the Torah had been legitimate, at least during the time of the old covenant. Like Philo, he believed that its figural meaning was much more substantial and lasting in significance. Unlike Philo, shadow and reality not only related to each other as surface and figural meanings to biblical texts. For him they also related to two periods of history. The literal meaning, the meaning of the shadows, pertained to the time before Christ. The figural meaning, the meaning of the true and the real to which the shadows pointed, pertained to the time after Christ.

There are a significant enough number of superficial parallels between Hebrews and Philo's writings that the question of influence has been a matter of longstanding debate. Was the author of Hebrews influenced by

---

overview, see Dillon, *Middle Platonists*.

23. The idea that Hebrews was a sermon comes not only from the fact that it lacks the typical opening greeting of a letter but also from the fact that it styles itself a "word of exhortation" in 13:22, which is what Acts 13:15 calls a synagogue homily that Paul gives. While there is no consensus on the destination of Hebrews, Rome currently commands the most support of the named options.

Philo directly or indirectly?[24] The majority of scholars at present think it unlikely that the author of Hebrews was directly influenced by Philo.[25] However, it is worth exploring whether Philo's notion of the literal sense of Scripture as a shadow of the figural sense is in any way similar to Hebrews' sense of the relationship between the Law as shadow of the true realities in the new covenant. A key here is to try to read the texts of the Torah as the author of Hebrews would have and to view him as a figural interpreter of biblical texts.

Before examining Hebrews, a brief detour into the New Testament book of Colossians may help frame our discussion. Colossians 2:17 comes in a passage in which Paul (or possibly a pseudonymous author) is telling a Gentile audience that it should not feel obligated to observe Jewish practices such as food laws or Sabbath observance.[26] These practices, Colossians says, are a "shadow" (σκιά) of things to come, while the reality to which they point, the "body" (σῶμα), was Christ. The rhetoric in this verse is strikingly similar to that which we saw in Philo's treatise *On the Confusion of Tongues* above (*Conf.* 130). The same Greek terms are in fact used. A key difference of course is that while Philo affirmed the literal practice of the Law, Colossians uses this imagery to indicate that Gentiles need not observe the Jewish Law. The deeper reality to which such practices pointed related to the Christ. Those in Christ thus need not observe the "shadows."

We arguably find the same imagery in Hebrews. In relation to the Jewish Law in general, Hebrews indicates that "the law has only a shadow [σκιά] of the good things to come and not the true form [εἰκών] of these realities" (10:1). As an example of such shadows in the Law, the earthly priests of Exodus "offer worship in a sanctuary that is a sketch and shadow of the heavenly one" (8:5). The pattern of the true tent (8:2; cf. 9:11), which is either in heaven or is heaven itself (9:24), was shown to Moses before he had it constructed (8:6).[27] The Most Holy Place of the earthly sanctuary was an "antitype" of the true one in heaven (9:24).

---

24. For an overview of the issue, see Schenck, "Philo and the Epistle to the Hebrews," 112–35; *Brief Guide*, 81–86.

25. As with many majority positions, however, we might speculate whether the majority of Hebrews scholars at present are really familiar enough with Philo's writings to make a solid judgment on the question.

26. Pseudonymity was the literary practice of writing a work under the name of an authority figure from the past. Scholars are divided on the question of whether Paul himself wrote the letter of Colossians or whether someone wrote the letter after his death to convey his authority to a subsequent time and situation.

27. For a thorough analysis of Hebrews' tabernacle language, see Schenck, *Cosmology and Eschatology in Hebrews*, 144–81.

While it is sometimes suggested that Hebrews is thinking Platonically here, the imagery seems to resist any straightforwardly Platonic scheme.[28] Plato saw material, observable things in the world as shadows of the more real patterns or ideas that we can access with our minds. However, for Plato, events did not take place in the world of ideas. So the idea that Christ might enter into a Platonic "archetype" would not have made any sense to Plato. While there is an undeniably Platonic feel to this imagery in Hebrews, it does not ultimately fit any straightforwardly Platonic scheme.[29] In the end, for Hebrews, the realities behind the shadows of the Law are not ideas.

However, Philo presents us with a different alternative. What if the language of shadow and reality relates less to metaphysics (questions of reality) and more to interpretation? What if the imagery here has more to do with the difference between literal and figural understandings of Scripture? Colossians gives us the model in its simplest form. The literal practices of the Jewish law were just shadows, "antitypes," if you would, of the more significant reality effected through Christ. The earthly sanctuary and its practices were only shadows, antitypes, of the realities associated with Christ (cf. Heb 9:24). For Hebrews, the events, settings, and other elements associated with Christ are the more substantial realities to which the literal practices and sense of the Torah as a text pointed.

From our perspective, the author of Hebrews is reading the Jewish Scriptures figurally. Nothing about the text of Exodus or Leviticus would have indicated to Israel that the literal sacrifices, sanctuary, or rituals of the Law were anticipatory or inadequate. For example, the Day of Atonement was a Jewish festival that occurred once a year (Lev 16). It was the one day a year when the high priest entered the innermost room of the sanctuary. Hebrews takes this event parabolically, figurally, of the onetime entrance of Christ into the true sanctuary in heaven (Heb 9:7–11). The literal practice of Scripture was only a shadowy meaning, especially since Hebrews did not consider any such sacrifices effective in their atonement (10:1–4). For Hebrews, the deeper meaning of the Day of Atonement—and indeed all the sacrifices of the Jewish Scriptures taken together—was the onetime "sacrifice" of Jesus.

28. Although his analysis is probably too simplistic, see especially Hurst, *Epistle of Hebrews*, 7–42.

29. The word ὑπόδειγμα (Heb. 8:5; 9:23) is often mistakenly translated "copy," which heightens the Platonic feel of Hebrews given that Plato considered the material things around us as copies and shadows of the ideal realities. However, Lincoln Hurst convincingly argued that this word, while similar to Plato's παράδειγμα, has more the sense of a sketch, as the NRSV translates it (Hurst, *Epistle of Hebrews*, 13–17). I have argued that it has more the sense of an illustration (e.g., Schenck, *Cosmology and Eschatology in Hebrews*, 117–21).

It is clear that Hebrews knows it is engaging in figural interpretations because the author at one point calls one such interpretation a "parable" (9:9). Hebrews was finding what we might call typological meanings in the texts of the Jewish Scriptures. The author knows that these are not the literal or first meanings of those passages, which he describes as a shadow of the reality in Christ.[30] Hebrews is making connections between elements of the biblical texts and elements of his own theology. In his mind, these were deep meanings of the text itself, understood on a symbolic level. However, from our perspective, these connections were not obvious in the texts themselves but are rather creative, metaphorical connections the author himself was making in relation to salvation events in his day.

Conclusion

We have seen in the preceding pages that both Philo and Hebrews use figural interpretation to interpret texts in the Jewish Bible and that both of them consider those metaphorical and symbolic meanings to be more substantial than the literal meanings. Both, however, considered the literal meanings to be legitimate as well, even if inferior in import. For Hebrews, the literal sacrificial practices of the Jewish Law were no longer necessary. Indeed, for this author, they were always foreshadowings and never actually efficacious for atonement. For Hebrews, the realities to which these biblical texts pointed figurally were recent salvation events relating to the death of Jesus. For Philo, the more important realities to which the surface stories and practices pointed tended to be truths about virtue and vice rather than events.

Philo, Hebrews, and even Colossians referred to the surface, literal sense of biblical texts and their practices as shadows. When they did so, they repurposed language Plato had used to express metaphysics and epistemology for an interpretive purpose. For Philo and Colossians, the figural reality that cast those shadows was the "body," the more substantial meaning. For Philo these were important truths about virtue and vice. For Colossians they anticipated Christ. Hebrews does not specifically use the word "body" but speaks in terms of the "true" version of the shadows (8:2) and the "things" themselves (10:1). For Philo, using a different metaphor, the literal practices could in turn be thought as the body in which the deeper truth was something like the "soul" that the physical practice inhabited. For

---

30. The self-referential participle that the author uses in 11:32 is masculine singular, making it overwhelmingly likely that the author of Hebrews was male.

all of them, figural interpretation allowed a text to point beyond itself to a more profound or more lasting meaning.

This chapter has demonstrated that some New Testament authors could use figural methods to hear meanings in the Jewish Scriptures. In particular, we have shown parallels between the ways in which Philo and Hebrews saw meanings in those texts. Without recognizing the potential for such "figural intertextuality," our understanding of certain New Testament texts will inevitably lack a certain depth. Even worse, we may find ourselves substantially misunderstanding the texts in the Jewish Scriptures with which those New Testament texts engage. Rather, we can only gain if we have a full appreciation of all these levels of multivalence—the original meaning of the Jewish texts, the meaning of the New Testament texts that draw on them, and the resonances that both of these meanings have with us in our interpretive communities today.

For the student of Scripture, the starting point is first to recognize when a New Testament text is engaging a text from the Jewish Scriptures. If it is a quotation, it will be easy enough to recognize. The study Bibles we use today, often with a "center reference," will usually tell us if the verse we are studying is alluding to a text from the Jewish Bible. The next step is to read those passages. However, we will want to bracket out the way those words were used in the New Testament. We will want to listen to them in their own context, reading the paragraphs and verses that lead up to the words in question. We will want to look at resources that help us get a fresh look at those words. We can then return to the New Testament passage again, exploring points of continuity and discontinuity in meaning. At what points has the New Testament author followed the meaning of the passage straightforwardly? Are there instances where the author has expanded the scope of the passage from the Jewish Bible? Are there instances where the author has performed a figural interpretation, taking the words in ways that go far beyond anything likely to have been in the original author's mind? Finally, the interpreter may want to ask, "How does my own interpretive community read these words? How are we in continuity or discontinuity? Does any discontinuity enrich our experience of these verses, or is some redirection in order?"

Recommended Reading

Borgen, Peder. "Philo—An Interpreter of the Laws of Moses." In *Reading Philo: A Handbook to Philo of Alexandria,* edited by Torrey Seland, 75–101. Grand Rapids: Eerdmans, 2014.

Hays, Richard B. *Echoes of Scripture in the Letters of Paul.* New Haven: Yale University, 1989.

———. *Reading Backwards: Figural Christology and the Fourfold Gospel Witness.* Waco: Baylor University, 2014.

Kamesar, Adam. "Biblical Interpretation in Philo." In *The Cambridge Companion to Philo,* edited by Adam Kamesar, 65–91. Cambridge: Cambridge University Press, 2009.

Robbins, Vernon K. *The Tapestry of Early Christian Discourse: Rhetoric, Society, and Ideology.* London: Routledge, 1996.

Young, Frances. *Biblical Exegesis and the Formation of Christian Culture.* Grand Rapids: Baker Academic, 2002.

7

Mimesis

Dennis R. MacDonald

The Roman poet Publius Vergilius Maro died in 19 BCE with his magnum opus, the *Aeneid*, unfinished. Even so, it had fulfilled the prediction of Propertius that "something greater than the *Iliad* is being brought to birth" (2.34.66). Vergil's brilliant recasting of the Homeric epics—as well as of previous Homeric imitations, such as the *Argonautica* by Apollonius Rhodius and the *Annales* of Ennius—soon became the textual foundation for the Roman Empire from Augustus to Augustine. By linking Julius Caesar and Octavian back to Homer's Aeneas and his mythological descendants, Vergil provided Romans a venerable past and the emerging Julio-Claudian dynasty ancient pedigree. Later poets, Greek and Latin, similarly imitated Homer, including Ovid, Quintus Smyrnaeus, and the author of the Christian *Homeric Centos*.

Most Homeric imitations, however, were in prose. "Who would claim that the writing of prose is not reliant on the Homeric poems?" This rhetorical question from the rhetorician Philodemus (*On Poetry* 5.30.36–31.2; first century BCE) anticipates the answer "no one." Although many prose imitations of the *Iliad* and the *Odyssey* antedate the *Aeneid*, they proliferated during the first two centuries of the Common Era. Best known, perhaps, are the Greek novels, but Jews, too, imitated Homer. At least eight examples appear in Josephus, and the *Testament of Abraham* provides a magnificent and extended imitation of *Od.* 19.[1] Christians, too, imitated the Greek bard,

---

1. For Josephus, see *J.W.* 3.516–19; 4.359–62; *Ant.* 1.246–248; 1.272–73; 2.224; 4.109–10; 6.362–63; 12.424–425. For the *T.Abr.* see chs. 2–7. Discussions of these texts appear in MacDonald, *Gospels and Homer*, 329–81.

including the authors of the Acts of the Apostles and the *Acts of Andrew (and Matthias).*[2]

This proliferation of Homeric imitations was not merely a literary fad but mimesis. As Tim Whitmarsh has shown, "The dominant notion in the literary aesthetic of Roman Greece was *mimēsis*, a complex term that covers both 'artistic representation' and 'imitation' of predecessors. . . . In literary terms, 'becoming Greek' meant constructing one's own self-representation through and against the canonical past."[3] Whitmarsh thus speaks of a "politics of imitation" that characterizes much of Roman Greek literature. "It was through writing literature (and writing about writing literature, and rewriting literature intertextually) that Greek cultural identity was most richly and intensively explored."[4]

Mimesis Criticism and the Gospel of Mark

In several publications I argue for Homeric imitations in the Gospel of Mark. For example, in *The Gospels and Homer: Imitations of Greek Epic in Mark and Luke-Acts*, I propose the following examples:[5]

Mark	Homer
1:9–11. The Holy Spirit comes to Jesus	*Od.* 1.11–324. Athena and Telemachus
1:13–15. Jesus's authoritative speech	*Od.* 1.325–402. Boldness of Telemachus
1:16–20. Jesus calls fishermen	*Od.* 2.260–387. Athena provides a ship
1:21–27. Jesus's authoritative speech	*Od.* 1.11—2.389. Boldness of Telemachus
1:22–34. Jesus's secret identity	*Od.* 13.306–406. Odysseus's disguise
1:40–45. Jesus's anger at the leper	*Od.* 18.1–123. Irus the rogue

2. For imitations in Acts see MacDonald, *Does the New Testament Imitate Homer*, and discussions in *Gospels and Homer* to Acts 6:9–15; 10:1–23; 12:1–17; 15:1–35; 16:9–12; 19:13–30; 20:7–12 and 18–38; 27:13–44; and 28:1–11 (see also the discussions of Luke 16:19–31 and 23:26–31). On the *Acts of Andrew*, see MacDonald, *Christianizing Homer.*

3. Whitmarsh, *Greek Literature and the Roman Empire*, 26–27.

4. Ibid., 38.

5. See MacDonald, *Gospels and Homer;* also ibid., *Homeric Epics*; ibid., *Mythologizing Jesus.*

2:1–12. The sinful paralytic	*Od.* 8.1–385. Hephaestus
3:6. The plot to kill Jesus	*Od.* 4.557–847. The plot of the suitors
3:13–17. The Boanerges	*Od.* 11.298–304. The Dioscuri
3:19. Judas Iscariot	*Od.* 17.1–260. Melanthius
4:35–41. Jesus awakes in a storm	*Od.* 10.1–77. Aeolus's bag of winds
5:1–20. The demoniac in the tombs	*Od.* 10.135–465. Polyphemus
5:21–43. Jairus's daughter / hemor-rhaging woman	*Il.* 16.433–683. Glaucus's wound
6:1–6. Jesus the carpenter	*Od.* 5.1–255. Odysseus the carpenter
6:14–29. The beheading of John the Baptist	*Od.* 11.385–464. Death of Agamemnon
6:30–44. Jesus feeds five thousand	*Od.* 2.427—3.124. Nestor's feast
6:45–52. Jesus walks on water	*Il.* 24.169–442. Hermes walks on water
6:53–56. Jesus disembarks to a warm reception	*Od.* 2.427—3.124. Pylians and Telemachus
7:24–30. The Syrophoenician woman	*Od.* 15.403–84. Eumaeus's nurse
8:1–9. Jesus feeds four thousand	*Od.* 4.1–144. Menelaus's feast
8:10–12. No sign for this generation	*Od.* 10.76–136. Laestrygonians
8:13–21. The disciples as foolish companions	*Od.* 9.62–107. Odysseus's foolish crew
8:22–26. The blind man at Bethsaida	*Od.* 8.454–555. Demodocus
8:27–30. Peter recognizes the messiah	*Od.* 19.320–505. Eurycleia's recognition
8:31. Jesus's courage	*Il.* 18.95–121. Achilles's courage
8:32–41. Peter's protest	*Od.* 12.16–305. Eurylochus's vow
9:2–13. Jesus's transfiguration	*Od.* 16.172–303. Odysseus's transfiguration
9:30–31. Jesus's courage	*Il.* 18.95–121. Achilles's courage
10:32b–34. Jesus's courage	*Il.* 18.95–121. Achilles's courage
10:35–40. Request of the Boanerges	*Od.* 11.298–304. Request of Dioscuri
10:46–52. Bartimaeus, the blind seer	*Od.* 11.1–151. Blind Tiresias
11:1–14. Jesus enters Jerusalem	*Od.* 6.251—7.328. Odysseus enters Phaeacia

11:15–18. Jesus ousts thieves from the temple	*Od.* 22.1–86. Slaying of suitors
12:1–12. The murderous vinedressers	*Od.* 16.363–417. Plot of the suitors
12:40–44. The widow's penny	*Od.* 17.534–47. Penelope
13:1–4. The disciples' request for the sign of the end	*Od.* 19.35–271. Penelope's request for a sign
13:24–26. Jesus the prophet return	*Od.* 19.296–319. Odysseus predicts his
13:28–32. The prophetic fig tree	*Od.* 19.296–319. The oak at Dodona
14:1–2. Jesus's enemies fear the crowd	*Od.* 16.363–417. Fears of the suitors
14:3–9. The anointing woman	*Od.* 19.320–505. Eurycleia
14:4–7. Resentment at the anointing woman	*Od.* 19.320–505. Melantho's resentment
14:12–17. The water carrier	*Od.* 10.76–136. Laestrygonian maiden
14:27–42. Jesus's disciples sleep as he prays	*Od.* 12.16–305. Odysseus at Thrinacia
14:32–41. Peter's vow	*Od.* 12.333–419. Eurylochus's vow
14:32–42. Gethsemane	*Od.* 10.466–550. Thrinacia
14:43–49. Hacking of the slave's ear	*Od.* 22.135–417. Hacking of Melanthius
14:50–52. The naked young man	*Od.* 10.551–74. Elpenor
14:60–62. Jesus's silence	*Od.* 17.453–87. Odysseus's silence
14:61–64. Jesus reveals his identity to his enemies	*Od.* 22.1–86. Slaying of suitors
14:66—15:1. Peter's broken vow	*Od.* 12.333–419. Eurylochus's failure
15:2–5. Jesus's silence	*Od.* 17.453–87. Odysseus's silence
15:7–20a. Jesus or Barabbas?	*Od.* 18.1–123. Irus the rogue
15:22–23. Jesus refuses wine mixed with myrrh	*Il.* 6.242–65. Hector refuses wine
15:29–32. The taunts at the cross	*Il.* 22.90–288. Hector's taunts
15:33–38. The death of Jesus	*Il.* 22.289–362. Death of Hector
15:39. The gloat of the centurion	*Il.* 22.364–404. Achilles's gloat
15:40–41. The women watching from afar	*Il.* 22.405–515. Trojan women

15:42—16:1. The rescue of Jesus's body	*Il.* 24.443–801. Priam and Achilles
15:46—16:4. The stone at Jesus's tomb	*Od.* 9.105–566. Polyphemus's door stone
16:5–8. The young man at the tomb	*Od.* 12.1–15. Elpenor

The number of possible imitations is breathtaking, which partially explains why few interpreters have adopted Mark's mimetic connection with the epics, favoring instead his debt to a combination of historical memory and oral traditions; Mark's literary models, if any, came from Jewish Scriptures. Such form critics thus are prone to view the Evangelist as a collector of lore about Jesus and not as a master of mimetic mythology.

But the same criteria that establish Homeric imitations in Lucian, for example, point to Mark's debt to the *Iliad* and the *Odyssey*. This methodology, which I call Mimesis Criticism, consists of seven criteria:

Criterion 1. The criterion of *accessibility* pertains to the likelihood that the author of the later text had access to the proposed antetext.

Criterion 2. *Analogy* likewise pertains to the popularity of the target. It seeks to know if other authors imitated the same mimetic model.

Criterion 3. *Density*: simply stated, the more parallels one can posit between two texts, the stronger the case that they issue from a literary connection.

Criterion 4. The criterion of *order* examines the relative sequencing of similarities in the two works. If parallels appear in the same order, the case strengthens for a genetic connection.

Criterion 5. A *distinctive trait* is anything unusual in the targeted antetext and the proposed borrower that links the two into a special relationship.

Criterion 6. *Interpretability* asks what might be gained by viewing one text as a debtor to another. As often as not, ancient authors emulated their antecedents to rival them, whether in style, philosophical adequacy, persuasiveness, or religious perspective.

Criterion 7. Often Greek readers prior to 1000 CE were aware of affinities between biblical narratives and their classical Greek models. Such *ancient and Byzantine recognitions* are useful for identifying mimesis in the original composition of the Gospels. This final criterion takes seriously the reception history of the proposed imitating text.

This chapter is not occasion to defend Mimesis Criticism and its relevance to the Gospel of Mark as a whole; instead, I will apply these criteria to one Markan tale.[6]

Mark 5:1–20 and Mimesis Criteria

The story of the Gerasene demoniac in Mark 5:1–20 strongly resembles the episodes of Polyphemus (the Cyclops) and Circe in the ninth and tenth books of the *Odyssey*. Both Homeric stories unquestionably satisfy mimetic criteria 1 and 2 insofar as they not only appear in one of the best known books from Greek antiquity (accessibility), they also were widely imitated (analogy): "The story of Odysseus and his men caught in the cave of the cannibal giant . . . is one of the most familiar, and most imitated, of the *Odyssey*'s narrative; it has become an iconic story for western narrative literature."[7] Examples appear in Euripides, Apollonius, Ovid, Petronius, and Apuleius.[8] Circe and her porcine-producing powers likewise inspired imitations in Apollonius, Achilles Tatius, Ovid, Petronius, Lucian, Apuleius, and the *Acts of Andrew*.[9]

Furthermore, the parallels between Mark 5 and *Od.* 9 and 10 are dense, sequential, and distinctive (criteria 3, 4, and 5).[10] Soon after disembarking on an island Odysseus discovered a monster; Jesus, too, discovered a monster after sailing to a desolate shore. Three times Mark mentions that the savage lived among the caves, like Polyphemus.

Od. 9.187–89 and 240–42	Mark 5:2b–5
On the islands of the Cyclopes, "live countless wild goats" (9.118–19).	
"There was a large / herd [πολλὰ / μῆλ'], sheep and goats rested there at night." (9.183–84)	cf. 5:11: "There on the mountain a huge herd of swine [ἀγέλη . . . μεγάλη]" was grazing.

6. I defend this methodology in MacDonald, *My Turn*.

7. Hunter, *Critical Moments in Classical Literature*, 53.

8. Euripides *Cyclops*; Apollonius *Argon.* 4.1638–88; Ovid *Metam.* 23.749–897; Petronius *Satyr.* 97; Apuleius *Metam.* 8.11–13.

9. Apollonius *Argon.* 4.557–752; Achilles Tatius *Leuc Clit.* 2.23; Ovid *Metam.* 14; Petronius *Satyr.* 127–34; Lucian *Ver. Hist.* 2.46; Apuleius *Metam.* 1.7–13. For the imitation in the *Acts of Andrew*, see MacDonald, *Christianizing Homer*, 39–40, 47–50, and my Appendix to *The Gospels and Homer*.

10. A fuller treatment of the following parallels appears in *Gospels and Homer*, 213–20.

The Cyclopes were shepherds.	Swineherds were present.
Odysseus discovered a cave, where "a monstrous man used to sleep, who shepherded his flocks / by himself far away. He did not engage with others / but lived apart and harbored cruel thoughts . . .	5:2: Immediately a man with an unclean spirit met him from the tombs. 3 He made his dwelling in the tombs,
[He was able to lift] a great door stone, / ponderous; two and twenty / excellent four-wheeled wagons might not raise it from the ground."	and no one ever was able to subdue him with chains, 4 for often he was bound in stocks and chains, but he ripped from him the chains and smashed the stocks. No one was strong enough to tame him.
When he discovered the intruders, he immediately crushed the skulls of two men and ate them.	5 Night and day he would be in the tombs and in the mountains crying out and cutting himself with stones.

For the element of fear, Mark borrowed from the story of Circe in *Od.* 10. Odysseus had sailed to her island, and the witch morphed most of his search party into swine. The left column presents her response to the hero after he drew his sword against her.

Od. 10.323–25 and 330–33	Mark 5:6–8
"She screamed loudly [μέγα ἰάχουσα], ran under the sword [ὑπέδραμε], took my knees, / and wailing away spoke to me winged words. /	When he saw Jesus far off, he ran [ἔδραμεν], fell down before him, 7 and crying out with a loud voice [φωνῇ μεγάλῃ] said,
'Who of men are you? . . .	"What have you to do with me,
Surely you are Odysseus of many devices, whom golden-wand Argeïphontes always / told me would come, returning from Troy on his swift black ship. /	Jesus, Son of the Most High God?
Come to me, put your sword in its sheath.'" [Odysseus had pulled his sword on Circe, threatening to kill her.]	I adjure you by God, do not torment me." 8 For he had said to him, "Unclean spirit, come out of the man!"

Circe knows that the stranger is Odysseus because of a prophecy of Hermes; the demons in Mark invariably recognize Jesus as the Son of God because of his preternatural powers. Both foes ask the hero not to do them harm ("Put your sword in its sheath"; "do not torment me"). The demoniac begs, "I adjure [ὁρκίζω] you by God, do not torment me [μή με]"; that is, he asks Jesus to swear an oath. The Greek verb ὁρκίζω, is the causal, verbal cognate to the noun Odysseus used to adjure Circe not the harm him: "Swear me an oath [ὅρκον] not to plan another plot to hurt me [μή τί μοι]." . . . "Once she had sworn and completed the oath [ὅρκον], at that point I went up to Circe's beautiful bed" (10.343–44 and 346–47).

The exchange that follows seems to be modeled after the famous pun in the story of Polyphemus in which Odysseus claims that his name was "Nobody." As a result, when the other Cyclopes ask the blinded giant who it was who was harming him, he replied, "O friends, Nobody is killing me by treachery" (9.408). The other Cyclopes mistook the statement to mean that no one was harming him; his affliction thus must be madness, "sickness from great Zeus" (9.411). Similarly, the demoniac dissimulates:

Od. 9.354–55, 363, and 366	Mark 5:9
"He asked me for it [the wine] again a second time: / 'Please give it to me	And he asked him,
again, and tell me your name [ὄνομα].' / . . . Then I spoke to him . . . ; / 'Nobody is my name [οὖτις ἐμοί γ' ὄνομα].'"	"What is your name [ὄνομα]?" And he said to him, "Legion is my name [λεγιὼν ὄνομά μοι], because we are many."

Odysseus's moniker indicates nonexistence; the demoniac's indicates a plethora of existences, "because we are many." The exchange of names in both stories gives the hero power over the monster. By naming himself Nobody, Homer's hero outwitted the giant so that he could not get assistance from the other Cyclopes. By learning the name of the demons, Jesus seems to have gotten power over them. Surely it is worth noting that at the end of the Polyphemus story Odysseus reveals his true name, which gives the Cyclops an opportunity to curse him to Poseidon, his father, a curse with dire consequences for the rest of the epic: "Grant that Odysseus, sacker of cities, not reach home, / the son of Laertes, who makes Ithaca his home" (9.530–531). Odysseus's "curse attains its full effect only when a victim's full name and identity have been given."[11]

The demons next ask Jesus to send them into swine, a task that should have reminded ancient readers of Circe.

> 5:10 And they begged him emphatically not to send them out of the region. 11 There, on the mountain, a huge herd of swine was

11. Heubeck, *Commentary on Homer's Odyssey*, 2.40.

grazing, 12 and the demons begged him, saying, "Send us into the swine so that we might enter them." 13 He let them do it. The unclean spirits left and went into the swine, and the herd rushed down the cliff into the sea—about two thousand of them—and drowned in the sea.

Whereas Circe used her powers to transform Odysseus's crew into swine, whom she later would likely eat, Jesus used his powers to cure the demoniac and to purge the region of swine.

According to Homer, Polyphemus shouted with pain when the strangers blinded him, and the other Cyclopes came to the cave to see what was happening. Similarly, after Jesus sent the demons into the swine and drowned them in the sea, the locals thronged to the site.

Od. 9.399–402	Mark 5:14–17
"[The giant] let out a great shout to the Cyclopes who lived around him / in the caves among the windy hills. /	The swineherds fled and told it in the city and in the country
When they heard his cry, they rushed from here and there, / and standing around the cave, they asked him what was troubling him."	The people came out to see what had happened. 15 They came to Jesus and saw the demoniac, the one who had had the legion, seated, clothed, and rational, and they were afraid.
	16 Those who had seen what had happened to the demoniac and the swine reported it to them. 17 Then they began asking him to leave their borders.

Mark's reference to the demoniac's now being clothed implies that he had earlier been nude, which is how ancient artists typically depicted Polyphemus the caveman.

Odysseus and Jesus both sail away.

Od. 9.471	Mark 5:18a
"They immediately boarded [εἴσβαινον] and sat on the benches."	After he boarded [ἐμβαίνοντος] the boat . . .

As Odysseus sailed away, he called back a gloat, and Polyphemus responded with a request that the hero return for a gift. Odysseus refused. As Jesus sailed away, the demoniac asked to be taken with him. Jesus refused. The following columns present speeches to the men who were left behind on terra firma.

Od. 9.501–5 and 523–25	Mark 5:18b–20
[Polyphemus asked Odysseus to return to receive a gift.] "I spoke back to him with a raging heart, / 'Cyclops,	The demoniac asked him that he might be with him. 19 But he would not let him, and says to him,
if some mortal man / should ask you	"Return home to your friends
about the disgraceful blinding of your eye, / say that Odysseus, sacker of cities, blinded it, / son of Laertes. /	and tell them how much the Lord has done for you
. . . O that I were able to deprive you of life and survival / and to send you to the house of Hades, / since not even the Earthshaker will heal your eye."	and had mercy on you."
	20 And he went out and began announcing in the Decapolis what Jesus had done for him, and everyone was amazed.

Whereas Odysseus told blind and naked Polyphemus to let others know that it was he who had blinded him, Jesus told the erstwhile demoniac, now clothed and rational, to let others know that God had healed him. The contrast could hardly be more transvaluative. The combination of similarities between these Homeric episodes and the Gerasene demoniac are too dense and distinctive to be attributed to accident (criteria 3, 4, and 5).

Criterion 6, interpretability, assesses why an author may have imitated the proposed model. In this case, Vergil's imitation of the Polyphemus story may provide a clue. Without his knowing it, Aeneas's flotilla "washed up at the shores of the Cyclopes" (*Aen.* 3.569), where they met Achaemenides, a haggard and pitiful Greek soldier whom Ulysses had failed to bring with him. He implored the Trojans to rescue him from the island, even though he was "from the land of Ithaca, comrade of luckless Ulysses" (3.613–15).[12] He described the ghastly cave of the Cyclops: "a house of blood and savage feasts, / inside dark and vast" (3.618–19). He also claimed to have witnessed the cannibalism that Homer had described in the *Odyssey*.

---

12. The soldier introduces himself with language similar to Odysseus's revelation of his identity to the Phaeacians (cf. *Od.* 9.19–21).

Od. 9.288–93	Aen. 3.623–27
"He jumped up and snatched two of my comrades with his hands. / Having grabbed two of them at once, like puppies, upon the ground / he smashed them. Their brains gushed out to the ground and soaked the earth. /	"I myself watched when two of our group / he seized in his huge hand as he reclined in the middle of the cave / and smashed them on a rock. The spattered thresholds swam in blood. /
And after butchering them limb from limb he prepared his dinner / and devoured them like a lion reared in the mountains. He left nothing— / no guts or flesh or marrowy bones."	I watched while he ate their body parts that dribbled black gore; / the warm limbs twitched below his teeth."

Suddenly the Cyclops himself came into view; Aeneas saw "a horrendous monster, misshapen, enormous, bereft of sight" (Aen. 3.658). The Trojans quickly took their suppliant on board and rowed furiously. Polyphemus heard the slapping of the oars and cried out; then "the race of Cyclopes, roused from the woods and high mountains, / run to the harbor and fill the shores" (3.675–76). Vergil used the story to contrast Homer's hero and his own. Whereas Odysseus abandoned his own countryman on Polyphemus's island, Aeneas helped his former enemy escape.

Mark's imitation, like Vergil's, makes his hero morally superior to Odysseus. Whereas Homer's hero, according to the Aeneid, abandoned another Ithacan on the Cyclops' island, Aeneas rescues Achaemenides. Whereas Odysseus blinded Polyphemus and stole his cattle, Jesus restored the caveman to his senses—and his wardrobe. One also should note that both Achaemenides and the demoniac ask to sail away with the protagonist. Aeneas takes the Ithacan about his ship, but Jesus commands the demoniac to stay and give witness to what his has done for him. Jesus's casting demons into swine imitates the transformative powers of Circe, who also appears in Aen. 7.10–20.

Parallels between two literary words satisfy criterion 7 of Mimesis Criticism (ancient recognitions) if affinities between the proposed model and its imitator were detected in the history of reading of the latter. The poets of the Homeric Centos found Od. 9 and 10 useful for retelling stories about Jesus (criterion 7). For example, they adapted lines from the episodes of Polyphemus and Circe for retelling Mark's story of the demoniac in the caves. The first thirteen lines in recension 2 are virtually sequential with Od. 9.181–192, the beginning of the Polyphemus story.

Hom. Cent. 2.782–793

(≅ *Od.* 9.181) But when they arrived at the area located among the Gerasenes,

(≅ *Od.* 9.182) here there was a headland where a cave lay next to the sea,

(≅ *Od.* 9.183) with cascading laurel as though encircling it.

(≅ *Od.* 9.184) In it swine and goats rested at night, and around it a high tomb

(≅ *Od.* 9.185) was built with large stones set deep in the earth,

(= *Od.* 9.186) with tall pines and high-foliaged oaks.

(≅ *Od.* 9.187) Here slept a monstrous man, whom a demon

(≅ *Od.* 9.188) shepherded by itself far away. He did not engage with others

(≅ *Od.* 9.189) but lived apart and knew only cruel thoughts.

(= *Od.* 9.190) For he had been made into a monstrosity and was not like

(= *Od.* 9.191) a man who eats bread, but like a wooded peak

(= *Od.* 9.192) of high mountains that looms larger than the rest.

The poets refrain from imitating *Od.* 9 for the rest of the poem; instead, they switch to *Od.* 10 and the episode with Circe:[13]

Hom. Cent. 2.801 and 803 (cf. 1.965–66)

(= *Od.* 10.229) So he [Jesus] spoke, and they [the demons] cried out and called to him,

(≅ *Od.* 10.251) "As you commanded, let us go into the crowd of the swine!"

These Byzantine poets clearly recognized affinities between the stories and mined the Homeric epic to retell the Gospel story.

Conclusion

What one reads in Mark 5:1–20 is neither historical memory nor antecedent oral tradition, as form critics would have one believe. Rather, it is a poster-child for early Christian Homeric mimesis. Homer's stories of Polyphemus and Circe were widely available and imitated (criteria 1 and 2), and the parallels between the *Odyssey* 9 and 10 and Mark 5 are dense, sequential,

---

13. It also is worth noting that the demoniac and the swineherds in *Homeric Centos* recension 1 are given Odyssean lines related to Eumaeus the swineherd (950–51, 968–71, 983–86; cf. *Od.* 13.409–10, 14.410, 412; 15.342–45).

and often unusual (criteria 3, 4, and 5). Mark's motivation for imitating Odysseus's adventures, like Vergil's imitations, was to portray his hero as more compassionate than Homer's (criterion 6, interpretability). The poets of the *Homeric Centos* recognized the affinities between these tales and borrowed from *Od.* 9 and 10 to retell Mark's exorcism (criterion 7).

If one grants this example, other parallels between the Gospels and the epics become more plausible. Furthermore, if this is the case, Mimesis Criticism belongs not on the fringes of Gospel scholarship but at its center, along with more traditionally accepted methodologies.

Recommended Reading

MacDonald, Dennis R. *Christianizing Homer: "The Odyssey," Plato, and "The Acts of Andrew."* New York: Oxford University Press, 1994.

———. *Does the New Testament Imitate Homer? Four Cases from the Acts of the Apostles.* New Haven: Yale University Press, 2003.

———. *The Gospels and Homer: Imitations of Greek Epic in Mark and Luke-Acts.* The New Testament and Greek Literature 1. Lanham: Rowman & Littlefield, 2014.

———. *The Homeric Epics and the Gospel of Mark.* New Haven: Yale University Press, 2000.

———. *Luke and Vergil: Imitations of Classical Greek Literature.* The New Testament and Greek Literature 2. Lanham: Rowman & Littlefield, 2014.

———. *My Turn: A Critique of Critics of "Mimesis Criticism."* IACOP 53. Claremont: The Institute for Antiquity and Christianity, 2009.

———. *Mythologizing Jesus: From Jewish Teacher to Epic Hero.* Lanham: Rowman & Littlefield, 2015.

Russell, Donald A. "De Imitatione." In *Creative Imitation and Latin Literature*, edited by David West and Tony Woodman, 1–16. Cambridge: Cambridge University Press, 1979.

Whitmarsh, Tim. *Greek Literature and the Roman Empire: The Politics of Imitation.* Oxford: Oxford University Press, 2001.

8

Poststructural Intertextuality

Gary A. Phillips

Poststructural intertextuality names a host of critical reading and writing practices that developed in post-World War II France. Poststructural intertextualists operate with diverse and expanded views of text, textuality, context, and interpretation. Texts are social products imbedded in culture, and critical reading is a social praxis that intervenes in various ways in the text and the social world. By contesting notions of the autonomous text, fixed meaning, and neutral reading, poststructural intertextualists privilege instability of texts, indeterminacy of meaning, the socially constructed roles of writers/readers, and the ethical urgency of interpretation. Poststructural intertextuality aims to expose unacknowledged structures, values, and forces that shape readers and the material worlds where both readers and texts live. In contrast to traditional critical practices marked by closure and boundaries, poststructural intertextuality aggressively opens text and reader to the outside. Transformation of text, reader, understanding, and world is the goal.

Crisis of Humanism

The turbulent events of May 1968 offer a context for situating poststructural intertextuality and the theory revolution that gave rise to it. Over a period of weeks, French civic life was convulsed by massive citizen demonstrations demanding national reform of the educational system, worker compensation, and the French political establishment. With the goal of transforming society, French citizens took to the streets in revolutionary fervor. At the height of the unrest the university system shut down; eleven million students, trade union workers, and civil servants went out on strike; and the government of President Charles De Gaulle, who briefly fled the country fearing a coup d'état, effectively collapsed. Although the paralysis proved temporary, the impact of the crisis on French intellectual, economic, political, and wider cultural life would be far-reaching. Even bedrock North American biblical studies would feel the aftershocks.

Poststructural theories of intertextuality emerged out of this social upheaval.[1] Broadly defined, poststructuralism is an umbrella term for a diverse set of critical responses to the crisis of humanism following World War II. The crisis of culture provoked a crisis of criticism. Poststructural theorists, many indebted and reacting to structural linguistic models, pursued alterative critical approaches to diagnose and transform society. Theorists aggressively advocated social reform in many sectors of French life with concern for prison reform, consumerist culture, colonial ideology, immigration policy, educational pedagogy, and literary interpretation.[2] Intertextual theory was one facet of a wider effort to reconfigure the relationship of literature to society, and the journal *Tel Quel* served as a crucible for the work.[3] Key contributors included Julia Kristeva, Jacques Derrida, Roland Barthes, Gérard Genette, and Tzvetan Todorov. They drew upon an eclectic pool of intellectual resources that included structural linguistics, cultural anthropology, Marxist and Maoist ideology, Freudian psychoanalysis, German phenomenology, as well as European philosophical and literary traditions. A shared feature among poststructural theorists was their outsider status in French culture—Derrida, Kristeva, and Todorov were North African and European immigrants; Derrida and Kristeva were Jewish. The poststructural preoccupation with issues of identity, otherness, and the urgency of ethical critique was intensely personal.[4]

Ingredient to the crisis of humanistic culture was the Holocaust. The specter of European antisemitism and the unresolved issues of French complicity in the Final Solution haunted poststructural theorists. French poststructuralism offered a complex response that "at once confronted, commemorated, deflected, and veiled the Holocaust."[5] Beyond France, the

1. On the diverse trajectories of intertextuality see Plett, "Intertextualities," 3–27.

2. Williams, *Understanding Poststructuralism*, 6.

3. See French, *Time of Theory*, 5–44.

4. Cornell, "Post-structuralism," 416–17. Derrida spurned the "poststructuralist" label ("Marx and Sons," 228–29).

5. Carton, "Holocaust, French Poststructuralism," 18.

Holocaust and the persistent "Jewish Question" influenced the migration of poststructural theory to North American shores and its subsequent adoption in literary critical circles.[6] Among biblical critics drawn to poststructuralist theory, however, questions of the Holocaust, antisemitism, and the ethical issues they raise for reading the Bible were not determining.[7] Biblical and theological scholarship's ambivalent relationship to Judaism and a long history of antisemitism tempered critical engagement with the Holocaust. A half century after Kristeva coined the term, the complicated connections between poststructural intertextuality, critique of post-war humanism, and the Holocaust remain under-acknowledged.

Employed by structuralist and poststructuralist literary critics alike, intertextuality is a malleable concept that has developed theoretically along several paths. Some critics (the unsettlers) use intertextuality iconoclastically to disturb fixed notions of text, reader, and meaning; others (the taxonomers), by contrast, want to limit an expansive notion of text and textuality by forging a rigorous scientific method of literary analysis; still others (the revolutionaries) actively promote socio-political change.[8] In this essay we concentrate on a group of unsettlers and their influence on a type of interruptive reading practice. We begin with Kristeva's definition of intertextuality and reworking of Mikhail Bakhtin's dialogical view of texts. We then look at Derrida's deconstructive critique of structural linguistics and the principle of textuality emblemized by his controversial statement, "There is nothing outside the text."[9] His concept of the trace, borrowed from Emmanuel Levinas, establishes a direct link to the Holocaust and to the ethical urgency of deconstructive and poststructural criticism more broadly. The aim is not to chart an exhaustive genealogy but to single out key figures, ideas, and concerns that illumine one kind of poststructural intertextual reading.

With the aid of these poststructural theorists we do an intertextual reading of Herod's slaughter of the innocent children in Matthew's infancy

6. For instance, the "Yale School" with Geoffrey Hartman, Harold Bloom, and Paul de Man.

7 The Bible and Culture Collective's *The Postmodern Bible*, mentions the Holocaust once in its poststructuralist criticism chapter. Similarly Moore's *Poststructuralism and the New Testament*. Contrast essays in Aichele and Phillips, *Intertextuality and the Bible* and Linafelt, *Strange Fire*.

8. Alfaro, "Intertextuality," 287. Plett proposes "progressive," "conventional," and "anti-intertextualist" as categories ("Intertextualities," 3–5); see Leitch, *Deconstructive Criticism*, 161.

9. On textualism see Vlacos, *Ricoeur*, 40–44.

narrative. Matthew 2:13–23 is a *crux interpretum* for traditional scholars.[10] It is a text knotted up with form critical, text critical, redaction critical, and theological difficulties that resist untangling. The infanticide story raises hard questions about gospel violence, God's justice, and responsible reading that have ethical implications for Christians who read the Bible in the wake of the Holocaust.[11] A poststructural lens presents Matt 2:13–23 as a fabric of interwoven citations. Matthew's text is an expansive surface inscribed with diverse narratives, contexts, voices, and lives, both ancient and modern, interacting and contesting one another. Holocaust survivor and painter Samuel Bak's artwork adds a disturbing voice to this space, a stunning visual thread woven into a disquieting Matthean tapestry.

The goal is two-part: first, to show Matthew's text as a productive and transformative rewriting of multiple texts and contexts that opens up reading and readers to the outside; and, second, to highlight the ethical challenge facing readers of violent New Testament texts after Auschwitz. Matthew's narrative presses us to ask—how do we make sense of and respond to "texts of terror" that depict and incite violence against Jewish children?[12] A poststructural intertextual reading conscious of recent history magnifies this ethical question. In the wake of transport trains, crematoria ovens, and a history of contempt for Jews, fueled by readings of Matthew's infanticide and blood libel (27:25) texts, what difference can intertextual reading of Matthew's gospel make? Or as Jewish philosopher Emil Fackenheim pointedly asks, is our reading of scripture responsive to the suffering of real children?[13]

Poststructural Intertextuality: A Theoretical Mosaic

Julia Kristeva introduced her notion of intertextuality into literary studies in the mid-1960s at a crisis point in the study of literature and the humanities more generally.[14] Traditional literary criticism in France was under pressure from structural linguistic approaches that promised greater objective knowledge about texts and their meanings. Despite sharp methodological differences, structuralist and traditional literary scholarship shared in common a view of texts as autonomous, aesthetic objects. Kristeva and other

10. Luz, *Matthew 1–7*, 148.

11. Ibid., 147: "It does not disturb Matthew that God saves his Son at the expense of innocent children."

12. Tribble's term, *Texts of Terror*.

13. Fackenheim, *Jewish Bible*, vi–viii.

14. See Aichele and Phillips, "Introduction," 7–15; Mai, "Bypassing Intertextuality," 33–46.

poststructural theorists contest this view and its conceptual underpinnings by reimagining the nature of text and critical reading praxis. At its core, the concept of intertextuality contests the closure of text and reading since every text contains something "already said" or "already written."

From Kristeva's sign-theory perspective, texts are complex social productions and meaning-making is fundamentally a contested social process. Every text "is constructed as a mosaic of citations, every text is an absorption and transformation of other texts;"[15] and "in the space of a text several utterances from other texts *intersect and neutralize* one another."[16] Responding to societal disruption, Kristeva forged the notion of an inter-ruptive intertextuality in conversation with structural linguistics, Marxist political theory, feminist criticism, and Freudian psychoanalysis. Her con-cept of intertextuality is a contextually shaped mosaic of diverse theories, interests, and concerns.

Kristeva views the literary text and interpretation as social production. Texts are relational and imbedded dynamically within networks of other texts. Textual meaning is the product of the webs of interference and illumi-nation created among texts. Moreover, texts are composite. They imbed and are imbedded within others texts, part and parcel of one another, at once inside and outside each other. Citing (and revising) Bakhtin, Kristeva ar-gues that writing and reading produce a "dialogue among several writings" in which "each word (text) is an intersection of other words (texts) where at least one other word (text) can be read."[17] A text's meaning is constituted as much by the absence of other voices and texts as by their presence. For example, Matthew's citation "Out of Egypt I called my son" (2:15) absorbs and transforms Exod 4:22 and Hos 11:1 producing an untidy cluster of textual differences and tensions. In Hosea (LXX) movement is *from* Egypt by *his son*; in Exodus flight is implied *from* Egypt by *my firstborn*; in Mat-thew's narration Joseph flees *to* Egypt with the *child son*. Matthew's word choices imply others not taken, thereby illustrating the linguistic principle that meaning is the *dynamic product of differences and absences*. Traces of absent words are ever present. Saussure's structural linguistic principle of difference and Derrida's transformation of difference into *différance*, his term for the dynamic force that powers all meaning-making, operate in the poststructural background.

Imagine the text as a palimpsest-like surface traced upon by mul-tiple voices and narratives. For example, Matthew's citation of Jer 31:15 in

---

15. Kristeva, *Desire in Language*, 146.

16. Ibid., 113. My emphasis.

17. Ibid., 66

2:18—"A voice is heard in Ramah, lamentation and bitter weeping. Rachel is weeping for her children; she refuses to be comforted for her children, because they are no more"—is inscribed onto the narrative, an outside prophetic voice vocalized through Matthew's narrator.[18] Different narrative commentaries on suffering and violence are evoked. Sixth century BCE recountings of Babylonian deportations and Matthew's gospel response to first century CE destruction of Jerusalem by Roman imperial forces name two. More recent lamentations can also be heard. Narratives of Nazi and Vichy deportations of Jewish mothers and their absent children overwrite antique others.[19] Traces of violence, sounds of silence, and profound experiences of loss mark a dynamic text and reading process whereby readers encounter an expanse of contested religious and national disaster stories, violent images and experiences, competing symbols and languages, and memories of maternal desperation and loss.[20]

Post-Holocaust readers bring other texts and experiences to Matthew's world in acts of interpretation and interruption. Samuel Bak's *Collective* (described below) intrudes into Matthew's narrative space. Bak paints a contemporary world where Jewish children appear only to dissolve before our very eyes, a miasma of faces and shapes that challenges readers to see Matthean text and narrative world with a different eye. Traditional literary and biblical scholarship privileges the objective eye in determining original authorship and textual meaning. But such reading has its blind spot. Intertextual reading perceives a fabric made up of numerous fibers that readers *weave into text* and *produce meaning*. Readers become aware of the constructed nature of texts and their creative work when we pixelate Matthean text and Bak canvas. Clarity and content of text and image are optical effects. Kristeva's notion of literary production thus challenges the objective eye—the *oculus dei*—that watches over the French literary tradition of *explication de texte* and its American New Critical counterpart influential in modern biblical scholarship. Traditional criticism sees a limited role for the reader; the clear objective determination of structure, style, and imagery; and the search for a single, historically determined meaning of a text. Kristevan poststructural intertextuality offers an alternative "vision of meaning, and thus of authorship and reading: a vision resistant to ingrained notions of originality, uniqueness, singularity and autonomy."[21] The intertextual reading eye views Matthew 2 as a constructed, contested, and con-

---

18. Davies and Allison characterize citation as "parasitic" (*Matthew*, 191).

19. Phillips "More than the Jews," 82.

20. Phillips, "Killing Fields," 249.

21. Allen, *Intertextuality*, 6.

tinuously reconfigured space of narratives, images, and voices of mothers, past and present, whose lamentations for their absent children unsettle.

In the hands of many traditional literary critics, intertextuality lacks this creative, disruptive force. Instead, it functions neutrally as a taxonomic tool for cataloging textual allusions and interconnections.[22] Kristeva associates such use with "banal" source, comparative, and influence criticism that, as Derrida suggests, protects rather than opens up reading. Ellen Van Wolde comments that for many biblical critics, intertextuality is little more than a "modern literary theoretical coat of veneer over the old comparative approach" intent on preserving a positivist notion of text and meaning. The venture into poststructural territory is a "superficial sightseeing tour."[23] We propose instead a different path through the poststructural theoretical terrain keeping eye and ear attuned to Saussure, Bakhtin, and Derrida as Kristeva's dialogue partners. Together with Bak's artwork, these voices facilitate not a conserving taxonomy of citations but an unsettling interruption of story and reader in the face of unfathomable violence directed against real children.

In the Beginning was Difference

The conceptual roots of poststructural intertextuality lie in the structural linguistics of Ferdinand de Saussure whose view of language as a system of differences fundamentally transformed linguistics, literary studies, and other disciplines.[24] Two Saussurean principles guide Kristeva and other poststructural theorists of texts—language is a structured system of signs, and meaning is fundamentally relational. For Saussure the sign is arbitrary and conventional. Composed of signifier (sound image) and signified (conceptual content), the sign is not made up of essential elements but characterized negatively by differences that distinguish it from other signs: "[I]n the linguistic system there are only differences, *without positive terms*."[25] Linguistic meaning is a function of the combinatory and associative differences between signifiers and signifieds within the language system. Structural literary criticism applied this insight to fashion texts as abstract

---

22. For example, Buchanan, *Introduction to Intertextuality*; Van Tilborg, "Matthew 27:3–10;" Luz, "Intertexts."

23. Van Wolde, "Trendy Intertextuality," 43. So Hays, *Reading the Bible*; Luz, "Intertexts."

24. See Still and Worton, "Introduction," 1–44.

25. Saussure, *Course*, 120. Emphasis his.

systems of signs.[26] Kristeva adopts Saussure's key concepts to argue that literary networks and social systems, not an author's intentions, are key to understanding textual production and meaning. The literary text is not an autonomous container of essential meanings; rather, it is a permutation and productivity of semiotic differences.

Kristeva's notion of intertextuality absorbs and transforms the ideas of Russian literary critic and semiotician Mikhail Bakhtin. Bakhtin's emphasis upon the dynamic social and historical dimensions of language is a corrective to Saussure's generalized and abstract view of language. Whereas Saussure diminishes the role of the speaking subject, Bakhtin accentuates the human–centeredness and dynamism of living speech.[27] He calls his theory of everyday language "dialogism." Dialogism is "another's speech in another's language, serving to express authorial intentions but in a refracted way."[28] Words never belong to a given speaker.[29] They are permeated by different intentions and accents carried forward and backward over time. A given word conveys the preferences and prejudices, positive and negative forces, inscribed in the language system. Tensions and contradictions are productively present not only between but within words themselves. Like the nucleus of an atom, a word is a bundle of discrete semantic elements held together by the elementary force of difference that powers a dynamic instability missing from Saussure's abstract, synchronic system. "Every concrete utterance is intersected by both centrifugal and centripetal, unifying and disunifying forces," Bakhtin writes.[30] The stable and fixed sense of words and their meanings associated with a lexicon or thesaurus is the effect of a particular ideological view of language, text, and meaning.

Bakhtin's dialogism enables Kristeva to describe the social reality "outside" of texts as an "infinity of textual structures."[31] This opens up a distinctive way for considering text and textuality. Culture itself is conceived as a "textual surface," and writers and readers are inscribed onto the "text of culture."[32] Assumed "natural" differences between literary text and social context are the effects of ideology, authorizing institutions, and policing power that enforces them. Unsettled by the idea of arbitrary distinctions,

26. Among biblical structuralists, Patte's *What is Structural Exegesis* is a classic example.

27. Allen, *Intertextuality*, 16. Mai, "Intertextualities," 31 doubts a strong Bakhtin influence.

28. Bakhtin, *Dialogic Imagination*, 324.

29. Ibid., 293.

30. Ibid., 272.

31. Alfaro, "Intertextuality," 271

32. Kristeva, *Desire in Language*, 65.

readers will appeal to disciplinary patrols to maintain fences that keep im-migrant ideas, voices, and texts outside and preserve a pure homeland and language. Derrida challenges notions of textual purity and natural borders when he asserts, "There is nothing outside of the text." By this oft-misun-derstood pronouncement Derrida says that the world, insofar as we know or speak about it, is so only by way of texts and systems of signs. There is no getting around or outside of texts or signifying processes to get to some independent "reality" free of texts. Derrida's principle of textuality upsets traditional critics who charge him, Kristeva, and other poststructuralists with "radical textualism" implying a denial of the material world.[33] This is a profound misreading of Derrida's view of text, textuality, and the activity of a deconstructive criticism whose aim is to expose creatively the constructed nature—as well as violent effects—of all reading and interpretation.

Deconstructive Intervention

Derrida's deconstructive criticism and principle of textuality shaped Kriste-va's intertextual theory and opened it up to wider application. Kristeva's aggressive rewriting of Bakhtin's "word" with "text" bears Derrida's decon-structive imprint. Deconstruction is a distinctive kind of philosophical reading. Unlike traditional philosophical or literary criticism that seeks to identify a text's unifying themes or content, deconstructive critique at-tempts to diagnose and disrupt deep governing assumptions at work in a text. It exposes the tensions created by rhetorical figures that point to out-side arguments that cannot be contained within the dominant operating assumptions.[34] A text's governing argument, for example, is necessarily supplemented by alternative views that the former subordinates but can-not fully manage or eliminate. What is "outside" of the text, deconstruction constructively shows is already "inside" the argument thereby disturbing inside/outside distinction and the notion of purity.

Deconstructive reading intervenes in the density and labyrinthine weave of reading and writing.[35] Derrida's readings intrude into the fabric of philosophical and literary texts to pull on various threads of their argu-ments thereby puckering the cloth, distorting old and creating new patterns of meaning. For example, he shows how the distinction between spoken and written language wobbles when Saussure cites written signs to support his point about verbal signs. Intertextual reading does something analogous by

33. Rorty, "Nineteenth-Century Idealism," in *Consequences of Pragmatism*, 139.

34. See further, Derrida, *Positions*, 6.

35. Hill, *Cambridge Introduction*, 22.

disruptively opening up texts and readings to expose the citation presence of outside texts and voices that are already inside.[36] Deconstructive reading prescribes a two-step process—first, the reader pays careful attention to what is expressed by the text (traditional reading stage); and, second, the reader goes beyond what is said to bring into the light and interrupt the text's controlling logic, values, and assumptions (intervening reading stage). Against detractors who charge Derrida and other poststructural readers with irresponsible "playing" with the text, he counters that although traditional criticism is an "indispensable guardrail" to interpretation, it "has always only *protected* . . . never *opened*, a reading."[37] The deconstructive drive to unsettle and open the text to the outside is motivated by "an ethical desire to enact the ethical relation."[38]

Derrida's principle of textuality is summed up in his much maligned pronouncement, "There is nothing outside the text." This statement has been a lightning rod for critics who interpret this as a denial of history, politics, truth, realty, and ethics. Derrida's admittedly "badly understood phrase"[39] means it is impossible to locate a final, absolute anchor point for textual interpretation and to still a text's ongoing permutation, absorption, and transformation by other texts. "There is nothing outside of the text" means "there is nothing that *stands* independent and outside of the text" unmediated by linguistic signs. To speak of the world is to speak of a world *already textualized, already interpreted in some way* inextricably imbedded in the dynamic networks of signifying structures.[40] While readers may hope to find the high ground of pure and assured meaning above the tumult of texts and reading, they can never extract themselves from the networks of textual structures into which they and their readings are already inscribed.[41]

With respect to Matthew's Gospel, traditional scholarship's effort to draw firm distinctions between reader and text, and text and context—to secure a definitive final meaning of Matthew's infanticide story or larger narrative purpose by appeal to historical, literary, theological, or any other (including "poststructural") grounds; to limit the gospel's permutation and transformation by appeal to authorial intent—fails to grasp the centrifugal and centripetal forces at work in texts of terror. Like deconstructive reading,

---

36. Leitch, *Deconstructive Criticism*, 161.

37. Derrida, *Of Grammatology*, 158 (emphasis his).

38. Cornell, "Post-structuralism," 416–17.

39. Derrida, *Limited Inc*, 137. For an overview, see Deutscher, "Il n'y as pas de hors-texte."

40. Margolis, "Text," 193.

41. Plotnitsky, *Complementarity*, 52.

intertextual reading intervenes in the oscillation of texts, lives, deaths, and memories that is Matthew's text.[42] Bak's visualization of the lost boys conjures them and Matthew's Jewish boys to mind. The faces of European Jewish children who are no more, Levinas reminds us, "thrusts us into the snake pit, into places that are no longer places, into places one cannot forget, but that do not succeed in placing themselves in memory, in organizing themselves in the form of memories. We have known such pits in this century."[43]

Intertextual Intervention in Texts of Terror

Few Gospel stories have exercised greater power to excite the Christian theological, artistic, and ethical imagination than the story of Herod's slaughter of the innocents.[44] It is the subject matter for poets, novelists, playwrights, composers, architects, song writers, film makers, singers, engravers, and painters across the centuries.[45] Few Gospel texts can claim greater impact, direct or indirect, upon Jewish lives. Paired with the blood libel in Matt 27:25—"And all the people answered, 'His blood be on us and our children!'"—the infanticide and blood libel stories frame Matthew's narrative and reader action. They are associated with pernicious fantasies about Jews, such as the ritual cannibalism of Christian children in the thirteenth century, and the scripting of Serbian slaughter of Kosovan women and children in the twentieth century.[46] That the innocents targeted could be Jewish or Muslim is a testament to the adaptive capacity of readers to enact texts of terror indiscriminately. Raymond Brown concedes as much in characterizing Matt 27:25 as "one of those phrases which have been responsible for oceans of human blood and a ceaseless stream of misery and desolation." This does not deter him, however, from praising Matthew as "the most effective theater among the Synoptics, outclassed in that respect

---

42. Nye, "Woman Clothed," 669, equates intertextuality with deconstruction. Cited in Mai, "Bypassing Intertextuality," 31

43. Levinas, "Beyond Memory," 85.

44. Boxall, *Discovering Matthew*, 76–7.

45. For example, *The Coventry Carol*; The Medieval *Rachel Plays*; Jacob Biedermann's 17th century epic drama *Herodiado libri iii*; The Serbian 19th century epic poem *The Mountain Wreath*; Vasily Grossmann, *Life and Fate*; Albert Camus, *The Fall*; the 1971 film, *Escape from the Planet of the Apes*; and countless painters that include Lucas Cranach the Elder; Matteo de Giovanni, Giotto, Rubens, Poussin, Pieter Bruegel the Elder, Reni, Tintoretto, Doré, Tissot, among many others (see http://www.textweek. com/art/massacre_of_innocents.htm.

46. Langmuir, *Antisemitism*, 266–317; Phillips, "More than the Jews," 80–84. Duarte, "Matthew," 354–59.

only by the Johannine masterpiece" while relegating historical Jewish suffering to a footnote.[47]

New Testament scholarship overwhelmingly shares Brown's appreciation for Matthew's aesthetic and narrative qualities. However, traditional scholarship's interests in the evangelist's passionate concern for justice (3:15) and peace (5:38) is disconnected from concern for the historical children who have suffered violence at the hands of Matthean readers. The history of Matthew's reception offers ample evidence that readers can separate aesthetic and literary qualities from anti-Jewish themes and narrative violence. For example, commentators readily transform the suffering of innocents in Matt 2:16 into martyrdom with the children a parenetic exemplar of the adult martyr.[48] Fackenheim calls such exegetical and theological readings of the Jeremiah citation and Herod's slaughter of the innocents "seamless": Holocaust reality fails to disrupt the continuity of exegetical and theological readings of Christian scripture.[49] Fackenheim argues that after Auschwitz Jewish and Christian readings must be shocked (*Erschütterung*) by the historical reality of real children, and literary and theological constructions and seamless readings must be disrupted. Irving Greenberg's hermeneutical principle is clear and direct: "No statement, theological or otherwise, should be made that would not be credible in the presence of the burning children."[50] In similar terms, Levinas calls for a "shaken" conscience in which the faces of the innocent and our excessive responsibility for others interrupt our interpretive schemes, institutional structures, and ego concerns.[51] This is the ethical demand—the demand for justice central to Matthew's imagination—to which an interruptive intertextual reading responds.[52]

Reading Inside the Guardrails

Our first move is to describe Matt 2:13–23 in traditional terms. Found exclusively in Matthew's gospel, Herod's slaughter of the innocents story forms the third of four narrative scenes making up the infancy cycle in chapter 2. Commentators differ marginally over whether it presents a

47. Brown, *Death of the Messiah*, 831 note 22. Contrast Crossan, *Who Killed Jesus?*, x, says scholarship must do better.

48. Luz, *Matthew 1–7*, 147–48. Luz, "Intertexts," lacks Kristeva's ethical urgency.

49. Fackenheim, *Jewish Bible*, 20.

50. Greenberg, "Cloud of Smoke," 23.

51. Levinas, "Ethics," 82; Phillips, "Killing Fields," 253.

52. See Mayordomo's intertextual reading in "Matthew 1–2"; Doane, "L'infanticide à Bethléem."

four- or five-part structure. The consensus is that place names are key to unlocking the chapter organization, which answers the question, "Whence Jesus?"[53] Each of the final three scenes, the focus of our reading, concludes with a formulaic biblical quotation related to the places featured in the episode—Egypt in 2:13–15; Bethlehem and Rama in 2:16–18, and Egypt and Nazareth in 2:19–23. The fulfilment quotation formula ("This was to fulfill what had been spoken by the Lord through the prophet" in vv. 15, 18, and 23) is a signature Matthean expression. The density of formula citations prompt critics to speculate that the chapter is a multi-layered composition of pre-Matthean text or tradition augmented by the formula citations added in the final editing.[54] Critics differ over whether Matthew engages in "free" midrashic exegesis or midrashic haggadic commentary similar to the *pesher* method of exegesis found in the Qumran library.[55] Critics also debate whether the fulfillment quotes function as the organizing principle of the narrative material or the narrative material is the motive for citation selection.[56] The interaction between narrative and citation invites broad questions about the ways texts act as intertexts with one another, the writer's intent in fashioning interconnections and transformations, and the reader's creative role in discovering alternative patterns of meaning.

Traditional scholarship finds disturbing knots in the quotation threads that raises questions about the Matthean writer's intent. The textual source of the first fulfillment question in v. 15 ("Out of Egypt I have called my son") is unnamed. Hosea's (11:1) *coming out* of Egypt is in tension with Matthew's *going to* Egypt. Matthew appears to draw from a Hebrew source (*my son*) and not the Greek (*children*).[57] One Christian commentator resolves these and other difficulties with a sweeping theological pronouncement: "When Matthew cites Hosea 11:1 he is citing the entire redemptive context, not only of Hosea but of the rest of the Old Testament. Citation of Hosea 11:1 reminds Israel of their double redemption from Egypt and Assyria/Babylon but also anticipates their final redemption from themselves."[58] This reductive resolution of the textual snags makes the Jews not only a problem in the text but ultimately to themselves.

---

53. Stendhal, "Quis," 95–100.

54. Brown, *Birth of the Messiah*, 97; 214. Luz, *Matthew 1–7*, 156–64.

55. Stendhal, *School of St. Matthew*, 12. Alternatively, France, "Formula Quotations," 239.

56. Hartman, "Scriptural Exegesis," 237.

57. Brown, *Birth of the Messiah*, 222.

58. Campbell, "Matthew's Use of the Old Testament."

The second fulfillment quotation in v. 18 ("A voice was heard in Ramah, wailing and loud lamentation, Rachel weeping for her children; she refused to be consoled, because they are no more") is the single longest citation in the infancy cycle, and it, too, presents numerous difficulties.[59] The citation does not agree with either the Hebrew or Greek text: the Hebrew text uses *children*, the Greek *sons*. The voice is heard in Ramah, Rachel's traditional burial site, not Bethlehem. In Jer 31:16–17, Rachel is told to stop weeping for the children who *return from Babylon* making this a hopeful prophecy. The citation seems to link up with other Old Testament allusions in Matthew 2—Micah 5:1 and 5:3 cited in v. 6 echo Jer 31:15 because of the association of Ramah near Bethlehem. But which Israelite deportation is in view is uncertain. Readers oscillate between the Babylonian and Assyrian tragedies. Unlike the fulfillment statements in 1:22; 2:15b; and 2:23b, the morphing of the purposeful "in order to fulfill" into a consequential "then" is perplexing.

Finally, the third fulfillment quotation in v. 23 ("He will be called a Nazorean") is, in Brown's words, the "most difficult formula citation in the Gospel since it is not indisputably related to an identifiable Old Testament text."[60] There is no reference to Nazareth or Nazarene in the Hebrew Scriptures. The scholarly consensus is that *Nazōraios* offers three possible meanings—the place-name Nazareth; *nazir* or one devoted to God (cf. Jud 13.5, 7); or *neser*, meaning "branch" and used with reference to the Messiah. Straining for a linguistic solution, Brown proposes that *Nazōraios* may have been written one way but pronounced another following the Masoretic pointing method known as Kethib-Qere. Harrington solves the problem in a different fashion: "It is likely that the readers were expected to keep all three connotations in mind rather than one alone. The latter two derivations would qualify the expression as a biblical quotation, and the first would tie them into the place where Jesus lived."[61] France treats the textual difficulties as "deliberate mistakes" and posits two levels of meaning. Most readers get the "surface" meaning intended by the writer, but only more "sophisticated" or "sharp-eyed" readers (like France, presumably) get the "bonus" meaning that leads to an unraveling of the textual knots. Like Jesus's disciples perplexed by his knotty parabolic stories, critics confused by Matthew's citational use must be "surface" readers.[62]

---

59. See Luz, *Matthew 1–7*, 147.

60. Brown, *Birth of the Messiah*, 223.

61. Harrington, *Matthew*, 46.

62. France, "Formula Quotations," 250.

Efforts to untangle these grammatical, text critical, and redactional knots by appeal to the Matthean writer's intent prove inconsistent and inconclusive. Commentators focus on the interweaving of narrative material and problematic formula quotations for clarifying intentional patterns. They identify threads of a geographical theme, a prominent Mosaic motif linking Exodus with Matthew in support of an extended Moses/Jesus typology, the midrashic use of Old Testament citations, Near Eastern infancy legends, and more.[63] Not surprisingly, readers perceive the fabric pattern differently and construe what was in the author's mind differently also. Taking up the weaving metaphor, Hartman suggests that the warp or vertical strand of Matthew 2 is "something like a midrashic haggadah based on the Moses haggadah and the first chapters of Exodus." Jewish midrash is the primary unifying thread with the geographical theme supplementing throughout.[64] France, by contrast, sees the geographical theme as the main organizing principle into which the woof of Mosaic and exodus typologies are cross-threaded.[65] He subordinates the Moses and Exodus typology and citational texts to the christological, geographical theme prominent in chapter 1. The christological warp supersedes Jewish midrashic woof. Echoing Brown, France affirms that Matthew's literary artistry delights audiences, although how infanticide possibly gives readers pleasure is not explained.

The traditional critical drive to locate authorial intent behind Matthew's slaughter of the innocents story is insistent but far from innocent. This brief episode is an unsettling narrative presence, an indigestible knot in the Gospel text and many readers' imaginations. The desire to rescue author, text, and tradition from complicity in this and other moments of violence in the Gospel call for interpretive dexterity. Some traditional commentators are confident that a disreputable Herod slaughtered Jewish children (although the actual numbers could have been no more than two dozen). They account for the story's inclusion in the Gospel, if not on artistic, theological, or ideological, then on historical grounds.[66] Most critics, however, dispute its historicity without resolving questions about narrative purpose.[67] The recurring theme of violence bubbles up repeatedly in Matthew's apocalyptic imagery, which makes Herod's violence then appear not so anomalous.[68] For some narrative critics, grammatical, linguistic, and thematic connec-

---

63. See Luz, *Matthew 1–7*, 152–55.

64. Hartman, "Scriptural Exegesis," 152.

65. France, "Formula Quotations," 240.

66. See France, "Herod." Hartman, "Scriptural Exegesis," 138.

67. Brown, *Birth of the Messiah*, 615.

68. Carter, "Construction of Violence," 98.

tions between 2:13–23 and the blood libel in 27:25 reinforce an anti-Jewish ideology implicating Herod, Pharisees, Jewish temple leadership, and even God in Jesus' death.[69] While commentators might agree on narrative grounds that the children's deaths anticipate Jesus's death, they differ over the theological significance of their deaths.[70]

The narrative linkage between 2:13–16 and 27:25 poses significant interpretative difficulties for commentators who wish to safeguard God and Jesus from direct narrative or theological involvement in the violence.[71] Interpreters are all over the map. "The best explanation of the story of the Slaughter of the Innocents (vv. 16–18)," Kingsbury writes, "is that it is an initial sign of the judgment that will befall Israel for having rejected its Messiah."[72] In other words, Jewish authorities, not God or Jesus, are to blame for the calamity that befalls them. For readers inclined to see something theologically redemptive in the violence, MacKinnon cautions: "Perhaps no event in the gospel more determinatively challenges the sentimental description of Christmas than the death of these children . . . Christians are tempted to believe that the death of the children of Bethlehem 'can be redeemed' by Jesus's birth, death, and resurrection. . . .[S]uch a reading . . . is perverse."[73] Hartman finds the textual evidence convincing in the Jeremiah 31:15 citation that God is willing and involved in making possible the children's deaths.[74] Even early second century CE readers go so far as to link the deaths directly to Jesus: "The elders of the Jews said to Jesus: . . . 'Your birth meant the death of the children in Bethlehem'" (*Acts of Pilate* 2.3).

Matthew's reception history suggests that the infancy cycle portends violence that will extend past the end of the story and beyond Matthew's first century setting. Once disconnected from a first century authorship or readership numbed by the disaster of Roman persecution, Matthew's texts of terror may be absorbed and transformed by other narrative texts and social contexts. The Serbian *Mountain Wreath*, German *Oberammergau Passion Play*, and American Westboro Baptist Church denunciations demonstrate how recent readers selectively morph Matthean scripture into scripts of physical and verbal violence.[75] This is not the full story. In tension with the violence against children recounted in 2:13–23 and 27:25 is Matthew's ex-

---

69. See Burnett "Anti-Jewish Ideology."

70. Harrington, *Matthew*, 49. Except for Carter, 98–99.

71. Carter, ""Construction of Violence," 85, 95.

72. Kingsbury, *Matthew*, 48, note 47. Compare Gundry, *Matthew*, 36.

73. MacKinnon, cited in Hauerwas, *Matthew*, 41; Luz, *Matthew 1–7*, 145.

74. Hartman, "Scriptural Exegesis," 141. See Burnett, "Anti-Jewish Ideology."

75. Phillips, "More than the Jews," 84–85.

plicit warning not to hinder (19:14) or despise (18:10) these little ones. The invitation to become child-like presents readers with a choice for or against violence against the children. Matthew makes clear the dire consequences of offence to disciples and readers alike (18:6). Which "Matthew" we read with and which against, which actions we follow and which we interrupt depends in part upon the intertexts we bring into dialog with the Gospel.

Collective Disappearance
Collective **Oil on Canvas 18 x 24"**[76]

Our next move is to interrupt Matthew with Bak's visual text. Forefronting the Holocaust reality in *Collective*, Bak confronts us with a scene that presses us to act. In 2006 Samuel Bak launched his artistic effort to memorialize each of the 1.5 million children murdered by the Nazi war machine. He described this series of paintings paradoxically as "monuments that could never exist," impossible memorials of the children whose faces can no longer be visualized.[77] *Collective* is one of more than a hundred canvases that give face to the murdered children who have disappeared. The impracticality of Bak's task is matched only by the incomprehensibility of the horror visited upon Jewish Children. Bak uses the iconic 1943

76. For a full color image go to http://puckergallery.com/pdf/Bak.Icon.2008.pdf

77. See Fewell and Phillips, "Bak's Impossible Memorials," 93–100.

photograph taken of a boy at the time of the Warsaw Ghetto cleansing as a template for giving the children face and form. *Collective* stands out prominently in the series in gathering onto one canvas and into one grim scene traces of the innumerable children who are no more.

What has Bak collected here? In the painting's foreground weathered, crisscrossed planks and rusty nails lie scattered upon a stone surface. Red-tinged wood, nails, and stone blocks more than hint of recent killing work. An ominous "X" marks the spot of more to come. Countless cutout cruciform figures crowd onto a platform, an imagined debarkation point for Jewish children headed for a destination with no return. Alternatively, we can picture wooden debris collected for burning. Compressed into a single mass onto one canvas, the bodies are too numerous to be distinguished and counted. Boys press uncomfortably close into our viewing space making it nearly impossible to avert our gaze from the difficult scene before us. A tangle of figures, many lacking eyes, noses, or any other discernible facial features, some barely distinguishable as human shapes, confront us. We discern children in varying degrees of detail and decomposition. Overwhelming in number, the children spill out toward the horizon. Scattered across the landscape cross-like wooden structures project upwards in the air. They evoke memories of a distant time of Roman mass murder of Jews and Christians and the iconic Golgotha, the place of Jewish torture rewritten as Christian redemption (Matt 27:33). In the far distance plumes of smoke rise up. Too numerous to be telltale signs of Kinder transports heralding rescue, the smoke clouds can only mean bonfires or crematoria chimneys and the certainty of no escape. The sky fills with cinders, traces of the burning children.

Read with and against Matthew's narrative, Bak's painting unsettles eye and sensibility. Past and present collide. Images of Hitler's murdered innocents are now inscribed onto Matthew's narrative surface. Traces of Rachel's lost children are rewritten with Bak's visualized lost ghetto boys. Rachel's lament for ancient Israelite children now reaches out to Bak's childhood friend Samek Epstein and the unnamed thousands liquidated across Europe. Real, historical children like Bak. Vilnius, Warsaw, Auschwitz, and Treblinka become the new geographical place names replacing Bethlehem, Egypt, Ramah, and Nazareth. These places structure an alternative infancy cycle—Primo Levi calls this a new story of the Bible—composed in the shadow of Auschwitz's chimneys and crosses.[78] If Matthew's second chapter once answered the question "Whence Jesus?," Bak's image answers a different, more pressing question, "Whence the children who are no more?" *Collective* invites us to refract Matthew's infanticide story making real, not

78. Levi, *Survival in Auschwitz*, 59.

narrative, children the center of our attention. We are left to absorb the import of what we see and, more importantly, what we are to do with the Matthean text.

Citing Texts and Inciting Justice

Collective encourages us to see the intertextually of Matt 2:13–23 as a rich mosaic of citations that transform and absorb one other. Its thickness extends beyond the presence of formula quotations marked by Matthean narrator and commentators. Multiple citations permeate Matthew's narrative giving it contour and depth. Masoretic and Septuagint variations within the quotations add their different inflections. More allusive textual citations, such as the Exodus Moses's infancy story and Jeremiah's Babylonian deportation narrative, echo in the references to Jesus' infancy story and the children who threaten powerful rulers. Other persecuted and rescued royal children stories populate the narrative space. Mithridates, Romulus and Remus, Nero and Cyrus legends offer alternative stories about Gentile children who also are persecuted and die.[79] Bak, too, was a legendary child. A precocious child artist, he was spirited out of the Vilnius ghetto and hidden in a Christian convent. Of the two hundred souls to survive the Vilnius liquidation, Bak was one of a handful of children.

Less obvious textual citations are to be noted. Alternative Hebrew and Greek text readings (wording, punctuation) and editor's emendations are collected at the foot of the Nestle-Aland Greek page. Being "on the page" but not "in" the text is an editorial conceit. Editorial sigla live both inside and outside the text, interrupting, however slightly, the seamless reading of the Greek text. Readers become adjusted to such intrusions and adjust their eyes accordingly. Critical commentaries by Brown, Stendhal, and Luz offer yet further citation. Once read, their grammatical, text critical, and theological comments supplement the Matthean narrative, compounding the mosaic of citations that is Matthew's text. Like the Kethib-Qere pointing system, readers hear different voices in the letters of the text. Points of difference make Matthew a dialogical space in Bakhtin's term. Bak's canvas functions as a visual citation of Matthew's text. A mosaic of brush strokes and colors, faces and hands, Bak's *Collective* is also citationally dense.

Matthew's narrative presents a citation-rich textuality that defies efforts to state definitively which context or frame finally determines its true meaning and who has the last word about its meaning. Subsequent readings of Matthew's gospel are possible, indeed inevitable—a next intertext will

---

79. See Luz, *Matthew 1–7*, 153.

happen, a supplement to a commentary upon a commentary upon a reading upon a painting upon an action. Citation, like textuality, is inexhaustible. Every text or word may be cited by another text with no outside limit to the possible citations of Matthew and Matthew's citations, no summative imbedding or framing, no final text or border that will close all inside. The borders cannot be secured. Matthean textuality knows no limit, for there is nothing outside of Matthew's text. Opting to read Bak's painting in relation to Matthew's narrative is a deliberate gesture of citing, reframing, and disturbing aesthetic and theological constructions that relegate murdered Jewish children seamlessly to footnotes or out of sight and mind altogether. His disappearing boys serve as a visual reminder of the reality that unseemly seamless reading obscures and what our responsibility as Matthean readers can be—to join with Bak in memorializing the faces of Matthew's missing children.

Conclusion

"A theoretical stance . . . is the only guarantee of ethics."
—JULIA KRISTEVA[80]

"Auschwitz has obsessed everything I have ever been able to think . . ."
—JACQUES DERRIDA[81]

A poststructural intertextual reading for citations, conflicts, and differences is key to opening up Matthew's text and readers. This is as much an ethical as a methodological matter. Rather than smoothing out knots in the textual fabric, intertextual reading pays careful attention to what breaks in from the outside. The outside is an important thread in Matthew's argument. The Gospel's opening genealogical references draw our eye to outsider Gentile, female, and morally suspect Tamar, Rahab, Ruth, and, indirectly, Bathsheba (1:3–6). Who is Jesus, Matthew's opening chapters ask? He comes from suspect outsiders, accentuating difference and destabilizing the distinction between Jewish and non-Jewish identity. Matthew's outward narrative push is evident as well at the conclusion when Jesus dispatches his disciples from

80. Kristeva, *Desire in Language*, ix.
81. Derrida, "Canons and Metonymies," 211–12 cited in Eaglestone, *Contest of Faculties*, 279.

atop the mountain outward to the nations (ἔθνη; 28:19–20). Matthew's centrifugal impetus means that disciple and narrative will be let loose in the world for better and for worse. Along with its injunction to not hinder the children, Matthew voices the pernicious blood libel directed against Jewish children. The creative and destructive potential of the text and how it lives on through its readers is forecast linguistically in 16:19 where Peter is handed heavenly power "to bind" and "to loose" (λύσῃς). The word that describes Peter's power to free carries the trace of its opposite sematic potential, namely to destroy. To untie and to tear down, to free and to destroy, to affirm peace or violence, to engage in excessive righteousness (5:20) or to kill. The uncertain, oscillating potential for good and evil presents readers with an ethical decision about how we will read and act responsibly. Will Matthew's readers, like the disciples given their marching orders in 28:19, exercise doubt ("οἱ δὲ ἐδίστασαν"; 28:17) about the authority, power, and story we read? Will we reject false constructions of the Jews? Will we open ours arms to (18:6) not raise them against children (2:16; 27:25)? Will we rewrite the story of Herod's infanticide by interrupting Matthew's text with intertexts, like Bak's *Collective*, that keep in memory the faces, names, and lives of children who are no more?

After Auschwitz, New Testament readers ever face the responsibility of signing off on Matthew's text with interpretations that incite violence or justice for the sake of the children. Bak signs his name on every canvas: *BAK*, an acronym, he was once told, of *Beney-Kedoshim*, "Children of the Martyrs." Writing in his memoir, Bak asks: "Could I have invented a more appropriate sign to leave on each of my paintings?" "Wasn't my signature a variant of those small stones that every Jew deposits on the tombs he visits, a memorial to the dead?"[82] Will our gospel readings add to his memorial stones? Will we interrupt seamless readings that continue to put children at risk? Will we intervene by rewriting Matthew's texts of terror with other texts that humanize and care for the innocent?[83] Poststructural intertextual reading interrupts. It moves toward these others to transform the world. It draws the threads of Matthew's textual fabric in the hope and with the urgency of responding to children, real and imagined, whose destinies are inescapably traced in the stories we choose to tell and to interpret.

82. Bak, *Painted in Words*, 128–29.
83. Levinas, *Humanism of the Other*, 45–47.

Recommended Reading

Aichele, George and Gary Phillips, eds. *Intertextuality and the Bible*. Semeia 69/70. Atlanta: Scholars, 1995.

Allen, Graham. *Intertextuality*. The New Critical Idiom. London: Routledge, 2000.

Boyarin, Daniel. *Intertextuality and the Reading of Midrash*. Indiana Studies in Biblical Literature. Bloomington: Indiana University Press, 1994.

Hays, Richard, Stefan Alkier, and Leroy Huizenga, eds. *Reading the Bible Intertextually*. Waco: Baylor University Press, 2009

Mai, Hans-Peter. "Bypassing Intertextuality. Hermeneutics, Textual Practices, Hypertext." In *Intertextuality*, edited by Heinrich F. Plett, 30–59. Research in Text Theory. Berlin: Walter de Gruyter, 1991.

Phillips, Gary. "The Killing Fields of Matthew's Gospel." In *The Labour of Reading. Desire, Alienation and Biblical Interpretation*, edited by Fiona Black, Roland Boer, and Erin Runions, 249–66. Semeia Studies 36. Atlanta: Society of Biblical Literature, 1999.

———. "What is Written? How are You Reading? Gospel, Intertextuality, and Doing Lukewise: Reading Lk 10:25–42 Otherwise." In *Intertextuality and the Bible*, edited by George Aichele and Gary Phillips, 111–48. Semeia 69/70. Atlanta: Scholars, 1995.

Still, Judith, and Michael Worton, eds. *Intertextuality. Theories and Practices*. New York: Manchester University Press, 1990.

9

Intertextuality Based on
Categorical Semiotics

Stefan Alkier

I ntertextual studies are not the solution to every exegetical problem. I regard intertextuality as a subfield of a categorical semiotics of biblical texts. This means that intertextuality is an inescapable aspect of biblical studies, but it is not the only perspective from which texts can and should be investigated. My vision of a semiotic conception of biblical studies rests upon a theory that bases all methodological steps involved in the interpretation of a text upon a consistent theory of texts. This text theory is grounded in a theory of signs, because signs comprise the universal, formal, fundamental elements of every instance of communication. Every sign production and sign reception occurs under the inescapable conditions of sign processes.[1] New Testament studies have to do primarily with linguistic signs, which when organized become texts that are received with the kinds of expectations that are appropriate to texts. The textual theorist János Petöfi writes:

> For us, *textuality* is no inherent characteristic of verbal objects. A producer or a recipient regards a verbal object as text when he or she believes that this verbal object is a cohesive and complete whole, which corresponds to an actual or assumed communicative intention in an actual or assumed communication situation. A text is—according to s terminology—a complex verbal sign

---

1. Cf. Alkier, "New Testament Studies" 223–48; ibid., *Wunder und Wirklichkeit*, 55–86.

(or a verbal sign complex), which corresponds to a given expectation of textuality.[2]

This definition of text permits all texts to be investigated on the basis of semiotic fundamentals, both according to their "system-immanent construction" as well as according to their "functional embedding," which means according to their "context of production and/or reception."[3] Such a perspective renders moot the conflict between diachronic and synchronic procedures of investigation.[4] It likewise renders moot the theoretical and semiotic tendencies to pit concepts and questions that view texts as autonomous aesthetic objects against those involving a reconstruction of the formation of texts. Furthermore, from the standpoint of this kind of theory of texts, the conflict of text-centered and reader-centered exegesis proves to be an unnecessary battle.

From the perspective of semiotics, texts are thus complex signs which themselves consist of signs, their relations to each other (syntagmatics), their relations to that which they designate (semantics), and their relations to sign users (pragmatics). These relations can be viewed respectively in a predominantly text-immanent perspective and in a primarily text-external perspective. These perspectives are not mutually exclusive but rather complement each other. The text-immanent perspective takes precedence in the sequence of investigation, but not in its importance. This approach inquires after the syntagmatics, semantics, and pragmatics of the text as a world for itself. Methodologically, the widest possible exclusion of its intertextual and text-external relationships is attempted. I call this world of the text, in dependence on Charles Sanders Peirce's concept, the text's *universe of discourse*.[5] I call the external relationships of the text, in dependence on Umberto Eco, its *encyclopedic relationships*.[6]

The level of the *universe of discourse* involves the global assumptions, values, and legalities that the perceptible signs of the text introduce. The text is here treated as an autonomous structure. In contrast, *encyclopedia* refers to the codified knowledge of a given culture. To a great extent, this knowledge assumes in equal measure not only intertextual competence but also extratextual competence, including, for example, the knowledge of cultural codes of conduct, as well as of geographical, societal, political, and other

2. Petöfi, "Explikative Interpretation," 184.

3. Ibid.

4. Diachronic studies investigate the development of language over time; synchronic studies analyze language as it exists at a particular point in time.

5. Cf. Alkier, *Wunder und Wirklichkeit*, 74–79.

6. Ibid., 72–74.

realities. When examined at the level of the *encyclopedia*, the intertextual and extratextual aspects of the autonomous structure of the universe of discourse of a given text can begin to be opened. After one decides to examine the text in terms of a particular encyclopedia, encyclopedic investigations can begin.

On the basis of categorical semiotics, one can thus differentiate three realms of investigation for the discipline of biblical studies—the *intratextual*, the *intertextual*, and the *extratextual* (*intermedial*).

Intratextual investigation is concerned with the text-immanent exploration of syntagmatic, semantic, and pragmatic textual relationships in connection with the models of analysis of literary-critical structuralism and with the inclusion of poetics, narratology, and rhetoric. Here one investigates the text in question under the widest possible methodological shielding from encyclopedic knowledge.

Intertextual investigation concerns itself with the effects of meaning that emerge from the references of a given text to other texts. One should only speak of intertextuality when one is interested in exploring the effects of meaning that emerge from the relating of at least two texts and that neither of the texts considered alone can produce. Within the paradigm of intertextuality, this goes in both directions. That is to say, the meaning potential of both texts is altered through the very intertextual reference itself. Since a text can be brought into relationship not only with one but also with many other texts, intertextuality involves the exploration of the *decentralization of meaning* through references to other texts.

Extratextual investigation concerns itself with the effects of meaning of the text that emerge from the reference of the text to other extratextual signs. Here belong the classic introductory issues of historical-critical biblical studies as well as the archaeological, social-scientific, and politico-historical questions; that is, all the questions that investigate the generation of meaning through acts of reference to text-external signs.[7]

Three Types of Intertextuality

The binding of the concept of intertextuality to a semiotic program enables the taking up of every plausible concern of unlimited and limited conceptions of intertextuality and assigning to them different tasks. For intertextual work in the framework of the semiotic concept, one should therefore distinguish among three perspectives without playing them off against each other: a production-oriented perspective, a reception-oriented perspective,

7. Cf. Alkier and Zangenberg, *Zeichen aus Text*.

and a generative (experimental) perspective. Every intertextual work on a biblical text can be approached from at least one of these perspectives.

Production-oriented intertextuality concerns text-to-text relationships established by such intertextual dispositions as quotations, allusions, and narrative.[8] In production-oriented perspectives a text may only be correlated with those texts the author demonstrably knew or could have known.

Reception-oriented intertextuality investigates textual relationships that were produced by actual readers or that could have been produced by hypothetical readers at particular times and places.

Generative intertextuality asks what effect a text-to-text relationship has on meaning, independent of the intertextual arrangement of the texts. Here text-to-text relationships are established neither through production-oriented nor through reception-oriented intertextuality. The criterion for generative intertextuality is whether interesting shifts in meaning are produced by the intertextual relationship. Whereas production-oriented and reception-oriented intertextual phenomena are investigated analytically and reconstructively and differentiate between legitimate and illegitimate intertextual relationships, generative intertextuality is in principal an unlimited, performative perspective that creates intertextual relations.

Intertextual Modes of Writing, Reading, and Composing

To find intertextual relations is only the starting point of the interpretation of those relations and of questions about their functions and effects. Questions concerning intertextual modes of writing, reading, or composition explore the ways and strategies of the implicit and explicit integration and connection of texts, along with the effects the recognition of these linkages has on meaning.

A glance back to the origins of this methodology in Mikail Bakhtin can help frame some key questions suggestive for guiding the different tasks of intertextual modes of writing, reading or composition.[9] Are texts monologically appropriated as proof texts for the appropriating text's own way of seeing things, or can their voices still be distinctly heard in the midst of the dialogue of interpretation? Are differences and dissonances between the related texts still perceptible, or are the correlated texts squeezed into a harmonious form by the laces of an interpretive corset? Is the intertextual correlation of texts beneficial for the texts? Do they complement each other, or are they in conflict with each other? Obviously, this unsystematic

8. Cf. Holthuis, *Intertextualität*, 29–36.
9. Bakhtin, *Dialogic Imagination*.

collection of questions is not exhaustive. Such questions indicate, however, the basic trajectory that further reflection on these matters should follow.

As one pursues the question of the *intertextual mode of writing*, one moves primarily into the realm of production-oriented intertextuality. At issue here is the generative poetics in play, not the question of the psychology or historical reconstruction of the act of writing by a real author. Moreover, this is not a question of style or literary criticism. It has much more to do with an analysis of texture, that is, of text as a tissue of symbol generating signs that point to other signs. By what art and manner, and with what intended effects and punchlines, were the common signs selected and organized so that, when read together, the impression of a coherent whole can arise? This concept of the mode of writing, which I have borrowed from Roland Barthes, stresses the aspect of choice in every act of writing, since it is never possible to link everything together. Therefore, because of the economy of language, every act of writing must always be eclectic and positional. Barthes writes:

> A language is therefore a horizon, and a style a vertical dimension, which together map out for the writer a nature, since he does not choose either. . . . Now every Form is also a Value, which is why there is room, between a language and a style, for another formal reality: writing. Within any literary form, there is a general choice of tone, of ethos, if you like, and this is precisely where the writer shows himself clearly as an individual because this is where he commits himself. . . . A language and a style are blind forces; a mode of writing is an act of historical solidarity.[10]

The specific question concerning intertextual modes of writing helps us grasp, correspondingly, how the selection, linking and integration of other texts in the writing process can reasonably function as a structuring element for writing in general. Because no authors can integrate every facet of every text known to them into their own text, the investigation of concrete ways in which the intertextual strategies of texts are carried out becomes an interesting perspective on the act of textual positioning.

The same applies for *intertextual modes of reading* when they are placed in the framework of reception-oriented intertextuality. For example, in Victorinus of Pettau's third-century commentary on Revelation, most of his quotes relate Revelation to Isaiah, Daniel, Psalms, Matthew, and some letters of Paul.[11] His intertextual strategy reads Revelation in harmony with

10. Barthes, "Writing Degree Zero," 13–14.

11. Cf. Poetovio, *Sur l'Apocalypse.*

those Scriptures that were well known and commonly accepted in Christian communities. He not only reads Revelation from the perspective of the quoted texts, but he also reads Paul from the perspective of Revelation. In this mode of reading all the texts he has collocated speak with one voice. There is no place for conflicts or dialogism among and between these texts.

On the other hand, Lactantius (d. 325) does not quote many other New or Old Testament Scriptures when he reads Revelation, but he does quote many Greco-Roman texts (*Liber Instituionum* VII.15–26).[12] There are more quotes from Cicero alone than all the biblical quotes combined. His intertextual strategy relates the prophecy of John to Roman discourses about the future and argues that they are very similar. Revelation in this intertextual relation becomes more trustworthy even if one is not a Christian. The meaning of a text in real existing interpretations depends highly on the intertextual connections the interpreter activates. But despite their significant differences regarding the texts they chose to correlate with Revelation, the mode of intertextual reading one finds in Lactantius works by way of the same harmonizing of the collocated texts as does that of Victorinus.

Questions about modes of intertextual writing and reading are primarily analytical questions. But reflection on *intertexual modes of composing*, while complex, is also very important. In religious education it is common for teachers to show or have students identify the intertextual combination of biblical texts within contemporary literature or other modern texts such as newspaper articles. Such experiments belong to generative intertextuality. If, however, we create a lesson, a sermon, or an article, we should always ask ourselves about our intertextual strategy. What will be the mode of intertextual composing? Do we want to show that the biblical text agrees with or says basically the same thing that other "good" and acceptable contemporary texts say? Or do we wish to show that the biblical text has it its own voice, one that questions our ways of thinking today?

In one such experiment of a generative intertextuality I brought together the story of Zacchaeus the tax collector (Luke 19:1–10) with the fascinating short story "Der Skorpion" ("The Scorpion") by Christa Reinig. My rationale for this mode of intertextual composition was to explore the anthropological or the soteriological question of the possibility of a healing, restorative change. The Lukan story offers a positive response to this question, but Christa Reinig's story provides a negative one. The intertextual experiment puts these different responses into dialogue, a dialogue that emphasizes the actuality and perspectives of both texts. In my experience, this

12. Cf. Lactantius, *Divinae institutiones*, 15–26.

experiment has proven itself to be quite suitable for teaching in schools and universities, as well as for work in the parish and for sermons.

Method

1. We Have to Choose

Before starting the exegetical work the exegetes should know what they are asking for. A lot of fruitless controversies in the field of biblical intertextual studies are the result of different points of view about the aims of such studies. Methods are ways to approach the task of answering questions. In order to choose the right method it is necessary to know and reflect on the question that is posed.

One thing must, however, be clear at the outset. There is no single method that can address at the same time all the intertextual questions one could pursue. Additionally, even when one narrows things down to a single question, one cannot fully exhaust the matter. The reason for this is not to be found in supposed weaknesses in any of the methods. Rather, this fact results from the reality that in principle any text can be correlated with any other text.[13] Intertextuality, with its awareness of semiotics and the decentralization of meaning, can teach humility and fascination at the same time. Intertextuality promotes humility when those who study it face their own limitations, and this develops out of their fascination with the apprehension they sense in the face of the ever growing potential for the meanings of a text within that text's world.

Intertextual studies offer a space within which to learn and practice a qualified pluralism. The first step, therefore, is to position oneself methodologically and, with all humility, to formulate one's own questions. One must then pursue these questions, plowing the textual fields with dedication, diligence, and passion. So, what questions would students and scholars like to ask? Do they want to pursue intertextuality at the level of the writing of a text, that is, at the level of an author? Do they want to engage in intertextual reading practices? Or, do they want to develop our own creativity and begin setting texts in conversation?

---

13. In keeping with Julia Kristeva's assumption.

2. Analyzing Intratextual Intertextuality

Before one can jump into an intertextual perspective, it is advisable to do some preparatory work. Texts that are to be evaluated intertextually should always be analyzed intratextually first. If one leaves this step out, it is all too easy to fall into the danger of failing to be guided by the text's own categories and substituting instead one's own highly limited preferences. When that happens the task quickly becomes boring. Those who want to find only themselves, will miss the miracle of facts, the richness of reality, the fascination of engaging with opponents, the inspiration of the other.

When one examines a text from the intratextual standpoint, it is necessary to hold one's own knowledge in abeyance. When, for example, Mark 1:2 identifies Isaiah as the source of the citation that follows, then this must be assumed to be true within Mark's universe of discourse without any "ifs" or "buts." Only then can one properly ask intratextual questions such as: What meaning does Isaiah have in Mark's Gospel? Where exactly is Isaiah's name mentioned in Mark? What authority is ascribed to Isaiah throughout Mark's Gospel? In short, what *generative* power does Isaiah have within the texture of Mark's Gospel?

One should use this intratextual study in order to note all the problems and ideas that could offer intertextual clues that might be fruitfully explored in the subsequent intertextual work. We might notice, for example, that Mark 1:2b–3 is a mixed citation and the locations of the individual components of the citation can then be identified so they can be read in their original contexts. Importantly, however, ideas from one's own knowledge must also be taken into account when engaging in the work of interpreting Mark. These can include intertextual associations made by other readers, but can also include links generated on our own. This was the case, for example, for my own reading of the Zacchaeus story I mentioned earlier. As far as I know, no one before me had thought to link the story of Zacchaeus with Christa Reinig's "The Scorpion." The connection between these two stories occurred to me, serendipitously, while reading Luke's story one day.

In this way one can uncover numerous intertextual possibilities. The descriptive and generative steps provide the materials for further work as we sort the initial ideas according to the appropriate approach for exploring them—that is, production-oriented intertextuality, reception-oriented intertextuality, or generative intertextuality.

3. Analyzing Intertextual Mode of Writing

Unlike the intratextual analysis just discussed, the initial step in doing intertextual study, examining the mode of writing, involves the identification of
all the known or plausible intertextual references in the text being studied.
This is true even when the text does not explicitly identify an intertextual
source, or, as is the case in Mark 1:2b–3, the sources have been obscured.
The criteria that Richard Hays has suggested for identifying echoes and allusions are very useful in helping one discover intertextual references.[14]

As a second step one should consider whether there is an intentional
and well-planned interplay of texts going on in particular places, or whether
the network of intertextual connections has been made in a more arbitrary
fashion.

The third step involves evaluating the frequency of quotations and allusions within the text being studied. Then the particular type of marking or
masking or lack of either, must be analyzed and interpreted. Once the references have been identified, they should be read carefully and thoroughly
in their own original contexts. In fact, these references should themselves
be studied intertextually within their own discourse universe. Only then
should they be examined intertextually with reference to the later text in
which they were included.

Finally, one should ask whether the voices of the citations or allusions
that are woven into the new text are respected or disappear into the monological perspective of the new text. The individual voices of the incorporated
texts can come into dialogue with the new text in manifold ways. They can
either enhance the text, they can add to it, or they can contradict it.

After this initial work has been done, one can ask how the text that
is being analyzed in the light of the text that has been incorporated into it
can now be read. It should also be considered how the text that has been
incorporated can be understood in fresh ways in the light of the text that is
being analyzed.

After these varied and complex analytical steps, we must again make
a decision. What should be investigated now? It is simply not reasonable to
think we can track down all the possible references and exhaustively explore
each of them. The reality of the uncontrollability of signs and the diverse
networks that they can form means that we must choose wisely which connections to explore in order to aim for productive interpretations at the end
of the process. One could certainly spend one's whole life in the academic
study of intertextual links in Mark's Gospel and never finish or achieve a

---

14. See the chapter above on Metalepsis.

degree! Working methodologically also means that one must carefully consider which questions and approaches are likely to be particularly profitable to pursue for a specific text. To cite Paul somewhat freely: All things are possible, but not all of them are beneficial (1 Cor 6:12).

4. Analyzing Intertextual Mode of Reading

Concerning the matter of intertextual mode of reading, we must first distinguish two possible approaches—does we want to read the text along lines already attested in past readings, or do we want creatively to imagine and apply new intertextual readings?

Real Readers

I have already noted examples of real readings of intertextual networks developed together with the book of Revelation in the textual worlds of Lactantius and Victorinus. It is important here to notice how often and how densely the text of the intertextual reader being analyzed cites or alludes to a particular text. The first step here is that one must consider the individual contexts, genres, and/or locations of the reader's text. The fact that the text of Revelation is constantly represented in a commentary on that book has a very different meaning than when one finds Revelation showing up at every turn in a letter dealing with different political forms of government. Second, the manner of marking (or not marking) intertextual references should be analyzed and interpreted. The third step consists in studying what other texts are cited or alluded to and how often these other texts occur. Only when one comes to the fourth step can one ask if and which references are connected to the text written by the intertextual reader being studied. One should also ask whether the connections have been done explicitly, or does the intertextual reader leave it to others who receive the text to uncover the intertextual references? Finally, it is important to ask how the texts have been put into relationship with each other by the reader. Does the reader produce more monological or dialogical relationships among the various texts?

Imagined Readers

It can also be a fruitful exercise to ask about readings that are not actually attested. That is, one can consider imagined readings. Clearly the results of this sort of approach must always be more hypothetical than those of actual readings. To ask heuristic questions concerning imagined readers naturally takes one into the realm of generative intertextuality. Importantly, however, the goal here is not freely to create new, uncontrolled or historically implausible combinations of texts, but instead to engage in an imagined historical experiment. How, for example, might a first-century Jewish reader in Asia Minor have read Revelation if he or she correlated it with the *Res Gestae* of Augustus? This approach must be executed with as much methodological rigor as the other approaches. Thus, both texts that one wants to correlate must be intensively studied and interpreted. Only then should one attempt to formulate a plausible historical situation, a task that requires a great deal of historical knowledge and a disciplined imagination. Only at this point can one propose a hypothesis regarding how the imagined reader in the presumed situation might have read the supposed texts intertextually.

5. Creating Intertextuality

The creative collocation of texts in which new meanings are produced— meanings that are plausible and also open up new perspectives—is an art in which one can be trained by learning particular methodologies. It is highly recommended that one keep a notebook in which to collect intertextual references, such as, for example, the literary processes at play in biblical texts. In this way I have identified points of comparison between the relevant elements of the parable of the prodigal son in Luke 15 and more recent literary works and poetry.[15] At this point interesting intertextual associations should be noted, especially those that do not lie immediately close to hand. The generation of these sorts of intertextual readings requires three important things. First, one needs to read widely so as to have a significant repertoire of good texts available. Second, one has to do more than read the Bible once. In fact, one has to live with the biblical texts on a daily basis in order to be able to bring them into association with other texts. Third, one needs to have patience and to enjoy doing creative work. Please give it a try. I promise that you will find it exciting, worthwhile, and valuable!

---

15. E.g., the work of André Gide, Rainer Maria Rilke, Rolf Rameder, Rose Ausländer.

Choosing a Production-Oriented
Intertextual Approach to Matthew 1

The Intratextual Structure of Matthew's Gospel

In my intratextual reading of Matthew's use of the term *biblos* (βίβλος//"book") in Matt 1:1, Matthew signals that his literary enterprise does not intend merely to relate some episodes of the life of Jesus, but to be a full story with a beginning, middle, and end. The word connotes that the reader will be informed of the whole story of Jesus Christ. The genitive construction that follows *biblos* indicates the content of this book. The term *genesis* (γένεσις/ "origin; state of being") implies the whole story of Jesus starting with its very beginning. "Jesus Christ" denotes the subject of the *genesis* of the story that is told, and at the same time explains why the story of Jesus is worthy to be told—Jesus is Messiah, the Christ. In light of a Jewish encyclopedic knowledge, the following genitive "son of David" (υἱοῦ Δαυίδ) indicates that Jesus is the Christ. Now that is not a sufficient argument, but rather a necessary one, and the following story has to show that it is plausible that this son of David is the Messiah. The final genitive "son of Abraham" (υἱοῦ Ἀβραάμ) denotes the starting point of the story of Jesus Christ. This starting point connotes that the story of Jesus is the sequel to the story of God's elected people. Matthew constructs his story as the continuation and transformation of the history of God with his elected people.

The mention of the names of Abraham, David, and Jesus serve to underline the very importance of the story. They function as the cornerstones of the structure of the genealogy in Matt 1:2–17. Because Matthew wants to show that this story is not a mere human story but the story of God and his people, he has to indicate that this story has a plan, a plan whose author is God himself. To show this, Matthew gives the genealogy the structure of 3 times 14 and expresses that explicitly in 1:17.

The following story in Matt 1:18–25 does not narrate the birth of Jesus but rather explains and interprets his conception. Matthew uses an imperfect verb tense in 1:18 in contrast to the aorist found in the genealogy, and this change of tense indicates that the interest in the story of the *genesis* of Jesus does not lie in the historical moment of the Virgin Birth, but in the durative aspect that Jesus is from the very start of the story the God who is with us. By this shifting of tenses, Matthew connects the human and the divine aspects of his story. Joseph must name the infant, but the name that he is to give as an act of adoption is supplied to him by the angel of God, and thus by God himself. This God-given name is a metonymy for what Jesus is, and this name, "Jesus," will be interpreted with the name Immanuel in

the fulfilment quotation. The "for" (γάρ) in 1:21b indicates that the following sentence provides the explanation for the name Jesus—he will save his
people from their sins.

This can happen because Jesus is the Immanuel: the *With-us-God*. This
theology of names gives the macrotext its structure. The book of Matthew
narrates *how* God is with us in the Immanuel, Jesus. Matthew's story transforms *With-us-God* into "I am with you all days until the end of this age" at
the very end of his book (28:20). The first transformation is that from God
to I. "I" denotes the resurrected Jesus Christ. That does not mean that Jesus
Christ is identified with God, but that he has the same relation to the "you"
that God has to the "us." That Jesus is not identified with God shows the
temporal limitation of this relation until the end of this age. At the beginning of the story "us" means Israel. But, by the end of the story it has been
transformed into "you." "You" means *everybody who believes in the story that
Matthew narrates in his book*. Matthew narrates the opening of the exclusive
relationship implied in the meaning of Immanuel into the open structure of
"I am with you". The Immanuel relationship is still valid for Israel, but it is
no longer an exclusive relationship. All those who believe in the Immanuel
Jesus Christ are accepted into this relationship.

The Intertextual Drive of Matthew 1 in the Limits of the Universe of Discourse of the Book of Matthew

If one ignores the encyclopedic knowledge of Israel's Scriptures and reads
Matthew 1 within the limits of the universe of discourse of Matthew's Gospel, it becomes clear that the intertextual network to Israel's Scriptures is
only explicitly referred to in 1:22–23. Verse 22 connects the episode that is
narrated in 1:18–21 with the quotation that is given in 23. The marker of the
quotation in the strict sense is, "what was spoken by the Lord through the
prophet, saying . . ." Only here and in 2:15 is the "Lord" (κύριος) mentioned
in the quotation marker—a term that emphasizes that the true source of the
following quotation is God himself. The prophet is only the medium that
God uses for his speech.

Matthew 1:22a suggests that the promise of the quotation was not
fulfilled until the things that are narrated in 18b–21 happened. The consequence of this is that Jesus alone is the Immanuel, nobody else before
or after him. Verse 22 denotes that the things that are narrated happened
because of the fulfilment of the promise that is quoted in 23. That means
that the word of God is the *causa* of Jesus' history. This implies a theology of the word of God—things happen because God has spoken through a

prophet. The history that Matthew narrates is not only an interesting story of a human author; it is the story of the fulfilment of the word of God. The quotation marker connotes not only Matthew's mode of reading Scripture, but also the hermeneutics he intends to be used for reading the story. In the universe of discourse of this book, the author of the story is God himself. Matthew is only the human narrator through whom this story of God is told. With regard to the quotation itself, 1:23a promises what the story fulfils in 1:18b–20. But there is a problem with 23b: "They shall call his name Immanuel." Yet, the story narrates that the angel says to Joseph that he should give him the name of Jesus, which Joseph in fact does in 25b. The solution to this problem lies in the commentary of the narrator in 23c: he translates the meaning of the name Immanuel: "with-us-God." The name of Jesus is explained by the angel in 21c. His name is Jesus, "for he will save his people from their sins." To understand the text of Matthew, it is not necessary to know that the name Jesus is derived from the Hebrew Yeshua, which can mean "Yahweh saves." On the level of the universe of discourse of the book of Matthew the readers know everything that Matthew wants them to know. Joseph has to give the child the name Jesus because he will save his people.

Reading Matthew 1 with Regard to
Production-Oriented Intertextuality

In this step of our intertextual method we have to use our encyclopedic knowledge about Israel's Scriptures. From this perspective not only the names and the quotation in Matt 1 function as intertextual dispositions, but the very first two words of the Gospel do so as well. The syntagm *biblos geneseōs* is an intertextual reference to Gen 2:4 and 5:1 (LXX), a phrase that repeats itself in Genesis and helps structure the entire book. Not only the first verse, but the entire first chapter of Matthew's Gospel can be read as an intertextual overture to the book. The numerous names in the chapter serve as abbreviations for the larger narratives that they invoke. The well-planned selection and arrangement of material evident in Matthew's intertextual mode of writing elicits a sense that God is the one at work behind the resulting sequence of the diverse stories that are represented. Both the careful selection of the names and the breaks in the standard genealogical form created by the insertion of specific names and important details—for example, "David begat Solomon by the wife of Uriah" (1:6b)—guide how one reads the genealogy. These phenomena intertextually direct the reception of the names found in the genealogy towards the very narratives with which they are connected in Israel's Scriptures. The appearance of the name of "Jesus, who is called Christ" (1:16b) in the genealogy interweaves Jesus in a dialogical way with the stories from the Scriptures. In this way the reception of these Scriptures is determined by the genealogy. The intertextual mode of writing of Matt 1 creates and enforces a theology of the gospel of Jesus Christ, a theology that is inextricably bound up with Israel's Scriptures. Moreover, their authoritative application within this theology forms an essential element of the logic that led to later concepts of a canon of the Old and New Testaments.

Matthew's mode of intertextual writing is dialogical in the sense that it refers to the voices of the Scriptures themselves. The history that the genealogy remembers is not only a history of triumph and faith, but also a history of catastrophes and sins. In light of this background it is plausible to conclude that the explanation of the name of Jesus is: *he will save his people from their sins.* The genealogy narrates the sins of this people by way of the intertextually inscribed voices selected from Israel's Scriptures. The history that the genealogy narrates cannot be foreseen from a human perspective. It is full of surprises, such as what the stories of the women in the genealogy connote. Or, if we consider Jacob, he is not the firstborn son, yet he gets the rights of the firstborn and therefore becomes part of the genealogy of the Messiah. The genealogy as a whole, then, leads readers with the proper intertextual competence to expect that Matthew's story will be a story full of complications, sins, and surprises in which God is the most important actor. The reader does not have to wait long for such a surprise; the genealogy provides one itself. We find the notion of begetting in the aorist active of γεννάω thirty-nine times—how boring! But then the verb changes to the passive voice: "Mary, of whom Jesus *was born* who is called Christ" (Matt 1:16b). In this surprising change we have an indication that God is the actor, for this is a divine passive, an action taken by a source not mentioned but assumed to be God, and the following story enacts this surprising *passivum divinum.*

Let us take another look at the quote from Isaiah in Matt 1:23. Which text of Isaiah should we use? Neither the Hebrew Masoretic Text nor one of the known LXX versions has exactly in Isa 7:14 what Matthew quotes in 1:23. Only Greek texts have "virgin," so we can surely say that Matthew used a Greek version. The LXX has "Behold the virgin will become pregnant and bear a son, and *you will call* (καλέσεις) his name Emmanuel (Ἐμμανουηλ)," Matthew's intertextual mode of writing transforms the quote. Instead of καλέσεις Matthew uses καλέσουσιν ("they will call") because he needs the plural in order to connect the name of Jesus with Immanuel as its interpretant. Notably, Matthew's interpretation of the quotation that translates the Hebrew name Immanuel as "With-us-God" shows that Matthew knew a Hebrew text of Isaiah. We do not know exactly what versions of Isaiah

Matthew knew, but we know that he used more than one version and that he reworked the quotations.

It is not possible here to examine the whole text of Isaiah, so I will look at Isaiah 6–8, as I think that will be sufficient to demonstrate what I wish to show. This section starts with Isaiah's call and his commission to bring about a hardening, a text that is quoted in Matt 13:14–15. In the immediate context of the quotation from Isaiah 7 we observe the account of the conflict between Damascus and Israel on the one side and Judah on the other. In Isaiah 8 we read about the birth of a son of Isaiah, but he is not Immanuel. Yet, Immanuel is mentioned again in 8:8 and its translation is given in 8:10. These are the only other occasions that Immanuel is mentioned in Isaiah. But who and what is "Immanuel" here? First, we should notice that Immanuel is not an identifiable person in Isaiah. Rabbinic exegesis and a lot of contemporary Old Testament scholars identify him with Hezekiah, the son of Ahaz. The fact remains, however, that Immanuel in 7:14 is not identified as a son of Ahaz and the mother of Immanuel is not a wife of Ahaz. Whoever the mother is, she is underdetermined as a young woman and nothing else is said about her. In 8:8 Immanuel is the addressee of Isaiah's prophecy of disaster about Judah, and Judah is said to be the land of Immanuel, but again nothing is said about the identity of Immanuel. The addressee Immanuel in the context of a prophecy of disaster about Judah looks ironic, but in 8:9–10 the meaning of "Immanuel" is used as an argument for the failure of the enemies of Judah. What, then, is Immanuel in 7:14?

The most important thing to say is that Immanuel functions as a prophetic sign given by God. Isaiah 7 narrates the first action of Isaiah after his call and his commission of hardening. The king of Damascus and the king of Israel are going to make war against Judah because they want to force Judah's king to take part in their alliance against Assyria (7:1). The king and his people react with great fear (v. 2). God responds to this fear by sending Isaiah to Judah's king with instructions on how to act and with a prophecy of disaster for Israel and Damascus. This part of the account ends with 7:9—"If you do not believe, you will not remain." Ahaz could be happy about this prophecy, if he were to believe. His reaction, however, is not given. What this gap in the story indicates in a sophisticated way is that Ahaz did not understand what he heard. His is the first example of a hardening after Isaiah's commission to be an instrument of hardening. Instead of detailing the reaction of Ahaz, what comes next in Isaiah is a speech of God directly to Ahaz. God asks Ahaz to choose a sign as a validation of the prophecy. But Ahaz does not follow the instruction of God; rather, he rejects God's request with pious words. Again, he does not understand and this shows that he does not believe. A careful reading of the account already makes it clear that

Judah will not remain, and 8:5–8 narrates exactly this with the ironic use of Immanuel. Despite God being with Judah, Judah will be destroyed because of unbelief in God; but despite its destruction, God is still with Judah and will save it from total dissolution (8:10).

In Isaiah 7, the reaction of God to the disobedience of Ahaz is not narrated, but Isaiah rebukes Ahaz and says that God will do the very thing Ahaz should have requested—provide a sign. This sign is the birth of Immanuel. He will eat butter and honey until he is grown up and then Damascus and Israel will be destroyed. Isaiah 7:18—8:4 deals with the same topic; Isaiah prophesies of the destruction of Israel and Damascus. So Immanuel is a sign of salvation for Judah and a sign of disaster for Israel and Damascus. Everything could turn out well for Judah, but in 8:5 Isaiah prophesies disaster for Judah, something the reader could expect because of Isaiah's commission to cause the hardening among the people in chapter 6, Ahaz's failure to understand after 7:10, and Ahaz's disobedience in 7:12. The time of salvation that is offered during the youth of Immanuel is a gift of God. Neither Israel nor Judah, however, believes God, so neither will remain. Nevertheless, God will remain and is still with them.

The sign of Immanuel, when viewed within the limits of the universe of the book of Isaiah, is not a messianic prophecy as Matthew has employed it. It is a sign in the same way that the names of the sons of Isaiah are signs. An intertextual reading of Matthew in relation to Isaiah cannot explain all the issues one might raise about these texts, but it opens the universe of discourse of the *biblos* of Matthew for nuances of meaning that cannot be seen within the closed structure of the text. Reading Matt 1 in relation to Isaiah 6–8 gives us some fresh aspects of meaning that are worthy of notice—Ahaz is a member of the genealogy of Jesus; he is one of his forefathers. Knowing the story of Ahaz, we see that Jesus did not become Messiah because his family was without sin. The opposite is the case. David, in the case of his liaison with Bathsheba (2 Sam 11), along with most of his descendants, failed to do what God wanted them to do. The people of Jesus and even lots of the members of his genealogy were sinners who were hardened for their sins, just as Matt 13:14–15 says using the very words of Isa 6:9–10. The result of this hardening will be death and destruction like Isaiah prophesied. This hardening can only be cancelled if the reason for the hardening comes to an end—the "he" mentioned in the prophecy has to "save his people from their sins," and that is the meaning of the God-given name of Jesus.

But who is "he" and what is the meaning of the name of Jesus with regard to the intertextual relation to Isaiah? In light of Isaiah, the "he" who saves his people is not Jesus, but God himself. The theocentric perspectives of the prophets are inscribed into the book of Matthew. As with the name

"Immanuel," the name "Jesus" becomes a sign for the activity of God. But in contrast to Isaiah's use of Immanuel, Matthew uses Jesus' birth and life to develop a narrative theology and narrates how God saves his people from their sins by means of the words and deeds of Jesus. Jesus tells of and declares the will of God in his words as well as in his deeds. He works against the hardening that has lain upon his people since Isaiah's time. God gave the hardening and only God can take it away. Jesus's name becomes a sign for what God does through Jesus for his people—in the words and deeds of Jesus, God is with his people.

What does Matthew do when he overwrites the Hebrew version of Isa 7:14 with a Greek version of this text? The most important thing he does is to depict the young woman of the Hebrew text precisely as a virgin. With this strategy, he emphasizes the divine nature of the sign. Further, by doing so he is able to indicate that Jesus is different from all the members of his genealogy despite the fact that he is from the house of David. What did Matthew do with the book of Isaiah? He does what every reader has to do in the act of reading: he determines the text by his readings. Isaiah does not narrate the fulfilment of the prophecy. He tells us nothing about the birth of Immanuel. Yet precisely this blank space in Isaiah allows Matthew to use the prophecy for his own *biblos*. Matthew determines the identity of the underdetermined Immanuel, and with that change his mode of intertextual writing transforms the prophecy of a sign into a messianic prophecy. With this identification and transformation every messianic prophecy in Isaiah is related to Jesus, the Christ of Matthew's *biblos*. But that is just the tip of the iceberg. With this identification Matthew overwrites the book of Isaiah with his own *biblos*. Isaiah becomes a prophet of Jesus Christ and at the same time provides an essential background for reading Matthew.

Conclusion

Intertextuality is not everything, but neglecting intertextuality makes one blind to the richness of the text being studied and explored. The short example from Matt 1 of a production-oriented intertextual analysis shows just how multifaceted, complex, and fruitful it can be to engage in tasks and questions that are central to reading according to an intertextual methodology. This approach opens up a variety of perspectives on and dimensions of meaning in texts. As should now be clear, it requires a lot of work and entails a great deal more than simply noticing that Matthew has cited Isaiah. That is only an initial step. One must go on to examine and research the details of the texts to see how and what impact the intertextual relationships have for detecting nuances of meaning. Further, it may be far from sufficient to examine only a few chapters from the text that is referenced. One must keep the whole book or books (in our case Isaiah) in view in order to do good intertextual work. The genealogy in Matt 1:2–17 offers a large collection of texts to read and to interpret, and Matthew's Gospel consists of much more than just this first chapter. That the texture of Matthew is crisscrossed with numerous intertextual references to Israel's Scriptures is hardly new news. One need only look at the so-called fulfilment sayings scattered throughout the Gospel to see that this is the case. Furthermore, our brief example of a production-oriented reading has only explored one intertextual approach, and that in a limited way. The possibilities of a reception-oriented intertextual approach or a generative intertextual approach multiply in a breathtaking way the potential for an array of meanings of the text to be explored.

So much should now be clear—intertextual work, as a decentralization of meaning, falsifies any interpretation that labors under the conviction that there can be only one correct interpretation. Intertextuality within the frame of a semiotic approach to studying the Bible is, however, anything but a blank check that funds arbitrary reading. One must always accept and work with the reality of the actual, given signs. This is an essential criterion for determining the plausibility and acceptability of one's interpretation. Precisely for this reason it is vital to consider carefully the different approaches to intertextuality and then to pursue a chosen approach methodically. The texts themselves together with their intertextual relationships will always remain far richer than any of our particular readings can ever capture.

Recommended Reading

Alkier, Stefan. "New Testament Studies on the Basis of Categorical Semiotics." In *Reading the Bible Intertextually*, edited by Stefan Alkier, Richard B. Hays, Leroy A. Huizenga, 223–48. Waco: Baylor University Press, 2009.

———. "Zeichen der Erinnerung—Die Genealogie in Mt 1 als intertextuelle Disposition." In *Bekenntnis und Erinnerung, Festschrift zum 75. Geburtstag von Hans–Friedrich Weiß*, edited by Klaus–Michael Bull and Eckart Reinmuth, 108–28. RTS 16. Münster: Lit, 2004.

Alkier, Stefan, and Richard B. Hays, eds. *Revelation and the Politics of Apocalyptic Interpretation* Waco: Baylor University Press, 2012.

Bakhtin, Mikhail. *The Dialogic Imagination: Four Essays*. Austin: University of Texas Press, 1981.

Barthes, Roland. *Writing Degree Zero*. New York: Hill and Wang, 2012.

Huizenga, Leroy. "The Old Testament in the New: Intertextuality and Allegory." *JSNT* 38 (2015) 17–35.

Kristeva, Julia. *Desire in Language*. New York: Columbia University Press, 1980.

Liszka, James Jakób. *General Introduction to the Semiotic of Charles Sanders Peirce.* Bloomington: Indiana University Press, 1996.

Petöfi, János S. "Explikative Interpretation: Explikatives Wissen." In *Von der verbalen KonstiAtution zur symbolischen Bedeutung—From Verbal Constitution to Symbolic Meaning,* edited by János S. Petöfi and Terry Olivi, 184–95. Hamburg: H. Buske, 1988.

Part II

Eclectic and Novel Strategies

10

Sociorhetorical Intertexture

Roy R. Jeal

The study of intertextuality tells us clearly that texts, including biblical texts, are never free-standing, independent communications.
Borrowing intertextually and reconfiguring a famous line from John
Donne, it is true for us to say that "No *text* is an island, entire of itself." One
of the things we can try in order to study and learn about the nature and
importance of intertextuality in the New Testament is the analytic of sociorhetorical interpretation, initiated and developed by Vernon K. Robbins,
which uses the term *Intertexture* to describe a full-bodied account of the
interweaving of the language of a New Testament text with things outside
the text.[1]

Robbins points out that "Every text is a rewriting of other texts, an
'intertextual' activity."[2] Crucial to the idea of intertexture is the recognition
that there is always an interactivity, an interplay, or, to focus on the sensory
metaphor of the "textures of texts," an "interweaving" of a broad range of
threads or lines of understanding that together make up the features, meanings, and rhetorical force in texts.[3] This interweaving suggests that the word
"text" refers broadly not only to words but to ideas or perceptions conveyed
by words, images, mental conceptions, cultures, societies, memories, and

---

1. Robbins, *Tapestry*, 30–32, 96–143; Robbins, *Exploring*, 40–70.

2. Robbins, *Tapestry*, 30. Cf. Kristeva, "Word, Dialogue, and Novel," 37: " . . . any
text is constructed of a mosaic of quotations; any text is the absorption and transformation of another."

3. Rhetorical force is the power of texts to move audiences by eliciting belief,
behavior, and community formation.

such like things. Intertextuality in the NT is a much bigger domain than direct language connections to the Hebrew Bible or LXX passages. It must consider not only literary connections among and between texts but also the extra-literary, indeed the entire environment, in which the NT was written.[4] According to Robbins, intertexture is "a text's representation of, reference to, and use of phenomena in the 'world' outside the text being interpreted."[5] Analysis involves determining the nature, functions, and effects of this texturing.

Intertextures

For Robbins, *intertexturality* involves a broadening of intertextuality that is not limited to locating and explaining sources, quotations, and references, nor by intertextual relationships only within the biblical tradition. It is about the interplay of all the intertextual features that make for argumentation and for the persuasiveness of argumentation. Robbins calls for the examination of a spectrum of four intertextures explained below, each with several sub-categories.[6]

Oral-Scribal Intertexture

Aspects of oral-scribal intertexture are most like what has typically been considered and analyzed by people interested in intertextuality in the NT. It considers the more obvious intertexturality of recitations, but also takes into account recontextualizations, reconfigurations, narrative amplifications, and thematic elaborations of language observed in other texts. The intertextural connections should not exclude Greco-Roman or other texts of the ancient Mediterranean since the NT was located in and addressed to persons living in the realm of Mediterranean texts and languages.

Recitation is about the employment of the exact words or at least the clear implication that the words are from spoken or written tradition found in another place.[7] Recitations often alter, omit, summarize, or use only

---

4. And also the contexts of reception and interpretation from the times when the NT documents were written until the present. The scope of intertextuality becomes so great that many connections cannot be identified and analyzed by one interpreter. It is very important therefore, as Robbins, *Tapestry*, 99, points out, to establish reasonable boundaries within which we consider ideas.

5. Robbins, *Exploring*, 40.

6. For many examples see ibid., 40–68.

7. Robbins, *Tapestry*, 103; Robbins, *Exploring*, 41.

some of the wording of the source texts. Some narrate the ideas of another text in the author's own words. Interpreters must analyze with considerable care the passages with which they work in order to identify recitations and the distinctions in them. *Recontextualization* occurs when there is no indication, explicit or implied, that wording from other texts is written anywhere else.[8] The intertextual wording is placed in a new context. *Reconfiguration* occurs when an earlier tradition or situation is restructured to indicate that a new situation or idea replaces or transcends the earlier one.[9] *Narrative amplification* is evident when recitations, recontextualizations, and reconfigurations are extended into longer sections of text.[10] Intertextual pieces become woven together to form intertextures within a narration or story. *Thematic elaboration*, according to Robbins, is an alternative to narrative amplification that is observed in complex argumentation that draws on intertextual and other resources to form its rationale.[11]

Cultural Intertexture

Texts interact not only with other texts but also with many features of cultures.[12] Cultural intertexture draws on people's knowledge of things that they understand because they live in or know implicitly about the features of a given cultural milieu. People "get" the ideas not necessarily because of direct, conscious knowledge of wording, but because they have a cultural familiarity with ideas that are "in the air." These intertextures frequently occur in references, allusions, and echoes from documents, sayings, inscriptions, images, or other symbols. *References* are words and phrases that point to culturally recognizable people, things, or traditions. *Allusions* presuppose and point to existing textual traditions, but interpret them rather than reciting or quoting them. *Echoes* occur when words or phrases can arouse memory of a cultural tradition. Echoes do not contain words or phrases undeniably from a cultural tradition, but are subtle, drawing on implicit memories of things in the minds of readers or listeners.

8. Robbins, *Tapestry*, 107; Robbins, *Exploring*, 48–50.

9. Robbins, *Tapestry*, 107; Robbins, *Exploring*, 50.

10. Ibid., 51.

11. Ibid., 52–53.

12. Robbins, *Tapestry*, 108–10; Robbins, *Exploring*, 58–60.

Social Intertexture

This intertexture is about the social knowledge people have by virtue of their direct interactions with each other. Social knowledge is attained because people have *social roles* or *social identities*, participate in *social institutions*, generally respect *social codes* and *conventions*, and engage in *social relationships*.[13] This means that readers and listeners recognize and interact easily with roles and identities such as soldier, slave, priest, Roman, and Jew, with institutions such as empire and church, with codes and conventions such as hospitality and table manners, and with relationships such as friendship and family.

Historical Intertexture

This intertexture is concerned with actual events that have occurred in specific times and places.[14] Analysis of historical intertexture considers the *multiplicity of the data*—the number of and relationships among the available accounts of events. It explores whether there is one or multiple accounts, whether the accounts are independent or indicate dependency, and whether independent accounts agree on facts. Likewise, this intertexture is concerned with the *nature of the data* whether from inscriptions, law, records of various kinds, literary works such as narrative, letters, speeches, and so on, along with the data's factuality and plausibility.

The task of our working with these various intertextures is to engage in the hard work of *intertextural analysis*. From the perspective of sociorhetorical interpretation this work is about rhetoric. That is, it is the analytical task of coming to understandings of how NT texts draw on and interact with other texts, the Mediterranean cultural milieu, social knowledge, and historical realities in order to move their audiences to beliefs and practices.[15] This approach is not about employing a method that produces predictable results. It is about analysis that examines the intertextural threads in order to see where they are located, how they interweave with other threads, and, most importantly, how they work to affect the audiences of the documents being examined. It aims to analyze and see what happens. In what follows in this chapter we will look at a specific NT text, Col 2:11–15, to demonstrate this analytic.

13. Robbins, *Tapestry*, 115–18; Robbins, *Exploring*, 62–63.

14. Robbins, *Tapestry*, 118; Robbins, *Exploring*, 63–68. In sociorhetorical interpretation, "historical" means actual events and does not include cultural and social phenomena as is often implied in the term "historical backgrounds."

15. Or, perhaps more correctly, how authors (with amanuenses) did these things in the production of their texts.

A Sociorhetorical Intertexture and Colossians 2:11–15

> 11 ... in whom you also were circumcised with a non-hand-made circumcision, in the stripping off of the body of the flesh in the circumcision of Christ, 12 being buried with him in baptism, in whom also you were raised through the faithful action of God, who raised him from the dead; 13 and you being dead in trespasses and the foreskin of your flesh, he made you alive together with him, forgiving us all our trespasses, 14 erasing the record in demands that opposed us, he removed it, nailing it to the cross; 15 disarming the rulers and authorities, disgracing them in boldness, triumphing over them in it.

Every discussion of intertextuality in Colossians notes that there are no quotations from the Hebrew Bible or the Septuagint in the letter.[16] The letter instead exhibits multiple points of contact with other texts and ideas outside of Colossians, certainly including links to the Old Testament. In Col 2:11–15, for example, we find there are oral-scribal, cultural, social, and historical intertextures that *shape the argumentation* and *impress the argumentative force* of the passage on audience members' minds. It is important that this be understood—*Intertexturality is about argumentation.* That is to say, the connection of ideas between and among texts is always aimed at making a point, at conveying an idea, at bringing about understanding, at bringing about or at least affecting what people believe and how they behave. It is therefore argumentative, persuasive, and psychological.

Colossians 2:11–15 uses particular intertextural features in order to make the persuasive argument that Christ-believers in Colossae should not be swayed by anyone who aims to capture them according to human and worldly thinking that stands against Christ (2:8).[17] What we have in this passage is more than the simple occurrence of intertexts. What we have is *interactivity* between and among intertextural features that functions argumentatively to achieve particular results. The interactivity is meant to be evocative, moving people to understanding and action.[18]

The first clear intertexture is about circumcision. *Oral-scribal recontextualization* ties this language to the practice and significance of circumcision

16. For example, see Sumney, "Writing 'In the Image' of Scripture," 189. See also Pizzuto, *Cosmic Leap of Faith*; Fee, "Old Testament Intertextuality in Colossians," 201–221; Gordley, *Colossians Hymn in Context*, 2007; Beetham, *Echoes of Scripture*; Beale, "Colossians," 841–70.

17. The wording is in the singular in 2:8, but it might be imagined that more than one person aims to "capture" the Christ-believers.

18. Moyise, *Evoking Scripture*.

that has been clear in the biblical story since Gen 17:1–27, where Abraham and every male of his house underwent the surgery as a sign of the covenant between themselves and God. According to the Torah, male children born to Israelite mothers were to be circumcised eight days after birth (Lev 12:3). The practice was known among some Gentile peoples, such as the Colchians, Egyptians, and Ethiopians (Herodotus *Hist.* 2.104).[19] Gentile residents of Colossae, as elsewhere, were aware of the practice (*cultural intertexture*), and the term and allusion were sensible to them.

Many interpreters claim that circumcision and some other Torah and Jewish practices were being imposed on or demanded of Colossian Christ-believers, particularly based on the language of 2:16–21. It does appear that they were being pressured to behave like and visually appear to be Jews or at least like Jews in some respects. The reasons for this pressure are not explicated, though many theories have been proffered. What is clear in 2:11 is that *cultural intertextual* knowledge regarding circumcision is employed to shape the persuasiveness of the argumentation, *not* directly to signify a practice that the letter's recipients were being urged to perform, even if they were under such pressure.[20] Here *oral-scribal reconfiguration* presents the image of the listeners or readers of the letter themselves as having been "circumcised with a non-handmade circumcision" (περιετμήθητε περιτομῇ ἀχειροποιήτῳ),[21] which is itself in turn described as the "stripping away of the body of the flesh." This complex interplay and blending of images becomes the foundation of the rhetorical argumentation. Non-handmade circumcision in the form, for example, of "circumcision of the heart," is a feature of the rhetoric of other texts in the Pauline corpus: "For a person is not a Jew who is one outwardly, nor is true circumcision something external and physical. Rather, a person is a Jew who is one inwardly, and real circumcision is a matter of the heart—it is spiritual and not literal" (Rom 2:28–29; cf. Phil 3:3). It is also a feature of the rhetoric of texts in the HB/LXX, and Jewish non-canonical texts:

> Circumcise, then, the foreskin of your heart, and do not be stubborn any longer. (Deut 10:16)

---

19. Cf. Strabo, *Geography* 17.2.5, which is nearly contemporaneous with the NT. Herodotus claims that ". . . the Syrians of Palestine themselves confess that they learned the custom from the Egyptians . . . ," an apparent allusion to the Jewish practice. Colchians (Colchis) lived in the southern Caucasus, on the eastern shore of the Black Sea (http://en.wikipedia.org/wiki/Colchis).

20. There is nothing in this passage that indicates pressure to practice circumcision.

21. The word περιετμήθητε is an aorist passive, the only instance of this use of the verb in the NT.

"Moreover, the LORD your God will circumcise your heart and the heart of your descendants, so that you will love the LORD your God with all your heart and with all your soul, in order that you may live." (Deut 30:6)

"Circumcise yourselves to the LORD, remove the foreskin of your hearts, O people of Judah and inhabitants of Jerusalem, or else my wrath will go forth like fire, and burn with no one to quench it, because of the evil of your doings." (Jer 4:4)

"The days are surely coming, says the LORD, when I will attend to all those who are circumcised only in the foreskin: Egypt, Judah, Edom, the Ammonites, Moab, and all those with shaven temples who live in the desert. For all these nations are uncircumcised, and all the house of Israel is uncircumcised in heart [= stubborn, obdurate]." (Jer 9:25–26)

"Say to the rebellious house, to the house of Israel, Thus says the Lord GOD: O house of Israel, let there be an end to all your abominations in admitting foreigners, uncircumcised in heart and flesh, to be in my sanctuary, profaning my temple when you offer to me my food, the fat and the blood. You have broken my covenant with all your abominations." (Ezek 44:6–7; see also 1QS 5:5; *Jub.* 1:23; Philo *Spec. Leg.* 1.305; Josephus *Ant.* 12.241)

The term "non-handmade" (ἀχειροποίητος) also occurs in Mark 14:58 and 2 Cor 5:1.[22] "Non-handmade" obviously contrasts with "handmade" (χειροποίητος), which implies humanly-produced things and deeds. In the LXX it is particularly used to refer to idols, but also refers to places of worship (Lev 26:1, 30; Isa 2:18; 16:12; 19:1; 21:9; 31:7; 46:6; Dan 5:4; 5:23; Bel 1:5), and in the NT it refers to a sanctuary made by human hands (Heb 9:24). These intertextures are more likely to indicate the cultural knowledge of the author of Colossians than of the recipients.[23] The intertextural terminology and imagery quite dramatically argue that a cutting off or cutting away has occurred and that, consequently, there is a new condition that exists wholly apart from human action.

22. In the discipline of art history the *acheiropoiēta* are images that are reputed to have been "made without hands." These include the Image of Edessa (the Mandylion), the Veil of Veronica, the Manoppello Image, and the Shroud of Turin. I thank Chris Nygren and Walter Melion for this connection.

23. It seems to be clear by now that a number of persons could be involved in the production of a NT letter. For Colossians, the real issue is not whether Paul was the singular author, but whether he was still alive when it was written, sent and received, and knew about the letter. He might have been.

The dramatic terminology of "stripping off" (noun ἀπεκδύσις, 2:11; verb ἀπεκδύομαι, 2:15; cf. 3:9) occurs only here. But the image of "stripping off the body of the flesh" is *social intertexture* that has a strong point of contact among Christ-believers. They would understand the social connections of this "flesh" language. The flesh is that aspect of human existence that damages and inhibits community living in human societies. It is echoed by "the passions of the flesh" and "the will of the flesh and of the mind" mentioned in Eph 2:3. This removal of "the flesh" is what the non-handmade circumcision accomplishes in bringing about their new condition. The language is a kind of apocalyptic discourse that was developing in the new Christ-believing society to convey what had happened in the circumcision of Christ. The "stripping off" functions as persuasive, apocalyptic, and social argumentation aimed at moving audiences to an understanding of their situation as believers. Their lives now function apart from "the flesh." Intertextural connections move the argument along.

Burial with Christ in baptism and resurrection with Christ through the faithful action of God (2:12)[24] are *social* and *historical intertextures* because they envision real social events that occurred in the past and exist vividly in the personal memories and experiences of the believers. This imagery also is a *thematic elaboration* (*oral-scribal intertexture*) of the ideas of Rom 6:3–4 (cf. 1 Cor 10:1–3). The argumentation is founded in the memory of their own baptism, in the burial "with" Christ it signifies to them, and in being raised with Christ out of death to the life they now live. This intertextural argumentation from their (collective) memory reinforces the reality of having undergone the non-handmade circumcision where the body of the flesh was stripped away.

The phrase "the foreskin of your flesh" is used only here (2:13), but is language that seems likely to have had social currency in the early churches. The noun ἀκροβυστία is here an *oral-scribal reconfiguration* of LXX and NT passages, the only places it is employed in Greek literature. It is likely a Jewish neologism that does not in fact mean "uncircumcision" despite this usual translation, but "foreskin" or "prepuce." Its linguistic source is probably the word *akroposthion*.[25] In the LXX the usage is more explicit and clearer: "and you shall circumcise the flesh of your foreskin" (Gen 17:11; see also 17:14, 23, 24, 25; 34:24; cf. Exod 4:25; Lev 12:3; Jdt 14:10). In Colossians the wording is reversed from "the flesh of your foreskin" to "the foreskin of your flesh," emphasizing the theological meaning of "your flesh"

---

24. I read ἐν ᾧ καὶ συνηγέρθητε as "in whom you were raised," not as "in which." This reading fits the context more accurately (see usage in vv. 9, 11).

25. See Schmidt, *TDNT* 1:225–26.

as the human proclivity to and connection with sin ("and you being dead in trespasses," cf. Eph 2:1, 5).[26]

We cannot know if the Colossian Gentile Christ-believers had so close a knowledge of the LXX as to be able to make an intertextural connection directly. It is unlikely that they could. But they would grasp the function of the argument because the images and knowledge of circumcision are a *cultural intertexture*, they were culturally "in the air," a phenomenon of the world outside the text, yet easily recognized. The life in "the flesh" has been cut off. They themselves are cut off from their former lives that were influenced and driven by the "traditions of humans" and the "elements of the cosmos," and they are now shaped by Christ, by the non-handmade circumcision, and by their burial and resurrection with Christ. Things are different now, in Christ.

The erasure of "the written record of rules that stood against us" (2:14) is often considered to refer to the removal of the effect of the Torah,[27] but Colossians does not explicitly or clearly set the Torah within its rhetoric. The terminology has many *oral-scribal, cultural,* and *social* intertextural connections that make it clear that a written document indicating and acknowledging obligations or indebtedness is to be envisioned (cf. Tob 5:3; 9:5). Very similar terminology for written records or books is found in a number of apocalyptic texts, referring to documents that are meant to be employed for passing judgment against persons because of their evil actions (*1 En.* 89.61–64; *2 En.* 53. 2–3; *T. Abr.* 12.7–18; *T. Job* 11.11; *Apoc .Zeph* 7.1–8).[28]

It is likely, then, that the "chirograph" (χειρόγραφον) is an *oral-scribal reconfiguration*, referring generally to an indicting record of any kind that demands judgment against evildoers.[29] Audiences understand this through *cultural* and *social* intertexture, because the idea of such indicting documents was part of their cultural milieu and their social experience. Here in Col 2:14 the idea and the imagery is taken up as a starkly contrastive and apocalyptic wiping out of such records. The persuasive-argumentative implication is that the expectation of judgment demanded by a written document has been removed by the action of God in making people alive with Christ and in forgiving their trespasses. Colossians takes up the apoca-

---

26. See Beetham, 186–89.

27. Cf. 3 Macc 1:3; 4 Macc 4:24, where δόγμα might refer to the Torah. See also Philo, *Leg. All.* 1.55; *Gig.* 52.

28. See also *Life of Aesop* 122; Exod 32:32–33; Rev 20:12.

29. It does not refer, *contra* Lincoln, "Colossians," 625–26, only to the indictments of heavenly powers. It includes indictments of all kinds, including those of cosmic-spiritual and earthly political-spiritual powers.

lyptic notion of judgment in its own use of apocalyptic rhetoric to show that judgment is quashed. The call for judgment against the listeners/readers has been removed, by means of "nailing it to the cross." The *historical intertexture* with the crucifixion of Jesus is obvious,[30] certainly in the imagery of the nailing of the *titulus* or indictment statement (epigraph/ ἡ ἐπιγραφή) to the cross (Mark 15:26). More particularly, the imagery focuses on the nailing of Jesus himself, on the judgment taken on in his own body, on the metaphorical "circumcision of Christ" (2:11) that removed both the "body of flesh" and the call for judgment against humans.

The canonical *oral-scribal intertexture* of the triumphal procession of 2:15, which describes the stripping off of powers and authorities, their disgrace, and their humiliating march, is found in 2 Cor 2:14 where Paul envisions himself and other believers being paraded among those conquered by God in Christ. Both passages *recite* forms of the verb θριαμβεύω. This picture is given rhetorical strength in the *historical intertexture* provided by Plutarch in his description of the three day triumphal procession of Aemilius Paulus (*Aemil.* 32–34). Included in the procession were wagon loads of plunder, sacrifices, money, the chariot and armor of the vanquished king, the king's children along with various attendants, the disgraced king himself (Perseus) followed by his grieving and similarly disgraced friends, followed in turn by the victorious, glorious-looking and highly praised Aemilius and his army. Here is an excerpt:

> After his children and their attendants came Perseus himself, clad all in black, and wearing the boots of his country, and looking like one altogether stunned and deprived of reason, through the greatness of his misfortunes. Next followed a great company of his friends and familiars, whose countenances were disfigured with grief, and who let the spectators see, by their tears and their continual looking upon Perseus, that it was his fortune they so much lamented, and that they were regardless of their own. Perseus sent to Aemilius to entreat that he might not be led in pomp, but be left out of the triumph; who, deriding, as was but just, his cowardice and fondness of life, sent him this answer, that as for that, it had been before, and was now, in his own power; giving him to understand that the disgrace could be avoided by death; which the faint-hearted man not having the spirit for, and made effeminate by I know not what hopes, allowed himself to appear as a part of his own spoils.[31]

30. This is also *cultural intertexture*, a feature of the cultural memory of Christ-believers.

31. John Dryden, trans. The Internet Classics Archive. http://classics.mit.edu/

Did the believers in Colossae know this particular example and its imagery? Once again, we cannot know. But the notion of a triumph was culturally understood, hence, this engages *cultural intertexture*. It is evident that they would grasp the idea when the letter was presented to them. The mental visuality of this intertexture makes the triumphal procession of the grandly disgraced powers and authorities described in 2:15 stand out in bold relief. The argument is that the victorious Christ Jesus has utterly conquered and disgraced the powers and authorities who wish to impose their views on others. His own apocalyptic circumcising-death-resurrection-erasure-of-indictments-nailing-to-the-cross has brought about the liberation and fullness of people. Colossians in this way employs the Roman triumphal procession to press home the vision, reality, and power of God's triumph that has brought about their freedom.[32] This intertextuality makes it clear that the Colossians can and should resist any pressure to add anything to what God in Christ has already done for them. There is no power or authority any longer available to stand against them with any requirements.

Persuasive Argumentation

The central argumentative rhetoric of Colossians (2:6—3:4) envisions the recipients in a *challenge-riposte* cultural situation,[33] where they face the likelihood of demands that they conform themselves to unnecessary, unhelpful, and dangerous binding philosophies, traditions, elemental realities, and behaviors (2:8, 16–18). The cultural and social expectations of time and place (Colossae; the *ekklēsia*) challenge people to conform to certain ideological and behavioral standards. They are called by the challenge to participate in thoughts and engage in practices that demonstrate that they meet social expectations. While they will feel social pressure to conform, the argument urges them to resist the demands. Colossians 2:11–15 forms an argumentative step (moving ahead from 2:9–10) where complete fullness, everything people require, is described as being located in Christ. In Christ there is a reconfigured existence where neither those who make the challenging demands, nor the behaviors themselves, nor the powers purported to be

---

Plutarch/paulus.html. See the artistic representation *The Triumph of Aemilius Paulus*, by Carle Vernet (Antoine Charles Horace, 1789) http://www.metmuseum.org/toah/works-of-art/06.144.

32. Cf. Maier, *Picturing Paul in Empire*, 33, 68.

33. On challenge-riposte environments see Robbins, *Exploring*, 80–81. A riposte is a resistance to a challenge.

behind the demands possess any authority or credibility at all. The argument makes its case in this progression:

> *Case:* (indicated in 2:6–7, 8–10) the letter recipients are likely to be faced with pressures challenging them to take on various humanly-produced, earthly, elemental views, and bodily practices that are perceived to fulfill their faith by means of self-generated actions. Against this it is argued that all the fullness of God is already present for them in Christ, in whom they are *already* full.

> *Rationale:* In Christ "the body of flesh," that part of human existence inclined toward and attracted to sin, evil, and the elemental things of the cosmos and that arrogantly aims to resolve human issues by its own efforts, has been cut away, circumcised, stripped off, in "the circumcision of Christ," a non-handmade circumcision (περιτομῇ ἀχειροποιήτῳ). This circumcision of Christ is a metaphor for Christ's death and burial with whom they themselves have been buried (represented in their baptism).[34] This cutting away of the body of flesh has been accomplished not by self-performance of the audience members themselves, but by the action of God who raised Christ Jesus, in whom and with whom they also have been raised.[35] While their former lives in the body of flesh were in fact dead existence, Christ's death, burial, and resurrection involved their own death, burial, and resurrection. They are now very much alive with Christ, and everything of the former fleshly existence has been removed. Existence in the flesh is characterized by the compulsion to obtain fullness through self-generated human performance, by the knowledge and guilt of unforgiven trespasses (2:13). It is pressured by the existence of written rules that call for strict observance (χειρόγραφον τοῖς δόγμασιν) and by rulers and authorities who demand recognition and obedience (2:14–15). All of these calls from the flesh have been cut off and led away in disgrace by the actions of God in Christ. The

---

34. Against Lightfoot, *Colossians*, 183, and many who have followed him for more than a century, 2:11 is not describing the "practical errors" of the Colossians who "do not need the circumcision of the flesh; for you have received the circumcision of the heart." Rather, the imagery of circumcision is argumentatively employed to demonstrate that the "body of the flesh" aspects of life have already been removed. The argument is not against the actual practice of circumcision (as in Galatians).

35. The genitival construction διὰ τῆς πίστεως τῆς ἐνεργείας τοῦ θεοῦ should be understood subjectively, where God is the subject of the activity. God has performed the faithful work of raising Christ Jesus and of raising believers with him. It does not refer to the faith of the Colossian believers.

argumentative rationale creatively employs *intertextural* topics to make its case.

Result: This intertextural argument demonstrates that the believers do not need to succumb to the pressures placed on them. Everything they need for fullness of life has been accomplished. All indictments of the flesh are cancelled, dead, and all cosmic-spiritual and political-spiritual powers are powerless. The audience members are already fully alive and free in Christ. Nothing else is required.

Even if impositions from the old, fleshly, elemental space seem to be attractive and wise, they are not to be taken on. What has been done is sufficient. The intertextures themselves make the argument, that is, they form the rationale for the argument, in Col 2:11–15 and do so with remarkably persuasive force. What we have is a series of specific intertextural, socially connected *topoi* understood implicitly by the Christ-believers that aims to evoke a focused understanding of their social and religious location in Christ. By employing the sequence of contact points—circumcision < non-handmade circumcision < stripping off < body of flesh < baptism < death < burial < resurrection < chirograph < erasure < nailing < crucifixion < triumphal procession in which the vanquished are disgraced—it is demonstrated that the audience already inhabits a space altogether free from the challenges they are likely to face. Their new cultural space of belief is already impervious to the challenges. Thus, they already inhabit a countercultural space where the challengers and challenging pressures can and should be resisted. A new society has been apocalyptically established where the "body of flesh" has been removed through actions outside the believers, performed for them and on them. The memory of their baptism indicates this to them. This makes for a grand, powerfully persuasive, psychological (and indeed mentally visual) argument.

The argument is that the new condition in Christ is not produced by or connected with any human actions that believers can perform, because all has been accomplished for them. They should not, therefore, submit to pressures to conform to what some insist they must do to fit in with religious, social, and cultural situations. Humanly produced actions may be, implicitly, idolatrous as "handmade." The argument works on the basis of the interactivity of the intertextural notions. The human traditions, the elements of the cosmos that are not "according to Christ" in whom the Christ-believers have been made full (2:10) but by which some other persons apparently wish them to be identified, have already been cut off, circumcised, stripped away. The things the Christ-believers are pressured to do are not for them distinctives or identifiers. Their distinctive is their connection with and in Christ. The intertexturality itself makes the argument in the ideas it conveys. Sociorhetorical intertextural analysis makes this clear.

Conclusion

The intertextural analysis demonstrates that argumentation in Col 2:11–15 functions in important ways by drawing on and interacting with texts and with cultural, social, and historical phenomena, knowledge, and understandings that are outside the passage itself. These interactions inform, support, and actually form features of the argumentation being made. This intertextural argumentation does something to people. It has a rhetorical force that creates an ideology. Believers are meant to understand that Christ has accomplished all that is needed, and they should not be persuaded by persons who demand additional requirements. In this way a kind of new world is created, perhaps even for us who read it at a distance. The lives of the Colossian believers and of people like us are enriched.

Recommended Reading

Jeal, Roy R. *Exploring Philemon: Freedom, Brotherhood, and Partnership in the New Society*. RRA 2. Atlanta: Society of Biblical Literature, 2015.

Oropeza, B. J. *Exploring Second Corinthians: Death and Life, Hardship and Rivalry*. RRA 3. Atlanta: Society of Biblical Literature, 2016.

Robbins, Vernon K. *Exploring the Textures of Texts: A Guide to Socio-Rhetorical Interpretation*. Valley Forge: Trinity International, 1996.

———. *The Tapestry of Early Christian Discourse: Rhetoric, Society and Ideology*. London: Routledge, 1996.

Sumney, Jerry L. "Writing in 'The Image' of Scripture: The Form and Function of References to Scripture in Colossians." In *Paul and Scripture: Extending the Conversation*, edited by Christopher D. Stanley, 185–229. Atlanta: Society of Biblical Literature, 2012.

Watson, Duane F., ed. *The Intertexture of Apocalyptic Discourse in the New Testament*. SBL Symposium 14. Atlanta: Society of Biblical Literature, 2002.

11

Narrative Transformation

J. R. Daniel Kirk

From Narrative Dynamics to Narrative Transformation

Narrative transformation is, first of all, a description of how writers use other texts and, in this chapter in particular, how New Testament authors use earlier texts. It depends on one primary, underlying idea—that texts of all kinds assume or participate in a set of narrative dynamics even when the genre of those texts is not a narrative genre (such as history writing or biography). In relation to NT writers, narrative transformation encapsulates the idea that the writers are aware of the larger narrative dynamics of the passages they cite, and in their use of those passages they rework the underlying narrative, often in a way that reflects their convictions of what God has done in Christ at the eschatological turning of the ages. As an interpretive method in this regard, narrative transformation seeks to identify both the original text narrative structure and the narrative structure of the NT text that cites it, and then this approach compares and contrasts the two narratives to shed light on the meaning of the NT passage.

Narrative and Biblical Interpretation

The roots of such an approach to biblical texts might be seen in the early- to mid-twentieth century, in various attempts to articulate a coherent biblical theology that makes sense of the whole Bible from Genesis through

Revelation.[1] Such a grand narrative sweep allows the reader to look for connections between earlier and later parts of a canonical story, but paints with too broad a brush to help us get hold of individual passages in which biblical citations are found. In working with such a big picture with general themes and narrative structures, it becomes easy either to neglect the amount of transformation that happens when an earlier text is reused in a NT context, or, alternatively to condemn the NT use of earlier texts as haphazard deployment of words and phrases that entirely neglect the original context.

A finer instrument was introduced by Richard Hays in a study of Galatians originally published in 1983.[2] The book is entitled, *The Faith of Jesus Christ: The Narrative Substructure of Galatians 3:1—4:11*. The phrase "narrative substructure" points to the new methodology he deployed. Hays used the structuralist theory of A. J. Greimas to help demonstrate that Paul's argument depended on an assumed narrative about how God was at work in the world through Christ.[3] In any given story there is an "initial sequence" in which the stage is set, often through a problem not being resolved. There is then a "topical sequence" in which the action of the story takes place and that initial lack or problem is rectified. A "final sequence" shows the rectification of the problem introduced in the initial sequence.[4]

Within these sequences the action can be further broken down. Someone wants to see a particular task accomplished. King Arthur wants to have a princess rescued. The person sends another to accomplish this task, and this agent stands in the middle of a conflict between various helpers and various opponents. Arthur is a "sender" who wants to bring an "object" (rescue) to a "recipient" (a princess) by means of a "subject" (knight) who will need a "helper" to overcome some "opponent."

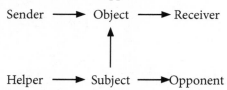

Any sequence of action within a larger narrative will have its own structure. Hays used this method to help shed light on how Paul's argument works in Galatians 3–4. God (*sender*) sends Christ (*subject*) to bring Abraham's blessing (*object*) to the Gentiles (*recipient*), and Christ finds help from "faith" or

---

1. Vos, *Biblical Theology*; Cullmann, *Christ and Time*; Cullmann, *Salvation in History*.

2. Hays, *Faith of Jesus Christ*.

3. Greimas, *Sémantique Structurale*; Greimas, *Du Sens 1: Essais Semiotiques*.

4. Hays, *Faith of Jesus Christ*, 82–90.

"faithfulness" (*helpers*) with which he overcomes the "elemental principles of the world" (*opponents*).[5]

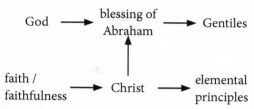

A significant contribution that Hays made with his study was in demonstrating that even a letter that does not deploy storytelling is nonetheless making arguments that depend on and disclose an underlying story.[6]

Narrative Dynamics and Intertextuality

When Hays turned to explore questions of intertextuality in subsequent work, his literary sensibility continued to inform his biblical interpretation, even though he no longer deployed structuralist literary analysis as his tool.[7] In *Echoes of Scripture in the Letters of Paul*, Hays regularly moves between the scriptural verse alluded to, the larger "narrative" of which that verse is a part, and the Pauline passage in which Paul refers to it. He discovers in this process that the meaning of the NT passage is enriched as the reader hears how the old story is reappropriated on behalf of Paul's argument.

Hays's reading of various NT texts shows a readiness to acknowledge the importance of the original Old Testament context for interpreting the NT passage, but without making the OT meaning determinative for how the verse functions when appropriated by a NT author. Without using this language, Hays in effect demonstrates that the narrative dynamics of the OT passages inform the narratives Paul articulates in his letters. However, Hays does not articulate a methodology for reading the NT and OT texts in concert with one another.[8]

5. Ibid., 105.

6. Readers interested in looking at another scholar who uses this narrative analysis, but with reference to the whole sweep of the canonical biblical story can see Wright, *New Testament and the People of God*, e.g., 221. For a wide-ranging exploration of how stories may or may not be functioning in Paul's letters, see Longenecker, *Narrative Dynamics in Paul*.

7. Hays, *Echoes of Scripture*; Hays, *Conversion of the Imagination*; Hays, *Reading Backwards*.

8. The language of Paul reading in concert with Israel's scripture is taken from the subtitle of Wagner, *Heralds of the Good News*. His work also builds on Hays's

This is the goal of "narrative transformation" as an interpretive method—to provide some guidelines for reading both the text cited and the passage containing the reference in concert with one another. In relation to NT use of the OT, for example, this goal allows the "story" of the OT to inform and enrich the significance of the NT "story" being told without allowing the OT to determine the claims put forth by the NT author. "Narrative transformation," in this case then, refers to the outcome of the interpretive process, in which we are able to articulate both the original narrative dynamics and how those have been changed in the NT context.[9]

For our study, the method entails naming the various narrative elements assumed or articulated by the OT passage and the NT passage that cites or alludes to it: (1) Who is the sender? (2) What is the object? (3) Who is the intended recipient? (4) Who is the subject who is sent to bring this about? In this process it will also be helpful as often as possible, to articulate (5) who the helpers are, and (6) who the opponents might be. However, starting with the points in numbers 1–4 above provides a basic entry point. A simplified way of conceptualizing this is to fill in the following sentence: "*x* wants to send *y* to *z* by means of *w*," where x is the sender, y is the object, z is the recipient, and w is the subject. To take an example from a verse that does not cite or allude to another, we might render John 3:16 like this: "*God* (sender) wants to send *eternal life* (object) to *the world* (recipient) by means of *his only son* (subject)." We might fill out the picture by saying that *belief* is the helper that enables the son to attain the end for which he was sent.

When articulating the narrative sequence for a passage that cites or alludes to another, we will need to compose such sentences for both OT and NT verses. Both the comparison and the contrast between the two sequences will point toward the significance of the OT passage in the NT context, a procedure that should both honor the contribution of the OT narrative sequence and enable us to view how the NT writer transforms it.

Transformed Stories: Gospels, Paul, and Acts

We will look at three examples to demonstrate how narrative transformation works as an interpretive method and its usefulness across different kinds of texts. From the Gospel of Mark we will look at the temple-clearing episode. Paul's letter to the Romans will offer us a particularly striking example of narrative transformation as Paul claims that the story of salvation adjusts

---

narratively-inclined hermeneutical approach.

9. See Kirk, "Toward a Theory," for another introduction to this methodology and its usefulness for interpreting the Pauline letters in particular.

its focus from Law to Christ. A final example comes from a sermon in Acts, in which Jesus' identity as resurrected son of God transforms an Old Testament enthronement psalm.

From House of Prayer to Den of Robbers

In Mark 11:15–17 Jesus enters the temple in Jerusalem. He overturns tables of moneychangers and those who are buying and selling the pure animals needed for sacrifice. He then teaches them by quoting scripture: "Isn't it written that 'my house will be called a house of prayer for all the peoples' (Isa 56:7)? But you have made it 'a robbers' den' (Jer 7:11)" (Mark 10:17).[10] The first passage Jesus cites is from Isaiah. We can represent the story by saying, "God (*sender*) wants to give a welcoming house (*object*) to the nations (*recipient*)." The broader context of Isaiah 56 can help us fill in the other parts of the story. The *subject* whom God sends is God's own salvation and righteousness (Isa 56:2, 8). The *helper* appears to be the Law, and faithfulness to God's covenant more generally (Isa 56:4, 6). Importantly, this is the final sequence, representing the culmination of the story that God intends to bring about.

Jesus' allusion to Jer 7:11 comes in four short words in English, two in the Greek text of Mark: "a den of robbers." This is not much to go on for articulating the narrative of Jeremiah 7. In the larger context, God is chiding the Jerusalem leadership for treating the temple like a good-luck charm. They steal, murder, commit adultery, perjure themselves, and sacrifice to other gods, but then they come into the temple that bears the sacred name and say, "We are safe!" One important thing to notice is that in the Old Testament passage, "den of robbers" means a place where people go who want to be safe after they have committed crimes elsewhere. It is not a place where robbery itself is performed.

Mapping out the narrative sequence is challenging here, because the actions that Jeremiah condemns do not represent the main sequence of the story. They represent actions that influence the plan of God, who remains the *sender*. The basic sequence of Jeremiah might be represented thus: "God (*sender*) wants to bring faithfulness (*object*) to Judah (*recipient*)." However, in Jeremiah 7 we are not reading the final sequence. Instead, we are learning how God is going to respond to Judah's rejection of God's plan. In this intermediate stage of the story, a topical sequence, we learn that "God (*sender*) is going to bring destruction (*object*) to Jerusalem and the temple (*recipient*)."

10. For a fuller discussion of this passage and its interpretation, see Kirk, "Time for Figs." See also Hays, "Can the Gospels Teach Us"; Hays, *Reading Backwards*, 6–9.

The subject of this sequence will be the Babylonian armies who destroy Jerusalem and carry the people into exile.

The citations from Isaiah and Jeremiah represent two different narrative sequences, and the reason for this is that they each represent a different stage in the overall storyline. Jeremiah 7 represents a topical sequence. Isaiah 56 represents a final sequence—Jeremiah prophesies a time of destruction, after which will come Isaiah's prophesied house for all nations.

When we return to the Jesus story, this realization helps us make sense of Jesus' actions. He has just overturned tables. This could be read as a "cleansing," as though Jesus' goal is to purify the temple court and restore the court of the Gentiles to the nations for whom the temple is intended. This is a common reading. However, another reading is possible, namely, that Jesus is prophesying the temple's destruction. The first option could be represented as, "God (*sender*) wants to bring purification (*object*) to the temple (*recipient*) through Jesus (*subject*)." The second option would then be, "God (*sender*) sends a prophecy of destruction (*object*) to the temple leadership (*recipient*) through Jesus (*subject*)."

By formulating the story in this way, we can see how the second option coheres well with Jeremiah. Jeremiah was prophesying the temple's destruction as well. Moreover, Jesus also indicates that the temple is *not* the temple of glorious restoration that Isaiah has prophesied. Thus, the idea of "cleansing" is less likely to be in view.

By combining the narratives of these two prophecies, denying the applicability of the one and appending the other, Jesus has written his own narrative about the Jerusalem temple. Rather than standing as the temple promised to the people after their exile—the glorious temple that comes at the culmination of God's saving work—the temple stands on the brink of another destruction, and the people on the brink of a fresh exile. This, then, coheres with other aspects of Mark's gospel, including the fact that Jesus goes on to explicitly prophesy the temple's destruction (Mark 13:1–2).

From God-Given Law to God-Given Christ

In Rom 10:6–10, Paul gives a running commentary on Deut 30:12–14.[11] I have italicized the OT references to help clarify where Paul's own interpretive hand is at work:

> But the righteousness from faith speaks thus: *"Do not say in your heart, 'Who will ascend into heaven?'"*—that is, to bring Christ

11. For a fuller discussion of this passage see Kirk, *Unlocking Romans*, 161–80.

down—"*or, 'Who will descend into the abyss?'*"—that is, to bring Christ up from the dead." But what does it say? *"The Word is near you, in your mouth and in your heart"*—that is, the word of faith that we preach, that if you confess with your mouth "Jesus is Lord" and you believe in your heart that God raised him from the dead, you will be saved.

The claim Paul makes in these verses can be represented as, "God (*sender*) sent Jesus (*subject*) to bring salvation (*object*) to Jews and Gentiles (*recipient*), aided by the proximity of the preached word, belief, and confession (*helpers*)."

The first half of the paragraph is spent underscoring the notion that God has already enacted the salvific plotline through the coming and resurrection of Jesus. Deuteronomy 30:12 and a rewritten 30:13 (or perhaps an allusion to another OT verse such as Ps107:26) are interpreted as prophecies of Jesus' arrival and resurrection. The Messiah does not need to be brought down or raised from the dead because God has already seen to both of these things. The second half claims that its arrival is made complete by Paul's proclamation and its reception. The "word" spoken of in Deuteronomy 30:14 is said to be the content of Paul's preaching that is available to all who hear him. Thus, the effect of this citation is to claim that Deuteronomy 30 anticipates quite specifically the arrival and resurrection of Jesus followed by its proclamation and the need to believe and confess that God has so acted.

How does this compare with the story told in Deuteronomy 30? Adding a couple of additional verses to provide some context to the citation, here is what 30:11–15 says in the Greek translation of the OT (the Septuagint) that Paul was likely citing:

> For this commandment which I am commanding you today is not difficult nor is it far away from you. It is not in heaven above so that you should say, "Who will go up for us into heaven and get it for us, so that hearing it we might do it?" Nor is it on the other side of the sea, so that you should say, "Who will cross over for us to the other side of the sea and get it for us and make it audible to us so that we can do it?" The word is exceedingly close to you, in your mouth and in your heart and in your hand so that you can do it. Behold! I have placed before you today life and death, good and evil.

Using our stereotyped formula we can summarize the storyline thus: "God (*sender*) has sent the commandment (*subject*) to bring life (*object*) to Israel (*recipient*)." The verses Paul cites are used, in their original context, to underscore the fact that God has already done what is necessary to bring Torah, the commandments and instructions, to the hearts, mouths, and hands of Israel so that they might keep that Law and live.

Both passages, Deut 30:11–15 and Rom 10:6–12, deploy imagery of traversing space in order to underscore that no person needs to go on a quest to do what God has already done to bring fullness of life to God's people. The people merely need to receive what God has given and respond appropriately. But this general level of coherence pales in comparison to the transformation Paul has wrought on his source text.[12]

Paul has replaced "the commandment" with "Christ" as the agent through whom God is bringing ultimate blessing to God's people. Moreover, Paul has replaced "doing" the commandments with belief and confession. Finally, Romans 10 replaces "Israel," the recipients of the Law, with both Jews and Gentiles as the recipients of God's eschatological salvation (Rom 10:12). These three moves are interrelated. At various junctures in Romans, and also in Galatians, Paul argues that salvation through Christ, which is received by faith, is what allows Jews and Gentiles equal access to the people of God. Doing what the Law of Moses requires marks out a uniquely Jewish identity, and Paul claims that Gentiles do not have to convert to Judaism to be part of the people of God.

In Romans 10 Paul is drawing a distinction between the righteousness that comes from the Law and the righteousness that comes by faith. The former offers life through keeping the commands (Rom 10:5). The latter offers eternal life through believing on the work of Christ. Earlier in the letter Paul had said that the Law and Prophets bear witness to God's righteousness as that is made known in Christ (Rom 3:21). This is precisely the role in which Paul has cast Deut 30:12–14 in Rom 10:6–10: he has made it a witness to his gospel. As such, it no longer tells the story of Israel's access to life through the Torah, but instead tells the story of everyone's access to salvation through Christ.

By recognizing both stories, we can see that the transformation Paul has worked on Deuteronomy 30 is precisely the transformation that Paul's gospel has introduced into his own thinking about how God is at work to bring salvation to the world. Salvation is not attained by joining the Jews in law-keeping, but in being united to the crucified and risen messiah. Moreover, the transformation marks the contrast in narratives between those in the early church who thought that Gentiles still needed to keep Torah and Paul who believed that Christ was enough. Both Paul prior to his conversion

---

12. For a brief overview of how other Jewish authors deployed Deuteronomy 30:12–14, see Bekken, "Paul's Use of Deut 30,12–14."

and the Christians who thought Gentiles needed to be circumcised and keep Torah believed that being Jewish, as demarcated by the Law, was necessary to belong to the people of God and to be saved. Paul is articulating an alternative narrative, and to tell it he has allowed the Christ event to transform the story of Deuteronomy 30, a passage which otherwise would have said exactly what his opponents claimed.[13]

From Begotten King to Resurrected Christ

Psalm 2 is cited or alluded to almost 20 times in the NT. It is widely regarded as an enthronement psalm, a song that was sung to commemorate, or even enact, the enthronement of Israel's king. In the face of hostile nations, God and the king each proclaim that God has established the king and that his kingship is thus inviolable. God speaks first, "I have established my king on Zion, my holy mountain!" The king speaks next, "I will declare the Lord's decree. He has said to me, 'You are my son, today I have begotten you.'" The language of God establishing the king and that of the king being begotten are parallel. In accordance with what we see, for instance, 2 Sam 7:14 and Ps 89:26, to be king of Israel was also to be God's son.

The narrative substructure of the psalm might be rendered like this: God (*sender*) begets and enthrones a king (*subject*) to establish kingship (*object*) in Zion/Israel (*recipient*). The rulers of the earth function as the opponents. In this instance, God has so identified with the king that God functions also as the king's helper, and the enemies who oppose the king oppose God who has enthroned him. The opposition of the nations and their rulers indicate the extent of the king's reign. God promises the ends of the earth as the king's possession.

Psalm 2 thus functioned in the time of Israel's monarchy as a narrative upholding the divine right of Israel's king to rule. Its reference is not to some future, hoped-for king, but to the current king of Israel. If the psalm articulates an unfulfilled hope, that hope is contained in the expectations that Israel's king was rightful heir of the whole earth. However, the narrative of God establishing kingship in Zion/Israel proved potent, and when the first Jewish followers of Jesus came to believe that he had filled that role, Psalm 2 provided words to help stake their claim.

Acts 13:16–41 contains a sermon that Paul preaches in a synagogue in Pisidian Antioch. It includes the following:

---

13. For further explorations of how narrative transformation illuminates Paul's letters, see Kirk, "Why Does the Deliverer Come"; and Kirk, "Toward a Theory."

> We proclaim the gospel to you, that God has fulfilled for us, the descendants, the promises made to our ancestors by raising Jesus, as also it is written in the second Psalm, "You are my son, today I have begotten you." Because he raised him from the dead, he is not going to turn back to corruption, so God said, "I will give to y'all the holy promises of David."

Several details are worth pointing out before articulating the storyline of this part of the sermon. First, I have used "y'all" here to underscore that the "you" to whom the promise comes is not singular, as though God is still talking to Jesus, but plural, indicating that God is talking to the people ("us, the descendants"). Second, and following the form of the first, this is a sermon squarely aimed at Jewish people. The ancestors, the descendants, and the "y'all" to whom the promises come and for whom they are fulfilled are all references to Israelites (Paul is speaking in a Jewish synagogue). Third, as Acts interprets the Psalm, the "begetting" of Jesus is referring to something that happens at his resurrection, not something that is true of Jesus for all eternity.

The narrative substructure, then, might be rendered like this: "God (*sender*) has established kingship (*object*) for Israel (*recipient*) through raising and begetting of Jesus (*subject*)." Moreover, the sermon clarifies that this kingship is what was promised to David and to the Israelites he ruled. Thus, Jesus' own kingship is playing an equivalent place in the story to that of the king in the psalm.[14]

The principal difference between the psalm and the sermon is that Jesus is enthroned through his resurrection. The resurrection itself is seen as an exaltation, the moment when Jesus is enthroned as heir to the promises of David.

What might come as a surprise to many Christian readers is that the meaning of divine sonship is equivalent in the two passages. In Acts 13, Jesus is not referred to as eternal son of God. Instead, "son" continues to function as a title bestowed upon the rightful Davidic king. In light of the narrative of the psalm, we can see that interpreting "You are my son, today I have begotten you" in terms of elevation to kingship is consistent across both texts. This correlates with other identifications of Jesus as God's son in Luke and Acts (see also Rom 1:3–4). The transformation the book of Acts works on the Psalm comes from aligning kingly enthronement with resurrection from the dead. The kingship is no longer established in Zion, but in the heavens. But in both texts it is this enthronement to kingship itself that qualifies someone as "son of God." The OT narrative helps us see the

---

14. See Janse, *"You Are My Son,"* 96–102.

significance of a Christological title that we might otherwise interpret quite differently.

Conclusion: The Importance of Both Contexts

Narrative transformation approaches questions of intertextuality seeking to do justice to the implicit or explicit narratives in each text and their broader contexts. As we have seen, articulating the narrative of the OT text often demands our reading more broadly than merely at the level of the verse(s) being referenced, which may or may not play a key role in the overall plot. That original plot is important for understanding what the NT writer is saying that is similar, and what the NT writer is saying that is different. Articulating the NT narrative will also at times demand that we look beyond the particular verse in question. In doing so, we must take care not to be unduly influenced by the OT narrative. Both contexts are important, and both must be allowed to speak with their own voice. When we allow both texts, and both contexts, to speak, we are in a position to see more clearly how the NT writers lay claim to an ancient text and story while proclaiming that a new, climactic scene has been orchestrated by Israel's God.

Recommended Reading

Hays, Richard B. *Echoes of Scripture in the Letters of Paul*. New Haven: Yale University Press, 1989.

———. *The Faith of Jesus Christ: The Narrative Substructure of Galatians 3:1—4:11*. 2nd ed. The Biblical Resource Series. Grand Rapids: Eerdmans, 2002.

Kirk, J. R. Daniel. "Toward a Theory of Narrative Transformation: The Importance of Both Contexts in Paul's Scriptural Citations." In *Searching the Scriptures*, edited by Craig. A. Evans and Jeremiah Johnson, 213–33. Studies in Scripture in Early Judaism and Christianity 19. London: T. & T. Clark, 2015.

———. "Why Does the Deliverer Come Εκ Σιών (Romans 11.26)?" *JSNT* 33 (2010) 81–99.

Longenecker, Bruce W., ed. *Narrative Dynamics in Paul: A Critical Assessment*. Louisville, KY: Westminster John Knox, 2002.

12

Orality and Intertextuality

James F. McGrath

Along with interest in intertextuality in all its forms, another major focus of interest in New Testament studies in recent years has been *orality*. Many associate orality with the period of oral storytelling and oral tradition that preceded the writing of the New Testament Gospels. But the study of orality in relation to the NT is much broader than this longstanding interest of NT scholars in oral tradition. In the world in which the NT writings were produced, literacy was rare, and writing was a highly specialized skill. As a result, most people who composed literature did so verbally while a scribe wrote down what they said, and more people heard literature read aloud than read it with their eyes on a page.

These two areas of scholarly interest—intertextuality and orality—are relevant to one another in ways that too frequently go unexplored, at least in relation to the study of the NT. The broader scholarly discussion of intertextuality, however, shows an awareness of the subject, if not always bringing the methods of orality studies to bear on it.[1] The study of orality intersects in turn with the psychology of memory, the role of storytelling in cultures, characteristics of oral tradition, and other subject areas which are given significant attention in relation to the NT, but once again, without

---

1. In relation to the Hebrew Bible, see e.g., Carr, *Writing on the Tablet of the Heart*; also several of the contributions to Schmidt, *Contextualizing Israel's Sacred Writings*. For ancient Greece, see Cooper, *Politics of Orality*; Lentz, *Orality and Literacy in Hellenic Greece*. Important works have also touched on orality and intertextuality in time periods and cultural settings even further afield, such as Persia, India, the Arab world, and sub-Saharan Africa. Such works at times yield insights that may be useful to the student of the NT.

intertextuality featuring prominently if at all. Kelly Iverson sums up well the reason why there is a need for deeper connections to be forged between intertextuality and orality as approaches to the NT:

> Despite a growing sensitivity to the oral context surrounding the Jesus tradition, discussions of intertextuality have yet to engage ancient media studies. Indeed, it is often assumed that intertextual techniques transcend media type and that the exchange between author and audience is not affected by the mode of delivery. . . . For both readers and hearers, intertextual association is a memory-rich process, but it is particularly demanding for audiences who must simultaneously access two contexts within the temporal flow of the performance and without recourse to written texts.[2]

The present chapter brings the interrelated aspects of intertextuality and orality to bear on Phil 2:6–11. The significance of the passage has often been tied to the question of whether the passage is a quotation from an already-existing hymn, and this is indeed an important matter as pertains to intertextuality.[3] But there are other important questions too.

First, there are potentially at least two layers of intertextuality with which the interpreter has to deal.[4] Paul may be quoting, alluding to, or echoing a hymn, but then the hymnic text itself features allusions or echoes of other texts. Bringing these multiple layers into the picture is important as we explore the text's range of possible meaning. Isaiah 45:23 is alluded to in the phrase "every knee shall bow, and every tongue confess." The story of Adam may also be echoed.[5] And indeed, whatever one's views on whether a pre-Gospel passion narrative might have been *written* in Paul's time, the story of Jesus even in oral form is a *text* in the broad sense, and it is also in view in this passage. Here we have the possibility that Paul is quoting a hymn which in turn is quoting one Scripture, while echoing still other parts of Scripture, and also making reference to the story of Jesus that Christians were telling. Multilayered intertextuality is thus, whether as a help or a hurdle, a major consideration for the interpreter. But it is not the only crucial methodological consideration.

---

2. Iverson, "An Enemy of the Gospel?" 27, 29, drawing heavily on Edenburg, "Intertextuality, Literary Competence."

3. See the classic study by Martin, *Carmen Christi*; also Duling, *New Testament*, 108–37.

4. On this multi-layered situation see Hayes and Holladay, *Biblical Exegesis*, 118.

5. In this study, I do not assume (as some scholars do) that allusions and echoes necessarily function in different ways.

Second, the points mentioned above bring orality into the picture. One of the "texts" echoed or alluded to in this passage—the story of Jesus—may have existed only in oral form at the time the letter was composed. But in addition, most people who encountered Paul's letter would have known Isaiah and Genesis through hearing them read aloud, rather than having read them for themselves. Orality is therefore relevant as the medium through which even written texts were known to most people who were familiar with them in this time period. Likewise, Paul's own letter would have been read aloud to a gathering of people most of whom could not and would not ever read the letter as words on a page. And so bringing our best knowledge about oral communication into the picture is crucial. So too is our relating the considerations from orality to the perspectives from intertextuality.[6] There are allusions which can be noticed—and connections which can be drawn—when reading texts, that simply cannot be *heard* in the same way, or *processed* in the same way, as is possible as when one can read a written text, consult another written text, then return to the first one and ponder the relationship between the two.[7] Intertextuality and orality are not only both important to the interpretation of Phil 2:6–11, but they are also interrelated.

Finally, the question of persuasion is another crucial consideration, and it must be treated in connection with the first two perspectives. What is involved in the rhetoric of *oral* persuasion, and did Paul write so as to accomplish his aim effectively when his letter would be presented orally? How do intertextual allusions/echoes in an oral presentation serve to make a speaker's case more persuasive? How would the Philippians' knowledge or lack thereof have had an impact on the effectiveness or otherwise of Paul's communication to them? What are the implications of such considerations for how we understand this part of Paul's letter, and the Christology it offers?

I will work through each of these points, and towards the end tie strands into a cord that I hope will result in a persuasive case being offered about the persuasiveness or otherwise of what Paul wrote.

Echoes from Hymns

Let us start with the question of what the quotation of a hymn means for an argument. I will proceed on the assumption that Paul is here quoting a hymn, since that has become the scholarly consensus (I hope, however, that

---

6. On the intersection see Bauks, "Intertextuality in Ancient Literature," 33–35.

7. On Paul's references to Scripture in his letters and the relevance of orality and literacy to the perception of them, see especially Stanley, "'Pearls before Swine'" 130, 132, 134–36. See too Edenburg, "Intertextuality, Literary Competence" 145.

the points I make in this chapter do not depend on one's view regarding that question.) The echoing of hymns in sermons is a widespread phenomenon that can be examined even in our time, and has been studied in the context of a number of different cultures, including predominantly oral ones which may provide useful analogies to Paul's own context.[8] Such studies offer an important challenge to our natural inclinations as readers living in a context of widespread literacy. How do echoes of hymns function within sermons, for instance, since Paul's letters often have a homiletic character? Paul's quotation is offered in support of his call to the Philippian recipients to think and behave in a particular way. A hymn echo can add emotional power if the hymn is well-known and widely cherished. The broader context of the other lines or verses of the hymn in question is not always relevant. Someone talking about perception of intertextual echoes might say that "we once were blind (in our ignorance of intertextuality), but now we see." The echo of a famous hymn may draw the attention of hearers to the point, reinforcing it and helping to fix it in the mind. This was one of the most important ways that communication in oral cultures made use of things already in the minds of hearers, using what hearers already knew as "pegs" on which to hang new information.[9]

The point in my example had nothing much to do with the content of the hymn "Amazing Grace," nor would the idea of being lost and subsequently found likely have come into your mind when I echoed the immediately-following line. The more familiar the words are, the more they can function on their own, decoupled from their original hymnic context. And the less familiar the hymn, the less likely it is that the allusion would be noticed, or that other parts of the hymn would be called to mind. This is just as well for the interpreter of Philippians, since we have no way of knowing what the remainder of the hymn may have been like, or whether there was anything else beside what we have quoted here. Whether this passage quotes an already-existing hymn or not, and whether the hymn was very, slightly, or not at all familiar to the Philippians, the likelihood of any conscious turning of thoughts to additional lines or stanzas is minimal, although in theory such a wider hymnic context may have provided resonances about which we as interpreters can, alas, never know.[10]

The main function of using a hymn quotation in communication is therefore not necessarily to call to mind other parts of the hymn, but to

8. See Buttrick, *Homiletic*, 143–45; Mieder, *"Making a Way Out of No Way,"* 7–8; Finnegan, *Why Do We Quote?*, 165–66.

9. See McGrath, "On Hearing (Rather than Reading)," 76.

10. For more on the role of hymns in religious communities in more recent times, see Brown, *Word in the World*.

fix the points made in conjunction with the quotation in the mind of the hearer. This may be less true of literary as opposed to hymnic allusions, where the point may actually be to call to mind a whole *story* through an allusion to a single line or turn of phrase. The passage in Philippians fits into both categories, since we have a proposed allusion to a hymn, allusions to one or more texts from the Jewish Scriptures, and to the story of Jesus. And so the use of a hymn may have served primarily to fix Paul's point in the mind of hearers, the theme of the hymn presumably being at least broadly relevant to that point. But the specific contents of the hymn, with its echoes of Scripture and of the story of Jesus, will have created a multi-faceted experience with multiple echoes, the impact of which must certainly have differed depending on who heard it, and what their prior knowledge was of the hymn and the Jewish Scriptures, among other things.

Echoes of Scripture from Hymns

Let us move from the level of the letter for a moment into the level of the hymn. What would the echoes of Scripture within the hymn have meant to those who sang it? Fortunately, once again we can ask what echoes of Scripture mean in hymns sung in other times and contexts including our own, to provide a basis for comparison. In a contemporary hymn, a phrase such as "Lamb of God" may bring to mind a specific story in the Gospel of John, or merely the broad theme of Jesus as sacrifice, or neither, depending not only on the contents of the other lyrics in the hymn, but also on the hearer's familiarity with Scripture in general, and with specific texts and their specific details. Many hymns which draw on specific Scriptures may fail to be fully understood or appreciated, despite the echo being unambiguous. For example, all who have sung the famous hymn "Come Thou Fount of Every Blessing" in its original form in its entirety will have uttered the words "Here I raise my Ebenezer."[11] But that certainly does not mean that most who have done so have recognized the reference to 1 Samuel, or understood its meaning.

There has been significant debate over whether the hymnic passage in Philippians includes deliberate echoes of the story of Adam. Are the connections being *found* or *concocted* by modern interpreters, or is it a bit of both? What is the likelihood that a first-century audience of "Christians" in Philippi could and would have done the same? The terminological echoes of Genesis are slim to non-existent. But it does not always take specific terminology to create an echo of a story. Often a pattern may be noticeable

11. Robinson, *Collection of Hymns.*

even in the absence of echoed vocabulary. Let us imagine encountering the phrase, "James McGrath so cared about intertextuality, that he wrote his only chapter in this book, that whosoever readeth it should not misunderstand but have unending illumination." The echo of John 3:16 is presumably obvious. Yet the verbal agreements with the prototype are largely in prepositions and conjunctions, and then in the overall structure, but not in the most important words in the original. So too, the terminological differences in Phil 2:6–11 have sometimes been considered decisive—being in the form (as opposed to image and likeness) of God, and grasping equality with God rather than a fruit that could make one like God. But the overall structure of the story, the mention of being like God, choosing whether to grasp at equality or submit to God in obedience, and the loss of status or being rewarded by God as a result, at each and every point involves either a structural echo of the Adam story, or what can be viewed as a deliberate inversion of that story. Since interpreters who agree about the Adamic echoes disagree about whether pre-existence and other such features are present in the hymn, ultimately this particular question has more to do with the resonances of the hymn for its hearers/singers, than with the settling of the wider array of Christological debates pertaining to this passage.

The question of how the hymn's Christology relates to monotheism, however, is directly connected to the intertextual echoes towards the end of the hymn. There, we find wording from an adamantly monotheistic passage in Second Isaiah, used to acclaim the universal recognition of *Christ's* lordship. It is perhaps not surprising that some have understood this passage in Paul as evidence for Paul's redefinition or reconfiguration of monotheism. But at this point, we must remind ourselves of what we have already emphasized about intertextuality and orality. If the context of the words quoted was brought to mind by the allusion, then that would have served to convey that the hymn's point was in line with the passage echoed. Conversely, if the echo was not sufficient to call the passage to mind, then no redefinition would have been detected by those who heard and sang it.[12] *Only if the words of the hymn conveyed disagreement with or modification of the outlook of the text echoed, and did so explicitly and clearly, would such a message have been detected.* Thus it is better (if possible) to understand the point of the hymn as in keeping with Jewish monotheism as understood in that time.[13] The same point applies to the oft-raised question of whether Paul and others of his contemporaries cared about the original contexts of their quotations.

12. On the possibility that Paul's echoes of Scripture may not have been detected by his audience in some instances, see Tolmie, *Persuading the Galatians*, 97, 111–12; Stanley, *Arguing with Scripture*.

13. On the use of the term "monotheism" see McGrath, *Only True God*, 1–54.

If they did not, then the monotheistic context in Isaiah becomes largely irrelevant to the meaning of the related words in this new context. And if they did care about the original context of their Scriptural quotations and allusions, then that monotheistic context must inform how the language is understood here.

Our interpreting the hymn as fully in line with Jewish monotheistic sensibilities is not at all difficult. It is God who exalts Jesus, above any status we are told that he previously held.[14] God does so for God's own glory. This is accomplished by bestowing the divine name on Jesus as God's supreme agent, who expresses the divine will and rule on the one hand, and on the other, ultimately directs all glory gained in this role away from himself and towards God. This is a pattern that has parallels in Jewish literature—the bestowal of the divine name is connected with figures such as Yahoel and Metatron, while the receipt of acclamation by the appointed viceroy can be seen in texts such as the Similitudes of Enoch. There is no reason to think that this hymn was thought to do anything other than to give Jesus the highest status it was possible to envisage a human being occupying within the framework of first-century Jewish monotheism. Envisaging the early Christians as redefining monotheism through echoes of Scripture in hymnic and creedal phrases alone seems implausible, when we consider the amount of detailed discussion and debate around Scriptural texts that was felt to be necessary in connection with the redefinition of the role of the Torah. Explicit and detailed argument is necessary when modifying or challenging a core conviction, and the absence of such arguments is itself evidence that no such modification was being undertaken.

Returning to the subject of Paul's quotation of the hymn, if it is implausible to see the hymn itself as redefining monotheism on the level of its own text, it is all the more implausible to envisage Paul as using a quotation of a hymn which echoes Scripture to redefine monotheism, one further step removed from Isaiah. Paul's own statements about Jesus elsewhere, such as in 1 Cor 15:20–28, match the pattern we have argued that the hymn sets forth. Christ is one to whom universal rule is given by God, over everything but God, in order to ultimately subject all things to God. Also relevant is Paul's other use of the same text from Isaiah in Rom 14:11, where the point made is that everyone is accountable to God.[15] It thus seems justified to

14. Note that it is God who honors Jesus, highly exalting him. And thus there is a marked difference from the way praise is offered to God, whose unique attributes and status are highlighted. See further Neyrey, "'First', 'Only,'" 59–87.

15. Also worth noting is the treatment of this text in post-NT Christian writings. Augustine and Eusebius of Caesarea interpret it in a solidly monotheistic way, while Theodoret of Cyrus recognizes the entanglement in his time with the question of the

conclude that no redefinition of monotheism is involved in Paul's use of the hymn, any more than in the use of Isaiah within the hymn itself.[16]

Moreover, the persuasive power of the hymn depended on its use of echoes of Scripture to reinforce its message.[17] Echoes of texts in a manner or context that subverted the very point of the text quoted, or which could be understood to do so, would have been counterproductive and detracted from the persuasive power of the author. If the hearers of Paul's words picked up on the echo, they would have understood Paul to be appealing to an emphatic affirmation of monotheism. If they failed to pick up on the echo, then they would simply have heard an acclamation of Christ's lordship which was ultimately "to the glory of God the Father." It is implausible to claim that Paul was making a subtle Christological point, much less one that no one is likely to have detected when the letter was read aloud to them.

Persuasion in the Hymn of Philippians 2:6–11

So what should we say about the message conveyed by Phil 2:6–11, its persuasive power, with its echoes of the story of Jesus and of monotheistic Scripture, and perhaps also of a hymn? The hymnic passage's relevance to Paul's point has been understood in a variety of ways—in salvation histori-cal terms or in terms of *imitatio Christi*. But few would dispute that Paul was seeking to persuade the Philippians to think and to live in a certain way. When considered in this context, the hymnic section can be understood as an example of epideictic rhetoric, and there is in fact no need to choose between the often starkly-posed alternatives.[18] On one level, the noble deeds of Christ do provide a model for obedience and humility, while the exaltation which is his reward is offered as motivation. But there is more to it in this case, due to the distinctive features of the theology that Paul and his readers shared. Unlike most examples of epideictic rhetoric, the Philippians

---

homoousion. See Elliott, *Ancient Christian Commentary,* 84–85.

16. Contra Fowl, "Use of Scripture in Philippians," 170, who claims "By connect-ing this language and imagery to Jesus in Phil 2:10–11, by ascribing to Jesus the name κύριος, Paul is, as Richard Bauckham says, including Jesus within the identity of the one God of Israel. From Paul's perspective it appears that he wants to emphasize that willed self-emptying and obedient suffering are elements of God's identity." The emphasis seems to be on connecting Jesus' story to humanity's on the one hand, and connecting the story of Christians with Jesus' on the other. On the theocentric character of Paul's Christology here, see Dunn, *Theology of Paul,* 254–55.

17. Cf. Fowl, "Use of Scripture in Philippians," 166–67.

18. On this passage as epideictic see especially Brucker, ›*Christushymnen‹ oder ›epideiktische Passagen‹?;* Reumann, *Philippians,* 362, 364–76. On the neglect of epide-ictic in NT studies, see Kern, *Rhetoric and Galatians,* 126–29.

would have believed that they were "in Christ," united with the one whose story was being depicted. This situated Paul's readers and hearers as more than mere observers of an exemplary life from a distance.[19] It is the logic of the eschatological tension—being united with Christ, being called to live as he did in the present age, being participants in a preliminary fashion with him in his entry into the age to come—that is offered as both theological context and motivation to the Philippian readers.

Paul does not, it seems to me, want his readers to see in Christ a unique divine incarnation whose unique mind leads to unique acts which accomplish salvation, as something external to them and which they could never hope to emulate. Rather, Paul wants them to recognize that Christ was a human being in whose new creation they are participants, and (in terms Paul articulates elsewhere) to allow the mind of the Last Adam to replace that of the First Adam in their own lives and experience. It is the one God who hyper-exalted Jesus, who has also connected them with him and allows them to experience this transformation in the present and hope for the future in their lives. Anything other than a genuinely monotheistic reading of Paul's argument here does more than just undermine the foundation of his point.[20] It also distracts from that point. The history of scholarship about this passage illustrates this well.[21] Rather than understanding how Paul uses the logic of the strict monotheism of Isaiah, and the obedience and reward of the Last Adam, to motivate Christians to live in a particular way, the Christology of the hymn, allegedly offering a radically new and innovative Christological monotheism, has been understood as an end in itself, and become the focus of our attention, bracketed out from its context in Paul's letter and the use to which Paul put it. And yet, for Paul to have been making an innovative Christological point here, he would have needed to defend and justify that point in relation to the talk of "one God" for which Jews were famous, and which Paul himself was known to have used. By recognizing that Paul here assumes rather than redefines Jewish monotheism, it frees the interpreter to see the persuasive power of the Christ hymn,

---

19. See most recently Lynn Cohick on participation in Christ and the hymn's meaning: Online: http://www.koinoniablog.net/2013/10/philippians-christ-hymn-lynn-cohick-new-commentary.html. See also Silva, *Philippians*, 95–97.

20. On the relevance of the other instance of Paul citing the same part of Isaiah, see McGrath, "On Hearing (Rather than Reading) Intertextual Echoes," 77.

21. So also Silva, *Philippians*, 20–21. For an example, see how Fowl, "Use of Scripture in Philippians," 171, is forced to focus on Christological debates and developments of subsequent centuries, and to suggest that Paul used this hymn or composed this passage without grasping the radical implications of what it was doing.

and of the monotheistic Scriptural echoes within it, in the context of Paul's letter.[22]

This is not to pose a false antithesis for the interpreter, as though there is a stark choice to be made, requiring that the passage be understood as one of two types of encomium. In ancient literature one finds praises offered to a divine figure for doing what mere mortals cannot, and praises offered to a human figure for accomplishing something that the hearer might also hope to. It is possible to see both ideas here by understanding the passage in a manner that is fundamentally in keeping with first-century Jewish monotheism. Jesus' life of obedience led, according to the hymn, to his being given the divine name and exalted to a place of universal rule on God's behalf. The sharing of the divine name might indeed be called a sharing of the divine identity, given how closely connected name and identity are. But this is presented, not as something that Jesus innately possesses, but as a reward for his obedience. This divine action in response to Christ's human action, when coupled with the conviction that the Philippian believers were united with Christ, would have provided a double motivation for the Philippians to let this mind be in them which also was in Christ Jesus. The monotheistic conviction of one God, at work in—and in response to—the story of Jesus, would have given Paul's words persuasive power for an audience which shared Paul's core convictions about God, Jesus, and Scripture.

Conclusion

Whether Paul quoted a familiar hymn or quoted an unfamiliar hymn or composed this encomium himself, Paul's echoes of the stories of Israel's one God, and of the First and Last Adams, were offered as motivation to the Philippians, asking them to respond in a particular way to a unique show of unmatchable divine power and an imitable display of human obedience. We have good reason to conclude that Paul's point, read aloud to the Philippians, would have been met with a response that he would have found satisfactory. I can only hope that my own written presentation, with its own quotations, echoes, and allusions, may be found persuasive by readers as well.

---

22. On whether Paul could be assumed to know and recognize the context of all his Scriptural allusions, see Stanley, "'Pearls before Swine'" 137.

Recommended Reading

Bormann, Lukas. "The Colossian Hymn, Wisdom, and Creation." In *Between Text and Text: The Hermeneutics of Intertextuality in Ancient Cultures and Their Afterlife in Medieval and Modern Times,* edited by Michaela Bauks, Wayne Horowitz, and Armin Lange, 243–56. JAJSup, 6; Göttingen: Vandenhoeck and Ruprecht, 2013.

Doane, A. N. "Oral Texts, Intertexts, and Intratexts: Editing Old English." In *Influence and Intertextuality in Literary History,* edited by Jay Clayton and Eric Rothstein, 75–113. Madison: University of Wisconsin Press, 1991.

Dunn, James D. G. *The Oral Gospel Tradition.* Grand Rapids: Eerdmans, 2013.

Horsley, Richard A., Jonathan A. Draper, and John Miles Foley, eds. *Performing the Gospel: Orality, Memory, and Mark: Essays Dedicated to Werner Kelber.* Minneapolis: Fortress, 2006.

Issacharoff, Michael. *Discourse as Performance.* Stanford: Stanford University Press, 1989.

Marmur, Michael. "Why Jews Quote." *Oral Tradition* 29.1 (2014) 5–46.

Niditch, Susan. *Oral World and Written Word.* Louisville: Westminster John Knox, 1996.

Ricard, Alain, and Flora Veit-Wild, eds. *Interfaces between the Oral and the Written/ Interfaces entre l'écrit et l'oral: Versions and Subversions in African Literatures 2.* Matatu 31–32. Amsterdam: Rodopi, 2005.

Rubanovich, Julia, ed. *Orality and Textuality in the Iranian World: Patterns of Interaction Across the Centuries.* Leiden: Brill, 2015.

Tsagalis, Christos. *The Oral Palimpsest: Exploring Intertextuality in the Homeric Epics.* Center for Hellenic Studies. Cambridge, MA: Harvard University Press, 2008.

13

Enunciation, Personification, and Intertextuality

Alain Gignac

Sometimes Scripture in the New Testament becomes a character and speaks, or more precisely, is made to speak. We see this, for example, in Paul's own discourse (e.g. Rom 3:9–20; 10:5–17; Gal 3:8, 22). Scripture, in other words, exhibits a process of *personification*. In such cases, one can use insights from narrative analysis—especially characterization—to study the workings of intertextuality.[1] We could ask the following questions regarding personification in this regard: What are the traits of Scripture as a character (revealed by its sayings and its doings)? What is its role in the plot of the miniature story told? How is the character progressively constructed in the flow of the discourse?

With this interpretative tact it can also be useful to draw attention to the workings of pronouns, inspired by the concept of *enunciation* developed by the French linguist Émile Benveniste. In this kind of discourse analysis, the key questions are these: Who is speaking to whom? How are they speaking? In such discourse an *I* speaks to a *you* (singular or plural) about an absent third party (*s/he* or *they*). Within this main conversation, the Old Testament is invited to speak under the guise of many figures, whether the Law, Scripture, prophet, and so on, including a divine *I*. Alternatively, our question could be formulated thus: how is the quotation *as discourse* integrated into the main discourse where it is quoted?[2]

---

1. Marguerat and Bourquin, *How to Read Bible Stories.*
2. By "discourse," we mean here its linguistic sense of "language in acting."

With these type of questions in mind I will explore how the enunciation analysis, Benveniste's theory, adds something to the understanding of the *mise en scène* of OT quotations in the letters of Paul. First, I will describe the theory and give two methodological examples taken from Rom 9 (how to proceed with this approach). Second, I will give two examples of how it is applied as concrete illustrations of the hermeneutical process (what the approach can do). I propose for this, Rom 10:5–13—with its personification of the two "righteousnesses" (δικαιοσύναι, 10:5–10) and the speech of Scripture (10:11)—and Rom 15:7–13, with its liturgical *mise en scène*. Who is speaking? To whom? How does the enunciative device give a twist to the intertextual material, and how does it help us understand the hermeneutical process within the Pauline discourse? The voice of Scripture speaks (literally) in the present of the Pauline predication.

Theory and Methodology

The Concept of Enunciation

The approach involved here is not rhetorical but linguistic, following the work of Émile Benveniste (1902–1976) on *enunciation*, still relatively unfamiliar in English-language circles.[3] This French scholar, professor at the Collège de France, was the first to reflect upon the significance of relationships between personal pronouns.[4] At first, this seems quite simple, but it can provide a sophisticated analytical tool that can lead to a more meaningful understanding of language. Why is language structured by the three personal pronouns (I, you, s/he)? What occurs in a communicative, speech act or enunciative situation? Benveniste describes the pronominal device thus:

> In the first two persons, there is both a person involved and a discourse concerning that person. "I" designates the one who speaks and at the same time implies an utterance about "I"; in saying "I," I cannot *not* be speaking of myself. In the second person, "you" is necessarily designated by "I" and cannot be thought of outside a situation set up by starting with "I"; and at the same time, "I" states something as the predicate of "you." But in the third person a predicate is really stated, only it is outside

3. For a comprehensive article on Benveniste, see Malkiel, "Lexis and Grammar."

4. Benveniste, *Problems in General Linguistics*; more specifically, see 223–30, 195–204, 217–22. There is a second volume of linguistic essays, to my knowledge not translated: Benveniste, *Problèmes de linguistique générale*, 2, with two interesting chapters: "L'appareil formel de l'énonciation," 79–88; "Le langage et l'expérience humaine," 67–78.

"I-you"; this form is thus an exception to the relationship by which "I" and "you" are specified. Consequently, the legitimacy of this form as a "person" is to be questioned.[5]

On the one hand, Benveniste perceives a correlation of personality, in which *I* and *you-singular* are persons, while *he, she* is a non-person, i.e. a third party absent from the conversation:[6]

I, you	$\neq$	he, she
Persons		non-persons

On the other hand, within this first correlation, Benveniste distinguishes a correlation of subjectivity: *I—you-singular*. *I* is the sign devoid of any stable referent (conceptual or individual)[7] that allows a human being to become subject, and so generating an interlocutor *you-singular*:

$$I \longrightarrow you$$

While the words "table" or "love" designate something, object or sentiment, the word *I* in a sentence designates only the origin of speech, literally, who is speaking. As Benveniste writes:

> What then is the reality to which *I* or *you* refer? It is solely a "reality of discourse," and this is a very strange thing. *I* cannot be defined except in terms of "locution," not in terms of objects as a nominal sign is. *I* signifies "the person who is uttering the present instance of the discourse containing *I*." This instance is unique by definition and has validity only in its uniqueness.[8]

Benveniste coined the word "enunciation" to express the act of speaking that manifests the existence of an *I*, the subject of speech. While speaking, this *I* is always located *here* and *now*, in a present time and an immediate space—even in the case of a discourse which a narrative places in the past of the reader. *I / here / now* are the markers of an engaged enunciation after which the other persons are defined—first the (implicit or explicit) counterpart *you-singular*, but also the absent third party *he, she* characterized by the negating *not I / elsewhere / formerly*. The plural *we* and *you* are, however,

---

5. Benveniste, *Problems in General Linguistics*, 197.

6. Ibid., 204.

7. "Now these pronouns are distinguished from all other designations a language articulates in that *they do not refer to a concept or to an individual*": ibid., 226 (italics his).

8. Ibid., 218.

particularly ambivalent since they derive from various combinations of the grammatical person singular.[9]

In other words, enunciation is a speech act where an *I* or a *we* situated "here and now" speaks with a *you* (singular or plural) about a third party, which can be characterized by the third grammatical person (also singular or plural).[10] The following formula expresses this relationship between enunciator and enunciatee:

enunciator	→	enunciatee	(→ third party)
I or *we*	→	*you* [sing. or pl.]	(→ *s/he* or *they*)

Enunciation is the manifestation of an enunciator who talks to an enunciatee. In the case of Pauline letters, this manifestation comes to us through a text which is called in linguistic terminology an *utterance*. "Enunciation is thus to be understood as the act of producing an utterance or text, an act which leaves behind its traces in the resultant utterance."[11] In other words, any act of enunciation always produces an utterance, which exists solely because of a foregoing enunciation—note here the circularity of the conceptual relationship between enunciation and utterance.

The pair "enunciator/enunciatee" is close to the pair "narrator/narratee" of a narrative, but it is not exactly the same. One must be careful not to confuse the enunciative device of a text with the rhetorical situation of a speaker and his audience—which focuses attention on the argumentation and the arguments, i.e. the "utterances." The focus of enunciative analysis is less *what* is said than *how* and *by whom* it is said. Consequently, regarding Pauline intertextuality, the emphasis will not be put on what Paul is saying but on his very speech act. In other words, stress will not be placed on the contents of the quotations *per se* but on the manner in which they are spoken. However, the utterances, which are the result of the enunciation and the only textual traces of it, will remain important as clues to the enunciative devices that are to be analyzed.

9. Ibid., 202, distinguishes principally two types of *we*: inclusive (*I* + *you*) and exclusive (*I* + *they*).

10. For a more comprehensive presentation of enunciation, see the excellent Wikipedia articles in French and in Italian (consulted on September 30, 2015): "énonciation" and "enunciazione." In English: Havercroft, "Énonciation/ Énoncé."

11. Havercroft, "Énonciation/ Énoncé," 540.

Two Methodological Examples (Rom 9:25–26, 27–29)

In the case of Paul's letters, after an address formulated in the "impersonal" third person—"The apostle *Paul*, to the church of [. . .], grace and peace"— the enunciator quickly manifests himself as an enunciator *I* who speaks to a community. That community is an enunciatee generally addressed as a *you-plural*, but eventually included in a large *we* that embraces enunciator and enunciatee. Such a device becomes complex with regards to intertextuality, i.e. when the Pauline *I* quotes the OT voices. To illustrate this, let us take two examples from Rom 9, for which we have to distinguish many levels of enunciation and use the enunciative formula explained above: I → you (⇒ he). At this stage, the purpose is not to furnish a complete intertextual interpretation, but to illustrate the mechanism of enunciation in hope of finding two interconnected facets of enunciation—the identification of *I* (and of its interlocutor) and their characterization.

The first example is from Romans 9—a sequence which tells the story of Israel called by God from the time of the patriarchs (9:6–13), to the exodus (vv. 14–24), and finally to the exile and the promise of a return (vv. 25–29). In his telling, Paul quotes many of God's sayings where the latter speaks in the first person, *I*.[12] In 9:24–26, we are in presence of a three-tier enunciative device.. The following table proposes a close analysis of these verses. One must locate the verbs indicating speech (in italics below) and try to separate the discourses that originate from different enunciators:

Table 1. Enunciation in Romans 9:24–26[13]

Line	Enunciative level (enunciator)	Formula	Text
1	0 (Paul)	*I*-Paul → *you*-Romans (pl.) (→ *us* [= I + you] vs God)	24 including us whom he [God] has *called*, not from the Jews only but also from the Gentiles?
2	0 (Paul)	*I*-Paul → *you*-Romans (pl.) (→ *he*-God)	25 As indeed he *says* in Hosea [cf. Hos 2:25 + 2:1],

12. Rom 9:9 (Gen 18:10, implicit divine *I*); 9:13 (Mal 1:2–3, implicit divine *I*); 9:14 (Exod 33:19, explicit divine *I*); 9:17 (Exod 9:16, *I* assimilated to . . . Scripture!); 9:25 (Hos 2:1, 25, explicit divine *I*); 9:33 (Isa 28:16 + 8:14, implicit divine *I*). About this "divine *I*," see Hübner, *Gottes Ich und Israel*.

13. Translations are from the NRSV, modified with italics and brackets.

3	-1 (God)	*I*-God → *you*-Hosea? (sing.) (→ *they*-Israel?, then)	"Those who were not my people I will *call,*
4	-2 (God)	*I*-God → *you*-Israel? (sing.)	'my people,'
5	-1 (God)	*I*-God → *you*-Hosea? (sing.) (→ *she*-Israel?, then)	and her who was not beloved I will *call:*
6	-2 (God)	*I*-God → *you*-Israel? (sing.)	'beloved.'"
7	-1 (God)	*I*-God → *you*-Hosea? (sing.) (→ *they*-Israel?, there, then)	26 "And in the very place where it was *said* to them,
8	-2 (God?)	*I*-? → *you*-Israel? (sing.)	'You are not my people,'
9	-1 (God)	*I*-God → *you*-Hosea? (sing.) (→ *they*-Israel?, there, then)	there they shall be *called,*
10	-2 (God?)	*I*-? → *you*-Israel? (→ *he*-God)	'children of the living God.'

First, there is the primary enunciation of the letter, a surface level toward which the reading constantly returns (level 0). Since the beginning of Romans 9, Paul is the primary enunciator who first uses the pronoun *I* (9:1–3), but goes on to be more discreet, assuming the position of a narrator (9:6–33). Although, note that just before 9:25, the enunciation is formulated with a resounding *us* that creates a solidarity between Paul and the Romans (9:24, line 1). In 9:25a (line 2), Paul talks about *he*, which refers to God (named in 9:22); more precisely, the apostle announces the enunciation of this *he*. Second, in 9:25b, within this primary level, there is a shift and God speaks, in a secondary enunciation inserted into the primary one. This is indicated by an underground level -1 (line 3; also 5, 7, 9). Third, there is a tertiary enunciation (level -2) that the enunciator of level -1 introduces as "myself" (lines 4, 6, 8, 10). The two underground levels have the same enunciator, at least at first glance. But they do not have the same enunciatee—the fact that Israel passes from a third-party status (level -1) to an enunciatee status (level -2) is crucial. Level -2 offers the climax of the enunciation: it is not Paul who says it, but God himself.

As we see, it is Paul (enunciative level 0) who indicates that the new and distinct *I* of the immediate lower enunciative level is God (level -1). It is God (level -1) who specifies that he is the one speaking in level -2, but it is not always so clear elsewhere as we will observe. Thus, the identification of the *I* is given by the immediate upper level of enunciation, although it is true that the word *I* itself has no specific reference. This is the very reason why the enunciation of citations is complex, as Benveniste foresees it:

> If I perceive two successive instances of discourse containing *I*, uttered in the same voice, nothing guarantees to me that one of them is not a reported discourse, a quotation in which *I* could be imputed to another. It is thus necessary to stress this point: *I* can only be identified by the instance of discourse that contains it and by that alone. It has no value except in the instance in which it is produced.[14]

This analysis, however, raises some caveats that will explain the many question marks in the table above. On the one hand, the identification of the enunciator is not always easy. Strangely enough, in lines 8 and 10, it is not clear who is the *I* speaking—since the passive voice (maybe divine) is used in lines 7 and 9, the upper level (-1) does not precisely identify the enunciator of the lower level (-2)—and consequently, God is referred to as a third person in line 10. On the other hand, the identification of the enunciatee and of the third party is complicated. At level -1 (lines 3, 5, 7, 9), is it obvious that the prophet Hosea has the role of enunciatee, or that the third party of the conversation is indeed Israel? In Hosea, it may perhaps be evident—and the Pauline discourse itself suggests to remember what God says "in Hosea" (9:25a). But at the same time, after 9:24 the reader might question: Does not the divine utterance indicate instead, as a third party, the new community, "us whom he has called, not from the Jews only but also from the Gentiles"? If so, at level -2 (lines 4, 6, 8, 10), could not the enunciatee be the Christians of Rome, particularly the Gentiles who were not the people of God (line 8)? That would mean a subversion of the plain sense of Hosea 2:1, 25, or, if not so, at least the possibility that the promises for the future made by God in Hosea are in part realized in the present of the Pauline enunciation. One thing is sure—we have to be extremely careful to analyze the enunciation as it appears in the present text and not to import the enunciation wholesale from the original context of Hosea.

Apart from this, the characterization of the divine *I* is constructed both by the upper level enunciation and, of course, by the enunciation proper— what the *I* says about itself. Here, in levels -1 and -2, God positions himself

---

14. Benveniste, *Problems in General Linguistics,* 218.

in relation to the collectivity of Israel (or to the collectivity of the Judean-Gentile Christian community), which is at first absent from the conversation but becomes, with a shift in the enunciation (level -2), the interlocutor (enunciatee). Interestingly enough, the divine enunciation emphasizes the fact that God is characterized by his very act of enunciation—he is the God who is calling. Level -2, the deepest one in the enunciative device, is here the place where the character God reveals himself the most concisely and the most intensively, when he says to Israel (and/or to the Roman church): "my people," "beloved," and (maybe) "children of God."

In short, in his own discourse to the Roman community (level 0), Paul gives the floor to God; in his own discourse addressed to the prophet Hosea (level -1), God reports his past or future discourse to Israel (level -2). It means that it is no longer Paul who is speaking, but God himself. The (almost narrative) discourse of Romans 9 about the story of divine calling borrows a scene from the Book of Hosea and makes God speak.

In light of these observations, one must ask the following questions: Why does Paul in his own discourse give the floor to God for direct speech? Why does he say, "God says" instead of, "it is written" or "Hosea says"? What is the effect of speaking about or to Israel alternately in the third and second persons? Why does a divine discourse conjugated in the first person end up in the third person (line 10)? Why are the identities of the enunciatee and of the third party blurred in levels -1 and -2?

The second example is from Rom 9:27–29, a quotation of Isaiah following the quotation of Hosea.

Table 2. Enunciation of Romans 9:27–29

Line	Enunciative level (enunciator)	Formula	Text
1	0 (Paul)	*I*-Paul → *you*-Romans (pl.) (→ *he*-Isaiah) (→ *he*-Israel)	27 And Isaiah *cries out* concerning Israel [cf. Isa 10:22–23]

2	-1 (Isaiah)	*I*-Isaiah → *you*-? (→ *he*-Israel, then) (→ *he*-Lord)	"Though the number of the children of Israel were like the sand of the sea, only a remnant of them will be saved; 28 for the Lord will execute his sentence on the earth quickly and decisively."
3	0 (Paul)	*I*-Paul → *you*-Romans (pl.) (→ *he*-Isaiah)	29 And as Isaiah *predicted*, [cf. Isa 1:9]
4	-1 (Isaiah)	*We*-Isaiah → *we*-? (→ *he*-Lord, then)	"If the Lord of hosts had not left survivors to us, we would have fared like Sodom and been made like Gomorrah."

Two remarks are worth mentioning on this table. First, the enunciative device is simpler here, with only two levels. Nevertheless, at level -1, the identification of the enunciatee is again not so evident: to whom does Isaiah speak? There even seems to be a kind of short-circuit in line 4, telescoping the enunciatee of level -1 and the enunciatee of level 0—as if Isaiah's prediction were addressed to Paul and the Romans (*us*: 9:24, 29). The possibility foreseen in the analysis of 9:25–26 seems to receive confirmation here.

Second, Isaiah is a character: "he cries out" (κράζει, in the present of the primary enunciation, line 1) and "he predicted" (in the past, line 3). At the same time, the prophet is a contemporary as well as an ancestor. He knows something about the Lord and stands with his people, the same way Paul stands with the Romans. Scripture is not a thing of the past; it speaks now, and it does it aloud. Scripture is neither a dead letter nor a discreet or cautious voice; it carries a public testimony, the kerygma (κήρυγμα), like a herald.[15]

Enunciation, personification,[16] and characterization are linked. The different *I*'s that take the floor are main characters of the epistolary discourse. Hence, it is crucially important the one describe their relationship with precision and accurately articulate their speeches in relation to each

---

15. Κήρυγμα has the same verbal stem as κράζει.

16. Resemblances here with the speech-in-character (προσωποποιία) of classical rhetoric are apparent. See Stowers, *Rereading of Romans,* 16–21, 264–72; Campbell, "Beyond Justification in Paul," 96–99; Anderson, *Ancient Rhetorical Theory,* 201–5.

other.[17] In conclusion of this section, let us summarize the methodological procedures I have followed to analyze the enunciation of quotations:

- Locate the verbs which indicate a speech.

- Look at the markers of enunciation *I, here, now*—if they are present.

- As in an archeological site, distinguish the different levels of enunciation.

- For each level, try to identify who is the enunciator, the enunciatee, and eventually (because it is not always present) the third party—take care, though, to rely on the clues from the utterances (from the level concerned and the level above it) and to evaluate the degree of certainty of the identification.

- Note the result in an enunciative formula: I → you (→ he).

- Describe the characterization of both enunciator and enunciatee.

- Be aware of the possibilities of telescoping between the different levels (either the enunciators or the enunciatees);

- Ask as many questions as possible on the how and the why of the enunciation.

Hermeneutical Applications

I will now analyze two other passages from Romans using the same method as in the previous section. I will take this one step further, however, showing how such close reading can foster theological reflection. Theology is not only a matter of utterances, but even more so a matter of enunciation.

17. For a more complete view, see Gignac, *L'épître aux Romains*, 348–69.

First Case: Romans 10:5–13

Table 3. Enunciation of Rom 10:5–13

Line	Enunciative level (enunciator)	Formula	Text
1	0 (Paul)	*I*-Paul → *you*-Romans (pl.) (→ *he*-Moses) (→ *it*-righteousness of Law)	5 Moses *writes* concerning the righteousness that comes from the law, that
2	-1 (Moses)	*I*-Moses → *you* (sing.) (→ *he*-doer, then)	"the person who does these things will live by them." [Lev 18:5]
3	0 (Paul)	*I*-Paul → *you*-Romans (pl.) (→ *it*-Rigtheouness)	6 But the [R]ighteousness that comes from faith *says*, [Deut 9:4 + 30:12–14]
4	-1 (Righ-teousness)	*I*-Righteousness → *you* (sing.)	"Do not *say* in your heart,
5	-2 (Inter-locutor)	*I* → *myself* (sing.) (→ *who*)	'Who will ascend into heaven?'
6	0 (Paul)	*I*-Paul → *you*-Romans (pl.) (→ *Christ*)	(that is, to bring Christ down)
7	-1 (Righ-teousness)	*I*-Righteousness → *you* (sing.)	7 "or
8	-2 (Inter-locutor)	*I* → *myself* (sing.) (→ *who*)	'Who will descend into the abyss?'"
9	0 (Paul)	*I*-Paul → *you*-Romans (pl.) (→ *Christ*)	(that is, to bring Christ up from the dead). 8 But what does it *say*?
10	-1 (Righ-teousness)	*I*-Righteousness → *you* (sing.)	"The *word* is near you, on your *lips* and in your heart"
11	0 (Paul)	*We*-Paul → *you*-Romans (pl.) (→ *Christ*)	(that is, the *word* of faith that we *proclaim*);

12	o (Paul) or -1 (Righ-teousness)?	I-Paul → *you* (sing.) I-Righteousness → *you* (sing.) (→ *Christ*)	9 because if you *confess* with your *lips* that Jesus is Lord and believe in your heart that God raised him from the dead, you will be saved
13	o (Paul)	I-Paul → *you-Romans* (pl.) (→ *believer*)	10 For one believes with the heart and so is justified, and one *confesses* with the mouth and so is saved. 11 For [S]cripture *says*, [Isa 28:16]
14	-1 (Scripture)	I-Scripture → *you* (sing.) (→ *believer*)	"No one who believes in him will be put to shame."
15	o (Paul)	I-Paul → *you-Romans* (pl.) (→ *Christ*)	12 For there is no distinction between Jew and Greek; the same Lord is Lord of all and is gener-ous to all who *call* on him. 13 For, "Everyone who *calls* on the name of the Lord shall be saved."

In 10:5–11, Paul quotes two books from Scripture (Lev 18:5; Deut 9:4 + 30:12–14), which point to two forms of righteousness—that which proceeds from the Law and that which comes from faith. In doing so, the apostle gives the floor respectively to Moses and to Righteousness of faith. Being thus personified, the latter becomes the main character of the discourse. Although both citations come from the Torah, they are not attributed to the same enunciator. Even in the original contexts, the enunciator of Leviticus 18:5 is God himself, whereas that of Deut 30:12–14 is Moses. Contrary to the other cases presented earlier (Hosea, Isaiah, and Moses), the discourse does not clearly signal the presence of a citation from Deuteronomy 30. Indeed, the sole marker here is the personification of Righteousness, and this is mainly triggered by the reader's/listener's memory. Moreover, the end of the discourse (10:13) conceals a citation from Joel 2:32 that is not revealed by syntax, rhetoric, or the enunciation itself—which is why it is not taken into consideration here. The citation of Joel is completely taken over by the enunciator Paul.

Both species of righteousness appear correlated here, implying a certain distinctness but without excluding complementarity. The righteousness of the Law may be typified as stemming from a written enunciation, and seems bound to acts, establishing an externalized relation between humankind and the commandments while involving a promise of life. Differently,

Righteousness of faith speaks in and of itself, is rather bound to the spoken word and to the heart, is centered on interiority, and effectively leads to salvation.

Whether it be presented as a direct or indirect discourse, the enunciation is important. Note particularly these verbs in italics above: "write," "say" (4 times), "word" (twice), "proclaim," "confess" (twice), "call on" (twice). Note also the substantive "lips" (twice). Several contributors are clearly identifiable while some enunciations are merely described or suggested (by the utterances):

1. The apostle acts as primary enunciator (level 0), generally addressing the *you-plural* of the Roman community, but there is also a *you-singular* (line 12). He comments on the words of Righteousness of faith (with a triple "that is," lines 6, 9, 11), and recalls the Christian kerygma (10:9–10, lines 12, 13).

2. Righteousness that comes from faith is a secondary enunciator (level -1), but is also an important character, a personified virtue or attitude,[18] who addresses an enunciatee in the second person: "Do not say this or that, because the word is near you" (lines 4, 7, 10). This discourse is immediately interpreted by Paul the primary enunciator as referring to the resurrection (lines 6, 9, 11, and 12).

3. *You-singular* is primarily the enunciatee of Righteousness of faith and must "not say" (lines 4, 6) but instead confess (line 12); its discourse is then embedded within that of Righteousness of faith as tertiary enunciator (lever -2), where it asks two questions (lines 5, 8).

4. There is a major enunciative ambiguity in 10:9 (line 12, in gray), where it becomes unclear who takes charge of the discourse. Is it still the secondary enunciator Righteousness of faith who continues to speak, or is Paul the primary enunciator describing "the word of faith"? In the first case, Righteousness of faith conveys the Christian discourse to a single *you-singular* enunciatee. In the second case, there is nevertheless a telescoping of two enunciatees (level 0 and -1): the enunciatee apparently addressed by Righteousness seems to be the same as the one Paul addresses. This is of some theological importance. One clearly understands that Righteousness of faith (like Scripture a little further on) speaks in the present-day of a believer's reading/proclamation. Righteousness of faith speaks directly to the community. Paul "would be demonstrating inductively that *Dikaiosune* [Righteousness] herself is speaking from the midst of their own situation, that is, from

18. Tobin, *Paul's Rhetoric*, 343

their experience of a trusting relationship with God."[19] It follows that the line of questioning initiated by Righteousness of faith—"Who will ascend into heaven? Who will descend into the abyss?" (lines 5, 8)—is the questioning of the community itself.

5. A *we* is said to proclaim "the word of faith," i.e., the story of Christ's fidelity (line 11).

6. A second *you-singular* appears as enunciatee (line 12)—and as we have just seen, possibly merges with the first *you-singular*. It would seem that, potentially, this enunciatee might adopt the posture of enunciator, by confessing Jesus as Lord.

7. Paul furthermore mentions the possibility for any believer to "confess" (line 13).

8. Scripture speaks and adds its voice to the others (line 14).

9. Finally, Paul the enunciator mentions all those who "call on" (line 15)—a multi-voiced choir that will grow larger still in 10:14–17.

Three features from the enunciative device just described are worth pointing out. First, despite the fact that he is present and speaking, the enunciator Paul remains discreet and does not manifest himself explicitly by the grammatical markers of the first person. Second, the reason he keeps to the background is because of the importance given to addressing the subjective *you* (10:6–9), which contrasts with the more impersonal, general, almost objective utterances in the third person (*he*, 10:5, 10–13). The enunciation therefore wavers between emotional argumentation (*pathos*)—which is more the purview of Righteousness of faith—and rational argumentation (*logos*)—which is more within the scope of the primary enunciator "Paul" and of Scripture. Third, the Pauline utterances clearly update and take over those of Righteousness of faith, on which they are based. In other words, it is clear that the enunciations of Paul and of Righteousness of faith are dovetailed, even telescoped or yet again merged.

There is in all these written instances of the spoken word a dramatization and an interplay involving the quoted scripture, the apostolic commentator, and the reader/listener. This hints to an ecclesiology related to a soteriology—not so much a discourse on the church and salvation as a discourse that creates a church and actualizes in the present day the notion of salvation. The text of Deut 30:12–14, repeated within a Christian assembly, is actualized to the point of personifying a righteousness that tells *you-singular* what must not be said (Rom 10:6–7) and what must be said

19. Dewey, "Re-Hearing of Romans," 117.

(10:9–10). Salvation is not in the future of a Christ who will descend from heaven to reveal his dominion at his *parousia*, nor in the past of a Christ who ascended from the abyss to show his resurrection, but it is instead in the present-day proximity and intimacy of a discourse set within the realm of belief (the heart) and of saying (lips) (10:8). It is a discourse permeated by the theme of faith/fidelity. This is the community discourse of *we* in which *you-singular* is invited to join. In short, the workings of pronouns and of nested voices have an impact on the identity of Paul's interlocutors. The Pauline discourse leads these interlocutors to assume a *discursive identity* by exposing them to a sophisticated enunciation and having them adapt to it. Given this multi-voiced choir, the reader is led to identify with the discourse in the second person, and so with the logic of the enunciative device, which goes on to build an inclusive community in the first person plural. To put it otherwise, being placed in the position of enunciatee (*you-singular*), the reader is in turn summoned to become a full-fledged enunciator (*I*), in the footsteps of Paul, righteousness of faith, and Scripture—and thus to join a community.

Such an enunciative device has still other theological repercussions. It reveals an oblique, intuitive teaching on the resurrection, not so much through the utterances themselves as in the way of formulating and saying them; which is after all the very characteristic of enunciation. The resurrection and the life is not to be sought out in remote places, but in this innermost discourse to which the faithful adhere, as it takes form in the words of Paul and Righteousness of faith. There is no need to rise to heaven or to descend into the abyss like Christ. In becoming the enunciator of this fidelity, the believer who confesses his faith adopts the same attitude of fidelity as Christ, and so identifies with the exalted righteous one, taking part in his righteousness and his salvation (10:10). Verses 9–10 suggest that adopting this discourse as a full-fledged enunciator and adhering to the same fidelity that Jesus espoused are two aspects of one and the same act of appropriation. In this manner, one can partake in the ways of Righteousness of faith and so, too, participate experientially in the resurrection.

Second case: Romans 15:7–13

Table 4. Enunciation of Romans 15:7–13

Line	Enunciative level (enunciator)	Formula	Text
1	0 (Paul)	*I*-Paul → *you*-Romans (pl.) (→ *he*-Christ) (→ *they*-Gentiles)	7 Welcome one another, therefore, just as Christ has welcomed you, for the glory of God. 8 For I tell you that Christ has become a servant of the circumcised on behalf of the truth of God in order that he might confirm the promises given to the patriarchs, 9 and in order that the Gentiles might glorify God for his mercy. As it is written, [Ps 18:49]
2	-1 (Christ?)	*I*-Christ → *you*-God (sing.)	"Therefore I will confess you among the Gentiles, and sing praises to your name";
3	0 (Paul)	*I*-Paul → *you*-Romans (pl.) (→ *he*-Christ)	10 and again he says, [Deut 32:43]
4	-1 (Christ?)	*I*-Christ → *you*-Gentiles (pl.) (→ *it*-Israel) (→ *he*-God)	"Rejoice, O Gentiles, with his people";
5	0 (Paul)	*I*-Paul → *you*-Romans (pl.)	11 and again, [Ps 117:1]
6	-1 (Christ?)	*I*-Christ → *you*-Gentiles (pl.)	"Praise the Lord, all you Gentiles, and let all the peoples praise him";
7	0 (Paul)	*I*-Paul → *you*-Romans (pl.) (→ *he*-Isaiah)	12 and again Isaiah says, [Isa 11:10]

| 8 | -1 (Isaiah) | *I*-Isaiah→ *you*-? (sing. or pl.)
(→ he-messiah)
(→ they-Gentiles) | "The root of Jesse shall come, the one who rises to rule the Gentiles; in him the Gentiles shall hope." |
| 9 | o (Paul) | *I*-Paul → *you*-Romans (pl.)
(→ *he*-God)
[*I*-Paul → *he*-God (pl.)
(→ *you*-Romans)] | 13 May the God of hope fill you with all joy and peace in believing, so that you may abound in hope by the power of the Holy Spirit. |

This Pauline discourse, the conclusion and high point of Romans, is divided into three sections: 1) an extended statement in which the enunciator is *personally* involved: "For I tell you" (line 1); 2) a scriptural collage (Ps 17:50 + Deut 32:43 + Ps 117:1 + Isa 11:10) in which an anonymous *I* speaks, followed by Isaiah (lines 2–8); 3) a salutation addressed by the primary enunciator directly to the Romans as enunciatees, but that also calls upon God as the implicit enunciatee of a prayer (line 9). Let us examine these three segments more closely.

First, 15:7–9a is a long statement in which the enunciator addresses an enunciatee in the second person plural, an inclusive *you-plural* that is meant to relate to Christ (15:7): "Welcome one another, therefore, just as Christ has welcomed you." Of course, this is Paul speaking to the Romans. Here, the Pauline *I* goes to the trouble of telling his enunciatees he has something to tell them (he could have just told them outright). What does he tell them? Essentially three things centered on three verbs in the infinitive (in a heavy syntax that makes coordination difficult to grasp) that form three utterances in the third person: "for Christ to become a servant," "for Christ to confirm the promises," and "for the Gentiles to glorify God." With these last two verbs, the enunciation "I tell" relates to a twofold declaration by Christ who confirms and by the nations that glorify: "I say that Christ and the Gentiles speak, as it is written . . ."[20] Yet this enunciation paradoxically goes on to refer back to *Scripture*. This reference to a textual enunciation brings about a downward shift leading to an enunciative level of -1.

Second, we see in 15:9b–12 a series of secondary enunciations (level -1) beginning with those quoted by a new *I*, whose indefinite identity needs to be specified according to the enunciative device (lines 2, 4, 6). I concur with commentators who see here a declaration by Christ, who was mentioned in the third person in 15:8, since this entire secondary enunciation

---

20. I interpret "to confirm the promises" as an utterance that describes an enunciation, a declaration, that is itself a reprise/confirmation of another enunciation encapsulated in the word "promises."

presents, by means of three declarations by an *I,* the utterance of 15:8–9a.
(This shows how enunciative analysis must sometimes make hermeneutical
choices which, though impossible to validate thoroughly, may be acceptable if they are explicit.) This new, secondary enunciator addresses himself
successively to God (15:9) and to the nations (15:10–11). The utterances
pronounced by Christ are enjoinders . . . once again to speak: "confess,"
"sing praises," "rejoice," "praise" (twice)—and again we see this *mise en scène*
cascade of enunciations. Immediately after Christ's three enunciations, a
second enunciator appears. Isaiah speaks of David's descendant (the son
of Jesse, i.e. the Messiah) and his relation to the nations. In a way, Isaiah's
intervention confirms that the previous secondary enunciator was indeed
Christ the Messiah.

Third, in 15:13, we return to the primary enunciation (level 0) with
a prayer in which *I* addresses *you-plural* directly and God indirectly (in
the third person) in hope that he will intercede in favor of the enunciatees. Paul's prayer effectively echoes Christ's and Isaiah's testimonies. Like
Christ who prays *with* the Gentiles, Paul prays for (and with) the Romans.
In accordance with Isaiah's testimony, the Gentiles of Rome are full of hope
on account of their trust in the Messiah. Once again, the utterances of the
quoted Scripture are fulfilled. Most importantly, the scriptural enunciative
gesture itself is actualized in the present-day of the Roman community, at
the exact moment this community receives the Pauline enunciation. In the
midst of an ecclesial assembly of praise, Paul's letter is read, reactivating an
enunciation which is itself the mirror of a liturgical enunciation set down
in Scripture. Two nested enunciations meet and coincide: the liturgy of the
community and the liturgy stated in the epistle.

In short, the discourse presents an enunciation from which slowly
emerge the features of a figure, Christ, of whom the Pauline *I* first speaks
in the third person, but who then speaks himself as *I,* and whom Isaiah
also speaks of in the third person. This Messiah, servant of the circumcised,
welcomes the Christians of Rome, confirms the promises, allows the nations
to glorify God, publicly confesses God among the nations, commands these
same nations, and is the object of their hope. The intrigue of this brief narration describes the triangular relationship between Christ, Israel ("the circumcised," "his people"), and the Gentiles. The Messiah not only concerns
Israel but all nations; by uniting Israel and the nations in a single motion of
praise to God, the Messiah fulfills the expectations of Scripture that Israel
should at last glorify her God, joined by all nations.

Of particular interest in this enunciative device is the fact that—notwithstanding the original enunciators who speak in Ps 17:50; Deut 32:43;
and Ps 117:1—these quotes become utterances spoken by the Messiah in

a way that actuates the initial Pauline affirmation: "Christ has become a servant of the circumcised . . . (15:8–9). We witness here, borrowed from Scripture, a liturgy in which Christ conducts a chorus of praise, the Gentiles being the choristers. And it is significant that once again—having seen this before in Romans 9 and 10—the declaration of Christ (as secondary enunciator within the actual Pauline discourse) is itself, as an utterance, about an enunciation. Christ says he will confess and praise God, and he invites the Gentiles to do the same.

Conclusion

Our taking enunciation into consideration has several advantages. First, this close analysis allows for the observation of certain details that might otherwise be overlooked. Second, it submits a theology of the Word (a logology!). The biblical discourse breathes life under our very eyes into the written word; Paul lends it his voice, and it lends Paul its words. The scriptural characters—Christ, the prophets, Moses, and so on—come to life before us through personification. It is an active, living Word. It concerns the reader/ listener in the present-day of the biblical enunciation. Third, it allows us to focus our attention not only on the statements of faith, but on the act of faith, which requires an act of language. If contemporary philosophy has rediscovered the importance of language, it would seem that the Bible, both Old and New Testaments, has long since understood the importance of the speech act. Fourth, it shows that Pauline intertextuality, namely, Paul's use of citations, often favors passages in which enunciation has an important role. Finally, as a hypothesis, it would be interesting to see if the enunciative device, which uses citations, might be in the habit of telescoping the various enunciative levels, from the enunciator's as well as the enunciatee's point of view. For example, does the Pauline *I* appropriate the utterance of the quoted prophetic *I*? Or yet again, is the *you* addressed by Scripture also (if not especially in Paul) meant for the interlocutors to whom the letter is destined?[21] In any case, by using the enunciative approach, one could study all the scriptural citations of biblical letters.

Recommended Reading

Dodson, Joseph R. *The "Powers" of Personification: Rhetorical Purpose in the Book of Wisdom and the Letter to the Romans*. BZNW 161. Berlin: de Gruyter, 2008.

21. I wish to thank Jacques-André Houle for the translation of this paper from the original French.

————. "The Voices of Scripture: Citations and Personifications in Paul." *Bulletin for Biblical Research* 20 (2010) 419–31.

Gignac, Alain. "The Enunciative Device of Rom 1:18–4:25: A Succession of Discourses Attempting to Express the Multiple Dimensions of God's Justice." *CBQ* (2015) 481–502.

————. "L'interprétation du récit d'Abraham en Ga 3,6–4,7: Tour de force ou coup de force? Le travail narratif du lecteur face à l'énonciation et à l'intertextualité pauliniennes." In *Le Lecteur. VIe Colloque international du RRENAB, Louvain-La-Neuve, 24–26 Mai 2012*, edited by Régis Burnet, Didier Luciani, and Geert Van Oyen, 309–30. BETL 273. Leuven: Peeters, 2014.

————. "'We Know That Everything That Law Says': Romans 3:9–20 as a Narrative Utilization of Intertextuality That Develops Its Own Theory of Intertextuality." In *Searching the Scriptures: Studies in Context and Intertextuality*, edited by Craig A. Evans and Jeremiah J. Johnston, 246–64. Studies in Scripture in Early Judaism and Christianity 19. LNTS. New York: T. & T. Clark, 2015.

Havercroft, Barbara. "Énonciation/ Énoncé." In *Encyclopedia of Contemporary Literary Theory: Approaches, Scholars, Terms*, edited by Irena R. Makaryk, 540–42. Theory/ Culture Series. Toronto: University of Toronto Press, 1993.

Loriggio, Francesco. "Benveniste, Émile." In *Encyclopedia of Contemporary Literary Theory: Approaches, Scholars, Terms*, edited by Irena R. Makaryk, 251–53. Theory/ Culture Series. Toronto: University of Toronto Press, 1993.

Lotringer, Sylvere and Thomas Gora, eds. *Polyphonic Linguistics: The Many Voices of Émile Benveniste*. Semiotica. Special Supplement. New York: Mouton, 1981.

14

Relevance Theory and Intertextuality

Peter S. Perry

Relevance Theory (RT) is a theory describing how human beings communicate. It was developed in the 1980s and has been used by literary
critics and translators to clarify the intertextual nature of texts.[1] RT has not
significantly impacted discussions of intertextuality in biblical studies.[2] In
this chapter I argue that RT complements, challenges, and clarifies discussions about intertextuality, especially: 1) how and why readers/hearers stop
at a particular interpretation; 2) why different readers'/hearers' interpretations diverge; and 3) how a reader's/hearer's awareness of intertextual references can both limit and liberate interpretation.[3] I will use examples from
the epistle of Jude to illustrate the benefits of RT for intertextual theory
since Jude contains many references to the Hebrew Bible and early Jewish
literature.

1. For example, Gutt, *Relevance Theory*; Pilkington, "Introduction"; and fuller treatment in Pilkington, *Poetic Effects*. See also Clark, "Stylistic Analysis"; García, "Dwelling"; Malik, "Fixing meaning"; and Koutrianou, "Intertextuality." A large bibliography
related to RT is maintained by Yus http://personal.ua.es/francisco.yus/rt.html.

2. RT has been used by various biblical scholars (e.g., Green, *Jude & 2 Peter*, 10;
Green, "Relevance Theory and Theological Interpretation."), but the only one I am
aware of to engage RT directly with intertextuality is Pattemore, "Relevance Theory,"
esp. 24–28; and Pattemore, *People of God,* esp. 36–43. Special thanks to Stephen and
Gene for their feedback on this chapter.

3. Henceforth, by "readers" we will normally assume "hearers" also.

Relevance Theory

When reading a text, the interpretive options can seem limitless. How does a reader settle on an interpretation? For example, someone reading the epistle of Jude encounters the first phrase of the first verse: "Jude, a slave of Jesus Christ . . ." This could be taken in various ways depending on how the reader understands the word "slave" and the phrase "slave of Jesus Christ":

1. Jude is the legal property of someone named Jesus Christ.

2. Jude works very hard for someone named Jesus Christ but is not paid for his work.

3. Jude's decision making is controlled by someone named Jesus Christ.

4. Jude is excessively emotionally dependent on someone named Jesus Christ.

5. Jude is an authoritative leader of the Christian Church.

We could add many more interpretive options for this phrase. By what process does a reader reach any of these conclusions? Why is it obvious to most scholars of Jude that (5) is the preferred reading?[4] Nothing in the statement "slave of Jesus Christ" seems to suggest a claim to authority; in fact, some readers may take the word "slave" as a sign of low status.

Theories of intertextuality, such as the one described in the classic *Echoes of Scripture* by Richard B. Hays, suggest that to reach (5) one must investigate the relationship of the phrase "slave of Jesus Christ" with other texts, for example, Rom 1:1 or Phil 1:1.[5] In those letters, "slave of Christ" is a title of leadership.[6] How does that work? Paul's authority is not encoded or even implied in the first phrase of Jude. While intertextual theories show that Paul's use of the phrase provides the necessary information for (5), they do not explain why most interpreters choose (5) over other choices.

Hays, Alkier, and others clarify intertextual theory by demonstrating that no text is autonomous.[7] The meaning of a text is always embedded in a network of texts, or as Jonathan Culler writes, "the discursive space of

---

4. E.g., Bauckham, *Jude, 2 Peter*, 23. Neyrey, *2 Peter, Jude*, 44. Green, *Jude & 2 Peter*, 46.

5. Hays's criteria for an "echo"—availability, volume, recurrence, thematic coherence, historical plausibility, history of interpretation, and satisfaction (*Echoes*, 29–31)—are all related in some way to what RT refers to as "accessibility." See Pattemore, *People of God*, 37–38, for discussion.

6. As demonstrated by Martin, *Slavery as Salvation*, 50–51.

7. Hays, Alkier, Huizenga, *Reading the Bible Intertextually*. Alkier, "Intertextuality," 3, writes, "intertextuality is an intrinsic characteristic of textuality."

a culture."[8] But this abstracts the text from concrete readers and fails to explain the process of comprehension by readers in specific situations. If a text exists in an essentially unlimited network of texts, interpreters would seemingly never reach conclusions. But this is not what happens in reality. As Rachel Malik writes, "it does not necessarily follow that interpretation is fundamentally unconstrained, 'open' and various, as is so frequently assumed. How meaning is disambiguated, determined or resolved is the central question."[9] Or, to put it another way, how and why do readers stop interpreting and arrive at a conclusion?

Relevance Theory (RT) is an ostensive-inferential theory of human communication developed by Deidre Wilson and Dan Sperber based on their study of human cognition. It is "ostensive" (think of a person clearing her throat to get a group's attention) because the behavior not only conveys information (an *informative intention*), but conveys the intention to communicate some information (a *communicative intention*).[10] Jude had his words put down in writing to create a letter and then handed it to someone. These actions indicate his intent to communicate, whether or not the person receiving the letter understood it in the same way as the author (or even read it at all).[11]

RT allows us to claim this limited authorial intent (the intent to communicate) while avoiding the intentional fallacy that readers have unrestricted access to the author's mind. A communicator, by definition, wants to be understood. Based on Jude's words, we can conclude someone identifying himself to be "Jude" desired to communicate with readers and be understood. That expression of *communicative* intention does not allow us to make definitive statements about what Jude was thinking, but allows us to compare conclusions that different readers may reach in order to evaluate what is most consistent with the author's communicative intention. The meaning and effect of the text is always mediated through the reader's cognition, that is, conscious and subconscious thought process. While some intertextual theorists (e.g., Barthes, Derrida) claim the text is

8. Culler, *Pursuit of Signs*, 103.

9. Malik, "Fixing Meaning," 15–16.

10. Sperber and Wilson, *Relevance*, 49; Pattemore, *People of God*, 16.

11. Following Petöfi, Alkier, and Pattemore, we are using the word "text" narrowly to refer to a linguistic object with the property of textuality (e.g., Pattemore, *People of God*, 22–31). I am transposing Sperber and Wilson, *Relevance*, regarding their speaker/hearer language into writer/reader for the sake of this "textual" discussion, but with the awareness that in many communication situations, ancient and modern, a written text would be often read aloud, performed, commented upon, with audience responses and other dynamics. RT as a descriptive communication theory works to explain cognitive processes in these situations as well.

entirely liberated from its author, RT maintains a relationship between the author and the text. RT allows us to assert the perception of the author's intent from the reader's side and how the reader processes the text as the author's communication.

Along with being an ostensive process, RT argues that human communication is an inferential process before it is a coding-decoding process. An inferential process starts from a set of premises, or logical statements, and results in conclusions drawn deductively from these premises. The phrase "logical statements" may make it sound like a computer can do the same work, but inference is "less a logical process than a form of suitably constrained guesswork" that happens almost instantaneously and often unconsciously.[12] Some communication theories conceive that a speaker sends a code and the hearer decodes the code, as if meaning is embedded in the words themselves, resulting in the recovery of the message associated with the signal.[13] RT does not deny that a coding-decoding process is involved in communication, but that words and phrases cannot encode the writer's meaning. Words, phrases, sentences, and paragraphs ("utterances") are cues that only assist the audience in the inferential process of deducing what the writer may mean.[14]

The priority of an inferential process helps to explain why interpreters of Jude so quickly pass over the literal options (1)–(4) above for a figurative meaning (5). Readers who have the premise that "a 'slave of Jesus Christ' is an authoritative leader of a Christian church," will not spend any time considering interpretations (1)–(4). They will immediately infer (5) based on their belief that their premise above, which we will call (6), is true.

The premises that a reader assumes to be true are called her *cognitive environment*. *Cognitive environment* may include memories, observations, inferences, assumptions, beliefs, values, ideas, and so on—whatever the reader can mentally represent as true or probably true. This type of environment is more conceptually sound than an amorphous "context" that is sometimes used in discussions of intertextuality. Not all aspects of a socio-historical context may be equally accessible to each reader or hearer of a text. For example, did members of Jude's first audience know that Paul also struggled with antinomian teachers and that Paul's first letter to the Corinthians is a possible intertext for Jude? Probably not, but a modern reader may. Each reader has a *cognitive environment* populated with information she assumes to be true. If a reader does not have any experience with "Jesus

---

12. Sperber and Wilson, *Relevance*, 69.

13. Ibid., 12–13.

14. Ibid., 27.

Christ," it is more likely that she will read Jude 1 and reach one of conclusions (1)–(4) rather than (5).

When a writer and reader share a set of information, this set is called a *mutually manifest cognitive environment*. When the writer and reader share premise (6), the reader with little effort will conclude (5), "Jude is an authoritative leader of a Christian church." As the reader continues to read a particular text, this *mutually manifest cognitive environment* grows as the text is added to the reader's cognitive environment. As a reader continues in Jude 1, she discovers that Jude is also the brother of James, and then processes the significance of this statement (perhaps to conclude that Jude is also the brother of Jesus). In this way, we can speak explicitly about the way the mutual cognitive environment is constructed in the process of reading a text.[15]

A reader who knows (6) quickly chooses interpretation (5) because this ostensive-inferential way of communicating is built into human beings. The *first principle of relevance* is that, "Human cognition tends to be geared to the maximization of relevance."[16] Our minds automatically search for how an input, whether written or spoken, a gesture or a signal, may relate to other information we know, observe, or infer. *Relevance* is defined by the greatest *cognitive effects* for the least amount of processing effort, or to put it differently, greater benefits at lower costs.[17] A *cognitive effect* may be an answer to a reader's question, improvement of knowledge about the world, confirmation of suspicions, or a correction of a mistake. Interpretations (1)–(4) yield no significant information to the reader and would require additional processing effort to obtain (6) or a similar premise to infer (5). For a reader who holds premise (6), the phrase "Jude, a slave of Jesus Christ" leads a reader to take the whole letter of Jude as a message from an authoritative leader of a Christian church. This has a more significant impact on the reader than the other options.

With the criteria of *cognitive effects* and *processing effort*, RT also asserts that there is an optimal interpretation. The *second principle of relevance* is that "every act of ostensive communication communicates a presumption of its own optimal relevance."[18] The writer wants to be understood and will write in such a way that the author believes will minimize the processing effort of the reader to reach the communicator's goal. Sperber and Wilson posit that *optimal relevance* is reached when two propositions are true:

15. See Pattemore, "Relevance Theory," 44.
16. Sperber and Wilson, *Relevance*, 260.
17. Ibid., 262.
18. Ibid., 260.

(A) The ostensive stimulus (in this case, words on a page or read aloud) is relevant enough for it to be worth the addressee's effort to process it.

(B) The ostensive stimulus is the most relevant one compatible with the communicator's abilities and preferences.[19]

Statement (A) asserts that there is an intersection of effort and effect that stops the cognitive process. This half of *optimal relevance* is focused on the reader. Subconsciously and sometimes consciously, a reader is always evaluating the relevance of a particular statement and following the path of least effort to interpret it. Once a reader reaches an interpretation that satisfies her expectations of relevance, she will stop. This does not mean that a phrase, sentence, paragraph, or text cannot ever be more than that, but that a reader subconsciously is calculating the payoff and the effort to reach that payoff. There may be signals of additional cognitive gains (for example, an awkward phrase that may suggest a deeper meaning), but the reader will calculate whether it is worth the processing effort. Consider the following statements:

(6) A "slave of Jesus Christ" is an authoritative leader of a Christian community.

(7) Paul refers to himself as a slave of Jesus Christ in Romans 1:1.

(8) Paul is an authoritative leader of a Christian community.

A reader may have added (6) to her cognitive environment by having prior experience with (7) and (8), but after (6) has been added to the reader's cognitive environment, it is no longer necessary to access (7)–(8) to reach (6). Naturally following the path of least effort, a reader of Jude 1 needs only to access (6) in order to reach conclusion (5).[20]

To restate in a way that may increase relevance for a discussion of intertextuality, a reader does not need to access a specific textual reference such as (7) to conclude with (5) that "Jude is an authoritative leader of a Christian community," although such access may strengthen (6). If a reader does not think in terms of (6) or questions (6), it may be necessary to exert the additional processing of (7) and (8) to reach optimal relevance. In short, relevance may be reached without specific access to intertextual references that support a premise. We will see that other statements in Jude will require more effort to access an intertext in order to reach optimal relevance.

---

19. Ibid., 270.

20. However, if the reader is a scholar writing a commentary on Jude, additional processing effort will be required as a part of the new communication situation!

However, if a reader cannot access (6) and cannot access (7) and (8) or anything that may result in (6), the reader may stop processing before optimal relevance is reached because the effort has become too great. The reader may settle for what feels like a less than satisfactory conclusion. For this reader, access to an intertextual reference would be necessary to reach optimal relevance.

Statement (B) concerns the writer's half of *optimal relevance*. The writer has communicative goals and produces a text that sends the reader on the search for those goals. But the writer is constrained by her abilities, preferences, and cognitive environment. For example, a writer may prefer particular vocabulary, syntax, style, and assumptions that may require more or less processing effort by different readers. There may be more relevant stimuli for a particular reader that the author does not know or think of when she writes. But out of the all the options available to the writer within these constraints, *optimal relevance* assumes that the writer chooses what seems to her to be most relevant to the addressee.

One of the options that is available to the author of Jude is:

(9) Jude, an authoritative leader of a Christian community, . . .

Certainly, this requires little processing effort. Why does the author not choose this formulation? Based on (B), RT suggests that (9) somehow does not maximize relevance, even though this phrasing eliminates processing effort. Since this phrasing was not chosen, processing effort is not the issue and some cognitive effect must be at stake. Either (9) has cognitive effects that do not meet the author's communicative goals, or "Jude, a slave of Jesus Christ" has cognitive effects that (9) does not have. RT, by the comparing effort and effects, illuminates the choices and assumptions of the author.

Which cognitive effects are at stake? Here, the study of ancient rhetoric, socio-historical criticism, and literary criticism offer some possible answers, and RT helps compare the effect of each relative to the effort:

(10) It is unacceptable to claim overtly leadership of Christian communities in the first century.

(11) "Slave of Christ" is an acceptable title for a Christian leader.

(12) To claim to be a "slave of Christ" is to identify with Paul, Peter, and other authoritative Christian leaders.

(13) Jesus said, "Whoever must be first among you must be slave of all" (Mark 10:44). Therefore, a "slave of all" may refer to a leader (someone who is "first").

(14) Prophets are called "slaves of the LORD" (Amos 3:7; Jer 7:25; Dan 9:6).

(15) A "slave of Caesar" was a title for an agent of the Emperor.

The first statement (10) is a negative cognitive effect that may explain why Jude avoided the direct phrasing of (9). The next statement (11) may be a positive corollary to (10) that motivates Jude's phrasing. The remaining (12)–(15) are possible positive cognitive effects that may have influenced the author to choose the formulation of Jude 1 over (9). Statement (13) requires knowledge of an intertext and further processing in order to relate "slave of all" to "slave of Jesus Christ." Statement (14) also requires knowledge of intertexts, but less effort to extend "slave of the LORD" to "slave of Jesus Christ." Therefore, RT suggests that statement (14) would have greater relevance (more effect for less effort) than statement (13). Statement (15) opens up another range of cognitive effects by comparing Jesus to the Emperor and Jude to agents of the Emperor. The reader, however, does not need to access any of these statements in order to reach optimal relevance, although accessing them may further enrich and extend the cognitive effects of Jude 1.

It should be clear by this point that RT provides a basis for comparing interpretations, but does not offer a quantitative or absolute reckoning for how a reader will interpret a statement. A reader does not compute a numerical value as to which interpretation is more relevant; a reader intuits which interpretation fits her background knowledge and the cues (explicit and implicit) provided by the author of the text.

The relevance of an utterance is maximized by more than explicit statements. The choice to use "slave of Jesus Christ" rather than a more direct (9) may also reflect what RT calls *poetic effects*. For example, rhetorical figures and style do not necessarily add propositions to the cognitive environment. They may influence the relationship between the communicator and hearer, for example, the emotional closeness or shared impressions. A speaker may also uses poetic effects (e.g., hyperbole, repetition, rhyme) when she expects them to reduce processing effort for hearers to reach the desired cognitive effect.

Some utterances represent another person's thoughts (e.g., a quotation) and the speaker's attitude or interpretation of it. These *echoic utterances* allow a speaker to express a whole range of emotions and attitudes towards another's opinion, "from outright acceptance and endorsement to outright rejection and dissociation."[21] Irony is an example of an echoic ut-

---

21. Ibid., 240; cf. Pilkington, *Poetic Effects*.

terance that uses particular words and phrases, but through tone, gestures, and other signals communicates the opposite of the words used. Without recognizing these attitudes and emotions, the hearer may not reach optimal relevance.

Within this framework of how human communication works, *intertextuality* refers to the connection made by a reader between an utterance and a remembered text within her cognitive environment that yields cognitive effects.[22] An *intertext* is an echoic utterance that represents another person's thought and the communicator's attitudes towards it. Recognizing the attitude towards the source text may be critical to a reader interpreting some intertexts. For some readers, the processing effort may be too great to reach significant cognitive effects, which may reflect the different cognitive environments or that the communicator's preferences do not match the readers' knowledge. Some authors may reduce the processing effort by making the author, source, and/or interpretation of a text explicit (as we will see with Jude's references to *1 Enoch*). In other cases, if the intertextual reference is only weakly signaled, in what some may call an echo or allusion, readers may reach a wider array of possible conclusions that fall short of optimal relevance.

Intertextuality in Jude

Jude is rich with connections to other texts, including those in Hebrew Bible as well as extra-canonical Jewish literature such as *1 Enoch*. Relevance Theory explains why readers stop processing intertextual references in different ways, reach different conclusions, and both limit and liberate meaning.
As described above, readers stop interpreting when they reach declining effect for increasing effort. Some readers stop short of optimal relevance because processing demands are too high or because further cognitive effects exceed optimal relevance. In contrast, scholars have the tendency to over-process an utterance and exceed optimal relevance, as illustrated below in the example of Jude's greeting.

Jude greets his readers with the phrase: "May mercy, peace, and love be yours in abundance" (v. 2). Readers aware of other early Christian letters note that this phrase is unique. "Grace and peace" is more common for the Pauline letters, while the triple formula "grace, mercy, and peace" is found

---

22. Pattemore, "Relevance Theory," 48, helpfully suggests that the term "'intertextuality' be reserved for relevance found within textually defined cognitive environments." This caveat prevents us from considering every experience as a source for intertextual reflection and draining the word "intertextuality" of any significance.

in 1 and 2 Timothy.[23] When a reader has Pauline greetings in her cognitive environment, the absence of "grace" may trigger a search for relevance. For example, Gene Green concludes, "Since the wish-prayer for 'grace' was a commonplace in Christian correspondence, Jude's omission is somewhat striking. Most likely he excludes the wish-prayer for grace since the fundamental problem that he addresses in the epistle is the distorted understanding of grace that the heretics had introduced into the church (v. 4)."[24] Green has inferred a cognitive effect of omitting "grace" from the greeting, but only after the entire letter is taken into consideration.

Is detecting the omission of "grace" necessary for optimal relevance? RT asserts not. Optimal relevance is reached in the greeting simply by processing the wish of the author for mercy, peace, and love. In a cognitive environment familiar with the Jewish greeting "mercy and peace," these two words would be familiar and tied to the memories of reading or hearing many such greetings. Jude adds the word "love," which Richard Bauckham argues is a more uniquely Christian greeting. Bauckham's conclusion is supported by the criteria of effort and effect: "No doubt Jude's readers would read the Jewish greeting with Christian overtones. God's mercy shown in Christ, and Christian salvation in Christ. The Christian interpretation is reinforced by the addition of ἀγάπη, 'love,' found in no Jewish salutation . . . "[25] These conclusions are accessible with a minimal amount of effort for a first-century Jewish Christian as well as for moderately educated modern Christian readers, and have significant impact. At this point in the letter, it is not necessary to understand the omission of "grace."

However, this is not to say that Green's conclusion cannot be reached by further processing of the letter. One of the strengths of using RT is that it emphasizes the linear nature of hearing and reading and the cumulative construction of a mutually manifest cognitive environment between author and reader. A reader may observe "grace" was omitted from the greeting, but decide (most likely subconsciously) at that point that processing this omission requires too much effort and so continues reading. If there is a lingering question, the reader may resolve the ambiguity when reading verse 4: some are "perverting the grace of God into licentiousness." In this way, if the reader noticed the omission of grace in verse 2 as a possible signal of Jude's concern, that conclusion is strengthened in verse 4: Jude's opponents are perverting God's grace so significantly that Jude is reluctant to include

---

23. Neyrey, 2 Peter, Jude, 46; Bauckham, Jude, 2 Peter, 20.

24. Green, Jude & 2 Peter, 49; see also Bauckham, Jude, 2 Peter, 11–13, on the antinomian character of Jude's opponents.

25. Bauckham, Jude, 2 Peter, 27.

it in his greeting.[26] But this conclusion is not necessary to reach optimal relevance of verse 2.

RT also predicts different conclusions that readers may draw and the strength of these conclusions. For example, consider verse 6:

> And the angels who did not keep their own position, but left their proper dwelling, he has kept in eternal chains in deepest darkness for the judgment of the great day.

To reach optimal relevance, the reference to "angels who did not keep their own position" requires access to traditions of Gen 6:1–4 and elaborations in Enochic Judaism (especially 1 *Enoch* 6–19, but the same story is told in *Jubilees* 5.1–2; 2 *Baruch* 56.10–16; CD 2.17–31; and in Josephus *Antiquities* 1.3.1.73).[27] Genesis 6 describes the "sons of God," called "Watchers" in 1 *Enoch*, who have sexual intercourse with human women, and as a result are bound and cast into the darkness until the Day of Judgment. A reader unfamiliar with even this one sentence summary might give up trying to process the details of verse 6. A different reader, however, will expend the effort to ignore what she does not understand in the verse and still conclude:

(16) God is willing to punish even the angels for disobedience.

The reader may not understand the specific references of "eternal chains" or "deepest darkness," but these words may still elicit the emotion of fear (a poetic effect) together with the implication:

(17) If God is willing to punish angels, how much more will God be willing to punish disobedient humans charged with authority (e.g., the false teachers)?

Without access to traditions expressed in 1 *Enoch* 6–19, the conclusion of (17) would be weak and have little persuasive force. It would be stronger and reach optimal relevance with at least a general awareness of the cosmic and eschatological scope of the Watchers' fall and their sexual transgression that reinforces Jude's accusation of his opponent's sexual immorality. Yet, it is not necessary to have specific, word-for-word access to 1 *Enoch* to reach optimal relevance, but only general and summary memory evoked by the references to "eternal chains," "deepest darkness," and sexual immorality.[28]

---

26. Pattemore, *People of God*, 53–54, calls this a "retrospective effect."

27. Green, *Jude & 2 Peter*, 67.

28. Pattemore, *People of God*, 42, describes this as "used conventionally," when an audience does not need access to the original context of the intertext. When an audience needs access, he calls it "contextually evoked."

The reference to 1 *Enoch* in Jude 14–16 is different. Here, Jude introduces a direct quote, "Enoch, in the seventh generation from Adam, prophesied . . ." Because Jude only assumes a general awareness of the story of the Watchers in verse 6, RT suggests that he does not assume his audience has specific access to the text of 1 *Enoch* itself.[29] As a result, the quotation requires a more substantial introduction to guide the reader to optimal relevance.

Jude refers to Enoch as "in the seventh generation from Adam." How does a reader process this statement?

> (18) This is a traditional description of Enoch found in 1 *Enoch* 60:8; 93:3; *Jub* 7:39; *Lev. Rab.* 29:11.[30]

Although true and interesting to scholars of intertextuality, this conclusion does not yield significant cognitive effects for a general reader and so does not explain why Jude would write this (see part B of optimal relevance described above). Better is:

> (19) Seven is a number of perfection; therefore,

> (20) A prophecy by a seventh son is more significant than other prophecies.[31]

If (19) is accessible in a reader's cognitive environment, statement (20) will lead a reader to conclude that the quotation from Enoch is significant. Then, consider:

> (21) Someone in the seventh generation from Adam, the first man, is very early in human history; therefore,

> (22) A prophecy by someone early in human history is more significant than other prophecies.

The cognitive effects of "seven" (20) and "from Adam" (22) suggest that the primary effect is to amplify the authority of the quotation that follows.[32] This conclusion is strengthened by Jude's use of "prophesied" in addition to "saying." Jude could have written simply, "said" or "wrote," but a reader is more likely to process the following quotation as a prophecy because Jude used the word "prophesied." Based on RT's understanding that an author chooses the preferred route to optimal relevance, we may conclude that Jude

---

29. Enochic ideas seem to be a part of the cognitive environment of the community to which Jude is writing and easily accessible ("in the air"). See Bauckham, *Jude, 2 Peter*, 97; Neyrey, *2 Peter, Jude*, 79–80.

30. Bauckham, *Jude, 2 Peter*, 96.

31. Ibid.

32. Ibid.

thought the audience may not receive the quotation as authoritative without amplifying Enoch as "in the seventh generation from Adam" and using
the verb "prophesied." Jude cues the audience to rank the quotation with
authoritative prophets, and in this way he maximizes the impact of Jude's
argument that the false teachers will be judged at the coming of the Lord.[33]
While optimal relevance limits interpretive options when a reader focuses
on the author's communicative intent, RT also explains why intertextuality
liberates interpretation. There is no theoretical limit to the kinds of intertextual relationships that an abstract reader may make with a given text.
RT concurs with literary theorists such as Kristeva, Barthes, and Derrida,
who claim that meaning is liberated by the limitless number of connections
a reader may make between one text and the whole universe of texts. For
example, it is possible to hear the Beatles' "Hey, Jude" in relationship with
the epistle of Jude:

(23) Hey Jude, don't make it bad. / Take a sad song and make it better. /
Remember to let her into your heart, / Then you can start to make it
better.

One could hear this in at least two ways (and probably many more) in relationship with the epistle of Jude, depending on how one decides the reference for the pronoun "her" and the phrase "sad song." Either:

(24) "Her" refers to "faith" that Jude wants to defend; "sad song" refers to
the message of the false teachers; or

(25) "Her" refers to sexual behaviors authorized by Jude's opponents;
"sad song" refers to Jude's message.

Depending whether one chooses (24) or (25), the hearer/reader may interpret the intertextual connection in opposite ways. Either:

(26) The singer encourages Jude to continue in his work in defending the
faith, making a sad song of his opponents better; or

(27) The singer is bummed out by Jude's prudishness and encourages him
to join in the behavior.

The possibilities are limitless, and one can imagine situations in which either interpretation may be used.

---

33. The long-term effects on audiences for Jude's decision to rank 1 *Enoch* with the
prophets can be seen in ancient and modern controversy about the status of 1 *Enoch* in
Christian communities. See Green, *Jude & 2 Peter*, 26–33.

Conclusion

RT does not replace existing theories of intertextuality but affirms and clarifies many aspects of them. What RT adds to intertextual theories is the framework of a cognitive communication theory that illuminates the three issues raised in the introduction.

How and why do readers/hearers stop at a particular interpretation? RT demonstrates that readers will stop when their expectations of relevance are satisfied based on the twin criteria of effort and effect. Each reader comes to a text with a cognitive environment that includes both general and specific knowledge other texts. The text being read is itself an ostensive signal that includes the presumption of optimal relevance, and the reader responds to cues in the text that are mutually manifest (i.e., texts that the reader recalls or is willing to expend the energy to access). Accessibility limits the relevance of the intertextual connection. When the expectation of relevance is satisfied the reader stops interpreting.

Why do different readers/hearers interpretations diverge? It is perhaps obvious that different readers bring different experiences and expectations to a text and thus diverge in the way that they interpret intertextual references. With RT, we can compare interpretations using the criteria of effort and effect and predict how different readers will respond. One reader may read a phrase and ignore it without awareness of an intertext. Another reader may think of an unrelated text and draw a conclusion based on this intertext. A different reader will detect a clue of additional cognitive benefit and search the Internet or the bookshelf to make a connection. It must be stated clearly that although RT predicts that there is optimal relevance for an intertextual reference, it also predicts a wide range of possible responses, from overly literal to wholly unintended.

RT illuminates also how the author's specific choices attempt to maximize relevance. The author makes it easier to detect an intertext by using a citation formula (for example, Jude's reference to 1 *Enoch* 1:9). An author may only weakly imply a connection to another text, perhaps out of a preference or poetic effect. With only a vague awareness of an intertext, the reader may have a difficult time discovering its significance. "Clearly, the weaker the implicatures, the less confidence the hearer can have that the particular premises or conclusion he supplies will reflect the speaker's thoughts, and this is where the indeterminacy lies."[34] The text represents the

34. Sperber and Wilson, *Relevance*, 200.

author's attempt to modify the reader's cognitive environment at the lowest effort, but the actual cognitive effects are not entirely foreseeable.[35]

How does a reader's awareness of intertexts both limit and liberate interpretation? On the one hand, each reader is confronted with the communicative intent of the author that suggests there is optimal relevance. The reader's pursuit of optimal relevance limits interpretation based on the criteria of effect and effort. On the other hand, each reader brings a cognitive environment populated with texts that may be more or less accessible in memory or practice. Texts can be connected that the author never imagined, such as connecting Jude to *Hey, Jude*. In this way, interpretation is liberated by the infinite possible combinations and connections to be made. Whether limiting or liberating, RT provides explanation for the cognitive processes of intertextuality.

Recommended Reading

Gutt, Ernst-August. *Relevance Theory: A Guide to Successful Communication in Translation*. Dallas, TX: SIL, 1992.

Malik, Rachel. "Fixing Meaning: Intertextuality, Inference and the Horizon of the Publishable." *RP* 124 (Mar/Apr 2004) 13–26.

Pattemore, Stephen. *The People of God in the Apocalypse: Discourse, Structure and Exegesis*. SNTMS 128. Cambridge: Cambridge University Press, 2004.

———. "Relevance Theory, Intertextuality and the Book of Revelation." In *Current Trends in Scripture Translation*, edited by Philip Noss, 43–60. UBS Bulletin 194/195. Reading, PA: UBS, 2003.

Sperber, Dan, and Deirdre Wilson. *Relevance: Communication and Cognition*. 2nd ed. Cambridge, MA: Blackwell, 1995.

35. See discussion in Sperber and Wilson, *Relevance*, 201–2, warning against looking only at the strongest implicatures. See the importance of poetic effects of weak implicatures above and in Sperber and Wilson, *Relevance*, 217–43.

15

Multidimensional Intertextuality

Erik Waaler

R e-use of the Old Testament in the New Testament is best described as re-contextualization of text. This is a complicated process involving many factors, and hence, it is a multidimensional approach to intertextuality. We start with a description of the nature of intertextuality, a concept borrowed from post-structuralism but to a certain degree used as an extended form of source-influence in New Testament studies from Richard Hays onwards.[1] The purpose of our approach is to make clear how the movement of words and sentences from one text to another changes the sentences that are moved in multiple ways. Such changes happen even when there is complete verbal agreement between texts. Our division of re-contextualized texts into the four different categories of citation, quotation, allusion, and echo is simplistic. We must therefore question whether ancient quotations that abide with our modern scholarly standards were ever really in existence.

The traditional approach to re-contextualization had predominantly emphasized the study of quotations and the *Vorlage* (prototype or prior version) of the author.[2] Focus on quotations was a narrow perspective, often chosen as a matter of convenience, diminishing the uncertainty of allusions and echoes. The focus on *Vorlage* is, to a large extent, inherited from literary criticism. Hays put allusion and echoes into focus. In his influential monograph, he developed a set of standard validating factors.[3] The emphasis on validation is probably intended to avoid accusations of paral-

1. Cf. Hatina, "Intertextuality," 28–43.

2. E.g. Stendahl, *School of St. Matthew.*

3. Hays, *Echoes,* esp. 29–32.

lelomania (i.e., the invention of unfounded parallels),[4] accusations that in our opinion often develop into parallelonoia (i.e., the aversion against uncertain parallels). Rather than focusing mainly on the question of validation of a source's link, we should study how intertextuality works and how it imposes meaning. The perspective we develop below focuses on the deeper structures of meaning: What is happening? How does it happen? What does it mean? Our work is dependent on the psychological perception of the acting subject, the perception of the subject's awareness of him- or herself.[5] It is dependent on anthropological concepts such as worldview and culture.[6] We use sociological models focusing on sociological impact on meaning,[7] and linguistic theory of meaning applied to lexemes, terminology and phrases.[8] This places our approach alongside the socio-rhetorical approach to Scripture as historically and culturally situated, and in our case to do re-contextualization.[9]

Textual Change and Continuity

Matthew 22:31–46 has multiple references, or so-called *quotations,* to the Old Testament; however, none of them is exactly *verbatim.* The way direct *reference* to the earlier text is made varies. Nevertheless, on the scale of *intent,* the references all score high. These factors are the main traditional elements in the discussion of citations, quotations, allusions, and echo, which should be renamed "re-contextualization." With just one category, we work towards a *thick description* of reused text.[10] We focus on intentional change and continuity rather than four external technical terms (i.e., citation, quotation, allusion, and echo). Below we will describe twenty-eight different aspects of change and continuity and apply them to the text of Matt 23:31–46.

1. Reference Formula (Matt 22:31, 41–42, 43)

The introduction to the "quotations" in Matt 22:31–46 follow the common twofold pattern for *explicit verbatim re-contextualizations* introduced by

4. See Sandmel, "Parallelomania," 1–13.
5. See further Hirsch, *Validity in Interpretation.*
6. As, e.g., Malina, *Cultural Anthropology,* proposes.
7. Such as in Linnell, *Approaching Dialogue.*
8. See Barr, *Semantics of Biblical Language.*
9. See further, Robbins, *New Boundaries,* 3; cf. *Exploring the Texture of Texts.*
10. Geertz, "Thick Description" 213–31; Ponterotto, "Brief Note," 538–49.

a composite reference formula. We have indirect reference to Exodus 3:6: *"That which was spoken to you by God . . ."* in Matt 22:31.[11] This is followed by explicit reference to Psalm 110: *"How is it then that David by the Spirit calls him Lord?"* (v. 43). Elsewhere in Matthew, we find formulae such as *"it is written . . ."* (e.g. Matt 4:4–10). Two of the reference formulae are followed by the verb "to say" (λέγοντος v. 31, λέγων v. 43). This part of the reference formula invites more verbatim repetition compared to the phrase *"it is written"*; but neither formula demands exact verbatim repetition.[12] However, often the reference formula is absent from verbatim as well as from less verbatim re-contextualizations, such as the reuse that has been claimed for Ps 2:2 in Matt 22:41–42.

2. Verbatimity (vv. 37, 44)

There is a relatively high degree of verbatimity in the four main re-contextualizations in our text, but it varies depending on which text-version we compare it with (MT, LXX, Qumran, etc.). For each version, there are text-critical issues. It is probable that Matthew had access to a version of the LXX, which we may try to re-construct by means of text-criticism. However, we may also compare Matthew with an early version such as the LXXA (Codex Alexandrinus). We do not have access to Matthew's *Vorlage*, thus both approaches are hypothetical, but the latter less so, for then we could compare it with an actual text and not a reconstructed one.

Matthew's version of the Great Commandment is at variance with the MT and the LXX. Matthew has ἐν (cf. בְּ), and the LXX has ἐξ. The main difference, however, is the translation of "of all your might" (מְאֹדֶךָ, δυνάμεως). Matthew reads, "with all your mind (διανοίᾳ)" (Matt 22:37).[13] Mark 12:30 includes both Matthew's διανοίᾳ and δυνάμεως of the LXX, adding a fourth part. The question is whether this is a pure source-critical issue, as Stendahl seems to think:

---

11. Here God's speaking is taken literally: The Lord spoke to the Israelites on the mountain. Elsewhere it might be indirect reference to inspired prophetical speech. Unless otherwise stated, all English quotations are from the NRSV.

12. Hence, we use the name *reference formulae*. The phrase τοῦ πατρός σου θεὸς (Exod 3:6: "God of your father") is absent from Matthew 22:32; the parallel to the LXX is closer in Matt 22:44. Reference may also come after the re-contextualization (Matt 22:38).

13. Gundry suggests that "mind" translates מַדָּעֶךָ, thus a different *Vorlage* (Gundry, *Matthew*, 449), whereas Gaechter (*Matthäus Evangelium*, 713) suggests that the two words are so similar that it could be a mistaken reading.

It is noteworthy that all the Synoptics, except the D text in Mark and Luke, include the synonyms καρδία and διάνοια both translations of the Hebrew לבב. It is very unlikely that any form of the shema containing such a repetition was known to the evangelists. The text of Matthew must therefore be a revision of the Marcan text.[14]

Does Mark add the last member? Or does Matthew reduce Mark's four parts to three, as in Deut 6:5?[15] The Synoptic Gospel versions are at variance with the MT, the Samarian Pentateuch, the Qumran texts, and the LXX. Possibly, the change is due to the Jesus tradition. Matthew's version is more pointed, as *mind* corresponds closer to *heart* and *soul* than the original *might*. This might speak for an intended interpretation in the direction of a person's inner being, which to some degree corresponds to loving your neighbour as yourself. Qumran's *Rule of the Community* interprets towards the exterior: "knowledge," "energies," and "riches" (1QS 1:11b–13a). It focuses on "God's decrees," "His perfect path" and "His just council," core values of the *Yahad* community (cf. 1QS 1:16–17a).[16] These are examples of interpretations rather than pure text-critical issues. If Matthew's text was prior to Mark, then Mark might have noticed the interpretation and expanded it in respect to both Matthew's Jesus and the Pentateuch (Mark 12:30; cf. Luke 10:27). Matthew (19:19) portrays the Shema as interpretation of the Decalogue in particular and as the core of the Law in general.[17] The idiosyncratic interpretation of Matthew's Jesus focuses on the attitude of the heart (cf. Luke 10:25–37).

Fitzmyer, among others, has described how the *Tetragrammaton* (יהוה) is replaced by the term "Lord" in the fourth re-contextualization (Matt 22:44, Κύριος). Extant Hebrew texts have: "Yahweh said to my lord." Matthew's version corresponds to the extant LXX text. This is a theological change, avoiding pronunciation of the name of God, a core value of Second Temple Judaism.[18] We agree that, "The Synoptic Gospels record an incident in the life of Christ which is difficult to understand apart from a directly

---

14. Stendahl, *School of St. Matthew*, 75–76.

15. Adding to the difficulty, Mark put yet another version in the mouth of the scribe (Mark 12:33), but here the text tradition is rather fluid.

16. Waaler, *Shema*, 253.

17. Ibid.

18. This custom is found in Qumran (1QS 4:27–5:1, 1QapGen 21:2/Gen 13:4; cf. 1QapGen 22:32/Gen 15:2) and the Elohistic psalter (Waaler, 423–28). This difference raises a huge discussion about the use of the term "Lord" in Hebrew, Aramaic, and Greek.

messianic interpretation of Psalm 110."[19] However, the text is not a perfect verbatim repetition of the LXX.[20] There is no material difference, though, and so we are left with stylistic change, possibly to avoid a pleonasm. This indicates how vocabulary is treated within a particular subculture (see vocabulary, worldview, sociologic dynamic below).

3. Intent and Awareness (vv. 43–44)

The discussion above leads on to the question of intent and awareness, which are evasive categories that do not focus on the text *per se*, but on the mind of the authors and their audiences. When a reference is made, it is relatively easy to identify intent, and then the story implies awareness for everyone (author, authorial audience, implied author and audience, narrator and narratee). However, the task of finding intent and awareness is not only relevant for the fact that *the text is used*, it is also relevant for the *way it is used*. One may be aware of some aspects of continuity and change, and unaware of others. The avoidance of the *Tetragrammaton* in Psalm 110 might be subconsciously intended due to cultural values. It is more difficult, however, to know whether the author and audience were aware of this. As Jews knew the *Shema* from Deut 6:4–5 by heart, most would notice a change in its text; consequently, both intent and awareness would be assumed on their behalf.

4. The Authority of the *Pretext*
from the Old Testament (vv. 29, 31, 35, 40)

As most Jews at the time, the authors of the New Testament had a perception of the Old Testament as the ultimate authority. This is self-evident and may go unnoticed. Our text has plentiful signs of this: (1) God's speaking from a burning bush is taken at face value (Matt 22:31, Exod 3:4); (2) The authority of the two great commandments is taken for granted; (3) There is no question mark with reference to the authority, clarity, and consistency of David, who speaks by the Spirit;[21] (4) The Sadducees go astray because they do not know the Scriptures (Matt 22:29), which implies that Scripture

---

19. Aloisi, "David's Lord," 103–23.

20. ὑποκάτω (ὑποπόδιον, Ps 109[110]:1) τῶν ποδῶν σου: Matt 22:44. Unless otherwise noted, the Greek text is from NA27.

21. "If David call him Lord, how can he be his son?" (Matt 22:45). It has been questioned if this quotation argues for Davidic descent or not (Albright and Mann, *Matthew*, 274).

has authority if properly used; (5) The third re-contextualization appeals to the *Law* (v.35; "and the *Prophets*" v. 40), as if to an authority. This kind of standard language implies a canonization process in process. Authority, taken for granted, is a major element in re-contextualization. Re-contextualized Scripture settles the case as if God himself had spoken. Thus, authority is good argumentative strategy. Use of such texts are at variance with texts which authority must be argued or is perceived to be absent.

5. Degree of Claimed Inspirational and Scholarly Interpretation and Agreeable Modes of Interpretation (vv. 32, 37)

Interpretation might be scholarly or simple; it might be inspired or mundane. In our text, we do find a scholarly interpretation of the double commandment that is based on rules similar to *gezerah shavah*. In its purest sense, *gezerah shavah* says that a particular word-form, found only twice in the Old Testament, indicate that the two verses are combined in interpretation. The strict limitation to two verses is often not respected in practice. The occurrence of one particular word-form often leads to similar combinations of texts for the purpose of interpretation. The verb form for love (וְאָהַבְתָּ) in the double commandment is found only four times in the OT and in two contexts (Deut 6:5; 11:1; and Lev 19:18, 34). From Philo we know that the double commandment was not an innovation made by Jesus; it was probably a well-known interpretation of the Decalogue (Philo *Decal.* 106–110, cf. *T. Iss.* 5:2).[22] It is quite common in the New Testament, often associated with the second part of the Decalogue. Not only does Jesus speak of loving one's fellow citizen (Deut 6:5; Lev 19:18), in the story of the Good Samaritan, he includes love towards the foreigner (הַגֵּר), probably based on Lev 19:34.[23] This interpretation is innovative and particular for the Christians, and it was probably resented by devout Jews at the time of the Second Temple period, but it is based on *gezerah shavah*. Such scholarly interpretations do not draw their authority from Jesus as a person or on any particular prophetic insight. However, as far as we know, the first re-contextualization (i.e. Matt 22:32) is neither traditional nor scholarly but rests on the prophetic authority of the speaker, namely Jesus.

22. With reference to several Jewish texts, Gundry, *Matthew*, 449, claims the origin to be Christian. See further Davies and Allison, *Matthew* 3.237; Luz, *Matthäus* 3.281.

23. Luz, *Matthäus* 3.283.

6. Metalepsis (vv. 32–40)

Metalepsis concerns the resonance of the quotation in its original context. It is implied that not only the part of the text that is moved from the pretext (i.e., referenced text) is important, but that the remaining original context functions as harmonic or disharmonic tones in a chord. In Matt 22:32–40 the double commandment is called the greatest commandment, but additionally reference is made to "the law and the prophets," thus the text explicitly signals a relationship between these two texts and the rest of the Old Testament. Such a relationship with context is often implicit rather than explicit. When the double commandment is interpreted as Decalogue interpretation, then the term "love" is interpreted in the direction of particular actions rather than feelings, and the larger context of Deut 6:5 is clearly invoked (i.e., Deut 5:7 and the following verses).

7. Norms of Language (v. 32)

With reference to the Hebrew text, as it is repeated in the LXX and in Matt 22:32, there is a major difference between the Hebrew and the Greek text. In Greek, one may use nominal sentences, but they are less common than in Hebrew. There is no way of avoiding an interpretation if a nominal sentence is translated to Greek by use of the copula. The copula is bound to be set in a particular verb form indicating mode and time, in this case an indicative present active—"I am (ἐγώ εἰμι / אָנֹכִי) the God of . . ." (Exod 3:6). The copula is important in Jesus' interpretation of the text by use of indicative present active: "He is (ἔστιν) not God of the dead but of the living." Hebrew norms of language do not exclude this interpretation, but this interpretation is neither necessary nor the only possible interpretation. In this sense, the reinterpretation is more limited and particular than the original.

8. Meaning of Words and Their Cultural Setting (vv. 32, 37, 44)

In order to sort out this issue, one often consults a good lexicon or word study volume. However, it is important to note that this issue is the meeting point of the diachronic and synchronic perspective. The meaning of the New Testament usage is based on its own contemporary cultural context, which most certainly was a development from a former state of the same culture. The term "Lord," as used in Ps 110:1, is dependent on the common translation of both the *Tetragrammaton* and the Hebrew term אֲדֹנִי by the Greek term κύριος. The second instance of lord from Matt 22:44 is clearly perceived as viceroy of God the Father; however, the identity of this viceroy is difficult to pinpoint in the original.

Another similar issue is the meaning of the term "heart" (לֵבָב) that in Greek is translated καρδία and διάνοια, the first of which might be taken literally or metaphorically. The second term is a genuine metaphorical translation. The metaphorical interpretation is genuinely Jewish in character, but is used also in other Greek texts.

9. Sociological Dynamics Adding Meaning (vv. 31–32)

This text is used in a context of sociological conflict between three separate groups that each treated the others with contempt: the Sadducees, the Pharisees and the disciples of Christ, who represent the Christians. This makes the sociological makeup of the text complicated. This context is irrelevant for the Old Testament texts that are under discussion, as these conflicting views did not exist at the time the texts came into being.[24] The Sadducees' question about resurrection and the answer given by Jesus does not make much sense apart from sociological and theological differences between Sadducees and Pharisees.[25] The question is based on the Jewish custom of levirate marriage (Deut 25:5). Thus, a woman could survive seven spouses, all brothers, still being barren.[26] The question seems odd if this core value is unknown.

Behind the question lies the issue of resurrection, which the Pharisees believed in, but not the Sadducees. This issue is raised in the text: ". . . as for the resurrection of the dead . . ." (Matt 22:31). Jesus uses a particular text to counter the argument of the Sadducees: *"I am the God of Abraham, the God of Isaac, and the God of Jacob."* This sentence is found in one particular OT text—the incident of the burning bush (Exod 3:6, cf. 3:15, 16, 4:5), a text that contains the self-revelation of God and his name (Exod 3:14). In this context, and with the Pharisees as onlookers, Jesus' reference to Exod 3:6 certainly puts him in line with the Pharisees and in opposition to the Sadducees. It is no wonder that the Pharisees approach Jesus.

---

24. It must be admitted that this conclusion is dependent on the dating of the texts, but the division between Pharisees and Sadducees is anyway somewhat removed from the text of Psalm 110 and the Pentateuch, even if the latter should have been written in the early postexilic period. From an NT perspective, however, it is evident that writers like the author of Matthew took the historic information of the OT at face value, that is, in the perceived sense it had in Second Temple Judaism.

25. See Albright and Mann, *Matthew*, 274.

26. Hagner, *Matthew* 2.640, points to a similar story about seven husbands in Tobit 3:7–9; however, her marriage with them was not consummated as they died on the wedding night.

10. Interpretive Addition of Meaning (v. 32)

The sociological dynamic described above influences the reading of the text from Exodus. Exodus 3:6, as it is found in the MT or the LXX, does not focus on life after death, an element that is explicitly raised by Jesus: "He is God not of the dead, but of the living" (22:32). An apparently similar interpretation, but in a different sociological context, is found in 4 Maccabees 16:25: "They knew also that those who die for the sake of God live to God, as do Abraham and Isaac and Jacob and all the patriarchs" (cf. 7:19).[27] Jesus's interpretation is traditional, as the original text does not speak about life after death. Thus, "it is not immediately clear how Jesus' citation of Exod. 3:6 . . . concerns resurrection at all."[28] Trick suggests a rather complicated interpretation based on the annulment of covenants at the time of death (cf. marriage), which leads him to suggest that the patriarchs have gone through "a kind of preliminary death, a death sufficient to experience resurrection, yet not so complete as to annul the covenant."[29] However, other covenants were not annulled by death, as the ancient vassal treaties clearly show. The protection of the offspring, in the case of the high king's death, is a main issue in these covenants. In ancient Israel, land could be sold, but the seller and his offspring still had a claim to the land. In our text, focus is not on covenant, but on resurrection. For the Jesus of Matthew, there must be some logic that implies that God would not be the God of the dead. God would not interact with the dead, but only with the living. If the premise is that God is God only of the living, then calling him God of the fathers implies they are alive; and thus that there is a resurrection. In my opinion, the premise is not deduced from Exodus 3:6 or its close context. *If* God is the God of the living only (which is Jesus's proposition), *then* Exodus 3:6 implies that the patriarchs are living and thus have tasted resurrection.

11. Worldview (vv. 44–45)

When a text is moved from its setting in a particular cultural context with a particular worldview to another such context with a somewhat different worldview, changes happens even if the text does not change. This is most evident in the case of 22:41–45. The text includes a re-contextualization of Ps 110:1. Stendahl describes the interpretation of the Matthean Jesus as

---

27. Ibid. This text is possibly dated to the first century (19–54 CE). See Anderson "4 Maccabees," 533–34.

28. Trick, *Death*, 234.

29. Ibid., 255.

"*deduction ad absurdum.*"[30] The problem is whether the original meaning of the Hebrew text could possibly have implied a reference to Jesus. Here Stendahl's modern worldview kicks in. Such a view seems to ask a modern question: "DID THE NEW TESTAMENT WRITERS violate the intent of the author of Psalm 110 when they identified the undesignated ('my Lord') of Ps 110:1 (and hence the focus of the entire psalm) as the Messiah, that is, Jesus Christ?"[31] This is probably "a pre-exilic royal psalm" describing the king of Israel in a sort of triumphant ideal state of victory over all enemies. The Psalm ascribes itself to David, and coming from him, such statements of a victory clearly describes a royal victory of unprecedented glory at the time.

We should ask, however, how Psalm 110 was perceived in Second Temple Judaism. Apart from later sources, there is little evidence for its early Jewish interpretation. There might be indirect evidence in 11QMelchizedek, a text that somehow links Melchizedek to the Messiah (11QMelch 2:18). "Whether Melchizedek is the same as the 'herald' in this text is difficult to say because of the fragmentary state of the document."[32] However, one element in this Qumran text has to come from Psalm 110, the only Old Testament text apart from Gen 14:18 that speaks of Melchizedek: "While Genesis 14 made Melchizedek a priest (11QMelch 2:6-8), Psalm 110—and it alone in the Bible—can account for his other role as international judge (esp. 11QMelch 2:13)."[33] Despite the fractured nature of the text, we know that it is *pesher* and thus that it applies OT references to the here and now of the community doing the referencing.[34] The Qumran community and the early church shared the expectancy of a Messiah, a common idea in Second Temple Judaism.[35]

The main issue in the early Christian worldview was the notion that Jesus was the Christ. If the messianic interpretation of Psalm 110 was viable in Second Temple Judaism, then application of this text to Jesus was inevitable. The NT portrays Jesus and the apostles as the origin of this perception that subsequently gave name to the emerging *Christian* movement (Acts 11:24). This self-designation, which the NT says had its origin among the non-believers (Acts 11:25), is profound proof that the doctrine that Jesus

30. Stendahl, *School of St. Matthew*, 78.

31. Davis, "Psalm 110," 157.

32. Fitzmyer, "Melchizedek," 25–41.

33. Rainbow, "Melchizedek," 179–94.

34. On pesher interpretation, see further, Brooke, "Pesharim," 778–82.

35. Other similar messianic interpretations are shared between Rom 10:15 and 11Q13 2:15–16, both of which apply Isa 52:7 to the Messiah (Rom 10:17; 11Q13 2:18).

was the Christ was a core value. Thus, we agree with Keener: ". . . this passage supplies the working Christological sense of 'Lord' elsewhere in Matthew's Gospel."[36]

12. Isolation of Text from Context— the Chosen Part to Repeat (vv. 37)

The way in which the Matthean Jesus chooses Deut 6:5 for re-contextualization, avoiding the following paragraph, is significant for the message he wants to proclaim. It is the meaning of the text that is important, not the phylacteries in which the *Shema* is found. With contempt, Jesus says of his opponents in the text, "They do all their deeds to be seen by others; for they make their phylacteries broad and their fringes long" (Matt 23:5). The point Jesus is making, in this sense, is the opposite of the point made in the context of the *Shema*. The scribes could have responded to Jesus, "It is written in the Scripture: 'Bind them as a sign on your hand, fix them as an emblem on your forehead'" (Deut 6:8). By avoiding this part of the text, which has more practical issues tied to it, Jesus focuses on the idea behind the custom of phylacteries, namely the teaching found in the *Shema* of practicing love wholeheartedly.

13. Embedding of Text in a New Context (vv. 32, 37, 39)

When embedding is possible, it is implied that extraction of a text from another context has been performed (i.e., de-contextualization) and a re-contextualization is being done. When Jesus raises the issue of resurrection (v. 31) before quoting Exod 3:6, he performs a new reading of the text. The issue is external to the text that is re-contextualized, thus the literary context gives a new and changed meaning to the Old Testament text. The love commandments come forward as part of plain texts in the OT, but in Matthew, they are set after a question: "Which is the greatest commandment?" In addition, the double commandment is set before Jesus's statement that the whole Law and the Prophets depend on these two commandments. In this manner, Jesus's particular emphasis changes the dynamic between one part of the OT and the whole text. Each time embedding happens, the new context impacts multiple new meanings on the embedded text.

36. Keener, *Matthew*, 532.

14. Change of *Gattung* (v. 32, 37, 39, 44)

The text of Matthew is typical of the conflict dialogues in the Gospels, often consisting in intricate questions from Jesus' opponents and convincing responses by Jesus. Chosen texts from Scripture are used as proof-texts to convince the onlookers, if not also the opponents of Jesus. However, the OT texts that are used in this context are taken from a Psalm and from the books of Exodus, Leviticus, and Deuteronomy. The former is possibly from a liturgical context and the latter from contexts belonging to Decalogue interpretation, thus legalistic in nature. This use in Matthew indicates a change from the original *Gattung* or genre of the OT texts.

15. Cohesion in the Text (vv. 37, 44)

Even though the challenge to monotheism posed by Christology is not explicitly present in the text, it lurks behind the scene. Whenever part of the *Shema* is used, the phrase "the Lord is one" lurks in the background. In the messianic interpretation, Psalm 110 is clearly taken to speak of the relationship between the Lord (meaning God the Father) and the L/lord (meaning the Messiah of God), as the Messiah is put on the heavenly throne. The issue of Christology and the role of Jesus is often focused in the conflict dialogues, thus it represents at cohesive element in the text.

16. Motive for the Use of Intertextuality

The question remains why Matthew includes these instances of intertextuality in his story about Jesus. According to Boring, "The chief function of this passage is to present Jesus as victor in the hostile series of dispute . . ."[37] The forceful use of Scripture ends this dispute in this chapter. However, this external motive is probably not the only one. Use of Scripture in this passage also adds to the fundamental picture of Jesus as the Christ and his relationship to God and the Jewish community. Implicitly, the text discusses the relationship of Christ to God on one side and his human relationship to King David on the other side.

---

37. Boring, *Matthew*, 8.

17. Perceived Response from the Community
(vv. 15, 22, 29, 33–34, 45–46)

In this text, there are two explicit descriptions of the reaction of the community: "And when the crowd heard it, they were astounded at his teaching" (Matt 22:33). "No one was able to give him an answer, nor from that day did anyone dare to ask him any more questions" (Matt 22:46). Earlier in the text, we find a similar reaction (Matt 22:22). This describes the shattering effect of Jesus's answers, describing him as an able teacher who was able to silence his opponents by his use of Scripture and astute replies. However, behind this responsive attitude from the crowd, we find those who are *silenced* (Matt 22:34), *those who do not dare to ask*, those who " . . . plotted to entrap him in what he said" (Matt 22:15). The Pharisees were angry at his parables that they interpreted to their own disadvantage, a point that the author of the Gospel indirectly seems to agree with (Matt 21:45). The rhetorical effect of this imbalance between Jesus and one part of the narrative audience is that the Christians reading the Gospel of Matthew must have sensed that their interpretation of the OT, represented by Jesus, is advantageous when compared to Pharisees or Sadducees. This is explicitly stated in the case of the Sadducees: "You are wrong, because you know neither the Scriptures nor the power of God" (Matt 22:29). In the case of the Pharisees the judgment is not towards their theoretical interpretation of the Scripture, which at times seems to agree with those of Jesus (cf. Mark 12:28–34). Rather, Jesus condemns the Pharisees for not practicing what they teach (Matt 23). Jesus's interpretation of Scripture, as it is retold by Matthew, is set to reconfirm the group identity of the Christians, those who follow the superior teaching of Christ, a group that is superior in theory and practice.

18. Mixed Quotations (vv. 36, 38)

We have no pure chain quotations in the text; the closest is the combination of the two love commandments. The two parts are divided by two sub-clauses. Putting two clauses together from different contexts is an act of interpretation that doubles many of the other factors of re-contextualization, bringing yet another context into the discussion. Deuteronomy 6:5 and Leviticus 19:18, 34 are set in contexts that have been considered to be Decalogue interpretation.[38] We may thus conclude that the two contexts are

38. "More specifically, the Shema is a summary of what Israel heard commanded of them in the Prologue and the First and Second Commandments, the exclusive and total commitment of one's whole being to the Lord alone, the one who had been seen

related in a more profound manner than merely through the term love. One may of course say that the Decalogue has little relevance for the author of Matthew, at least in our text. However, it is significant that the question is for the *greatest commandment* (v. 36) and that the reply of Jesus is that this is the "*first* and greatest commandment" (v. 38). As the *Shema*, especially Deut 6:4–5, is often considered an interpretation of the *first* commandment, the *Ten Commandments* are not so far removed from our text as we may think.[39] In Matthew both text come forward as apodictic, even though this is less so in their original context, especially Leviticus.

19. Changed Actual Context from Referenced Text (Pretext) to Referencing Text (Phenotext), Physical and Historical Context (vv. 44–45)

The New Testament is set in the post-Maccabean period, after national freedom had been lost again, this time to the Romans. This laid the ground for a messianic hope that was vividly present in several of the Jewish sects—in Qumran as well as in later rabbinic sources, and of course among early Christians. At the time of Jesus's birth, the current ruler was not a Jew by birth, but an Idumean. In the Maccabean period, Idumea had been ruled by the Jews, and the people there had been forced to accept Judaism.

At the time of the NT, it is possible that Psalm 110 was indicative of messianic hope. It had been used to describe the priestly Maccabean ruler: "The Jews and their priests have resolved that Simon should be their leader and high priest forever, until a trustworthy prophet should arise" (1 Macc 14:41). The *eternal* ruler and *priest* might well be under influence of Psalm 110:4b (cf. v. 1).[40] The enemy of the people, the nations (Ps 110:5–6), is a general concept even though it must have been written in a particular historical context with a particular set of enemies in view. However, when the old enemies are gone and new and different ones appear, then the reading of Psalm 110 easily changes with the new political context. A messianic text read in the political realm of the Romans cannot avoid the backdrop of the

---

to be their God powerfully in the Exodus from Egypt." (Johnson, "Use of Leviticus," 234). "In some cases, one finds a summary or collection of other commandments, as in Leviticus 19:3–4, where the Fifth, Fourth, First, and Second Commandments are gathered together. Indeed, Leviticus 19 contains many of the commandments in some form or other" (235).

39. So Hagner, *Matthew*, 2.647

40. *Contra* Gnilka, *Matthäusevangelium*, 265–6, who holds the messianic interpretation of Psalm 110 to be a Christian innovation.

current political conflict, especially for a psalm with such a general message about the enemy peoples and their kings.

20. Application of the Text to the Here and Now
(vv. 37–38, 44–45)

Such application may be divided into two different categories. First, we have the prophetic application of an OT text on the actual situation in question. Secondly, we have the application of certain norms and regulations on the present community. The best example of a prophetic application on the here and now in our text is Jesus's application of Ps 110:1 on the Messiah, which in the Gospel is implicit of Jesus himself. However, our text does not say so explicitly. The question of the greatest commandment in the Law leads to an application of an OT text to the here and now, but then within the realm of practical ethics. Jesus seems to use this kind of love language to lay greater emphasis on the intention behind an ethical act that is on the "heart," "soul" and "mind," of the inner being.

21. Patterns of Association Attached to the Text
by the Actual Audience (vv. 37–38)

As one part of a text might summon the whole text or a larger part of it forming metalepsis, a fraction of a text might summon a set of ideas that are common in the author's contemporary culture.[41] It seems probable that any reading of the *Shema* would imply several concepts in Second Temple Judaism, such as the Decalogue and monotheism. In this setting, any speech that focuses on "loving God wholeheartedly" would imply monotheism as its context. In the early Christian movement, the issue of monotheism and Christology is related and sometimes treated together, often with the invocation of language from the *Shema* (cf. 1 Cor 8:1–6).[42] In this aspect our text, with its inclusion of *Shema* language and Christology enters into a pattern that is culturally conditioned.

41. Carter, *Evoking Isaiah*, 503–20.
42. Waaler, *Shema*, 253.

22. Pattern Association Connected to the Phenotext

It has been suggested that the larger structure of Matthew is divided into five sections based on the structure of the Pentateuch.[43] Such structural patterning is more vivid in so-called rewritten Scripture. If proven true, this views the writing of the text from a different perspective, as it is modelled on "Scripture" and thus has a function that mirrors that of Scripture. Ellens has suggested that the story of John's Gospel is based on the Ezekiel story and the ordination ritual described in Leviticus 8–9.[44] Such structural patterns might influence interpretation of the Old Testament.

23. Focalization (vv. 44–45)

Reuse of text is also subject to Gérard Genette's three perspectives of focalization, "zero focalization providing the narrator with unrestricted access to information, internal focalization restricting the narrator's access to information provided by one or several focal characters, and external focalization restricting the narrator's access to the external information available to an uninvolved bystander."[45] The use of Psalm 110 seems to come close to zero focalization, as the author of Matthew knows about issues that apparently were unknown to David as the author, as well as to his audience. An example of this is its application to the Messiah, in this case, to Jesus.

24. Finality of the Text (v. 44–45)

In the age of printing, the text is final and all copies of a book are identical, at least in one edition. This was not the case with first-century handwritten copies of the Old Testament, as is well documented from the Qumran texts, where different versions of a text and even rewritten scripture is plentiful. Naturally, the *Vorlage* of the New Testament re-contextualizations are not directly available to us.

A translation might influence our reading of the original, especially if it is read in advance of the original. In the case of the *Tetragrammaton*, it appears that the reading of the Hebrew text influenced the translation. When the Hebrew text has YHWH, the Jews at the time read *Lord* or *God* or *the Name*, avoiding pronunciation of the name of God. This is probably

43. Beaton, *Matthew*, 116–34, with reference to Bacon.
44. Ellens, *Second Temple Texts*, 131–49.
45. Horstkotte and Pedri, "Focalization," 330–57.

an interpretation of one of the Ten Commandments: "You shall not make wrongful use of the name of the LORD your God, for the LORD will not acquit anyone who misuses his name" (Deut 5:11). In Second Temple Judaism, it seems common to set a fence around the Law. In order to keep this commandment, the Jews avoided any use of the name of God outside the Temple. This custom is known from this period, and it may be suggested at the time when the Elohim Psalms came into existence, psalms characterized by the use of the Hebrew word *Elohim* for God rather than YHWH. The existence of these psalms might indicate that a shift happened at some point in history, and that the original psalms used the name of the LORD (YHWH) more freely.

25. Narrative or Argumentative Patterns in the Book (vv. 15–45 and beyond)

The narrative plot in our text is rather complicated. To begin with, it is the opponents of Jesus that take the initiative, first the Pharisees (vv. 15–22), then the Sadducees (vv. 23–33), and then again the Pharisees (vv. 34–40). In the end, however, Jesus takes the initiative (vv. 41–45). All through this Gospel, however, the general argumentative pattern is that Jesus's re-contextualizations are treated with respect, as if coming from an authority. Thus, consent to his interpretations are expected from the reader, and so also in our text. This general pattern is slowly created throughout the Gospel. Such narrative and argumentative patterns influence the reading of Matthew's re-contextualizations.

26. Continuity within Change (vv. 44–45)

We maintain that change and continuity works on various scales. Thus, a fair amount of change and a fair amount of continuity might be found at the same time. Actually, both change and continuity might be highly present at the same time. Psalm 110:1 uses the term "Lord" twice, first with reference to God in line with the use of the Tetragrammaton in the Hebrew text, which is something that is not always the case in the New Testament.[46] In its original setting, it is probable the second "lord" was used about David or the following kings of Judah. However, the messianic reading of this psalm invites a particularity that applies the term "lord" to the current contender to the title "Christ," in this case Jesus. This is implicit in the text, but prob-

---

46. See Capes, *Yahweh Texts.*

ably evident for the early church. Even if this is a possible reading of the OT text, it is not the only possible reading and thus more limited than the text itself. In this manner, continuity and change work together in our text. It is notable that most of the different perspectives that we have discussed might end up in the category of continuity or change, and that some categories will testify to continuity and change at the same time, namely in different parts of the same text.

27. Humor, Irony and So On . . . (vv. 31–32, 44–45)

Deep knowledge of the actual culture is needed in order to understand irony and humor.[47] Two of the re-contextualizations are clearly polemical in form and conclusion. Both may be constructed as statements drawn from Scripture and interpreted by a negative statement (v. 32) or a rhetorical question (v. 45) immediately following the re-contextualization. The reaction implies that the rhetorical effect was a *silenced* opposition (ἐφίμωσεν Matt 22:34; cf. 22:46). This speaks for a profound and shattering rhetorical effect. I think part of this rhetorical impact was due to the irony of the apparent question that might be reformulated: "Is God the God of the dead?" Irony influences interpretation, in this case by pushing a new perspective on the text, a perspective Jesus's audience apparently did not see coming. An Abraham that is alive in the after-life is a common element in the teaching of Jesus (Matt 8:11; cf. Luke 13:28; 16:22–31).

Similarly, the Pharisees gave Jesus a simple answer to a straightforward question, and they were cornered by a rhetorical question that had some kind of ironic power, implying an elevated status for the Messiah, more so than David himself (22:41–45). By the rhetorical question that precedes the text-reading, Jesus forces the audience to read Psalm 110 in a messianic manner.[48] The polemical perspective is situated in the then current situation, the conflict between Jesus and his Jewish opponents. This perspective is not lifted from the OT texts; they are foreign to these text. However, they are deeply rooted in the worldview of Jesus and his followers.

28. The Modern Angle

The modern angle on the text sometime imports readings that are dependent neither on the culture of the Old Testament nor the culture of the New

---

47. So Leithart, *Deep Exegesis.*
48. Cf. Luz, *Matthäus* 3.287.

Testament. This third angle is the modern perspective that imports readings into the combined text that are modern rather than textual interpretation. We cannot read the term "grace" without being influenced by Luther's biblical interpretation. The modern concept of love is difficult to describe, but it is possible to focus on some sort of positive and graceful feeling, rather than law observance and covenantal prophetic statements coming to pass (the reality of any kind of prophecy is often downplayed or denied by the modern mind). We read the NT with knowledge of the totality of its interpretation of the OT, whereas the NT writers wrote from a different perspective. We might even read the NT "quotations" as if they abide by our scientific standards, but they are set in a different culture with different rules for the engagement with pretexts. Post-knowledge and lost-knowledge—everything that has happened after the text was written that we have access to, and everything that was known to them that we have no access to—tends to distort the message for us.

Conclusion

The discussion above shows that there are multiple factors at work when Matthew's Jesus uses Scripture in dialogue. Some factors such as Christology is so inherent to our thinking that we do not immediately recognize the change that happens when Old Testament texts are applied to Jesus within an emerging Christocentric worldview. Other factors, such as our perception of what a quotation is like, are well known and sparsely commented on, leading to fundamental misunderstandings and misrepresentations of such re-contextualizations. One of the main focuses that needs to be dealt with in intertextuality is the issue of the reading of the earlier text (e.g., pretext) within the context of the text referencing it (phenotext), including the traditional way of reusing the OT texts that was present in that particular culture.

The multiple factors described above contributes to the change of meaning, changes that are bound to happen when a text is applied to a new situation and cultural context. This does not mean that analogy is not happening nor that continuity is not present. What we have seen is that some factors move in the same direction, adding emphasis, and in this case on Christology. Such interaction between various verses from the OT and various modes of interpretation makes the issue of re-contextualisation and re-interpretation more complex. In my opinion, a reused text is never totally stable but always carries added meaning. If that was not the intent, there would be no need to create a new text including the old one. At the same time, there is no point in invoking Scripture for authority if some sort of continuity is not implied. In Second Temple Judaism there was no Davidic king, thus for an application to the here and now, the only sensible application would be messianic. The Messiah to come was the new Davidic king. In order to describe this the authors of the New Testament used contemporary literary devices. They show no awareness of higher criticism, nor any other modern way of perceiving the text; rather, their mode of interpretation was inherited from their contemporary cultural context.

Recommended Reading

Barr, James. *The Semantics of Biblical Language.* Reprint. Eugene: Wipf and Stock, 2004.

Beale, G. K. *Handbook on the New Testament Use of the Old Testament: Exegesis and Interpretation.* Grand Rapids: Baker Academic, 2012.

Leithart, Peter J. *Deep Exegesis: The Mystery of Reading Scripture.* Waco: Baylor University Press, 2009.

Linell, Per. *Approaching Dialogue: Talk, Interaction and Contexts in Dialogical Perspective.* Amsterdam: John Benjamins, 1998.

Phillips, Gregory Y., Fika Janse van Rensburg, and Herrie F. Van Rooy. "Developing an Integrated Approach to Interpret New Testament Use of the Old Testament." *In die Skriflig* 46, (2012) 1–10.

Porter, Stanley E. "The Use of the Old Testament in the New Testament: A Brief Comment on Method and Terminology." In *Early Christian Interpretation of the Scriptures of Israel: Investigations and Proposals*, edited by Craig A. Evans and James A. Sanders, 79–96. Sheffield: Sheffield Academic, 1997.

16

Reference-Text-Oriented Allusions

Korinna Zamfir and Joseph Verheyden

This chapter uses the intertextual method developed by Annette Merz, biblical scholar and theologian from the University of Utrecht, in her analysis of the Pastoral Epistles as a fictitious self-exposition of Paul.[1] Her approach draws from Julia Kristeva, who has coined the notion of intertextuality and has argued that texts have a dialogical character—they are by definition a mosaic, an absorption and a transformation of other texts.[2] Intertextual references to earlier texts produce an increasing complexity in meaning.[3] These references or allusions "constitute, enhance and colour the meaning."[4] The meaning of a given text is determined by its intratextual position (the literary context), by the situational context, and, more importantly, by its intertextual relationships. Merz departs from purely reader-oriented approaches, which use intertextuality to "de-centre" the text and deconstruct the author asserting that the intertextual interpretation needs to take into account the communicative triad of the author, the text, and the recipients.[5] This perspective should be upheld notably for texts

1. Merz, "Fictitious Self-exposition," 113–32; ibid., *Fiktive Selbstauslegung*, 1–71.

2. Kristeva, *Révolution*, 59–60; ibid., *Sèméiôtikè*, 84–85; Merz, *Fiktive Selbstauslegung*, 1–2, 17, 36–37.

3. Merz, *Fiktive Selbstauslegung*, 3, 35–36 (though she also refers to intertextuality as a generic term for all the relationships between texts: 5).

4. Merz, "Fictitious Self-exposition," 116.

5. Merz, *Fiktive Selbstauslegung*, 27. Kristeva, *Sèméiôtikè*, 84–85, argued that studying the text means defining the three dimensions of the textual space: the subject of the writing, the addressee, and the external texts. These elements participate in the dialogue.

with a pragmatic function that aim to achieve a particular goal and compel the interpreter to take into account the question of author and authorial intention.[6] This is clearly the case with the Pastoral letters—1–2 Timothy and Titus—which have gained their authority and have had an impressive, effective history because of their purported author and their inclusion in the Pauline corpus. The intertextual reading of the Pastoral letters requires a distinction between "Paul" as the implied author and the empirical or real author, and between fictitious addressees ("Timothy" and "Titus") and intended readers.[7] We will first explicate Merz's intertextual approach and then examine the Pastoral Epistles (henceforth, PE).[8]

The Intertextual Reading of Annette Merz

According to Merz, intertextuality may be latent (unintended) or intended.[9] The latter aspect is more significant. In this case the author deliberately uses earlier texts, either marked by quotation formulae, or unmarked, to create and enhance meaning. In an ideal situation the readers will have the knowledge that is needed to recognise these references. A special case of intended intertextuality is that of veiled intertextuality. This implies that, for various reasons, the author conceals from the readers the references to other texts.[10] Perhaps the most obvious and extreme form of veiled intertextuality is plagiarism. But there are also other ways of using unnamed sources. For the New Testament one might refer to Matthew's and Luke's use of Mark. A special case is that of literary forgeries, which may contain both open and veiled references. In the PE intended intertextuality, partly open and partly veiled, creates the impression of authenticity.[11] Although this is not an issue directly related to intertextuality, it should be noted that Merz rejects the idea of open pseudepigraphy, as is sometimes claimed for the PE,[12] but

---

6. Merz, *Fiktive Selbstauslegung*, 31–33. This is where she differs from Julia Kristeva.

7. Ibid., 27.

8. On the PE as a corpus, see Roloff, *1 Timotheus*, 43–45; Ehrman, *Forgery*, 192–217; Marshall, "Crete," 784. The corpus-hypothesis is challenged by Johnson, *Letters*, 63–64, 98–99; Towner, *Letters*, 88–89.

9. Ibid., 29–35.

10. Ibid., 34–35.

11. Merz, "Fictitious Self-exposition," 122.

12. The possibility of deliberate deception is often rejected on theological and/ or moral grounds: cf. Meade, *Pseudonymity*, 2; Porter, "Pauline Authorship," 105–23. Those who admit pseudepigraphy explain it with the need to preserve and adapt the apostolic teaching to new contexts: e.g., Pokorný, "Problem," 122. Others regard the PE

rather regards them as literary forgeries written with the aim of being taken for authentic letters of Paul.[13]

Intertextuality can take the form of textual references.[14] This form takes up more or less explicitly a *pre-text*, also known as the reference-text (citation, allusion, echo). Textual references may be quotations or allusions to particular texts, references to titles of earlier writings, or allusions to names or places.[15] *Onomastic references* re-use biblical characters, for example, Adam and Eve in 1 Timothy, or personalities known to the community, such as Paul, Timothy, Titus. These allusions have a low degree of specificity, but are important because they contribute to the creation of the fictitious world of the text. Moreover, they evoke not only specific texts, but larger textual corpora or traditions associated with these persons.[16]

In terms of function, Merz distinguishes between two types of intertextual references, as instruments of relecture, of creating and enhancing meaning—*text-oriented allusions* and *reference-text-oriented allusions*.[17] A text-oriented allusion is mainly used to consolidate the authority of the new text and/or to underscore its message and position. Reference-text-oriented allusions are typical for pseudonymous writings, more specifically for literary forgeries. This latter form is meant to reinterpret the pre-text by a one-sided emphasis on elements in the original text, by its interpretation, or by corrections of "misinterpretations" and even "retractions." Reference-text-oriented allusions change the meaning of the primary text.

---

as instances of school pseudepigraphy with no intention to deceive (i.e., open pseudepigraphy): e.g., Herzer, "Fiktion," 521–23, 533–36.

13. See Merz, *Fiktive Selbstauslegung*, 221, 224, 383–84; also Donelson, *Pseudepigraphy*, 22, 24, 55, *passim*; Frenschkowski, "Pseudepigraphie," 251, 262; Marshall, "Crete," 781–803. Forgery implies that the real author is not the same as the purported author, and pseudonymity is not used for literary purposes but with the intention to deceive in order to promote certain ideas (Speyer, *Fälschung*, 13; Ehrman, *Forgery*, 128–32). Baum, *Pseudepigraphie*, 81–93, 131, shows that forgeries were not accepted in early Christianity except in cases where the content could be linked to the purported author, notably when the apostle authorized the real author to write a letter. If Paul did not authorize the writing of the PE, according to ancient standards, then these were forgeries. On persona information as an instrument of pseudepigraphy, see Brox, "Notizen," 272–94; Donelson, *Pseudepigraphy*, 24–29.

14. Merz, *Fiktive Selbstauslegung*, 22, 25–26. This she calls "Einzeltextreferenz."; "Systemreferenz" refers to other forms of intertextuality: references to linguistic codes, discourse types, or literary genres.

15. Merz, 22–25, speaks of "allusive Intertextualität," "titulare Intertextualität," and "onomastische Intertextualität,."

16. Ibid., 23.

17. Ibid., 57–60.

The PE use both types of intertextual references. Text-oriented allusions to genuine Pauline letters and other traditions confer Pauline authority to pseudepigraphic texts.[18] The reference-text-oriented allusions are by far a more important and less analyzed form of intertextuality. These references produce a fictitious self-exposition and interpretation ("*Selbstauslegung*") of "Paul" by means of pretended self-references to information found in the authentic letters. In doing so, they reinterpret the genuine epistles, most often in a restrictive way, and eliminate other possible interpretations. Fictitious self-references influence decisively the interpretation of the authentic letters of Paul, even to the point of modifying their original meaning.[19] As pseudonymous writings that aim to close and reinterpret the Pauline corpus after its first edition, the PE display both elements of continuity and discontinuity with the authentic letters of Paul.[20] They are therefore from the very beginning conceived as an intertextual enterprise—they deliberately take up certain Pauline themes, but also keep an independent profile and wish to defend one interpretation of Paul against competing readings.[21] They become Paul's final words to readers of all times and the interpretative lens through which his genuine letters will be read.[22]

By way of illustration, this intertextual approach will be applied to 2 Tim 4:1–8 showing the links between this passage and Phil 1:23–24, 30; 2:16–17, 19–24.

Reading 2 Timothy Intertextually

The Pastoral letters are concerned with preserving sound doctrine when it was apparently being challenged by certain unnamed opponents. This is said to be the task of the leaders of the community who can claim to stand in continuity with Paul.[23] From this perspective 2 Timothy can be read as a fictitious theological testament of the apostle in epistolary form.[24]

18. We use forgery not as something different from pseudepigraphy, but pseudepigraphy is the broader term that comprises forgery—forgery is one specific form of pseudepigraphy. On the two, see further, footnote 13 above.

19. Merz, "Fictitious Self-exposition," 126–27.

20. Merz, *Fiktive Selbstauslegung*, 201–13, 220

21. Ibid., 221–43.

22. Ibid., 239.

23. Donelson, *Pseudepigraphy*, 127–28, 142–43, 151; Oberlinner, "Paulus," 173, 176–77.

24. E.g., Collins, *Commentary*, 7, 181–5; Marshall, *Pastoral Epistles*, 797; Wolter, *Pastoralbriefe*, 222–41. *Pace* Smith, *Timothy's Task*, 3, 73–97, 147. For the objections to his argument, see Zamfir, Review, 190–94.

It closes the Pastoral corpus and, eventually, the Pauline corpus.[25] Second Timothy 4 is an intertextual composition that integrates elements from the undisputed letters of Paul, particularly from Philippians and 1 Corinthians.[26] The intertextual references to the authentic letters are aimed at making 2 Timothy look like a "real" letter of Paul. More importantly, the author creates the figure of Timothy as the ideal disciple of Paul and the guardian of the deposit of faith received from the apostle. "Paul" gives his last instructions before his death to his faithful collaborator, who will have to appoint reliable leaders (2:2). The readers will know that in Paul's absence after his death, these officials will continue his mission and lead the community. In this strategy, 2 Tim 4, as the spiritual testament of Paul, plays a decisive role. An intertextual reading of 4:1–8, especially vv. 6–7, shows that the author takes up motifs from Philippians to create the image of the apostle who faces death and hands over his mission to Timothy, the type of the ideal community leader.

The Context, Plot, and Message of 2 Timothy 4:1–8

In 2 Timothy the polemic against the opponents (2:16–18, 24–25; 3:1–9, 13; 4:3–4) alternates with exhortations to Timothy to follow Paul's example, rebuke the false teachers, keep the deposit, and teach the doctrine that has been entrusted to him (1:13–14; 2:2, 14–15; 3:14–15; 4:1–2). The letter is pervaded by a sense of urgency and gravity, underscored by repeated references to time and to exemplary figures and attitudes from the past. Paul exhorts Timothy to steadfastness, to relentless preaching, and readiness to suffer, after the model of the apostle. Several motifs are typical for the testament genre.[27] The reader feels that a turning point has been reached.

Time (καιρός, ἡμέρα) has mostly dramatic connotations. In the last days, believers face terrible times—people will reject sound doctrine and turn to false teachers (3:1–9, 4:3–4; cf. 1 Tim 4:1–4). That is why Timothy is expected to proclaim the word in season and out of season. "Paul" refers several times to *that day*, the day of judgement, when the Lord will reward his faithful servants (1:12; 1:18; 4:8). This is also the day of Christ's coming and a new epiphany, when his rule (βασιλεία) will be manifested (see

---

25. Wolter, *Pastoralbriefe*, 240–41; Puskas, *Letters*, 193.

26. Weiser, *2 Timotheus*, 298, 304, 306–8.

27. These motifs include references to evil times, remembering, evoking the past, looking at the life of exemplary figures, foretelling unfortunate events, calling upon close relations to join the dying hero, and exhortations. See Weiser, *2 Timotheus*, 36, 38–40, 298.

4:1; also 2 Thess 1:10).[28] For Paul, the day of his encounter with Christ the judge coincides with the time of his approaching death (4:6–8). Under these circumstances, the true disciples should hastily gather around Paul (1:17; 4:9, 21).

Timothy is the spiritual child, model disciple, trusted co-worker and follower of Paul (1:2, 13; 2:1; 3:10, 14). As Paul's continuator and teacher of the sound doctrine, Timothy has to be ready to share in Paul's suffering (1:8; 2:3; 3:11, 14; 4:5). Paul and Timothy's ministry, full of hardship, is described with military and athletic metaphors (2 Tim 2:3–5; 4:7).[29] The theme of perseverance while suffering for the faith, up to the point of martyrdom, runs through the letter. Paul is imprisoned for his faith, for the gospel, and for his mission (1:8, 11–13; 2:3, 9–10). He has been persecuted in Antioch, Iconium, and Lystra, and is now in chains in Rome (3:11). He is the suffering righteous and assailed by enemies (4:14). He is also deserted by friends. All have abandoned him including those in Asia, notably Phygelus and Hermogenes (1:15), just as have most of his co-workers. Demas deserted him out of love for this world (4:10).[30] Crescens and Titus have also left for some unspecified reason.[31] No one stood by Paul at his first defence (4:16).

This is the context of Paul's final address to Timothy, whom he summons to preach the word. Timothy has to be vigilant and ready to suffer, and he has to do the work of the evangelist, precisely because Paul will soon face death.

Paul's Departure and Legacy

The summary of Paul's spiritual testament is in 2 Tim 4:1–8. He is imprisoned, facing impending death, and passes on his final exhortations to Timothy. The apostle conjures him to proclaim the word (4:1–2).[32] His

---

28. Collins, *Commentary*, 202–3. The PE do not use *parousia* (παρουσία), but speak of the immediacy of Christ's coming to judge (2 Tim 4:1) and his new and final manifestation (ἐπιφάνεια, 2 Tim 4:1, 8; also 1 Tim 6:14; Tit 2:13); ἐπιφάνεια is both the initial manifestation of God's grace and saving will in Christ in his incarnation, death, and resurrection (2 Tim 1:10; compare φανερόω in 1 Tim 3:16), and the final manifestation of Christ as judge.

29. Marshall, *Pastoral Epistles*, 807; Seesengood, "Contending," 87–118.

30. This solitude is at odds with what is said about Christians sending greetings to Timothy (4:21).

31. Marshall, *Pastoral Epistles*, 816, assumes a missionary task.

32. Against a number of English translations, "I charge you" is not the best translation of διαμαρτύρομαι in this context. French and German ecumenical translations are probably closer to the intention of the text when translating with (an equivalent of)

faithful disciple has to follow his example in spite of expected suffering and opposition, and he must defend sound doctrine against the threats posed by heterodox teachers and their followers. Timothy is expected to rebuke and censure the false teachers and their adherents, and to exhort and encourage the believers. The topic is not that Timothy is commissioned for the first time to do something, but that he has to fulfil this mission with determination, notwithstanding the inopportune circumstances and the adversities he will have to face. The summoning is particularly solemn and is framed with eschatological words.[33] Paul conjures Timothy in the presence of God and Christ, the coming judge of the living and the dead, on behalf of Christ's manifestation (ἐπιφάνεια) and kingdom. Attention is directed toward eschatological judgement and the manifestation of divine power. Timothy is responsible before God and Christ.[34] He should hasten to come to Paul (v.9). His character sets him on the side of Paul and of the truth. His expected travel to join Paul is contrasted with the departure of Demas.

The context contains both onomastic and textual allusions. Onomastic allusions to Paul and Timothy evoke known details about their life and mission without explicitly mentioning any of these. The references to Demas and Luke are onomastic allusions to Philemon 24 (also taken up by Col 4:14). There are several other such allusions in 4:10–12, 19–21. They recall the missionary commitment of Paul and his co-workers, notably Timothy and Luke. Paul is concerned with the success of the gospel even at the time of his impending death, but this success depends on finding reliable helpers to continue the work. This is also stressed through a negative example— the case of Demas shows how easily some of these have abandoned Paul in difficult times. The passage functions mainly as a reference-text-oriented allusion, a fictitious self-reference which takes up the situation envisaged in Philippians and modifies the pre-text. At the same time, it works as a self-text-reference enhancing the authority of 2 Timothy.

The Pre-text of Philippians 1:21–25, 30; 2:16–24

In Philippians Paul is bound and imprisoned (Phil 1:7, 13–14, 17). The place of his detainment is debated, but Rome has good arguments for it.[35] The defence mentioned in 1:7 may refer to a court hearing, and a final decision

---

"conjure." See also LSJ *ad loc*; Weiser, *2 Timotheus*, 267, 298.

33. See Collins, *Commentary*, 265–66.

34. Weiser, *2 Timotheus*, 298.

35. For an overview: O'Brien, *Philippians*, 19–26; Silva, *Philippians*, 3–7.

is still ahead (2:23).[36] Paul thinks that his situation has advanced the cause of the gospel (1:12–18). He faces oppositions with some teaching the gospel out of jealousy, rivalry and ambition (1:15, 17). The outcome of Paul's trial is uncertain. The trial may either lead to his release or to his condemnation and death. Although Paul has some confidence that he will be able to continue to minister the gospel to the community (1:25), he also several times refers to the possibility of an imminent death (1:20–21, 23; 2:17–18). The meaning of σωτηρία (1:19) is ambiguous—it may refer to a rescue, to eschatological salvation, or to the ability to be a bold witness of Christ before the Roman court.[37] Given this uncertain future, Paul regards both life, which would allow for the ministry to go on, and death, which would unite him with Christ, as equally desirable alternatives (1:21–24). Dying is described euphemistically with ἀναλύω (depart, 1:23). The verb literally means "to unloose" and thereby release, but it may also refer to departure from life.[38] There can be no doubt that in this context the verb refers to the possibility of his death (cf. 1:21).[39]

The course of this life full of suffering is metaphorically described as an ἀγών (an athletic contest) and a race that may soon come to its completion (2:16; cf. 1:30; 3:12–14). The faithfulness of the Philippians to the word will be a source of pride for Paul on the day of judgement, attesting that his mission was not "run" in vain.

The possibility of his impending death is described in terms of an offering.[40] His life may be "poured out" as a libation (σπένδομαι 2:17),[41] accompanying the sacrifice and ministry of the Philippians' faith.[42] In the LXX, σπένδω commonly refers to pouring out a drink offering both in Jewish and non-Jewish contexts.[43] The cultic-sacrificial background is obvious. In the NT the verb occurs only twice, in Phil 2:17 and 2 Tim 4:6. The reference to death in these passages is supported by cases when σπένδω is used in connection with death, or metaphorically for dying.[44] Other texts associate

36. Schnelle, *Einleitung*, 153.

37. Hellerman, *Philippians*, 58–59.

38. On the former, LSJ *ad loc*; the latter, e.g., *Pythagorean sentences* 68a; Philo, *Flacc.* 187; Clement, *Strom.* 3.9.65; cf. Spicq, *Épîtres* II.804; Weiser, *2 Timotheus*, 305.

39. O'Brien, *Philippians*, 129–30; Hellerman, *Philippians*, 69.

40. Weiser, *2 Timotheus*, 305; Hellerman, *Philippians*, 139–41.

41. For this meaning of *spendomai*, see e.g., O'Brien, *Philippians*, 305–6.

42. Merkel, *Pastoralbriefe*, 81: The faith of the Philippians is a spiritual sacrifice offered to God, and Paul's death is in a sense a drink offering accompanying this sacrifice.

43. E.g., Gen 35:14; Exod 25:29; Num 4:7; Hos 9:4; (non-Jewish): Jer 7:18; 51:17, 19, 25; Ezek 20:28.

44. Because libations involved the pouring out of other liquids rather than blood,

the verb with pouring out blood.[45] Metaphorically, σπένδω may refer to a dedicated ministry or a life consecrated to God, but the metaphor is based on the association between libation and blood.[46] In some sources σπένδω refers metaphorically to dying due to the association between the libation of wine (the juice of crushed grapes) and death.[47] Historical and literary sources may openly describe the voluntary death of a person as a libation.[48] These examples show that σπένδω could be used as a metaphor for death.

The metaphorical use of σπένδω in Phil 2:17 and 2 Tim 4:6 for Paul's death is confirmed by early Christian interpretations of these passages and by Christian lexicographers.[49] The repeated references in the context of Phil 2:17 to Paul's death show that he does not merely speak of his dedicated ministry of the gospel. He is clearly envisaging death as a real possibility, though not as a certainty, as indicated by the conjunction εἰ ("if").

Since he may as well be rescued, Paul hopes that he will stay in touch with the community in Philippi in the near future. He will send Timothy, his child and trusted co-worker (2:19–23). Upon his return, Timothy will provide Paul with news from the beloved community. Paul also hopes that he will be able to visit them in the near future (2:24). He will also send Epaphroditus, his other devoted co-worker (2:25–30; 4:18).

---

it has been argued that the expression does not necessarily refer to Paul's death, but to his committed life: e.g., Prior, *Paul*, 92–93. Yet the metaphorical use is clear from the examples referenced here, and Marshall, *Pastoral Epistles*, 806 rightly notes that Prior confuses the literal meaning of the verb and its metaphorical application.

45. 2 Sam 23:13–17; cf. 1 Chron 11:18; 4 Macc 3:14–16. There is a strong connection between the pouring of the libation and the potential death of the warriors: the water is poured out as a libation to God because it is seen as a symbol of the men risking their life (their blood); *Pace* Prior, *Paul*, 93; Smith, *Timothy's Task*, 104–5.

46. LXX Sir 50:15; Philo, *Vit. Mos.* 2.150; *Quis rer. div.* 183.

47. Dionysus is poured out as a libation (σπένδεται) to the gods to the benefit of humans (Euripides *Bacc.* 284–85). Teiresias implicitly associates here wine, the juice of the vine, with the blood of Dionysus. Plutarch claims that in earlier times Egyptians did not drink or offer libations of wine, as they regarded wine as the blood of those who had once fought against the gods (*De Is. et Osir.* 353b).

48. Tacitus, *Ann* 16.35; Dio Cassius 62.26.4 is more explicit: "To thee, Jupiter, Patron of Freedom, I pour this libation of blood" (LCL, tr. E. Cary). See further examples in Michel, *TDNT* 7.530–36; Spicq, *Epîtres* II, 804; Quinn, Wacker, *Letter*, 785.

49. E.g., John Chrysostom, *De laudibus sancti Pauli apostoli* 1.3.15(PG 50, 474); *Hom. Rom.*, Argument, PG 60, 393.9, Ioannes Damascenus, PG 95, 868.46–51; Severianus, *Fragmenta in epistulam ii ad Timotheum (in catenis)*, 344.12. All examples from a TLG search, December 12, 2014. See also Ignatius *Rom* 2.2; Marshall, *Pastoral Epistles*, 806. For lexicographers, Photius, *Lexicon*, 530 *l.* 7; the *Suda*, 920, *l.* 1; [Zonaras], *Lexicon*, 1666, l. 24, s.v. σπένδομαι (TLG search, December 12, 2014).

2 Timothy 4:6–8 as a Fictitious Self-Reference
to Philippians 1:21–25, 30; 2:16–24

In 2 Timothy, just as in Philippians, Paul is a prisoner bound and in chains (2 Tim 1:8, 16; 2:9). But the situation has changed in a number of ways. This time Timothy is not with the imprisoned apostle, but is expected to join him. He is not the co-sender of a letter, but the recipient of Paul's exhortations. Most importantly, Paul is now certain that he is going to die. The similarities suggest that 2 Tim 4:6 is a reference-text-oriented allusion to Phil 2:17. The εἰ ("if") of Philippians has become ἤδη ("now," "already"). The adverb functions here as an indicator that the event foretold is soon coming to completion (ἤδη σπένδομαι), stressing the imminence of Paul's death, his "being poured out."[50]

A further reference in 4:6 points to the same—the time of his departure (ἀνάλυσις) is at hand. This ἀνάλυσις refers back to Phil 1:23.[51] Yet, the allusion modifies the pre-text in Philippians. There Paul desires to depart ("τὸ ἀναλῦσαι . . .") to be with Christ, but he immediately asserts that in spite of his personal longing for Christ there is a greater need to remain in the flesh (to live in this world) for the benefit of advancing the believers' faith (1:24–25). Paul still seems rather confident that eventually he will be released from prison. Second Timothy 4:6 picks up on Phil 1:23 and 2:17,[52] but leaves no hope anymore for such an outcome—Paul knows that his death is imminent, and so does the reader. At this point 2 Timothy substantially modifies the pre-text making it clear that Paul is soon to die. It lends particular weight and gravity to Paul's exhortations in this letter and to his commission of Timothy. They sum up the last will of the apostle facing martyrdom.[53]

A third allusion to Philippians is contained in 2 Tim 4:7–8, which takes up the theme of Paul's ἀγών and race and his reward on the day of Christ (1:30; 2:16).[54] Paul has successfully fought the good competition (καλόν ἀγών); he has completed the race and kept the faith (4:7).[55] The crown of

---

50. Marshall, *Pastoral Epistles*, 805–6 (σπένδομαι refers to Paul's imminent death; against Prior, *Paul*, 93–94).

51. Weiser, *2 Timotheus*, 305; Quinn, Wacker, *Letter*, 785. For early Christian interpretations in this sense: Gregory of Nazianzus, *Funebris oratio in laudem Basilii Magni Caesareae in Cappadocia episcopi* (*Orat.* 43) 78.1.2; Eusebius, *H.E.* 2.22.5; cf. 1 Clement 44.5; Collins, *Commentary*, 273; *pace* Smith, *Timothy's Task*, 127–29, 133–42.

52. Collins, *Commentary*, 272–273; Oberlinner, *2 Timotheus*, 160.

53. Merkel, *Pastoralbriefe*, 81; Weiser, *2 Timotheus*, 304–5.

54. Collins, *Commentary*, 272; Merkel, *Pastoralbriefe*, 81.

55. The phrase "τὴν πίστιν τετήρηκα" involves both keeping the faith in Christ

righteousness awaits him (4:8).[56] The metaphors, taken from the world of sports, emphasize again that Paul has completed his mission and the course of his life. In Philippians, Paul's ἀγών still goes on, and his pride after the completion of the course, on the day of Christ, a rather remote event, will be the perseverance of the believers. In 2 Tim 4:7 three verbs are in the perfect tense (ἠγώνισμαι, I have fought; τετέλεκα, I have completed; τετήρηκα, I have kept). They indicate that the competition is over, and they direct the attention to the near future, to the crown that Paul will receive from the eschatological judge in recognition of his merits and victory.[57]

Based on 4:18 one could argue that Paul is confident that God, who has rescued him from previous persecutions, will also set him free this time (3:11; 4:17a). Rescue from the mouth of the lion would refer to deliverance from imperial authorities (4:17b). But in this context it is rather more a complex intertextual allusion to the salvation of the suffering righteous, as in Ps 21[22]:22 (LXX), thereby associating the martyrdom of Paul with early Christian interpretations of this Psalm as portraying the passion of Christ. This rescue may also take up the rescue of Daniel (Dan 6:21 Theodotion), a passage that was later applied to Jewish and Christian martyrs.[58] None of these allusions imply salvation in this world. As a matter of fact, Paul trusts that God will rescue him to go to the heavenly kingdom (4:18).

In sum, the author of 2 Timothy, knowing that Paul has already died, presents the apostle as facing imminent death.[59] As a consequence, it is now the task of "Timothy" (4:1–2) and of the legitimate leaders he appoints (2:2) to carry out the ministry of the word and to guard the faith. This shift explains a further difference—Philippians envisages Paul in dialogue with a community, but in 2 Timothy Paul addresses Timothy, who typifies the leader of the church in that letter. The empowering of the leaders is all the more urgent as the opposition of heterodox teachers goes far beyond that which Paul faced in Philippians, and indeed it has reached apocalyptic dimensions.

(faithfulness; as indicated by the athletic and military metaphor) and preserving the deposit of faith (Marshall, *Pastoral Epistles*, 807–8).

56. See also 1 Tim 6:12. The suggestion that 6:12 would draw on the authentic 2 Tim 4:7, as argued by Luttenberger, *Prophetenmantel*, 318–20, lacks support.

57. Merkel, *Pastoralbriefe*, 81; Weiser, 308–9; Marshall, *Pastoral Epistles*, 809.

58. See the detailed analysis in Merz, *Selbstauslegung*, 46–57.

59. Marshall, *Pastoral Epistles*, 805; Merz, *Fiktive Selbstauslegung*, 55.

Conclusion

The intertextual analysis of 2 Tim 4:6–8 and its context takes us beyond a biographical reading of the passage. In Philippians Paul looks back at a life dedicated to the ministry of the gospel, which is described with athletic metaphors, and ponders on his possible death, which is interpreted in liturgical-sacrificial terms. Yet he still hopes he will be released. The reference-text-oriented allusion in 2 Tim 4 picks up on these themes, but changes the pre-text in several ways. The most important difference is that Paul's death is no longer a mere possibility but an imminent fact. In this way the author creates the setting for Paul's final will. Timothy is ordered to come to Paul as soon as possible. He is solemnly summoned to proclaim the gospel and to preserve sound doctrine. Earlier in the letter he is also mandated to appoint trustworthy local leaders. Times are utterly dramatic. The opposition faced by Paul according to Philippians has turned here into apocalyptic antagonism.

The PE refer several times to the absence of Paul, a void filled by the appointed ministers (Tit 1:5; 1 Tim 1:3; 3:15). The intertextual reference to Paul's impending death in 2 Timothy is part of a strategy. The certitude about the apostle's death indicates that the church has entered a new era. Timothy has received Paul's legacy and authority via this (fictitious) letter from Rome. This legacy is now preserved by the appointed leaders (2:2). The officials take the place of the apostle; they continue his ministry and the fight against heterodoxy with full authority. The content of 2 Tim 4 guarantees the doctrinal and ministerial continuity in a Pauline community based on Timothy's fictitious succession to Paul.

Recommended Reading

Alfaro, María Jesús Martínez. "Intertextuality: Origins and Development of the Concept." *Atlantis* 18.1–2 (1996) 268–85.

Brodie, Thomas L., Dennis R. MacDonald, and Stanley Porter, eds. *The Intertextuality of the Epistles. Explorations of Theory and Practice.* New Testament Monographs 16. Sheffield: Sheffield Phoenix, 2006.

Ehrman, Bart D. *Forgery and Counterforgery: The Use of Literary Deceit in Early Christian Polemics.* New York: Oxford University Press, 2012.

Kristeva, Julia. *Revolution in Poetic Language.* New York: Columbia University Press, 1984.

Merz, Annette. "Fictitious Self-exposition of Paul: How Might Intertextual Theory Suggest a Reformulation of the Hermeneutics of Pseudoepigraphy?" In *The Intertextuality of the Epistles. Explorations of Theory and Practice*, edited by Thomas L. Brodie, Dennis R. MacDonald, and Stanley Porter, 113–32. New Testament Monographs 16. Sheffield: Sheffield Phoenix, 2006.

17

Probability of Intertextual Borrowing

Elizabeth A. Myers

The study of New Testament intertextuality is founded on the belief that connections exist between NT texts and other texts. While such connections often are inferred from verbal and conceptual parallels, a demonstration of the likelihood of a real connection is difficult, especially when the parallels occur between NT documents. On the one hand, many scholars claim that without explicit indicators of a direct connection it is impossible to discern any more than a possibility that the authors may have had some experience with a common milieu. Claims of direct dependence of one document upon another are frequently dismissed as outstretching the evidence, not only because parallels may exhibit varying degrees of correspondence, but also because there are no commonly accepted criteria or methods for assessing the nature of the relationship between parallel texts. On the other hand, with the prospect of contributing important historical and hermeneutical insights, much scholarly ink has been spilled over potential exegetical implications of parallels involving NT books. In the absence of strict controls, or even the most general of guidelines, the results have been inconsistent and often lack credibility, so much so that charges of speculation and misuse have been laid upon the field of parallels-study.

Perhaps most notable is the indictment leveled by Samuel Sandmel in his Presidential Address to the annual meeting of the Society of Biblical Literature in 1961. In this frequently quoted speech, Sandmel accuses NT scholarship of "parallelomania," which he describes as "that extravagance among scholars which first overdoes the supposed similarity in passages and then proceeds to describe source and derivation as if implying literary connection flowing in an inevitable or predetermined direction."[1] Although the details of Sandmel's argument might be disputed, he is right to advise caution in dealing with perceived parallels. The chaotic state of this field of study has been widely recognized and has prompted attempts to establish clear criteria for classifying parallels and for determining their significance.[2]

The research conducted for this project, however, shows that the study of parallels still suffers from the lack of sound methodology. Among other things, published studies reveal that there is no consensus either for what constitutes a parallel or for what conclusions may be drawn from parallels. Only rarely are the criteria stated explicitly, and even rarer is the inclusion of underlying rationale for stated criteria. Most puzzling is the fact that identical criteria may be viewed differently by different scholars—as positive indicators of literary dependence for some and as negative indicators for others. Without a more disciplined approach to the problem, claims of intertextual borrowing based on perceived parallels will continue to invite charges of speculation and misuse.

Methodology

The two-part methodology described below is intended to provide a means of evaluation that is capable of generating consistent and reliable results. Part 1 addresses the question, "what is the likelihood of a direct literary connection between two documents?" Part 2 follows with the obvious question, "who is most likely to have used whom?"

Part 1: Determining the Likelihood of Literary Dependence

This methodology is both similar and dissimilar to what has been applied in related areas of intertextual research. In studies of the use of the OT in the NT, it is most common to find what might be referred to as a "reference" approach. Such an approach classifies parallels according to generally understood definitions of "citation," "quotation," "allusion," or "echo," which are based on preciseness of correspondence and perceptions about the author

---

1. Sandmel, "Parallelomania," 1.

2. Notable for their attention to methodology and criteria for evaluating intertextual parallels are the following works: Beetham, *Echoes*, 17–35; Berding, *Polycarp*, 27–32; Gilmour, *Significance*, 47–80; Gregory and Tuckett, "Reflections," 61–82; Köhler, *Rezeption*, 1–17; Leonard, "Identifying," 246–57; Lindemann, *Paulus*, 15–19; Schutter, *Hermeneutic*, 35–36; Shimada, "1 Peter?" 90–91; Stein, *Synoptic*, 29–42; Thompson, *Clothed*, 30–37.

and the intended readers. Although exact definitions can vary, the following summary captures the basic idea behind the reference approach:

> Texts can rehearse other texts in a variety of ways. As such, a first point of call will be to define the terms "citation," "allusion," and "echo." By *citation*, I mean a *direct* and deliberate lifting of one text into another with some kind of marker to signify the use of a second text such as "as it is written," "as the Lord said,"or "as the apostles taught." An *allusion* is a figure of speech that makes *indirect* extratextual references by activating awareness of a second text through its particular choice of subject, language, and grammar. Unlike citation, allusion is indirect and requires shared knowledge of a second text between the author and reader in order to be discernible. An *echo* invokes a particular text through the *general* thematic coherence between the subject matter of the two texts.[3]

While a reference approach is most typical for evaluating NT use of the OT,[4] it has also been applied to use of the NT in the NT and in other early Christian writings.[5] The methodology described here is similar in that some of the same criteria are employed for evaluating preciseness of correspondence. The major difference is that conclusions are not based on the likelihood that an author is intentionally drawing the audience's attention to a "referenced" document. Unlike references to the OT, it cannot be assumed that the recipients are aware of a "referenced" NT document or that the author's intention is to "activate awareness of" or "invoke" a particular text with which the reader is assumed to be familiar.[6] Determinations of literary dependence between NT documents, then, cannot be based on the likelihood of an intended reference signal from author to reader.

Another approach that has been used for intertextual studies evaluates relationships according to quantifiable stylistic features of the written language. Such stylometric methods often are used to discern authorship of disputed documents. For example, in a study that seeks to determine authorship of the disputed Federalist Papers (1787–1788), certain common stylistic features of the writings are compared in order to establish which

---

3. Bird, "Reception," 74.

4. E.g., Hays, *Echoes*, 29–32; Koch, *Schrift*, 13–15; Moyise, *Evoking*, 1–5; Porter, "Use," 79–96.

5. E.g., Berding, *Polycarp*, 31–32; Thompson, *Clothed*, 30–37.

6. Gilmour, *Significance*, 49, also draws attention to this issue for parallels between NT and other early Christian writings, specifically noting that "quotations and borrowings are not identical."

of two authors is most likely to have penned the disputed papers.[7] The basic idea is to compare, based on the selected stylistic features, the relative strength of the relationship of the twelve disputed papers with each of the fifty known to be written by James Madison and the fifty-six known to be written by Alexander Hamilton. In this case, there is sufficient comparable data of known authorship by which to make statistically significant assessments of how the twelve disputed papers relate.

Stylometric methods have also been applied to NT documents.[8] Such applications, however, are not completely reliable for establishing NT authorship. With the possible exception of the Pauline corpus, there are not enough documents known to be written by the same person with which to make confident comparisons. Variations of the stylometric approach have also been applied in the fields of NT Textual Criticism and Septuagint studies in order to evaluate relationships between manuscripts.[9] The methodology established here is similar to stylometric approaches in that analysis is based on observable, measurable features of the texts. The main difference is in the criteria used to evaluate significance. Since stylometric approaches are comparative in nature, reliability depends on having a confident basis for comparison which links a particular stylistic profile to a known reference of interest (e.g., a particular author or manuscript tradition). In the case of literary dependence between NT documents, a confident basis for comparison is even less tenable than for NT authorship because there are no undisputed cases of literary dependence between NT documents. For this reason, the significance of parallel stylistic features must be established on other grounds.

Rather than depending on assumptions regarding authorial intention and reader awareness, or on statistical comparisons with known references, the present methodology determines the likelihood of literary dependence through a mathematical probability analysis, with the parallel texts themselves supplying the necessary data.[10] Since not all parallel relationships support literary dependence, the methodology is designed to establish the probability that two documents exhibit the particular type of parallel relationship that is required for literary dependence, namely, a direct genealogical relationship. In such a relationship, parallels are not mediated through

7. Fung, "Disputed," 42–46.

8. See, e.g., Kenny, *Stylometric*; Mealand, "Extent," 61–92.

9. See, e.g., Donker, *Text*; Jobes, "Quantitative," 73–95.

10. This chapter gives an overview of the methodology. For a complete description, including the rationale underlying all components of the methodology, specific procedures for application, and detailed analyses and results for the test cases, see Myers, *Probability*.

some other source such as a common tradition. Rather, they arise from a direct line of influence between the parallel elements. Therefore, in order to demonstrate literary dependence between two documents, there must be evidence of a direct connection.[11] Since a direct literary relationship between two documents can be established with just one direct-connect parallel, the objective of the methodology is to determine the overall likelihood that *at least one* of the parallels derives from a *direct* literary connection.

Suitable evidence is identified by recognizing the fact that directness can be measured by the degree to which a relationship between two elements is exclusive—the higher the degree of exclusivity, the higher the degree of probable directness because the possibility of influence from other sources diminishes. The degree of exclusivity for literary parallels is evidenced by the rarity of the parallel and the degree of correspondence between the parallel elements. While such characteristics are frequently cited as indicators of literary dependence, the strength of the evidence is rarely, if ever, quantified in comparable terms.[12]

In this methodology, the degree of rarity is represented by a number that reflects the parallel item as a proportion of all the occurrences found in other Greek bodies of literature that might have been available to the NT writers. The degree of correspondence is represented by a sum of numbers which indicate how closely the lexical, grammatical, structural, semantic, and pragmatic features of the parallel elements resemble one another. Since common clusters of parallels present stronger evidence of relational directness than do isolated parallels, each parallel is also assigned a number that represents the degree of correspondence between higher-order clusters of which they are members.[13]

The likelihood of literary dependence between two documents is determined by applying probability theory to the evidence of directness observed in parallel texts, as shown in figure 1.

11. For a good explanation of different types of parallel relationships and the requirement of a direct connection for genealogical influence of one element upon another, see Donaldson, "Parallels," 199–201.

12. For example, Kahmann, "Second Peter and Jude," 106; Leonard, "Identifying," 251–52; Mitton, *Ephesians: Authorship*, 179–84; Thompson, *Clothed*, 31–37; Wand, *Peter and Jude*, 24–25; Witherington, "Influence," 146, 148.

13. Common clusters of parallels are viewed as indicators of direct literary relationships by Barnett, *Paul*, 65–66; Berding, *Polycarp*, 150–51; Gilmour, *Significance*, 52, 90.

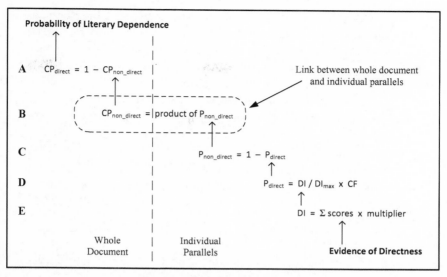

Figure 1. Probability of literary dependence

The ultimate parameter of interest is the overall probability that at least one of the parallels derives from a direct connection.[14] This is the cumulative probability of directness, denoted CPdirect on line A. The data needed for the probability analysis is extracted from individual parallels in the form of a "Directness Index," denoted DI on line E. This represents the degree of directness for an individual parallel. The Directness Index is based on a summary score that is assigned to each parallel according to the indicators of directness, that is, the rarity of the parallel and the degree of correspondence between the parallel elements. Since a high degree of correspondence over a long string of words is more significant than a similarly high degree of correspondence over a short string of words, a multiplier is used to account for the length of the parallel (line E).[15]

The methodology uses the notion of a "perfect" parallel to calibrate the process so that the result is meaningful. A "perfect" parallel is defined as a parallel that earns the highest possible score for rarity of occurrence and correspondence of parallel elements and consists of at least thirty-two verbatim words. The number thirty-two is based on the length of the parallel

14. Berding, *Polycarp*, 203–4, employs a similar method of computing the probability of literary dependence as a way of demonstrating the cumulative effect of many parallels.

15. That more extensive parallels offer stronger evidence of a literary relationship is noted by Gilmour, *Significance*, 52, 83, 90; Leonard, "Identifying," 252–23; Lincoln, *Ephesians*, lv.

between Eph 6:21–22 and Col 4:7–8, which is widely viewed as having derived from a direct literary connection.[16] Although only one direct-connect
parallel is required to demonstrate literary dependence between two documents, a conservative approach is adopted and the minimum critical condition for literary dependence is set at a probability of directness equal to that
of *two* perfect parallels. The probability scale is calibrated using a calibration
factor, denoted CF on line D, so that a probability of 0.5 reflects, not a 50
percent chance of literary dependence, but rather the same probability of
directness as the critical condition of two perfect parallels. Hence, if the
analysis yields a result greater than or equal to 0.5, it is safe to conclude that
at least one of the parallels derives from a direct literary connection.

Part 2: Determining the Most Likely Direction of Borrowing

Given that a relationship of direct literary dependence has been established
as highly probable between two documents, the question of who used whom
becomes valid. Although the nature of the question is quite different than
the question of literary dependence, the methodology used to discern the
direction of borrowing is similar. In this case, the methodology is designed
to assess which of two directional scenarios is most likely—that the author
of document A borrowed from document B, or that the author of document
B borrowed from document A. Since an author's position as borrower can
be established with just one clearly borrowed parallel, the objective is to
determine for each directional scenario the overall likelihood that *at least
one* of the parallels was borrowed.

Suitable evidence may be identified by first considering the different
ways in which the question of directionality has been approached. Research
conducted for this project highlights five major approaches, which can
be distinguished according to the mode and directness of assessment, as
shown in figure 2.

---

16. So, e.g., Best, "Who?" 92–93; Hoehner, *Ephesians*, 867–68; Lincoln, *Ephesians*, lv; Mitton, *Ephesians: Authorship*, 58–59; O'Brien, *Ephesians*, 491.

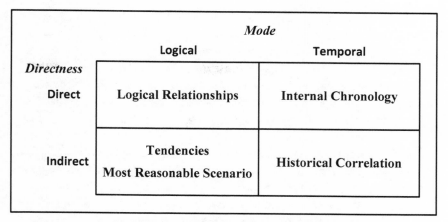

Figure 2. Major approaches to assessing directionality

The "Internal Chronology" approach determines directionality from common temporal markers contained directly in the texts. Directionality of the relationship is based on the position of each document relative to the common temporal marker. Markers of this type might include references to the reign of a particular ruler, the passing of certain laws or edicts, specific battles, or other recorded events. Since conclusive evidence of this type is quite rare in the NT, the internal chronology approach is of little use for determining directionality of interdependent NT documents.

The "Historical Correlation" approach assesses directionality indirectly by attempting to show temporal correlation of the writing of each document with an external historical marker. Many examples of historical correlations appear in studies of NT writings. Some of the more prominent cases include correlation of the occasion for writing with a particular period of persecution,[17] correlation of the grammar with an earlier or later dialect of Greek,[18] correlation of the conveyed theological ideas with the presence of popular philosophical teachings,[19] and correlation of the instructions given to readers with major periods of church development.[20]

Indirect-logical approaches establish directionality by evaluating the parallels according to externally derived logical criteria. This category is dominated by two particular methods. The "Tendencies" method evaluates

17. For example, scholars have attempted to correlate the writing of 1 Peter to periods of Christian persecution during the reigns of Nero, Domitian, and Trajan. See, e.g., Holtzmann, *Einleitung*, 522–24.

18. E.g., Daube, "Participle," 467–88.

19. E.g., DeMaris, *Colossian*; Fossum, "Colossians," 183–201; Martin, *Philosophy*.

20. E.g., Orchard and Riley, *Order*, 275–77.

parallels according to the tendencies or practices exhibited by scribes or authors when transmitting or utilizing another work in their own writing. While application of observed tendencies is most common in analyses of the Synoptic Problem,[21] it also shows up in studies of other NT intertextual relationships. In particular, it is not unusual to find references to the commonly acknowledged tendencies of increasing length,[22] increasing detail,[23] and increasing theological development.[24] The "Most Reasonable Scenario" method establishes the direction of borrowing by evaluating which of the two directionality scenarios offers the best explanation of both the similarities and the differences between two documents. Attention is focused on explaining the redactional practices of each author, assuming that he or she leveraged the work of the other author, and then determining which scenario seems most reasonable in the eyes of the person doing the evaluation.[25]

The "Logical Relationships" approach establishes directionality directly from the logical relationships observed in parallels and their host documents. This approach is the most reliable and therefore is selected for the present methodology.[26] For the purpose of assessing directionality, logical relationships are evaluated according to four categories of indicators: (1) Evidence that the parallel material is foreign to the host document (e.g., disturbances of language, style, meaning, or function);[27] (2) Evidence which demonstrates consistency with the author's borrowing practices in known cases of borrowing (e.g., use of OT texts);[28] (3) Evidence of logical progression of events or circumstances between parallel elements, as indicated by language, structure, thought, or function in the host documents;[29] and (4) Identification of a likely external source for just one of the parallel

---

21. E.g., Stein, *Synoptic*, 48–84. For a critique, see Sanders, *Tendencies*.

22. E.g., Kelly, *Peter and Jude*, 226.

23. E.g., Hagner, *Use*, 187; Kahmann, "Second Peter and Jude," 109.

24. E.g., Kümmel, *Introduction*, 360; Mitton, *Ephesians: Authorship*, 68–71.

25. For example, Davids, *2 Peter and Jude*, 141–2; Goodacre, *Synoptic*, 81–82; Neville, *Mark's Gospel*.

26. For detailed evaluation of the various approaches, see Myers, *Probability*.

27. Examples are noted in Coutts, "Relationship," 201; Crossan, *Birth*, 105–6; Ellingworth, "Hebrews and 1 Clement," 262–69; Gilmour, *Significance*, 53–54; Goodacre, *Case*, 40–43; Lane, *Hebrews 1–8*, cli; Masterman, *First Peter*, 39; Thompson, *Clothed*, 31–37.

28. Consistency of borrowing practices is viewed as evidence of borrowing in Goodacre, *Case*, 86–94; Hill, *Johannine Corpus*, 70; Leonard, "Identifying," 262; Miller, "Attestation?" 623; Sanders, *Tendencies*, 146, 259.

29. E.g., see Hagner, *Use*, 218; Attridge, *Hebrews*, 7; O'Day, "Jeremiah," 265.

elements.[30] It is important to keep in mind, however, that none of the indicators is decisive in and of itself. A skilled author could have incorporated external material seamlessly into the discourse without any disturbance, chosen to diverge from a normal pattern of OT usage, incorporated an illogical progression, or even disguised the use of an ancient source. That is why the overall probability of borrowing is based on cumulative evidence of all indicators across entire documents rather than solitary indicators of direction or selected individual parallels.

The probability of borrowing is computed in much the same way as the probability of directness, as shown in figure 3.

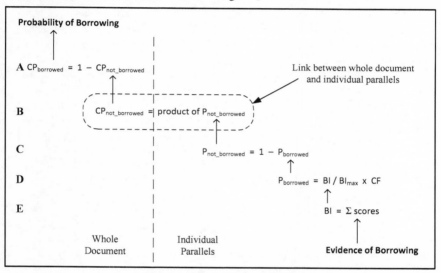

Figure 3. Probability of borrowing

The ultimate parameter of interest is the overall probability that at least one of the parallels is borrowed, denoted CPborrowed on line A. The data needed for the probability analysis is extracted from individual parallels in the form of a "Borrowing Index," denoted BI on line E. This represents the degree to which parallel material looks like it was borrowed. The Borrowing Index is a summary score that is assigned to each parallel based on the direct-logical indicators of borrowing, with 1 point awarded for each observed indicator.

The methodology again uses the notion of a "perfect" parallel to calibrate the process to produce a meaningful result. The minimum critical condition for borrowing is conservatively set at a probability of borrowing

---

30. See, e.g., Mitton, *Ephesians: Authorship*, 186–87.

equal to that of *two* perfect parallels, that is, two parallels, each of which exhibits evidence of all the borrowing indicators. The probability scale is calibrated so that a probability of 0.5 reflects the same probability of borrowing as the critical condition of two perfect parallels (CF on line D). Hence, if the analysis yields a result greater than or equal to 0.5, it might safely be concluded that the author borrowed material from the other document for *at least one* of the parallels.

In order to determine the most likely direction of borrowing, it is necessary to evaluate both directional scenarios because both authors are potential borrowers. The procedure is relatively straightforward. First, the probability of borrowing is calculated for each directional scenario. Then the respective probabilities of borrowing are evaluated to determine which scenario, if any, is more likely. Final assessment of directionality depends on the combination of the two results.

	Document_B	
	$CP_{borrowed\_B} \geq 0.5$	$CP_{borrowed\_B} < 0.5$
Document_A $CP_{borrowed\_A} \geq 0.5$	doc_A ↔ doc_B (co-development?)	doc_A ← doc_B (doc_B is prior)
$CP_{borrowed\_A} < 0.5$	doc_A → doc_B (doc_A is prior)	doc_A ? doc_B (inconclusive)

Figure 4. Significance of borrowing probabilities

As indicated in figure 4, directionality between the two documents may be established when the CPborrowed value is ≥ 0.5 for one document and < 0.5 for the other document. For the two cases where this occurs, the document with the CPborrowed value ≥ 0.5 is the borrower and the other document is prior. The other two cases are inconclusive for discerning directionality. In the case where both of the CPborrowed values are < 0.5, the evidence is insufficient to conclude borrowing on the part of either author. In the case where both of the CPborrowed values are ≥ 0.5, both documents are shown to contain material that looks like it was borrowed, in which case the possibility of co-development or mutual sharing between the authors must be considered.

Application

The methodology described above provides a disciplined analytical approach to evaluating parallels between NT books for the likelihood of intertextual borrowing. Its usefulness for NT scholarship, however, requires that it can be applied in a consistent manner and that it is capable of producing credible results. The best way to demonstrate such usefulness is to apply the methodology to selected pairs of NT documents where the likelihood of intertextual borrowing is already fairly certain. These cases occur at the two extremes of the probability scale, where the result is either strongly negative or strongly positive.

Negative Test Case: James and Philippians

The letters of James and Philippians present an excellent negative test case for the methodology because they have very little in common. Indeed, nowhere in the research conducted for this project is it suggested that one of these authors borrowed material from the other document. Therefore, when the documents are analyzed for the likelihood of literary dependence, we should expect a negative result indicating that a direct literary connection is unlikely. Analysis of the parallels between these two letters should produce a very low value for CPdirect, certainly less than 0.5.

Part 1 of the methodology was applied to 20 parallels that meet the established qualifying condition.[31] Arrangement of the parallels is illustrated in figure 5, in the order in which they occur in each document. The boxes representing the parallels include the reference where the parallel Greek text is found, a descriptive label that represents the parallel texts, and the assigned parallel number.

---

31. In order to be included in the analysis, a parallel must meet a minimum condition for rarity of occurrence and/or verbal correspondence. For specific criteria and rationale, see Myers, *Probability*.

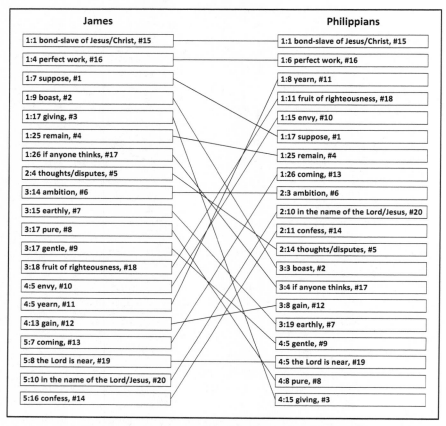

Figure 5. Arrangement of parallels (James and Philippians)

From the disorderly arrangement of parallels it is easy to see that none of the parallels are clustered closely together in groups of three or more to form higher-order parallel clusters. Hence, the probability analysis does not include any clusters, only individual first-order parallels consisting of single words (#1–14) and groups of words (#15–20).

The resulting probability of directness, CPdirect, falls in the range 0.12–0.14. Since this is well below 0.5, the analysis has produced the expected negative result that a direct literary connection between James and Philippians is highly unlikely. Thus, the case of James and Philippians demonstrates credibility of the methodology at the low end of the probability scale. Application of the methodology to two documents that bear little resemblance to one another does indeed yield an expected negative result. The negative result for James and Philippians also signals completion of the analysis for these two documents. Since literary dependence is highly unlikely, there is no warrant for proceeding to the next step of the methodology, which assesses the most likely direction of borrowing. Instead, we turn our attention to demonstrating credibility at the high end of the probability scale with a positive test case.

Positive Test Case: Jude and 2 Peter

The documents selected for the positive test case are Jude and 2 Peter, two letters that are strikingly similar. Given the remarkable degree of similarity, it comes as no surprise that the strong likelihood of an intertextual relationship is frequently mentioned in commentaries and focused studies of the two letters. Although a few published works claim that the parallels are best explained by both authors having relied upon a common source,[32] direct literary dependence between Jude and 2 Peter is commonly accepted in NT scholarship.[33] Thus, Jude and 2 Peter present an excellent test case. When the documents are analyzed for the likelihood of literary dependence, we should expect a positive result indicating that a direct literary connection is likely. Analysis of the parallels between these two documents should produce a very high value for CPdirect, certainly higher than 0.5. Moreover, the weight of scholarly opinion favors the scenario in which the author of 2 Peter borrowed from Jude.[34] Hence, when the documents are further analyzed to determine the most likely direction of borrowing, we should expect a result which points to the author of 2 Peter as most likely to have borrowed from Jude.

Part 1 of the methodology was applied to 25 first-order parallels that meet the qualifying condition established for the project. Arrangement of the parallels is illustrated in figure 6, in the order in which they occur in each document.

---

32. So M. Green, *Second Peter and Jude*, 50–55; Reicke, *James, Peter, and Jude*, 189–90; Spicq, "La Ia Petri," 197 n1.

33. So, e.g., Bauckham, *Jude, 2 Peter*, 141–3; Davids, *2 Peter and Jude*, 136–43; Gilmour, *Significance*, 5, 83–91; G. Green, *Jude and 2 Peter*, 152, 159–62; Jobes, *Letters*, 258, 380–86; Kelly, *Peter and Jude*, 225–27.

34. So, e.g., Bauckham, *Jude, 2 Peter*, 141–43; Davids, *2 Peter and Jude*, 141–43; G. Green, *Jude and 2 Peter*, 159–62; Gilmour, *Significance*, 83–91; Kahmann, "Second Peter and Jude," 106–7; Moffatt, *Introduction*, 351; Neyrey, *2 Peter, Jude*, 120–22; Schreiner, *1, 2 Peter, Jude*, 418–19; Thurén, "Relationship," 451–60; Wand, *Peter and Jude*, 135–37; Watson, *Invention*, 160–87; but Bigg, *Peter and Jude*, 216–24; Moo, *2 Peter and Jude*, 16–21.

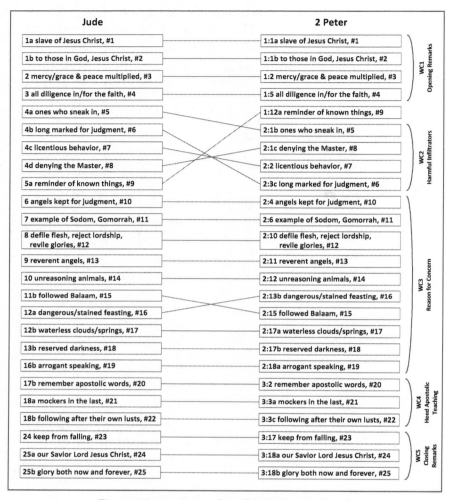

Figure 6. Arrangement of parallels (Jude and 2 Peter)

As shown in figure 6, the parallels between Jude and 2 Peter exhibit a much higher degree of correspondence in their arrangement than do those between James and Philippians (cf. figure 5). In the case of Jude and 2 Peter, only seven of the 25 first-order parallels do not appear in the same order in both documents. Furthermore, most of the first-order parallels also combine to form five additional higher-order parallel clusters (WC1–5).

The resulting probability of directness, CPdirect, is in the range 0.81–0.84. Since this is well above 0.5, the analysis has produced the expected positive result that a direct literary connection between Jude and 2 Peter is highly likely. Therefore, although the non-deterministic nature of probability disallows specific claims about direct literary connections between individual parallels, it may be concluded that at the whole document level Jude and 2 Peter are very likely to be related through direct literary dependence. This does not preclude the possibility that some of the parallels might derive from independent use of common traditions or from coincidence. The analysis shows only that it is highly likely that *at least one* of the parallels is due to a direct literary connection.

Since literary dependence is highly likely, part 2 of the methodology may be applied to the same set of parallels in order to determine the most likely direction of borrowing. For the scenario in which Jude borrowed from 2 Peter, evidence of borrowing is limited to four parallels that exhibit progression of language tense, where Jude 4 seems to suggest completion of what appears to be foretold in 2 Pet 2:1–3. The probability of borrowing for Jude, CPborrowed, is only 0.11. For the scenario in which 2 Peter borrowed from Jude, evidence is found in 18 parallels that exhibit 24 indicators of borrowing. Five parallels show disturbance of style, as evidenced by unexpected writing or awkward editing. An example is found in parallel #20, where the author of 2 Peter writes that readers should remember τῆς τῶν ἀποστόλων ὑμῶν ἐντολῆς τοῦ κυρίου καὶ σωτῆρος ("the commandment of your apostles, of the Lord and Savior"). The double genitive in this expression is widely recognized as syntactically difficult and awkward.[35] Furthermore, the reference to "your apostles" is unexpected in a letter that claims to be written by an apostle who normally refers to himself with first-person verbs and pronouns. Whether or not the reference is intended to include the author, the expression seems out of place in the letter.[36] Borrowing from Jude is further evidenced by 15 indicators of logical progression, which are found in 14 parallels that exhibit progression of structure, thought, or function. For example, one way in which progression of structure may be indicated is when parallel texts exhibit a significant difference in the use of *portability* features, such as parallelism and rhyme, with the direction moving from more to less portable. This phenomenon is evident in parallel #12, where Jude uses a triplet of expressions to show that the behavior of the infiltrators is similar to that of those mentioned in vv. 5–7, who were judged and destroyed by God for their sinful behavior. As shown in figure 7, lines 2–4

---

35. See, e.g., Bauckham, *Jude, 2 Peter*, 287; Davids, *2 Peter and Jude*, 261; Kelly, *Peter and Jude*, 354.

36. Scholars have attempted to explain the odd reference as evidence of pseudonymous authorship or as reflecting a much broader definition of "apostle" than is implied in 2 Pet 1:1, 16. See, e.g., Kelly, *Peter and Jude*, 354; Bauckham, *Jude, 2 Peter*, 287; Davids, *2 Peter and Jude*, 262; Moo, *2 Peter and Jude*, 164–65.

all have structures of the form: feminine-accusative noun + conjunction + present-active-indicative third-person plural verb.

1	Ὁμοίως μέντοι καὶ οὗτοι ἐνυπνιαζόμενοι		
	Yet in the same way even these dreamers		
2	σάρκα	μὲν	μιαίνουσιν
	the flesh		defile
3	κυριότητα	δὲ	ἀθετοῦσιν
	lordship		reject
4	δόξας	δὲ	βλασφημοῦσιν.
	glories		blaspheme.

Figure 7. Parallelism in Jude 8 (Parallel #12)

Through the use of parallel structures and rhyming of the noun and verb endings (-α/-ας, -οῦσιν), the triplet in Jude 8 exhibits a style of parallelism that makes the entire expression highly portable. Since the parallel text in 2 Pet 2:10 lacks such portable features, the parallel provides evidence of structural progression from more to less portable. Finally, for four of the parallels, the element in Jude has a likely external source while the parallel element in 2 Peter does not. These all involve Jude's likely use of pseudepigraphal literature, *1 Enoch* and *Testament (Assumption) of Moses*. The probability of borrowing, CPborrowed, based on all of these indicators is 0.51.

Having determined the probability of borrowing for each of the two directional scenarios, the next step is to evaluate the results to see which, if any, scenario is more likely. Since the probability that Jude borrowed is less than 0.5 and the probability that 2 Peter borrowed is greater than 0.5, the significance of the borrowing probabilities is found in the bottom-left quadrant of the chart in figure 8. Here the combination of results indicates that the author of 2 Peter most likely borrowed from Jude. Accordingly, Jude is most likely to be the prior document.

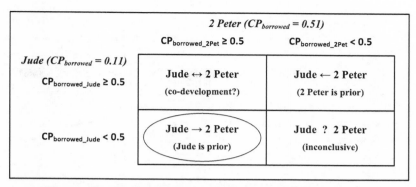

Figure 8. Significance of borrowing probabilities for Jude and 2 Peter

Although the identity of the borrowed parallel(s) remains unknown due to the non-deterministic nature of probability, application of the methodology has produced the expected result that the author of 2 Peter is more likely to have borrowed from Jude. The fact that the final value of CPborrowed for 2 Peter just barely meets the threshold value of 0.5 also is not surprising, given the shortness of the letters and the uncertainty reflected in historical studies of the literary relationship between these two books. Thus, the case of Jude and 2 Peter demonstrates credibility of the methodology at the high end of the probability scale. Application of the methodology to two documents that are strikingly similar does indeed yield an expected positive result for the likelihood of literary dependence and for the most likely direction of borrowing.

Conclusion

The methodology described above adds a degree of objectivity to the task of evaluating NT literary parallels for the likelihood of intertextual borrowing. The test cases involving parallels between James and Philippians and between Jude and 2 Peter show that it is feasible to determine the likelihood of direct literary connections and the most likely direction of borrowing between two documents through mathematical analysis based on probability theory and relevant literary indicators. Rather than basing conclusions on what seems most reasonable in the eyes of individual interpreters, the methodology allows for consistent and reliable results, regardless of who performs the assessment. Application to other pairs of NT documents has the potential to shed new light on some of the most intriguing mysteries of the NT, including the Synoptic Problem, background of thought and chronology of the NT epistles, and even authorship of the writings.[37] Since the methodology can easily be adapted for intertextual relationships with and between other bodies of literature such as the Septuagint, the Pseudepigrapha, and the Hebrew Bible, the scope of application may extend to include multiple dimensions of biblical intertextuality. It is hoped that through the use of analytical methodologies such as this, future studies of New Testament intertextuality will avoid charges of speculation and misuse that are often associated with "parallelomania."

Recommended Reading

Donaldson, Terence L. "Parallels: Use, Misuse and Limitations." *EvQ* 55 (1983) 193–210.

Gilmour, Michael J. *The Significance of Parallels between 2 Peter and Other Early Christian Literature*. Academia Biblica 10. Leiden: Brill Academic, 2002.

Gregory, Andrew F., and Christopher M. Tuckett. "Reflections on Method: What Constitutes the Use of the Writings That Later Formed the New Testament in the Apostolic Fathers?" In *The Reception of the New Testament in the Apostolic Fathers*, edited by Andrew F. Gregory and Christopher M. Tuckett, 61–82. Oxford: Oxford University , 2005.

Myers, Elizabeth A. *Authorship of 1 Peter and Hebrews: New Evidence in Light of Probable Intertextual Borrowing*. Forthcoming.

———. *Probability of Intertextual Borrowing between New Testament Books: A Methodology for Determining the Likelihood of Literary Dependence and the Direction of Borrowing*. Forthcoming.

Sandmel, Samuel. "Parallelomania." *JBL* 81 (1962) 1–13.

---

37. See, e.g., Myers, *Authorship*.

Bibliography

Aichele, George, and Gary A. Phillips, eds. *Intertextuality and the Bible*. Semeia 69/70. Atlanta: Scholars, 1995.

———. "Introduction: Exegesis, Eisegesis, Intergesis." In *Intertextuality and the Bible*, 7–18. Semeia 69/70. Atlanta: Scholars, 1995.

Aichele, George. "Canon as Intertext: Restraint or Liberation?" In *Reading the Bible Intertextually*, edited by Richard Hays, Stefan Alkier, and Leroy Huizenga, 139–56. Waco: Baylor University Press, 2009.

Albl, Martin C. *And Scripture Cannot Be Broken: The Form and Function of the Early Christian Testimonia Collections*. NovTSup 96. Leiden: Brill, 1999.

Albright, W. F., and C. S. Mann. *Matthew*. AB 26. Garden City: Doubleday, 1971.

Alfaro, María Jesús Martínez. "Intertextuality: Origins and the Development of the Concept." *Atlantis* 18.1/2 (1996) 268–85.

Alkier, Stefan and Jürgen Zangenberg, eds. *Zeichen aus Text und Stein. Studien auf dem Weg zu einer Archäologie des Neuen Testaments*. TANZ 42. Tübingen: Francke Verlag, 2003.

Alkier, Stefan. "Intertextuality and the Semiotics of Biblical Texts." In *Reading the Bible Intertextually*, edited by Richard Hays, Stefan Alkier, and Leroy Huizenga, 3–21. Waco: Baylor University Press, 2009.

———. "New Testament Studies on the Basis of Categorical Semiotics." In *Reading the Bible Intertextually*, edited by Stefan Alkier, Richard B. Hays, Leroy A. Huizenga, 223–48. Waco: Baylor University Press, 2009.

———. *Wunder und Wirklichkeit in den Briefen des Apostels Paulus. Ein Beitrag zu einem Wunderverständnis jenseits von Entmythologisierung und Rehistorisierung*. WUNT 134. Tübingen: Mohr Siebeck, 2001.

Allen, Graham. *Intertextuality*. 2nd ed. New Critical Idiom. London: Routledge, 2011.

Allison, Dale C. Jr. *The New Moses: A Matthean Typology*. Minnaepolis: Fortress, 1993.

———. *Studies in Matthew: Interpretation Past and Present*. Grand Rapids: Baker, 2005.

Almazán García, Eva M. "Dwelling in Marble Halls: A Relevance-Theoretic Approach to Intertextuality in Translation." *Revista Alicantina de Estudios Ingleses* 14 (2001) 7–19.

Aloisi, John. "Who Is David's Lord? Another Look at Psalm 110." *Detroit Baptist Seminary Journal* 10 (2005) 103–23.

Anderson, H. "4 Maccabees (First Century AD) A New Translation and Introduction." In *The Old Testament Pseudepigrapha*, edited by James H. Charlesworth, II, 531–43. Garden City: Doubleday, 1985.

Anderson, R. Dean. *Ancient Rhetorical Theory and Paul*. Rev. ed. Contributions to Biblical Exegesis and Theology 18. Louvain: Peeters, 1999.

Attridge, Harold W. *The Epistle to the Hebrews: A Commentary on the Epistle to the Hebrews*. Hermeneia: A Critical and Historical Commentary on the Bible. Philadelphia: Fortress, 1989.

Auerbach, Erich. "Figura." In *Scenes from the Drama of European Literature*, translated by Ralph Manheim, 11–77. Minnaepolis: University of Minnesota, 1984.

———. *Mimesis: The Representation of Reality in Western Literature*. Translated by Willard R. Trask. Princeton: Princeton University Press, 1953.

Aune, David. *Revelation 1–5*. WBC 52A. Dallas: Word, 1997.

Bak, Samuel. *Painted in Words—A Memoir*. Bloomington: Indiana University Press, 2001.

Bakhtin, Mikhail. *The Dialogic Imagination: Four Essays*. Edited by Micahel Holquist. Translated by Caryl Emerson and Micahel Holquist. Austin: University of Texas, 1984.

Bannister, Andrew G. *An Oral-Formulaic Study of the Qur'an*. Lanham, MD: Lexington, 2014.

Barnett, Albert E. *Paul Becomes a Literary Influence*. Chicago: University of Chicago Press, 1941.

Barr, David L. "The Lamb Looks Like a Dragon." In *The Reality of Apocalypse. Rhetoric and Politics in the Book of Revelation*, edited by David L. Barr, 205–20. Atlanta: Society of Biblical Literature, 2006.

Barr, James. *The Semantics of Biblical Language*. Eugene: Wipf and Stock, 1961.

Barrera, Julio Trebolle. *The Jewish Bible and the Christian Bible: An Introduction to the History of the Bible*. Translated by Wilfred G. E. Watson. Leiden and Grand Rapids: Brill and Eerdmans, 1998.

Barrett, C. K. "The Interpretation of the Old Testament in the New." In *The Cambridge History of the Bible, Vol. 1: From the Beginnings to Jerome*, edited by Peter R. Ackroyd and Craig F. Evans, 377–411. Cambridge: Cambridge University Press, 1980.

Barthes, Roland. *Image-Music-Text*. Translated by Stephen Heath. New York: Hill & Wang, 1977.

———. *The Pleasure of the Text*. Translated by Richard Miller. New York: Hill & Wang, 1975.

———. *Writing Degree Zero*. Translated by Annette Lavers and Colin Smith. New York: Hill and Wang, 2012.

Barton, J. "Déjà Lu: Intertextuality, Method or Theory?" In *Reading Job Intertextually*, edited by K. Dell and W. Kynes, 1–16. Library of Hebrew Bible/Old Testament Studies 574. New York: T. & T. Clark, 2013.

Bates, Matthew W. "Getting Some Fatherly Advice: Refining 'Intertextuality' in the Study of Paul's Scriptural Interpretation." Paper presented at the SBL. Atlanta, GA. Nov. 2012.

Bauckham, Richard J. *The Climax of Prophecy: Studies on the Book of Revelation*. Edinburgh: T. & T. Clark, 1993.

———. *God Crucified: Monotheism and Christology in the New Testament.* Grand Rapids: Eerdmans, 1998.

———. *Jude, 2 Peter.* WBC 50. Nashville: Thomas Nelson, 1983.

———. "Tamar's Ancestry and Rahab's Marriage: Two Problems in the Matthean Genealogy." *NovT* 37 (1995) 320–29.

Bauks, Michaela, Wayne Horowitz, and Armin Lange, eds. *Between Text and Text: The Hermeneutics of Intertextuality in Ancient Cultures and Their Afterlife in Medieval and Modern Times.* JAJSup 6. Göttingen: Vandenhoeck & Ruprecht, 2013.

Bauks, Michaela. "Intertextuality in Ancient Literature in Light of Textlinguistics and Cultural Studies." In *Between Text and Text: The Hermeneutics of Intertextuality in Ancient Cultures and Their Afterlife in Medieval and Modern Times*, edited by Michaela Bauks, Wayne Horowitz, and Armin Lange, 27–46. JAJSup 6. Göttingen: Vandenhoeck and Ruprecht, 2013.

Baum, Armin Daniel. *Pseudepigraphie und literarische Fälschung im frühen Christentum.* WUNT 2.138. Tübingen: Mohr Siebeck, 2001.

Bauman, Richard. *A World of Others' Words: Cross-Cultural Perspectives on Intertextuality.* Oxford: Blackwell, 2004.

Bazerman, Charles. "Intertextuality: How Texts Rely on Other Texts." In *What Writing Does and How It Does It: An Introduction to Analyzing Texts and Textual Practices*, edited by Charles Bazerman and Paul A. Prior, 83–96. Mahwah: Lawrence Erlbaum, 2003.

Beal, Timothy K. "Ideology and Intertextuality: Surplus of Meaning and Controlling the Means of Production." In *Reading Between Texts: Intertextuality and the Hebrew Bible*, edited by Danna Nolan Fewell, 27–39. Literary Currents in Biblical Interpretation. Louiseville: Westminster John Knox, 1992.

———. "Intertextuality." In *Handbook of Postmodern Biblical Interpretation*, edited by A. K. M. Adam, 128–30. St. Louis: Chalice, 2000.

Beale, Gregory K. "Colossians." In *Commentary on the New Testament Use of the Old Testament*, edited by G. K. Beale and D. A. Carson, 841–70. Grand Rapids: Baker Academic, 2007.

———. *Handbook on the New Testament Use of the Old Testament: Exegesis and Interpretation.* Grand Rapids: Baker Academic, 2012.

———. *John's Use of the Old Testament in Revelation.* JSNTSup 166. Sheffield: Sheffield Academic, 1998.

Beare, Frank. *The Gospel According to Matthew.* New York: Harper & Row, 1981.

Beaton, Richard C. "How Matthew Writes." In *The Written Gospel*, edited by Markus Bockmuehl and Donald A. Hagner, 116–34. Cambridge: Cambridge University Press, 2005.

Beentjes, Pancratius C. *The Book of Ben Sira in Hebrew.* VTSup 68. Leiden: Brill, 1997.

Beetham, Christopher A. *Echoes of Scripture in the Letter of Paul to the Colossians.* Biblical Interpretation Series 96. Leiden: Brill, 2008.

Bekken, Per Jarle. "Paul's Use of Deut 30:12–14 in Jewish Context: Some Observations." In *The New Testament and Hellenistic Judaism*, edited by Peder Borgen and Søren Giversen, 183–203. Aarhus: Aarhus Universtiy, 1995.

Belleville, Linda L. "1 Cor 10:4 and the Exodus-Wilderness Rock Tradition." Paper presented at the Society of Biblical Literature conference. Baltimore, MD, 2013.

Ben-Porat, Ziva. "The Poetics of Literary Allusion." *PTL: A Journal for Descriptive Poetics and Theory of Literature* 1 (1976) 105–28.

Benveniste, Émile. *Problèmes De Linguistique Générale*, 2. Tel 47. Paris: Gallimard, 1974.

———. *Problems in General Linguistics*. Translated by Mary Elizabeth Meek. Miami Linguistics Series 8. Coral Gables: University of Miami, 1971.

Berding, Kenneth. *Polycarp and Paul: An Analysis of Their Literary and Theological Relationship in Light of Polycarp's Use of Biblical and Extra-Biblical Literature*. Supplements to Vigiliae Christianae 62. Leiden: Brill, 2002.

Best, Ernest. "Who Used Whom? The Relationship of Ephesians and Colossians." *NTS* 43 (1997) 72–96.

The Bible and Culture Collective. *The Postmodern Bible*. New Haven: Yale University Press, 1995.

Bigg, Charles. *The Epistles of St. Peter and St. Jude*. Edinburgh: T. & T. Clark, 1987.

Bird, Michael F. "The Reception of Paul in the Epistle to Diognetus." In *Paul and the Second Century*, edited by Michael F. Bird and Joseph R. Dodson, 70–90. New York: T. & T. Clark, 2011.

Borgen, Peder. *Philo of Alexandria: An Exegete for His Time*. SNT 86; Leiden: Brill, 1997.

———. "Philo—An Interpreter of the Laws of Moses." In *Reading Philo. A Handbook to Philo of Alexandria*, edited by Torrey Seland, 75–101. Grand Rapids: Eerdmans, 2014.

Boring, M. Eugene. "The Gospel of Matthew." In *The New Interpreters Bible: General Articles & Introduction, Commentary, & Reflections for Each Book of the Bible Including the Apocryphal / Deuterocanonical Books in Twelve Volumes, vol. 8*, edited by Leander E. Keck et al., 87–505. Nashville: Abingdon, 1995.

———. *Revelation. Interpretation: A Bible Commentary for Teaching and Preaching*. Louisville: John Knox, 1989.

Bormann, Lukas, "The Colossian Hymn, Wisdom, and Creation." In *Between Text and Text: The Hermeneutics of Intertextuality in Ancient Cultures and Their Afterlife in Medieval and Modern Times*, edited by Michaela Bauks, Wayne Horowitz, and Armin Lange, 243–56. JAJSup 6. Göttingen: Vandenhoeck and Ruprecht, 2013.

Boxall, Ian. *Discovering Matthew: Content, Interpretation, Reception*. Grand Rapids: Eerdmans, 2014.

Boyarin, Daniel. *Intertextuality and the Reading of Midrash*. Bloomington: Indiana University Press, 1990.

Bredin, Mark. *Jesus, Revolutionary of Peace. A Nonviolent Christology in the Book of Revelation*. Carlisle: Paternoster, 2003.

Brettler, Marc Zvi. "The New Testament Between the Hebrew Bible (Tanakh) and Rabbinic Literature." In *The Jewish Annotated New Testament*, edited by Amy–Jill Levine and Marc Zvi Brettler, 504–06. New York: Oxford University Press, 2011.

Brodie, Thomas L., Dennis R. MacDonald, and Stanley E. Porter, eds. *The Intertextuality of the Epistles: Explorations of Theory and Practice*. New Testament Monographs 16. Sheffield: Sheffield Phoenix, 2007.

Broich, Ulrich, and Manfred Pfister, eds. *Intertextualität: Formen, Funktionen, anglistische Fallstudien*. Tübingen: Niemeyer, 1985.

Brooke, George J. "Hypertextuality and the 'Parabiblical' Dead Sea Scrolls." In *In the Second Degree: Parabiblical Literature in Ancient Near Eastern and Ancient Mediterranean Culture and its Reflections in Medieval Literature*, edited by Philip S. Alexander, Armin Lange, and Renate J. Pillinger, 43–64. Leiden: Brill, 2010.

———. "Pesharim." In *Dictionary of New Testament Background*, edited by Craig A. Evans and Stanley E. Porter, 778–82. Downers Grove, IL: InterVarsity, 2000.

Brown, Candy Gunther. *The Word in the World: Evangelical Writing, Publishing, and Reading in America, 1789–1880*. Chapel Hill: University of North Carolina Press, 2004.

Brown, Jeannine K. "Creation's Renewal in the Gospel of John." Catholic Biblical Quarterly 72 (April, 2010) 275–90.

———. "Genesis in Matthew's Gospel." In *Genesis in the New Testament*, edited by Maarten J. J. Menken and Steve Moyise, 42–59. New York: T. & T. Clark, 2012.

———. "Matthew's 'Least of These' Theology and Subversion of 'Us/Other' Categories." In *Matthew: Texts @ Contexts*, edited by Nicole Wilkinson Duran and James P. Grimshaw, 287–301. Minnaepolis: Fortress, 2013.

———. *Matthew*. Teach the Text Commentary Series. Grand Rapids: Baker, 2015.

———. *Scripture as Communication: Introducing Biblical Hermeneutics*. Grand Rapids: Baker Academic, 2007.

———. "Silent Wives, Verbal Believers: Ethical and Hermeneutical Considerations in 1 Peter 3:1–6 and Its Context." *Word and World* 24 (2004) 395–403.

Brown, Raymond. *The Birth of the Messiah. A Commentary on the Infancy Gospels of Matthew and Luke*. AB Reference Library. New Haven: Yale University Press, 1993.

———. *The Death of the Messiah. From Gethsemane to the Grave: A Commentary on the Passion Narratives*. AB Reference Library. Garden City: Doubleday, 1994.

Brox, Norbert. *Die Pastoralbriefe*. Regensburg: Pustet, 1969.

———. "Zu den persönlichen Notizen der Pastoralbriefen." In *Pseudepigraphie in der heidnischen und jüdisch-christlichen Antike*, edited by Norbert Brox. Wege der Forschung 484. Darmstadt: Wissenschaftliche Buchgesellschaft, 1977.

Brucker, Ralph. *Christushymnen oder epideiktische Passagen? Studien zum Stilwechsel im Neuen Testament und seiner Umwelt*. Göttingen: Vandenhoeck & Ruprecht, 1997.

Brueggemann, Walter. "A Fissure Always Uncontained." In *Strange Fire: Reading the Bible after the Holocaust*, edited by Tod Linafelt, 62–75. New York: New York University Press, 2000.

Buchanan, George Wesley. *Introduction to Intertextuality*. Lewiston: Mellen, 1994.

Budd, Philip J. *Numbers*. WBC 5. Dallas: Word, 1984.

Burgess, Jonathan S. *The Death and Afterlife of Achilles*. Baltimore: Johns Hopkins University Press, 2009.

Burnett, Fred. "Exposing the Anti-Jewish Ideology of Matthew's Implied Author: The Characterization of God the Father." *Semeia* 59 (1992) 155–91.

Buttrick, David G. *Homiletic: Moves and Structures*. Minneapolis: Fortress, 1987.

Caird, George B. *A Commentary on the Revelation of St John the Divine*. 2nd ed. London: A. & C. Black, 1984.

Campbell, Douglas A. "Beyond Justification in Paul: The Thesis of the Deliverance of God." *Scottish Journal of Theology* 65 (2012) 90–104.

Campbell, Lee. "Matthew's Use of the Old Testament: A Preliminary Analysis." Online: http://www.xenos.org/essays/matthews-use-old-testament-preliminary-analysis.

Capes, D. B. *Old Testament Yahweh Texts in Paul's Christology*. WUNT 2.47. Tübingen: Mohr Siebeck, 1992.

Carr, David M. "The Many Uses of Intertextuality in Biblical Studies: Actual and Potential." In *Congress Volume Helsinki 2010*, edited by Martti Nissinen, 505–35. Supplements to Vetus Testamentum 148. Leiden: Brill, 2012.

———. *Writing on the Tablet of the Heart: Origins of Scripture and Literature.* Oxford: Oxford University Press, 2005.

Carter, Warren. "Construction of Violence and Identities in Matthew's Gospel." In *Violence in the New Testament*, edited by Shelly Matthews and E. Leigh Gibson, 81–108. New York: T. & T. Clark, 2005.

———. "Evoking Isaiah: Matthean Soteriology and the Intertextual Reading of Isaiah 7–9 and Matthew 1:23 and 4:15–16." *JBL* 119 (2000) 503–520.

Carton, Evan. "The Holocaust, French Poststructuralism, the American Literary Academy, and Jewish Identity Poetics." In *Historicizing Theory*, edited by Peter Herman, 17–47. Albany: SUNY, 2004.

Case-Winters, Anna. *Matthew. Belief. A Theological Commentary on the Bible.* Louisville: Westminster John Knox, 2015.

Childs, Brevard S. "Critique of Recent Intertextual Canonical Interpretation." *ZAW* 115 (2003) 173–84.

Christensen, Sean M. "Solidarity in Suffering and Glory: The Unifying Role of Psalm 34 in 1 Peter 3:10–12." *Journal of the Evangelical Theological Society* 58 (2015) 335–52.

Clark, Billy. "Stylistic Analysis and Relevance Theory." *Language and Literature* 5 (1996) 163–78.

Clayton, Jay, and Eric Rothstein, eds. *Influence and Intertextuality in Literary History.* Madison, WI: University of Wisconsin, 1991.

Cockerill, Gareth L. *The Epistle to the Hebrews.* Grand Rapids: Eerdmans, 2012.

Collier, Gary D. "'That We Might Not Crave Evil': The Structure and Argument of 1 Cor 10:1–13." *JSNT* 55 (1994) 55–75.

Collins, Raymond F. *1&2 Timothy and Titus: A Commentary.* Louisville: Westminster John Knox, 2002.

———. *First Corinthians.* Sacra Pagina 7. Collegeville: Liturgical, 1999.

Colson, F. H., and G. H. Whitaker. *Philo.* Cambridge: Harvard University Press, 1985.

Cook, Johann. "Intertextual Readings in the Septuagint." In *The New Testament Interpreted: Essays in Honour of Bernard C. Lategan*, edited by Cilliers Breytenbach, Johan C. Thom, and Jeremy Punt, 119–34. NovTSup 124. Leiden: Brill, 2007.

Cooper, Craig, ed. *Politics of Orality: Orality and Literacy in Ancient Greece.* Mnemosyne BCB, 280. Leiden: Brill, 2005.

Cornell, Drucilla. "Post-Structuralism, the Ethical Relation and the Law." *Cordoza Law Review* 9 (1988) 1587–628.

Coutts, John. "The Relationship of Ephesians and Colossians." *NTS* 4 (1958) 201–7.

Crossan, John Dominic. *The Birth of Christianity: Discovering What Happened in the Years Immediately after the Execution of Jesus.* New York: HarperSanFrancisco, 1998.

———. *Who Killed Jesus? Exposing the Roots of Anti-Semitism in the Gospel Story of the Death of Jesus.* San Francisco, CL.: HarperSanFrancisco, 1991.

Culler, Jonathan. *On Deconstruction. Theory and Criticism after Deconstruction.* Ithaca: Cornell University Press, 1982.

———. *The Pursuit of Signs: Semiotics, Literature, Deconstruction.* Ithaca: Cornell University Press, 1981.

Cullmann, Oscar. *Christ and Time: The Primitive Christian Conception of Time and History.* Rev. ed. Philadelphia: Westminster, 1964.

————. *Salvation in History. The New Testament Library.* London: SCM, 1967.

Daube, David. "Appended Note: Participle and Imperative in 1 Peter." In *The First Epistle of St. Peter: The Greek Text with Introduction, Notes and Essays,* edited by Edward Gordon Selwyn, 467–88. London: Macmillan, 1955.

Davids, Peter H. *The Letters of 2 Peter and Jude.* The Pillar New Testament Commentary. Grand Rapids: Eerdmans, 2006.

Davidson, Harriet. *T. S. Eliot and Hermeneutics: Absence and Interpretation in the Waste Land.* Baton Rouge, LA: Louisiana State University Press, 1985.

Davies, W. D., and Dale Allison. *The Gospel According to Saint Matthew.* Vol 1. ICC. Edinburgh: T. & T. Clark, 1988.

————. *The Gospel According to Saint Matthew.* Vol 3. ICC. Edinburgh: T. & T. Clark, 1997.

Davies, W. D. *Paul and Rabbinic Judaism.* London: SPCK, 1962.

Davis, Barry C. "Is Psalm 110 a Messianic Psalm?" *Bibliotheca Sacra* 157 (2000) 160–73.

Delorme, Jean. "Intertextualities about Mark." In *Intertextuality in Biblical Writings. Essay in Honour of Bas van Iersel,* edited by Sipke Fraisma, 35–42. Kampen: Kok, 1989.

DeMaris, Richard E. *The Colossian Controversy: Wisdom in Dispute at Colossae.* JSNTSup 96. Sheffield: Sheffield Academic, 1994.

Derrida, Jacques. "Canons and Metonymies: An Interview with Jacques Derrida." In *Logomachia: The Contest of Faculties,* edited by Richard Rand, 195–211. Lincoln, NE: University of Nebraska, 1992.

————. *Of Grammatology.* Translated by Gayatri Chakravorty Spivak. Baltimore, MD: Johns Hopkins University Press, 1974.

————. "An Interview with Derrida (from Le nouvel observateur)." Translated by David Allison, et al. In *Derrida and Différance,* edited by David Wood and Robert Bernasconi, 71–82. Evanston: Northwestern University Press, 1988.

————. *Limited Inc.* Evanston: Northwestern University Press, 1977.

————. "Marx and Sons." In *Ghostly Demarcations,* edited by Michael Sprinker, 213–69. London: Verso, 1999.

————. *Positions.* Translated by Alan Bass. Chicago: University of Chicago, 1972.

Deutscher, Max. "'Il n'y a pas de hors-texte'—Once More" Symposium. *Canadian Journal of Continental Philosophy* 18.2 (2014) 98–124.

Dewey, Arthur J. "A Re-Hearing of Romans 10:1–15." *Semeia* 65 (1994) 109–27.

Dillon, John M. *The Middle Platonists: 80 BC to AD 200.* Ithaca: Cornell University Press, 1996.

Doane, A. N. "Oral Texts, Intertexts, and Intratexts: Editing Old English." In *Influence and Intertextuality in Literary History,* edited by Jay Clayton and Eric Rothstein, 75–113. Madison: University of Wisconsin, 1991.

Doane, Sébastien. "L'infanticide à Bethléem: quand l'intertextualité devient critique impériale." Unpublished paper. 72nd ACÉBAC Congress, University of Lava, May 29–31, 2015.

Dodson, Joseph R. *The "Powers" of Personification: Rhetorical Purpose in the Book of Wisdom and the Letter to the Romans.* BZNW 161. New York: de Gruyter, 2008.

————. "The Voices of Scripture: Citations and Personifications in Paul." *Bulletin for Biblical Research* 20 (2010) 419–31.

Doeve, Jan Willem. *Jewish Hermeneutics in the Synoptic Gospels and Acts*. Assen: Van Gorcum, 1954.

Donaldson, Terence L. "Parallels: Use, Misuse and Limitations." *Evangelical Quarterly* 55 (October 1983) 193–210.

Donelson, Lewis R. *Pseudepigraphy and Ethical Argument in the Pastoral Epistles*. Tübingen: Mohr Siebeck, 1986.

Donfried, Karl Paul. "Rethinking Scholarly Approaches to 1 Timothy." In *1 Timothy Reconsidered*, edited by Karl Paul Donfried, 153–82. Colloquium Oecumenicum Paulinum 18. Leuven: Peeters, 2008.

Donker, Gerald J. *The Text of the Apostolos in Athanasius of Alexandria*. The New Testament in the Greek Fathers 8. Atlanta: Society of Biblical Literature, 2011.

Draisma, Sipke, ed. *Intertextuality in Biblical Writings: Essays in Honour of Bas van Iersel*. Kampen: Kok, 1989.

Duarte, Alejandro. "Matthew." In *The Global Bible Commentary*, edited by Daniel Patte, 350–60. Nashville: Abingdon, 2004.

Duling, Dennis C. *The New Testament: History, Literature, and Social Context*. Belmont: Thomson/Wadsworth, 2003.

Dunn, James D. G. *The Oral Gospel Tradition*. Grand Rapids: Eerdmans, 2013.

———. *The Theology of Paul the Apostle*. Grand Rapids: Eerdmans, 2006.

Eaglestone, Robert. *The Contest of the Faculties*. London: University of Nebraska, 1992.

———. *The Holocaust and the Postmodern*. Oxford: Oxford University Press, 2004.

Edenburg, Cynthia. "Intertextuality, Literary Competence and the Question of Readership: Some Preliminary Observations." *JSOT* 32 (2010) 131–48.

Ehrman, Bart D. *Forgery and Counterforgery: The Use of Literary Deceit in Early Christian Polemics*. New York: Oxford University Press, 2012.

Ellens, J. Harrold. "Exegesis of Second Temple Texts in a Fourth Gospel Son of Man Logion." In *Biblical Interpretation in Judaism and Christianity*, edited by Isaac Kalimi and Peter J. Haas, 131–49. Library of the Hebrew Bible / Old Testament Studies 439. New York: T. & T. Clark, 2006.

Ellingworth, Paul. "Hebrews and 1 Clement: Literary Dependence or Common Tradition?" *Biblische Zeitschrift* 23.2 (1979) 262–69.

Elliott, John H. *1 Peter*. AB. New Haven: Yale University Press, 2007.

Elliott, Mark W., ed. *Ancient Christian Commentary on Scripture, Vol. XI: Isaiah 40–66*. Downers Grove, IL: InterVarsity, 2007.

Ellis, E. Earle. *Paul's Use of the Old Testament*. Reprint. Eugene: Wipf & Stock, 2003.

———. *Prophecy and Hermeneutic in Early Christianity*. WUNT 18. Tübingen: Mohr Siebeck, 1978.

Elman, Yaakov. "Classical Rabbinic Interpretation." In *The Jewish Study Bible*, edited by Adele Berlin and Marc Zvi Brettler, 1844–63. Oxford: Oxford University Press, 2004.

Emadl, Samuel. "Intertextuality in New Testament Scholarship: Significance, Criteria and the Art of Interpretation." *Currents in Biblical Research* 14 (2015) 8–23.

Enns, Peter E. "The Moveable Well in 1 Cor 10:4: An Extrabiblical Tradition in an Apostolic Text." *Bulletin for Biblical Research* (1996) 23–38.

Evans, Craig, and James A. Sanders, eds. *Early Christian Interpretation of Israel: Investigations and Proposals*. JSNTSup 148. Studies in Scripture in Early Judaism and Christianity 5. Sheffield: Sheffield Academic, 1997.

Evans, Craig A. and Shemaryahu Talmon, eds. *The Quest for Context and Meaning: Studies in Biblical Intertextuality in Honor of James A. Sanders.* Leiden: Brill, 1997.

Evans, Craig A., and Jeremiah J. Johnston, eds. *Searching the Scriptures: Studies in Context and Intertextuality.* Studies in Scripture in Early Judaism and Christianity 19; LNTS. New York: T. & T. Clark, 2015.

Fackenheim, Emil. *The Jewish Bible After the Holocaust: A Re-Reading.* Bloomington: Indiana University Press, 1991.

———. *To Mend the World. Foundations of Post-Holocaust Jewish Thought.* Bloomington: Indiana University Press, 1994.

Farmer, Ron. *Beyond the Impasse: The Promise of a Process Hermeneutic.* Macon: Mercer University Press, 1997.

Fee, Gordon D. "Old Testament Intertextuality in Colossians: Reflections on Pauline Christology and Gentile Inclusion in God's Story." In *History and Exegesis: New Testament Essays in Honor of Dr. E. Earle Ellis,* edited by Sang-Won Son, 201–21. London: T. & T. Clark, 2006.

Féral, J. "Kristevian Semiotics: Toward a Semanalysis." In *The Sign: Semiotics Around the World,* edited by R. W. Bailey, Ladislav Matejka, and P. Steiner, 271–79. Ann Arbor: Michigan Slavic, 1980.

Fewell, Danna Nolan, and Gary A. Phillips. "Bak's Impossible Memorials: Giving Face to the Children." In *Representing the Irreparable: The Shoah, the Bible and the Art of Samuel Bak,* edited by Danna Nolan Fewell, Gary A. Phillips, and Yvonne Sherwood, 93–124. Boston: Pucker Art Publication, 2008.

Fewell, Danna Nolan, ed. *Reading Between Texts: Intertextuality and the Hebrew Bible. Literary Currents in Biblical Interpretation.* Louisville: Westminster John Knox, 1992.

Fielder, Peter. *Das Matthäus-Evangelium,* vol 1. Theologishcer Kommentar Zum Neuen Testament. Stuttgart: W. Kohlhammer, 2006.

Finnegan, Ruth. *Why Do We Quote?: The Culture and History of Quotation.* Cambridge: Open Book, 2011.

Fiore, Benjamin. *The Pastoral Epistles. First Timothy, Second Timothy, Titus.* Sacra Pagina 12. Collegeville: Liturgical, 2007.

Fish, Stanley. *Is There a Text in this Class? The Authority of Interpretive Communities.* Cambridge: Harvard University Press, 1980.

Fishbane, Michael. *Biblical Interpretation in Ancient Israel.* Oxford: Clarendon, 1985.

———. "Types of Intertextuality." In Congress Volume: Oslo 1998, edited by André Lemaire and Magne Saebø, 39–44. VTSup 80. Leiden: Brill, 2000.

———. "Use, Authority and Interpretation of Mikra at Qumran." In *Mikra: Text, Translation, Reading and Interpretation of the Hebrew Bible in Ancient Judaism and Early Christianity,* edited by Martin Jan Mulder and Harry Sysling, 339–77. Minnaepolis: Fortress, 1988.

Fisk, Bruce N. "Synagogue Influence and Scriptural Knowledge Among the Christians of Rome." In *As It Is Written: Studying Paul's Use of Scripture,* edited by Stanley E. Porter and Christopher D. Stanley, 157–85. SBLSymp 50. Atlanta: Society of Biblical Literature, 2008.

Fitzmyer, Joseph A. "Further Light on Melchizedek from Qumran Cave 11." *JBL* 86 (1967) 25–41.

———. *The Gospel According to Luke.* AB 28–28A. Garden City: Doubleday, 1985.

Fossum, Jarl. "Colossians 1.15–18A in the Light of Jewish Mysticism and Gnosticism." *NTS* 35 (1989) 183–201.

Fowl, Stephen. "The Use of Scripture in Philippians." In *Paul and Scripture: Extending the Conversation*, edited by Christopher D. Stanley, 163–84. Atlanta: Society of Biblical Literature, 2012.

France, Richard T. "The Formula Quotations of Mt 2 and the Problem of Communication" *NTS* 27 (1981) 233–51.

———. "Herod and the Children of Bethlehem." *NovT* 21 (1979) 98–120.

French, Patrick. *The Time of Theory: A History of Tel Quel (1960–1983)*. Oxford: Clarendon, 1995.

Frenschkowski, Marco, "Pseudepigraphie und Paulusschule. Gedanken zur Verfasserschaft der Deuteropaulinen." In *Das Ende des Paulus. Historische, theologische und literaturgeschichtliche Aspekte*, edited by Friedrich Wilhelm Horn, 239–272. BZNW 106. Berlin: Walter de Gruyter, 2001.

Friedman, Susan Stanford. "Weavings: Intertextuality and the (Re)Birth of the Author." In *Influence and Intertextuality in Literary History*, edited by Jay Clayton and Eric Rothstein, 146–80. Madison: University of Wisconsin Press, 1991.

Frow, John. "Intertextuality and Ontology." In *Intertextuality. Theories and Practices*, edited by Michael Worton and Judith Still, 44–55. New York: Manchester University Press, 1990.

Fung, Glenn. "The Disputed Federalist Papers: SVM Feature Selection Via Concave Minimization." In *TAPIA '03 Proceedings of the 2003 Conference on Diversity in Computing, Atlanta, GA, October 15–18, 2003*, 42–46. New York: The Association of Computing Machinery, 2003.

Gadamer, Hans-Georg. *Truth and Method*. 2nd ed. Translated by J. Weinsheimer and D. G. Marshall. London: Bloomsbury, 1989.

Gaechter, Paul. *Das Matthäus Evangelium*. Innsbruck: Tyrolia, 1963.

Gamble, Harry Y. *Books and Readers in the Early Church: A History of Early Christian Texts*. New Haven: Yale University Press, 1995.

Gaskin, Richard. *Language, Truth, and Literature. A Defence of Literary Humanism*. Oxford: Oxford University Press, 2013.

Gathercole, Simon. "The Titles of the Gospels in the Earliest New Testament Manuscripts." *Zeitschrift für die Neutestamentliche Wissenschaft und die Kunde der älteren Kirche* 104.2 (2013) 33–76.

Geertz, Clifford. "Thick Description: Toward an Interpretive Theory of Culture." In *Readings in the Philosophy of Social Science*, edited by Michael Martin and Lee C. McIntyre, 213–31. Cambridge: MIT, 1994.

Gélin, A. "Osée." In *Dictionnaire de la Bible, Supplément*, edited by L. Pirot and F. Vigouroux, 926–40. Paris: Letouzey 1960.

Genette, Gérard. *Palimpsests: Literature in the Second Degree*. Translated by Channa Newman and Claude Doubinsky. Lincoln, NE: University of Nebraska, 1982.

———. *Paratexts: Thresholds of Interpretation*. Cambridge: Cambridge University Press, 1997.

Gignac, Alain. "The Enunciative Device of Rom 1:18—14:25: A Succession of Discourses Attempting to Express the Multiple Dimensions of God's Justice." *Catholic Biblical Quarterly* (2015) 481–502.

———. *L'épître Aux Romains. Commentaire Biblique*. Nouveau Testament 6. Paris: Cerf, 2014.

———. "L'interprétation du récit d'Abraham en Ga 3,6–4,7: Tour de force ou coup de force ? le travail narratif du lecteur face à l'énonciation et à l'intertextualité pauliniennes." In *Le Lecteur. VIe Colloque internatinal du RRENAB, Louvain-La-Neuve, 24–26 Mai 2012*, edited by Régis Burnet, Didier Luciani, and Geert Van Oyen, 309–30. BETL 273. Leuven: Peeters, 2014.

———. "'We Know That Everything That Law Says': Romans 3:9–20 as a Narrative Utilization of Intertextuality That Develops Its Own Theory of Intertextuality." In *Searching the Scriptures: Studies in Context and Intertextuality*, edited by Craig A. Evans and Jeremiah J. Johnston, 246–64. Studies in Scripture in Early Judaism and Christianity 19. London: T. & T. Clark, 2015.

Gillmayr-Bucher, Susanne. "Intertextuality: Between Literary Theory and Text Analysis." In *The Intertextuality of the Epistles. Explorations of Theory and Practice*, edited by Thomas L. Brodie, Dennis R. MacDonald, Stanley Porter, 13–23. New Testament Monographs 16. Sheffield: Sheffield Phoenix, 2006.

Gilmour, Michael J. *The Significance of Parallels between 2 Peter and Other Early Christian Literature*. Academia Biblica 10. Leiden: Brill, 2002.

Gnilka, Joachim. *Das Matthäusevangelium: II. Teil*, edited by Alfred Wikenhauser, Anton Vögtle, and Rudolph Schnackenburgh. Vol. 2. Herders Theologischer Kommentar zum Neuen Testament. Freiburg: Herder, 1988.

Goodacre, Mark S. *The Case Against Q: Studies in Markan Priority and the Synoptic Problem*. Harrisburg: Trinity, 2002.

———. *The Synoptic Problem: A Way Through the Maze*. New York: T. & T. Clark, 2001.

Goppelt, Leonhard. *Typos: The Typological Interpretation of the Old Testament in the New*. Translated by Donald H. Madvig. Grand Rapids: Eerdmans, 1982.

Gordley, Matthew E. *The Colossians Hymn in Context: An Exegesis in Light of Jewish and Greco-Roman Hymnic and Epistolary Conventions*. WUNT 2.228. Tübingen: Mohr Siebeck, 2007.

Green, Barbara. *Mikhail Bakhtin and Biblical Scholarship*. Atlanta: Society of Biblical Literature, 2001.

Green, Gene L. *Jude & 2 Peter*. BECNT. Grand Rapids: Baker, 2008.

———. "Relevance Theory and Theological Interpretation: Thoughts on Metarepresentation." *Journal of Theological Interpretation* 4.1 (2010) 75–90.

Green, Michael. *The Second Epistle General of Peter and the General Epistle of Jude: An Introduction and Commentary*. Grand Rapids: Eerdmans, 1968.

Greenberg, Irving. "Cloud of Smoke, Pillar of Fire: Judaism, Christianity, and Modernity after the Holocaust." In *Auschwitz: Beginning of a New Era? Reflections on the Holocaust*, edited by Eva Fleischner, 7–57. New York: KTAV, 1977.

Greene, Thomas M. *The Light in Troy: Imitation and Discovery in Renaissance Poetry*. New Haven: Yale University Press, 1982.

Gregory, Andrew F. and Christopher M. Tuckett. "Reflections on Method: What Constitutes the Use of the Writings That Later Formed the New Testament in the Apostolic Fathers?" In *The Reception of the New Testament in the Apostolic Fathers*, edited by Andrew F. Gregory and Christopher M. Tuckett, 61–82. Oxford: Oxford University Press, 2005.

Greimas, Algirdas Julien. *Du Sens 1: Essais Semiotiques*. Seuil edition. Paris: Seuil, 2012.

———. *Sémantique Structurale*. Paris: Universitaires de France, 2002.

Gundry, Robert. *Matthew. A Commentary on His Literary and Theological Art*. Grand Rapids: Eerdmans, 1982.

Guthrie, George H. "Hebrews." In *Commentary on the New Testament Use of the Old Testament,* edited by Gregory K. Beale and Donald A. Carson, 919–95. Grand Rapids: Baker Academic, 2007.

Gutt, Ernst-August. *Relevance Theory: A Guide to Successful Communication in Translation.* Dallas: SIL, 1992.

Hagner, Donald A. *Matthew 14–28.* WBC 33B. Dallas: Word, 1995.

———. *The Use of the Old and New Testaments in Clement of Rome.* Leiden: Brill, 1973.

Hance, Kenneth G., David C. Ralph, and Milton J. Wiksell. *Principles of Speaking.* 3rd ed. Belmont, CA: Wadsworth, 1989.

Harrington, Daniel. *The Gospel of Matthew.* Sacra Pagina 1. Collegeville: Liturgical, 1991.

Harris, William V. *Ancient Literacy.* Cambridge: Harvard University Press, 1989.

Hartman, D. L. "Scriptural Exegesis in the Gospel of St. Matthew and the Problem of Communication." In *L'Évangile selon Mattieu. Rédaction et Théologie,* edited by M. Didier, 131–52. Gembloux: Duculot, 1972.

Hatina, Thomas R. "Intertextuality and Historical Criticism in New Testament Studies," *Biblical Interpretation* 7 (1999) 28–43.

Havercroft, Barbara. "Énonciation/ Énoncé." In *Encyclopedia of Contemporary Literary Theory: Approaches, Scholars, Terms,* edited by Irena R. Makaryk, 540–42. Theory/ Culture Series. Toronto: University of Toronto, 1993.

Hauerwas, Stanley. *Matthew.* Brazos Theological Commentary on the Bible. Grand Rapids: Brazos, 2006.

Hay, David M. "Philo's References to Other Allegorists." *SPh* 6 (1979–80) 41–75.

Hayes, John H., and Carl R. Holladay. *Biblical Exegesis: A Beginner's Handbook.* Louisville: Westminster John Knox, 2007.

Hays, Richard B. "Can the Gospels Teach Us How to Read the Old Testament?" *Pro Ecclesia* 11 (2002) 402–18.

———. *The Conversion of the Imagination: Paul as Interpreter of Israel's Scripture.* Grand Rapids: Eerdmans, 2005.

———. *Echoes of Scripture in the Letters of Paul.* New Haven: Yale University Press, 1989.

———. *The Faith of Jesus Christ: The Narrative Substructure of Galatians 3:1—4:11.* 2nd ed. The Biblical Resource Series. Grand Rapids: Eerdmans, 2002.

———. "On the Rebound: A Response to Critiques of Echoes of Scripture in the Letters of Paul." In *Early Christian Interpretation of Israel: Investigations and Proposals,* edited by Craig A. Evans, and James A. Sanders, 93–111. JSNTSup 148. Studies in Scripture in Early Judaism and Christianity 5. Sheffield: Sheffield Academic, 1997.

———. "Psalm 143 and the Logic of Romans 3." *JBL* 99 (1980) 107–15.

———. *Reading Backwards: Figural Christology and the Fourfold Gospel Witness.* Waco: Baylor University Press, 2014.

Hays, Richard, Stefan Alkier, and Leroy Huizenga, eds. *Reading the Bible Intertextually.* Waco: Baylor University Press, 2009.

Hebel, Udo J. *Intertextuality, Allusion, and Quotation: An International Bibliography of Critical Studies.* Bibliographies and Indexes in World Literature 18. New York: Greenwood, 1989.

———. "Towards a Descriptive Poetics of Allusion." In *Intertextuality,* edited by Heinrich F. Plett, 135–64. Berlin: Walter de Gruyter, 1991.

Hellerman, Joseph H. *Philippians.* Nashville: Broadman & Holman, 2015.

Herzer, Jens. "Fiktion oder Täuschung? Zur Diskussion über die Pseudepigraphie der Pastoralbriefe." In *Pseudepigraphie und Verfasserfiktion in früchristlichen Briefen / Pseudepigraphy and Author Fiction in Early Christian Letters*, edited by Jörg Frey, et al., 489–536. WUNT 1.246. Tübingen: Mohr Siebeck, 2009.

Heubeck, Alfred. *A Commentary on Homer's Odyssey.* Vol. 2. Books IX–XVI, edited by Alfred Heubeck and Arie Hoekstra. Oxford: Oxford University Press, 1990.

Hezser, Catherine. *Jewish Literacy in Roman Palestine.* Tübingen: Mohr Siebeck, 2001.

Hill, Charles E. *The Johannine Corpus in the Early Church.* Oxford: Oxford University Press, 2004.

Hill, Leslie. *The Cambridge Introduction to Jacques Derrida.* Cambridge Introductions to Literatures. Cambridge: Cambridge University Press, 2007.

Hirsch, E. D. *Validity in Interpretation.* New Haven: Yale University Press, 1967.

Hoehner, Harold W. *Ephesians: An Exegetical Commentary.* Grand Rapids: Baker Academic, 2002.

Hollander, John. *The Figure of Echo: A Mode of Allusion in Milton and After.* Berkeley, CA: University of California, 1981.

Holquist, Michael, ed. *The Dialogic Imagination.* Austin: University of Texas, 1981.

Holthuis, Susanne. *Intertextualität. Aspekte einer rezeptionsorientierten Konzeption.* Stauffenburg Colloquium 28. Tübingen: Stauffenburg, 1993.

Holtzmann, Heinrich Julius. *Einleitung in das Neue Testament.* Freiburg: Mohr Siebeck, 1886.

Horsley, Richard A., Jonathan A. Draper, and John Miles Foley, eds. *Performing the Gospel: Orality, Memory, and Mark: Essays Dedicated to Werner Kelber.* Minnaepolis: Fortress, 2006.

Horstkotte, Silke and Nancy Pedri. "Focalization in Graphic Narrative." *Narrative* 19.3 (2011) 330–57.

Hübner, Hans. *Gottes Ich Und Israel: Zum Schriftgebrauch Des Paulus in Römer 9–11.* FRLANT 136. Göttingen: Vandenhoeck & Ruprecht, 1984.

———. "Intertextualität—Die hermeneutische Strategie des Paulus." *TLZ* 116 (1991) 881–98.

Huizenga, Leroy A. "The Old Testament in the New, Intertextuality and Allegory." *JSNT* 38 (2015) 17–35.

Hultgren, Arland J. *The Parables of Jesus: A Commentary.* Grand Rapids: Eerdmans, 2000.

Hunter, Richard. *Critical Moments in Classical Literature: Studies in the Ancient View of Literature and its Uses.* Cambridge: Cambridge University Press, 2009.

Hurst, Lincoln. *The Epistle of Hebrews: Its Background of Thought.* SNTSMS 65. Cambridge: Cambridge University Press, 1990.

Hurtado, Larry W. *Lord Jesus Christ: Devotion to Jesus in Earliest Christianity.* Grand Rapids: Eerdmans. 2003.

Instone-Brewer, David. "Hermeneutics, Theology of." In *Encyclopaedia of Midrash: Biblical Interpretation in Formative Judaism.* 2 Vols, edited by Jacob Neusner and Alan J. Avery-Peck, 1.292–316. Leiden: Brill, 2005.

Issacharoff, Michael. *Discourse as Performance.* Stanford: Stanford University Press, 1989.

Iverson, Kelly R. "An Enemy of the Gospel? Anti-Paulinisms and Intertextuality in the Gospel of Matthew." In *Unity and Diversity in the Gospels and Paul: Essays in*

Honor of Frank J. Matera, edited by Christopher W. Skinner and Kelly R. Iverson, 7–32. Atlanta: Society of Biblical Literature, 2012.

Jakobson, Roman. "Closing Statement: Linguistics and Poetics." In *Style and Language*, edited by Thomas Sebeok, 350–77. New York: Wiley, 1960.

Janse, Sam. *"You Are My Son": The Reception History of Psalm 2 in Early Judaism and the Early Church*. Leuven: Peeters, 2009.

Jeal, Roy R. *Exploring Philemon: Freedom, Brotherhood, and Partnership in the New Society*. RRA 2. Atlanta: Society of Biblical Literature, 2015.

Jervis, L. Ann. "'But I Want You to Know...' Paul's Midrashic Intertextual Response to the Corinthian Worshipers (1 Cor 11:2–16)." *JBL* 112 (1993) 231–46.

Jobes, Karen H. 1 Peter. BECNT. Grand Rapids: Baker Academic, 2005.

———. *Letters to the Church: A Survey of Hebrews and the General Epistles*. Grand Rapids: Zondervan, 2011.

———. "Quantitative Methods for Exploring the Relationship Between Books of the Septuagint." In *The Bible As Book: The Transmission of the Greek Text*, edited by Scot McKendrick and Orlaith A. O'Sullivan, 73–95. New Castle: Oak Knoll, 2003.

Johnson, Luke T. *The First and Second Letters to Timothy*. AB 35A. Garden City: Doubleday, 2001.

———. "The Use of Leviticus 19 in the Letter of James." *JBL* 101 (1982) 391–401.

Johnson, Marshall D. *The Purpose of the Biblical Genealogies: With Special Reference to the Setting of the Genealogies of Jesus*. Cambridge: Cambridge University Press, 1969.

Kahmann, Johannes. "The Second Letter of Peter and the Letter of Jude: Their Mutual Relationship." In *The New Testament in Early Christianity: La réception des écrits néotestamentaires dans le christianisme primitive*, edited by Jean-Marie Sevrin, 105–22. BETL 86. Leuven: Peeters & Leuven University Press, 1989.

Kaiser, Walter C., Darrell L. Bock, and Peter Enns. *Three Views on the New Testament Use of the Old Testament*. Grand Rapids: Zondervan, 2008.

Kamesar, Adam. "Biblical Interpretation in Philo." In *The Cambridge Companion to Philo*, edited by Adam Kamesar, 65–91. Cambridge: Cambridge University Press, 2009.

Kasher, Rimon. "The Interpretation of Scripture in Rabbinic Literature." In *Mikra: Text, Translation, Reading and Interpretation of the Hebrew Bible in Ancient Judaism and Early Christianity*, edited by Martin Jan Mulder and Harry Sysling, 547–94. Van Gorcum, Assen and Minnaepolis: Fortress, 1988.

Keener, Craig S. *A Commentary on the Gospel of Matthew*. Grand Rapids: Eerdmans, 1999.

———. 1–2 Corinthians. NCBC. Cambridge: Cambridge University Press, 2005.

Kelly, J. N. D. *A Commentary on the Epistles of Peter and of Jude*. BNTC. London: A. & C. Black, 1969.

Kenny, Anthony. *A Stylometric Study of the New Testament*. New York: Oxford University Press, 1986.

Kern, Philip H. *Rhetoric and Galatians: Assessing an Approach to Paul's Epistle*. SNTSMS 101. Cambridge: Cambridge University Press, 1998.

Kern-Ulmer, Rivka. "Hermeneutics, Techniques of Rabbinic Exegesis." In *Encyclopaedia of Midrash: Biblical Interpretation in Formative Judaism*, edited by Jacob Neusner and Alan J. Avery-Peck, 1.268–92. 2 Vols. Leiden: Brill, 2005.

Kingsbury, Jack. *Matthew: Structure, Christology, Kingdom.* Philadelphia: Fortress, 1975.

Kirk, J. R. Daniel. "Conceptualising Fulfillment in Matthew." *Tyndale Bulletin* 59 (2008) 77–98.

———. "Time for Figs, Temple Destruction, and Houses of Prayer in Mark 11:12–25." *Catholic Biblical Quarterly* 74 (2012) 509–27.

———. "Toward a Theory of Narrative Transformation: The Importance of Both Contexts in Paul's Scriptural Citations." In *Searching the Scriptures. Studies in Context and Intertextuality,* edited by Craig A. Evans and Jeremiah J. Johnston, 213–33. London: T. & T. Clark, 2015.

———. *Unlocking Romans: Resurrection and the Justification of God.* Grand Rapids: Eerdmans, 2008.

———. "Why Does the Deliverer Come ἐκ Σιων (Romans 11.26)?" *JSNT* 33 (2010) 81–99.

Kittel, Gerhard, and Geoffrey W. Bromiley. *Theological Dictionary of the New Testament.* 10 vols. Grand Rapids: Eerdmans, 1964–76.

Koch, Dietrich-Alex. *Die Schrift als Zeuge des Evangeliums: Untersuchungen zur Verwendung und zum Verständnis der Schrift bei Paulus.* Beiträge zur historischen Theologie 69. Tübingen: Mohr Siebeck, 1986.

Köhler, Wolf-Dietrich. *Die Rezeption des Matthäusevangeliums in der Zeit vor Irenäus.* WUNT 2.24. Tübingen: Mohr Siebeck, 1987.

Koutrianou, Elena. "Intertextuality and Relevance Theory in the Interdisciplinary Approach to Surrealist Literature and Painting. A Case-Study: Nikos Engonopoulos' 'Bolivar.'" *Research Notebooks* 29 (2009) 145–54.

Kristeva, Julia. *Desire in Language. A Semiotic Approach to Language and Art.* Edited by Leon S. Roudiez. Translated by Thomas Gora, Alice Jardine, and Leon S. Roudiez. New York: Columbia University Press, 1980.

———. La révolution du langage poétique. L'avant-garde à la fin du XIXe siècle: Lautréamont et Mallarmé. Paris: Seuil, 1974.

———. *Revolution in Poetic Language.* Translated by M. Waller. New York: Columbia University Press, 1984.

———. *Sèméiôtikè—Recherches pour une sémanalyse.* Points Essais. Paris: Seuil, 1969.

——— "Word, Dialogue, and Novel." In *The Kristeva Reader,* edited by Toril Moi, 34–61. New York: Columbia University Press, 1986.

Kugel, James L. *The Idea of Biblical Poetry: Parallelism and Its History.* New Haven: Yale University Press, 1981.

Kümmel, Werner Georg. *Introduction to the New Testament.* Rev. ed. Translated by Howard Clark Kee. Nashville: Abingdon, 1975.

Lactantius. *Divinae institutiones et epitome divinum institutionum.* Edited by S. Brandt. CSEL 19. Prague, 1890.

Lakoff, George, and Mark Johnson. *Metaphors We Live By.* Chicago: University of Chicago, 1980.

Lane, William L. *Hebrews 1–8.* WBC 47A. Nashville: Thomas Nelson, 1991.

Langmuir, Gavin. *Toward a Definition of Antisemitism.* Berkeley, CA: University of California, 1990.

Larsson, Kristian. "Intertextual Density, Quantifying Imitation." *JBL* 133 (2014) 309–31.

Leitch, Vincent. *Deconstructive Criticism: An Advanced Introduction.* New York: Columbia University Press, 1983.

Leith, Dick, and George Myerson. *The Power of Address: Explorations in Rhetoric.* London: Routledge, 1989.

Leithart, Peter J. *Deep Exegesis: The Mystery of Reading Scripture.* Waco: Baylor University Press, 2009.

Lentz, Tony M. *Orality and Literacy in Hellenic Greece.* Carbondale: Southern Illinois University Press, 1989.

Leonard, Jeffery M. "Identifying Inner-Biblical Allusions: Psalm 78 as a Test Case." *JBL* 127 (2008) 241–65.

Levi, Primo. *Survival In Auschwitz.* Translated by Stuart Woolf. New York: Touchstone, 1996.

Levinas, Emmanuel. "Beyond Memory. From the Tractate Berakhot, 12b–13a." In *The Time of the Nations,* translated by Michael B. Smith, 76–91. Indianapolis: Indiana University Press, 1994.

———. "Ethics as First Philosophy." In *The Levinas Reader,* edited by Seán Hand, 75–82. Oxford: Blackwell, 1989.

———. *Humanism of the Other.* Translated by Nidra Poller. Chicago: University of Illinois, 2003.

———. *Totality and Infinity. An Essay on Exteriority.* Translated by Alphonso Lingis. Dordrecht: Kluwer Academic, 1991.

Lieberman, Saul. *Hellenism in Jewish Palestine: Studies in the Literary Transmission, Beliefs, and Manners of Palestine in the I Century BCE–IV Century CE.* New York: The Jewish Theological Seminary of America, 1950.

Lightfoot, J. B. *Saint Paul's Epistles to the Colossians and to Philemon.* London: Macmillan, 1880.

Linafelt, Tod, ed. *Strange Fire: Reading the Bible after the Holocaust.* New York: New York University Press, 2000.

Lincoln, Andrew T. "Colossians." In *The New Interpreters Bible. Vol. 11,* edited by Leander E. Keck, 551–669. Nashville: Abingdon, 2000.

———. *Ephesians.* WBC 42. Dallas: Word, 1990.

Lindemann, Andreas. *Paulus im ältesten Christentum. Beiträge zur historischen Theologie 58.* Tübingen: Mohr Siebeck, 1979.

Linell, Per. *Approaching Dialogue: Talk, Interaction and Contexts in Dialogical Perspective.* Amsterdam: John Benjamins, 1998.

Liszka, Jakób James. *A General Introduction to the Semiotic of Charles Sanders Peirce.* Bloomington: Indiana University Press, 1996.

Litwak, Kenneth D. "Echoes of Scripture? A Critical Survey of Recent Works on Paul's Use of the Old Testament." *Currents in Research: Biblical Studies* 6 (1998) 260–88.

———. *Echoes of Scripture in Luke-Acts: Telling the History of God's People Intertextually.* JSNTSup 282. London: T. & T. Clark, 2005.

Longenecker, Bruce W., ed. *Narrative Dynamics in Paul: A Critical Assessment.* Louisville, KY: Westminster John Knox, 2002.

Longenecker, Richard. *Biblical Exegesis in the Apostolic Period.* 2nd ed. Grand Rapids: Eerdmans, 1999.

Lord, George DeForest. *Classical Presences in Seventeenth-Century English Poetry.* New Haven: Yale University Press, 1987.

Loriggio, Francesco. "Benveniste, Émile." In *Encyclopedia of Contemporary Literary Theory: Approaches, Scholars, Terms*, edited by Irena R. Makaryk, 251–53. Theory/ Culture Series. Toronto: University of Toronto Press, 1993.

Lotringer, Sylvere, and Thomas Gora, eds. *Polyphonic Linguistics: The Many Voices of Émile Benveniste*. Semiotica. Special Supplement. New York: Mouton, 1981.

Lucas, Alec J. "Assessing Stanley E. Porter's Objections to Richard B. Hays's Notion of Metalepsis." *Catholic Biblical Quarterly* 76 (2014) 93–111.

Lust, Johann. "Ezekiel 36–40 in the Oldest Greek Manuscript." *Catholic Biblical Quarterly* 43 (1981) 517–33.

Luttenberger, Joram. *Prophetenmantel oder Bücherfutteral? Die persönlichen Notizen in den Pastoralbriefen im Licht antiker Epistolographie und literarischer Pseudepigraphie. Arbeiten zur Bibel und ihrer Geschichte*. Leipzig: EVA, 2012.

Luz, Ulrich. *Das Evangelium nach Matthäus (Mt 18–25). Vol. 3*. Evangelisch-Katholischer Kommentar zum Neuen Testament I/3. Zürich: Benziger, 1997.

———. "Intertexts in the Gospel of Matthew." *Harvard Theological Review* 97 (2004) 119–37.

———. *Matthew 1–7. A Commentary*. Translated by Wilhelm Lins. Minnaepolis: Augsburg, 1989.

Lyotard, Jean-François. "Discussions, or Phrasing 'after Auschwitz'." In *Auschwitz and After: Race, Culture, and 'the Jewish Question' in France*, edited by Lawrence D. Kritzman, 149–74. New York: Routledge, 1995.

MacDonald, Dennis R. *Christianizing Homer: "The Odyssey," Plato, and "The Acts of Andrew."* New York: Oxford University Press, 1994.

———. *Does the New Testament Imitate Homer? Four Cases from the Acts of the Apostles*. New Haven: Yale University Press, 2003.

———. *The Gospels and Homer: Imitations of Greek Epic in Mark and Luke-Acts*. The New Testament and Greek Literature 1. Lanham, MD: Rowman & Littlefield, 2014.

———. *The Homeric Epics and the Gospel of Mark*. New Haven: Yale University Press, 2000.

———. *My Turn: A Critique of Critics of "Mimesis Criticism."* Claremont: The Institute for Antiquity and Christianity, 2009.

———. *Mythologizing Jesus: From Jewish Teacher to Epic Hero*. Lanham, MD: Rowman & Littlefield, 2015.

MacKinnon, Donald. *Explorations in Theology*. Vol 5. London: SCM, 1979.

Mai, Hans-Peter. "Bypassing Intertextuality. Hermeneutics, Textual Practices, Hypertext." In *Intertextuality*, edited by Heinrich F. Plett, 30–59. Research in Text Theory. Berlin: Walter de Gruyter, 1991.

Maier, Harry O. *Picturing Paul in Empire: Imperial Image, Text and Persuasion in Colossians, Ephesians and the Pastoral Epistles*. London: T. & T. Clark, 2013.

Maier, Johann. "Early Jewish Biblical Interpretation in the Qumran Literature." In *Hebrew Bible/Old Testament: The History of Its Interpretation*. Volume 1: From the Beginnings to the Middle Ages (Until 1300), edited by Magne Sæbø, 108–29. Gottingen: Vandenhoeck & Ruprecht, 1996.

Malherbe, Abraham J. "'In Season and Out of Season': 2 Timothy 4:2." *JBL* 103 (1984) 235–43.

Malik, Rachel. "Fixing Meaning: Intertextuality, Inference and the Horizon of the Publishable." *Radical Philosophy* 124 (2004) 13–26.

Malina, Bruce J. *The New Testament World: Insights from Cultural Anthropology*. 3rd ed. Louisville: Westminster John Knox, 2001.

Malka, Salomon. *Emmanuel Levinas. His life and Legacy*. Translated by Michael Kigel and Sonja Embree. Pittsburgh: Duquesne University Press, 2006.

Malkiel, Yakov. "Lexis and Grammar—Necrological Essay on Émile Benveniste (1902–76)." *Romance Philology* 34 (1980) 160–94.

Mallen, Peter. *The Reading and Transformation of Isaiah in Luke-Acts*. New York: T. & T. Clark, 2008.

Margolis, Joseph. "Texts." *Poetics Today* 14.1 (1993) 193–211.

Marguerat, Daniel, and Adrian Curtis, eds. *Intertextualités: La Bible en échos*. Le Monde de la Bible 40. Geneva: Labor et Fides, 2000.

Marguerat, Daniel, Yvan Bourquin, and Marcel Durrer. *How to Read Bible Stories: An Introduction to Narrative Criticism*. London: SCM, 1999.

Marmur, Michael, "Why Jews Quote." *Oral Tradition* 29.1 (2014) 5–46.

Marshall, I. Howard. *The Pastoral Epistles*. ICC. London: T. & T. Clark, 1999.

Marshall, John W. "'I Left You in Crete': Narrative Deception and Social Hierarchy in the Letter to Titus." *JBL* 127 (2008) 781–803.

Martin, Dale B. *Slavery as Salvation: The Metaphor of Slavery in Pauline Christianity*. New Haven: Yale University Press, 1989.

Martin, Ralph P. *A Hymn of Christ: Philippians 2:5–11 in Recent Interpretation & in the Setting of Early Christian Worship*. Downers Grove: InterVarsity, 1997.

Martin, Troy W. *By Philosophy and Empty Deceit: Colossians as Response to a Cynic Critique*. JSNTSup 118. Sheffield: Sheffield Academic, 1996.

Masterman, John Howard Bertram. *The First Epistle of S. Peter: Greek Text, with Introduction and Notes*. London: MacMillan, 1900.

Mayordomo, Moisés. "Matthew 1–2 and the Problem of Intertextuality." In *Infancy Gospels: Stories and Identities*, edited by Claire Clivaz et al., 257–79. WUNT 281. Tübingen: Mohr Siebeck, 2011.

McAfee, Noëlle. *Julia Kristeva*. Routledge Critical Thinkers. New York: Routledge, 2004.

McEwen, Alastair. "Paul's Use of the Old Testament in 1 Corinthians 10:1–4." *Vox Reformata* 47 (1986) 3–10.

McGrath, James F. "On Hearing (Rather Than Reading) Intertextual Echoes: Christology and Monotheistic Scriptures in an Oral Context." *Biblical Theology Bulletin* 43 (2013) 74–80.

————. *The Only True God*. Urbana, IL: University of Illinois Press, 2009.

McKay, Niall. "Status Update: The Many Faces of Intertextuality in New Testament Study." *Religion & Theology* 20 (2013) 84–106.

Meade, David G. *Pseudonymity and Canon: An Investigation into the Relationship of Authorship and Authority in Jewish and Earliest Christian Tradition*. Grand Rapids: Eerdmans, 1986.

Mealand, D. L. "The Extent of the Pauline Corpus: A Multivariate Approach." *JSNT* 59 (1995) 61–92.

Meek, Russell L. "Intertextuality, Inner-Biblical Exegesis, and Inner-Biblical Allusion: The Ethics of a Methodology." *Biblica* 95 (2014) 280–91.

Meeks, Wayne A. "'And Rose up to Play': Midrash and Paraenesis in 1 Corinthians 10:1–22." *JSNT* 16 (1982) 64–78.

Memar Marqah. *The Teaching of Marqah*. Edited and translated by John Macdonald. BZAW 84. Berlin: Töpelmann, 1963.

Merkel, Helmut. *Die Pastoralbriefe*. NTD 9.1. Göttingen: Vandenhoeck & Ruprecht, 1991.

Merz, Annette. "Fictitious Self-exposition of Paul: How Might Intertextual Theory Suggest a Reformulation of the Hermeneutics of Pseudoepigraphy?" In *The Intertextuality of the Epistles. Explorations of Theory and Practice*, edited by Thomas L. Brodie, Dennis R. MacDonald, Stanley Porter, 113–32. New Testament Monographs 16. Sheffield: Sheffield Phoenix, 2006.

―――. *Die Fiktive Selbstauslegung des Paulus: Intertextuelle Studien zur Intention und Rezeption der Pastoralbriefe*. NTOA 52. Göttingen: Vandenhoeck & Ruprecht, 2004.

Michel, Otto. "σπένδομαι." In *TDNT* 7.528–36.

Mieder, Wolfgang. *"Making a Way Out of No Way": Martin Luther King's Sermonic Proverbial Rhetoric*. New York: Peter Lang, 2010.

Mihaly, Eugene. "A Defense of Israel's Election: An Analysis of Sifre Deuteronomy 32:9, Pisqa 312." *HUCA* 35 (1964) 103–43.

Miller, G. D. "Intertextuality in Old Testament Research." *Currents in Biblical Research* 9 (2011) 239–309.

Miller, Robert J. "Is There Independent Attestation for the Transfiguration in 2 Peter?" *NTS* 42 (1996) 620–25.

Mitton, C. Leslie. *The Epistle to the Ephesians: Its Authorship, Origin and Purpose*. Oxford: Clarendon, 1951.

Mody, Rohintan Keki. "The Case of the Missing Thousand': Paul's Use of the Old Testament in 1 Corinthians 10:8—A New Proposal." *Churchman* 121 (2007) 61–79.

Moffatt, James. *An Introduction to the Literature of the New Testament*. The International Theological Library. New York: Charles Scribner's Sons, 1911.

Moi, Toril, ed. *The Kristeva Reader*. New York: Columbia University Press, 1986.

Moltmann, Jürgen. *The Crucified God—40th Anniversary Edition*. London: SCM, 2015.

Montrose, Louis. "Professing the Renaissance: The Poetics and Politics of Culture." In *The New Historicism*, edited by H. Aram Vesser, 15–36. New York: Routledge, 1989.

Moo, Douglas J. *2 Peter and Jude*. NIV Application Commentary. Grand Rapids: Zondervan, 1996.

―――. *The Old Testament in the Gospel Passion Narratives*. Sheffield: The Almond, 1983.

Moore, Stephen. *Poststructuralism and the New Testament. Derrida and Foucault at the Foot of the Cross*. Minnaepolis: Augsburg Fortress, 1994.

Moore, Stephen D., and Y. Sherwood. *The Invention of the Biblical Scholar: A Critical Manifesto*. Minnaepolis: Augsburg Fortress, 2011.

Morgan, Thaïs E. "Is There an Intertext in this Text? Literary and Interdisciplinary Approaches to Intertextuality." *American Journal of Semiotics* 3.4 (1985) 1–40.

Moyise, Steve. "Does Paul Respect the Context of His Quotations?" In *Paul and Scripture: Extending the Conversation*, edited by Christopher D. Stanley, 97–114. Atlanta: Society of Biblical Literature, 2012.

―――. *Evoking Scripture: Seeing the Old Testament in the New*. London: T. & T. Clark, 2008.

―――. "Intertextuality and Biblical Studies: A Review." *Verbum et Ecclesia* 23 (2002) 418–31.

——. *The Later New Testament Writings and Scripture: The Old Testament in Acts, Hebrews, the Catholic Epistles and Revelation.* Grand Rapids: Baker, 2012.

——. *The Old Testament in the Book of Revelation.* JSNTSup 115. Sheffield: Sheffield Academic, 1995.

Mulder, Otto. *Simon the High Priest in Sirach 50: An Exegetical Study of the Significance of Simon the High Priest as Climax to the Praise of the Fathers in Ben Sira's Concept of the History of Israel.* JSJSSup 78. Leiden: Brill, 2003.

Murphy, Frederick J. *Fallen is Babylon. The Revelation to John.* Harrisburg: Trinity International, 1998.

Myers, Elizabeth A. *Authorship of 1 Peter and Hebrews: New Evidence in Light of Probable Intertextual Borrowing.* Forthcoming.

——. *Probability of Intertextual Borrowing between New Testament Books: A Methodology for Determining the Likelihood of Literary Dependence and the Direction of Borrowing.* Forthcoming.

Nadella, Raj. *Dialogue Not Dogma: Many Voices in the Gospel of Luke.* London: T. & T. Clark, 2011.

Neville, David J. *Mark's Gospel—Prior or Posterior?: A Reappraisal of the Phenomenon of Order.* JSNTSup 222. London: Sheffield Academic, 2002.

Neyrey, Jerome H. *2 Peter, Jude.* AB 37C. Garden City: Doubleday, 1993.

——. "'First', 'Only', 'One of a Few', and 'No One Else': The Rhetoric of Uniqueness and the Doxologies in 1 Timothy." *Biblica* 86 (2005) 59–87. Online: http://www3. nd.edu/~jneyrey1/first-only.htm.

Niditch, Susan. *Oral World and Written Word.* Louisville: Westminster John Knox, 1996.

Nye, Andrea. "Woman Clothed with the Sun: Julia Kristeva and the Escape from/to Language." *Signs* 12 (1987) 664–86.

O'Brien, Peter T. *The Epistle to the Philippians: A Commentary on the Greek Text.* NIGCT. Grand Rapids: Eerdmans, 1991.

——. *The Letter to the Ephesians.* The Pillar New Testament Commentary. Grand Rapids: Eerdmans, 1999.

O'Day, Gail R. "Jeremiah 9.22–23 and 1 Corinthians 1.26–31: A Study in Intertextuality." *JBL* 109 (1990) 259–67.

Oakes, Peter. *Philippians. From People to Letter.* SNTSMS 110. Cambridge: Cambridge University Press, 2001.

Oberlinner, Lorenz. *Die Pastoralbriefe. Kommentar zum zweiten Timotheusbrief.* HThK XI/2.2. Freiburg: Herder, 1995.

——. "Paulus versus Paulus? Zum Problem des Paulinismus der Pastoralbriefe." In *Pneuma und Gemeinde: Christsein in der Tradition des Paulus und Johannes,* edited by Jost Eckert, Martin Schmidl, Hanneliese Steichele, 170–99. Festschrift für Josef Hainz zum 65. Geburtstag. Düsseldorf: Patmos, 2001.

Ong, Walter J. *Orality and Literacy: The Technologizing of the Word.* 30th Anniversary Edition. London: Routledge, 2012.

Orchard, Bernard, and Harold Riley. *The Order of the Synoptics: Why Three Synoptic Gospels?* Macon, GA: Mercer University Press, 1987.

Oropeza, B. J. *Exploring Second Corinthians: Death and Life, Hardship and Rivalry.* RRA 3. Atlanta: Society of Biblical Literature, 2016.

——. *First Corinthians.* New Covenant Commentary. Eugene: Cascade, forthcoming.

————. "Intertextuality." In *The Oxford Encyclopedia of Biblical Interpretation*, edited by Steven L. McKenzie, 1.453–63. Oxford: Oxford University Press, 2013.

————. "Laying to Rest the Midrash: Paul's Message of Meat Sacrificed to Idols in Light of the Deuteronomic Tradition." *Biblica* 79 (1998) 57–68.

————. *Paul and Apostasy: Eschatology, Perseverance and Falling Away in the Corinthian Congregation*. WUNT 2.115. Tübingen: Mohr Siebeck, 2000.

Orr, Mary. *Intertextuality: Debates and Contexts*. Cambridge: Polity, 2003.

Patte, Daniel. *What is Structural Exegesis? Guides to Biblical Scholarship*. Philadelphia: Fortress, 1976.

Pattemore, Stephen. *The People of God in the Apocalypse: Discourse, Structure and Exegesis*. SNTMS 128. Cambridge: Cambridge University Press, 2004.

————. "Relevance Theory, Intertextuality and the Book of Revelation." In *Current Trends in Scripture Translation*, edited by Philip Noss, 43–60. UBS Bulletin 194/195. Reading: UBS, 2003.

————. *Souls Under the Altar: Relevance Theory and the Discourse Structure of Revelation*. UBS 9. New York: UBS, 2003.

Perelman, Chaïm, and Lucie Olbrechts-Tyteca. *The New Rhetoric: A Treatise on Argumentation*. Notre Dame: University of Notre Dame, 1969.

Perrot, Charles. "Les examples du désert (1 Co. 10.6–11)." *NTS* 29 (1983) 437–52.

Petöfi, János S. "Explikative Interpretation: Explikatives Wissen." In *Von der verbalen KonstiAtution zur symbolischen Bedeutung—From Verbal Constitution to Symbolic Meaning*, edited by János S. Petöfi and Terry Olivi, 184–95. Hamburg: H. Buske, 1988.

Pfister, Manfred. "How Postmodern is Intertextuality?" In *Intertextuality*, edited by Heinrich F. Plett, 207–24. Research in Text Theory 15. Berlin: Walter de Gruyter, 1991.

Phillips, Gary. "Biblical Studies and Intertextuality: Should the Work of Genette and Eco Broaden Our Horizons?" In *The Intertextuality of the Epistles: Explorations of Theory and Practice*, edited by Thomas L. Brodie, Dennis R. MacDonald, and Stanley E. Porter, 36–45. NTM 16. Sheffield: Sheffield Phoenix, 2006.

————. "The Killing Fields of Matthew's Gospel." In *The Labour of Reading. Desire, Alienation and Biblical Interpretation*, edited by Fiona Black, Roland Boer, and Erin Runions, 249–66. Semeia Studies 36. Atlanta: Society of Biblical Literature, 1999.

————. "More Than the Jews. . . . His Blood be upon all the Children: Biblical Violence, Bosnian Genocide, and Responsible Reading." In *Confronting Genocide: Judaism, Christianity, Islam*, edited by Steven Leonard Jacobs, 77–91. Lanham, MD: Lexington, 2009.

Phillips, Gregory Y., Fika Janse van Rensburg, and Herrie F Van Rooy. "Developing an Integrated Approach to Interpret New Testament Use of the Old Testament." *Die Skriflig* 46.2 (2012) 1–10.

Phua, Richard Liong-Seng. *Idolatry and Authority: A Study of 1 Corinthians 8.1—11.1 in the Light of the Jewish Diaspora*. London: T. & T. Clark, 2005.

Pietersen, Lloyd. *Reading the Bible after Christendom*. Milton Keynes: Paternoster, 2011.

Pilkington, Adrian. "Introduction: Relevance Theory and Literary Style." *Language and Literature* 5 (1996) 157–62.

————. *Poetic Effects: A Relevance Theory Perspective*. Amsterdam: John Benjamins, 2000.

Piotrowski, Nicholas G. "'After the Deportation': Observations in Matthew's Apocalyptic Genealogy." *Bulletin for Biblical Research* 25 (2015) 189–203.

Pizzuto, Vincent A. *A Cosmic Leap of Faith: An Authorial, Structural, and Theological Investigation of the Cosmic Christology in Colossians 1:15–20.* Leuven: Peeters, 2006.

Plag, Christoph. "Paulus und die Gezera shawa." *Judaica* 50 (1994) 135–40.

Plett, Heinrich F., ed. *Intertextuality. Research in Text Theory 15.* Berlin: Walter de Gruyter, 1991.

———. "Intertextualities." In *Intertextuality*, edited by Heinrich F. Plett, 3–29. Research in Text Theory. Berlin: Walter de Gruyter, 1991.

Plotnitsky, Arkady. *Complementarity. Anti-Epistemology after Bohr and Derrida.* Durham, NC: Duke University Press, 1994.

Plottel, Jeanine Pariser, and Hanna Charney, eds. *Intertextuality: New Perspectives in Criticism.* New York Literary Forum 2. New York: Literary Forum, 1978.

Poetovio, Victorin De. *Sur l'Apocalypse et autres écrits.* Edited and translated by M. Dulaey. SC 423. Paris: Cerf, 1997.

Pokorný, Petr. "Das theologische Problem der neutestamentlichen Pseudepigraphie." In *Bibelauslegung als Theologie*, edited by Petr Pokorný, Josef Souček, Bohumil, 121–32. WUNT 1.100. Tübingen: Mohr Siebeck, 1997.

Pokorný, Petr, Ulrich Heckel. *Einleitung in das Neue Testament: seine Literatur und Theologie im Überblick.* Tübingen: Mohr Siebeck, 2007.

Ponterotto, Joseph G. "Brief Note on the Origins, Evolution, and Meaning of the Qualitative Research Concept Thick Description." *The Qualitative Report* 11.3 (2006) 538–49.

Porter, Stanley E. "Allusions and Echoes." In *As it is Written: Studying Paul's Use of Scripture,* edited by Stanley E. Porter and Christopher D. Stanley, 29–40. SBLSS 50. Atlanta: Scholars, 2008.

———. "Further Comments on the Use of the Old Testament in the New Testament." In *The Intertextuality of the Epistles. Explorations of Theory and Practice,* edited by Thomas L. Brodie, Dennis R. MacDonald, Stanley Porter, 98–110. New Testament Monographs 16. Sheffield: Sheffield Phoenix, 2006.

———. "Paul and His Bible: His Education and Access to the Scriptures of Israel." In *As It Is Written*, edited by Stanley E. Porter and Christopher D. Stanley, 29–40. Society of Biblical Literature Symposium Series 50. Atlanta: Scholars, 2008.

———. "Pauline Authorship and the Pastoral Epistles: Implications for Canon." *Bulletin for Biblical Research* 5 (1995) 105–23.

———. "The Use of the Old Testament in the New Testament: A Brief Comment on Method and Terminology." In *Early Christian Interpretation of Israel: Investigations and Proposals*, edited by Craig Evans and James A. Sanders, 79–96. JSNTSup 148. Studies in Scripture in Early Judaism and Christianity 5. Sheffield: Sheffield Academic, 1997.

Porter, Stanley E., and Christopher D. Stanley, eds. *As it is Written: Studying Paul's Use of Scripture.* Society of Biblical Literature Symposium Series 50. Atlanta: Scholars, 2008.

Porton, Gary G. "Hermeneutics, A Critical Approach." In *Encyclopaedia of Midrash: Biblical Interpretation in Formative Judaism*, edited by Jacob Neusner and Alan J. Avery-Peck, 1.250–68. 2 vols. Leiden: Brill, 2005.

Powell, Mark Allan. *Following the Eastern Star: Adventures in Biblical Reader-Response Criticism.* Louisville: Westminster John Knox, 2001.

Prior, Michael. *Paul the Letter-Writer and the Second Letter to Timothy.* JSNTSup 23. Sheffield: Sheffield Academic, 1989.

Propp, William H. *Exodus 1–18.* AB. Garden City: Doubleday, 1999.

Puskas, Charles B. *The Letters of Paul: An Introduction. Good News Studies 25.* Collegeville: Liturgical, 1993.

Quinn, Jerome D., and William C. Wacker. *The First and Second Letter to Timothy.* Grand Rapids: Eerdmans, 2000.

Rainbow, Paul. "Melchizedek as a Messiah at Qumran." *Bulletin for Biblical Research 7* (1997) 179–94.

Reicke, B. *The Epistles of James, Peter, and Jude.* AB. Garden City: Doubleday, 1964.

Resseguie, James L. *Revelation Unsealed: A Narrative Critical Approach to the Apocalypse.* Leiden: Brill, 1998.

Reumann, John. *Philippians.* AB. New Haven: Yale University Press, 2008.

Ricard, Alain, and Flora Veit-Wild, eds. *Interfaces Between the Oral and the Written /* Interfaces entre l'écrit et l'oral. Versions and Subversions in African Literatures 2. Amsterdam: Rodopi, 2005.

Ricoeur, Paul. *Interpretation Theory: Discourse and the Surplus of Meaning.* Fort Worth: Christian University Press, 1976.

———. *The Rule of Metaphor.* London: Routledge & Kegan Paul, 1978 [Fr. 1975].

———. *Time and Narrative,* vol. 1. Translated by K. McLaughlin and D. Pellauer. Chicago: University of Chicago Press, 1984.

Riffaterre, Michael. *Semiotics of Poetry. Advances in Semiotics.* Bloomington & Indianapolis: Indiana University Press, 1978.

Robbins, Jill. *Altered Readings: Levinas and Literature.* Chicago: University of Chicago Press, 1999.

Robbins, Vernon K. *Exploring the Texture of Texts: A Guide to Socio-Rhetorical Interpretations.* Harrisburg, PA: A. & C. Black, 1996.

———. *New Boundaries in Old territory: Form and Social Rhetoric in Mark.* Vol. 3. Frankfurt: Peter Lang, 1973.

———. *The Tapestry of Early Christian Discourse: Rhetoric, Society and Ideology.* London: Routledge, 1996.

Robinson, Robert. *A Collection of Hymns Used by the Church of Christ in Angel Alley.* Bishopgate, 1759.

Roloff, Jürgen. *Der erste Brief an Timotheus.* EKK XV. Zürich: Benzinger e.a., 1988.

Rorty, Richard. *Consequences of Pragmatism (Essays: 1972–1980).* Minnaepolis: University of Minnesota Press, 1982.

Rubanovich, Julia, ed. *Orality and Textuality in the Iranian World: Patterns of Interaction Across the Centuries.* Leiden: Brill, 2015.

Sanders, E. P. *The Tendencies of the Synoptic Tradition.* Cambridge: Cambridge University Press, 1969.

Sandmel, Samuel. "Parallelomania." *JBL* 81.1 (1962) 1–13.

Sartre, Jean-Paul. *Anti-Semite and Jew.* Translated by George G. Becker. New York: Shocken Books, 1948.

Saussure, Ferdinand de. *Course in General Linguistics.* Edited by Charles Bally and Albert Sechehaye. Translated by Roy Harris. Chicago: Open Court, 1998.

Schechter, Solomon, and Wilhelm Bacher. "Gamaliel I." In *Jewish Encyclopedia*. Online: *http://www.jewishencyclopedia.com/articles/6494-gamaliel-i.*

Schenck, Kenneth. "The Allegory of the Tent in Hebrews 9:6–10: Two Rooms, Two Ages, Two Realms." In *Studies in Hebrews*. Tübingen: Mohr Siebeck, forthcoming.

———. *A Brief Guide to Philo*. Louisville: Westminster John Knox, 2005.

———. *Cosmology and Eschatology in Hebrews: The Settings of the Sacrifice*. SNTSMS 143. Cambridge: Cambridge University Press, 2007.

———. "Philo and the Epistle to the Hebrews: Ronald Williamson's Study after Thirty Years," *SPh* 14 (2002) 112–35.

Schmidt, Brian B., ed. *Contextualizing Israel's Sacred Writings: Ancient Literacy, Orality, and Literary Production*. Atlanta: Society of Biblical Literature, 2015.

Schmidt, Karl Ludwig. ἀκροβυστία. In *Theological Dictionary of the New Testament. Vol 1*, edited by Gerhard Kittel and Gerhard Friedrich; translated by Geoffrey W. Bromiley, 225–26. 10 vols, Grand Rapids: Eerdmans, 1964–1976.

Schnelle, Udo. *Einleitung in das Neue Testament*. Göttingen: Vandenhoeck & Ruprecht, 2005.

Schreiner, Thomas R. *1, 2 Peter, Jude*. New American Commentary 37. Nashville: Broadman & Holman, 2003.

Schutter, William L. *Hermeneutic and Composition in 1 Peter*. WUNT 2.30. Tübingen: Mohr Siebeck, 1989.

Seesengood, Robert P. "Contending for the Faith in Paul's Absence: Combat Sports and Gladiators in the Disputed Pauline Epistles." *Lexington Theological Quarterly* 41 (2006) 87–118.

Shapiro, James. *Oberammergau. The Troubling Story of the World's Most Famous Passion Play*. New York: Vintage, 2000.

Sherwood, Yvonne. *The Prostitute and the Prophet: Reading Hosea in the Late Twentieth Century*. Edinburgh: T. & T. Clark, 2004.

Shimada, Kazuhito. "Is 1 Peter Dependent on Romans?" *Annual of the Japanese Biblical Institute* 19 (1993) 87–137.

Shroyer, Montgomery J. "Alexandrian Jewish Literalists." *JBL* 55 (1936) 261–84.

Shuart-Faris, Nora, and David Bloome, ed. *Uses of Intertextuality in Classroom and Educational Research*. Greenwich: Information Age, 2004.

Silva, Moisés. *Philippians*. BECNT. Grand Rapids: Baker Academic, 2005.

Smith, Craig A. *Timothy's Task, Paul's Prospect: A New Reading of 2 Timothy*. Sheffield: Sheffield Phoenix, 2006.

Sparks, James T. *The Chronicler's Genealogies: Toward an Understanding of 1 Chronicles 1–9*. Academia Biblica 28. Atlanta: Society of Biblical Literature, 2008.

Sperber, Dan, and Deirdre Wilson. *Relevance: Communication and Cognition*. 2nd ed. Cambridge, MA: Blackwell, 1995.

Speyer, Wolfgang. *Die literarische Fälschung im heidnischen und christlichen Altertum. Ein Versuch ihrer Deutung. Handbuch der Altertumswissenschaft 1.2*. München: Beck, 1971.

Spicq, Ceslas. "La Ia Petri et le témoignage évangélique de Saint Pierre." *Studia Theologica* 20 (1966) 37–61.

———. *Les Épîtres Pastorales II*. Paris: Gabalda, 1969.

Stahlberg, Lesleigh Cushing. *Sustaining Fictions: Intertextuality, Midrash, Translation, and the Literary Afterlife of the Bible*. Library of Hebrew Bible/Old Testament Studies. New York: T. & T. Clark, 2008.

Stamps Dennis L. "The Use of the Old Testament in the New as a Rhetorical Device." In *Hearing the Old Testament in the New Testament,*edited by Stanley E. Porter, 9–27, Grand Rapids: Eerdmans, 2006.

Standhartinger, Angela. "Join in imitating me" (Philippians 3.17) Towards an Interpretation of Philippians 3." *NTS* 54 (2008) 417–35.

Stanley, Christopher D. *Arguing with Scripture: The Rhetoric of Quotations in the Letters of Paul.* New York: T. & T. Clark, 2004.

———. *Paul and the Language of Scripture: Citation Technique in the Pauline Epistles and Contemporary Literature.* SNTSMS 74. Cambridge: Cambridge University Press, 1992.

———. "Paul's 'Use' of Scripture: Why the Audience Matters." In *As It Is Written, Studying Paul's Use of Scripture,* edited by Stanley E. Porter and Christopher D. Stanley. 125–55. Society of Biblical Literature Symposium Series 50. Atlanta: Brill, 2008.

———. "'Pearls before Swine': Did Paul's Audiences Understand His Biblical Quotations?" *NovT* 41:2 (Apr. 1999) 124–44.

———. "The Rhetoric of Quotations: An Essay on Method." In *Early Christian Interpretation of the Scriptures of Israel: Investigations and Proposals,* edited by Craig A. Evans and James A. Sanders, 44–58. Sheffield: Sheffield Academic, 1997.

Stein, Robert H. *The Synoptic Problem: An Introduction.* Grand Rapids: Baker Books, 1987.

Stegner, William R. "Romans 9,6–29—A Midrash." *JSNT* 22 (1984) 37–52.

Stemberger, Günter. *Introduction to the Talmud and Midrash.* Translated and edited by Markus Bockmuehl. 2nd ed. Edinburgh: T. & T. Clark, 1996.

Stendahl, Krister. *The School of St. Matthew and Its Use of the Old Testament.* 2nd ed. Acta Seminarii Neotestamentici Upsaliensis 20. Lund: Gleerup, 1967.

———. "Quis et Unde? An Analysis of Mt 1–2." In *Judentum Urchristentum Kirche. Festscrift für Joachim Jeremias,* edited by Walther Eltester, 94–105. Berlin: Verlag Alfred Töpelmann, 1960.

Stern, David. "Midrash and Jewish Interpretation." In *The Jewish Study Bible,* edited by Adele Berlin and Marc Zvi Brettler, 1863–75. Oxford: Oxford University Press, 2004.

Still, Judith, and Michael Worton. "Introduction." In *Intertextuality. Theories and Practices,* edited by Michael Worton and Judith Still, 1–44. New York: Manchester University Press, 1990.

Stockhausen, Carol K. *Moses' Veil and the Glory of the New Covenant: The Exegetical Substructure of II Cor. 3:1–4, 6.* Analecta Biblica 116. Rome: Gregorian University Press, 1989.

Stoops, Robert F., and Dennis R. MacDonald, eds. *The Apocryphal Acts of the Apostles in Intertextual Perspectives.* Atlanta: Scholars, 1997.

Stowers, Stanley K. A *Rereading of Romans: Justice, Jews, and Gentiles.* New Haven: Yale University Press, 1994.

Suggit, John. "Jesus the Gardener: The Atonement in the Fourth Gospel as Re-Creation." *Neotestamentica* 33 (1999) 161–68.

Sumney, Jerry L. "Writing 'In the Image' of Scripture: The Form and Function of References to Scripture in Colossians." In *Paul and Scripture: Extending the Conversation,* edited by Christopher D. Stanley, 185–229. Atlanta: Society of Biblical Literature, 2012.

Sweet, John P. M. *Revelation*. 2nd ed. London: SCM, 1990.

Tajra, Harry W. *The Martyrdom of Saint Paul*. WUNT 2.67. Tübingen: Mohr Siebeck, 1994.

Thatcher, Tom. "Cain and Abel in Early Christian Memory: A Case Study in 'The Use of the Old Testament in the New.'" *Catholic Biblical Quarterly* 72 (2010) 749–50.

Thiessen, Matthew. "'The Rock Was Christ': The Fluidity of Christ's Body in 1 Corinthians 10.4." *JSNT* 36 (2013) 103–26.

Thompson, Michael. *Clothed with Christ: The Example and Teaching of Jesus in Romans 12.1–15.13*. JSNTSup 59. Sheffield: Sheffield Academic, 1991.

Thurén, Lauri. "The Relationship between 2 Peter and Jude—A Classical Problem Resolved?" In *The Catholic Epistles and the Tradition*, edited by Jacques Schlosser, 451–60. BETL 176. Leuven: Peeters, 2004.

Tobin, Thomas H. *Paul's Rhetoric in Its Contexts: The Argument of Romans*. Peabody, MA: Hendrickson, 2004.

Tolmie, D. Francois. *Persuading the Galatians: A Text-centred Rhetorical Analysis of a Pauline Letter*. Tübingen: Mohr Siebeck, 2005.

Towner, Philip. *The Letters to Timothy and Titus*. NICNT. Grand Rapids: Eerdmans, 2006.

Tribble, Phyllis. *Texts of Terror. Literary-Feminist Readings of Biblical Narratives. Overture to Biblical Theology*. Minneapolis, MN: Fortress, 1984.

Trick, Bradley R. "Death, Covenants, and the Proof of Resurrection in Mark 12: 18–27." *NovT* 49 (2007) 232–56.

Trummer, Peter. *Die Paulustradition der Pastoralbriefe*. BETL 8. Frankfurt: Peter Lang, 1978.

Tsagalis, Christos. *The Oral Palimpsest: Exploring Intertextuality in the Homeric Epics*. Center for Hellenic Studies. Cambridge: Harvard University Press, 2008.

Vahrenhorst, Martin. *Kultische Sprache in den Paulusbriefen*. WUNT 1.230. Tübingen: Mohr Siebeck, 2008.

Van Tilborg, Sjef. "Matthew 27.3–10: an Intertextual Reading." In *Intertextuality in Biblical Writings. Essay in Honour of Bas van Iersel*, edited by Sipke Fraisma, 159–74. Kampen: Kok, 1989.

Van Wolde, Ellen. "Texts in Dialogue with Other Texts: Intertextuality in the Ruth and Tamar Narratives." *Biblical Interpretation* 5 (1997) 8–28.

———. "Trendy Intertextuality?" In *Intertextuality in Biblical Writings. Essay in Honour of Bas van Iersel*, edited by Sipke Fraisma, 43–50. Kampen: Kok, 1989.

Vanhoozer Kevin. *Is There a Meaning in This Text? The Bible, the Reader, and the Morality of Literary Knowledge*. Grand Rapids: Zondervan, 1998.

Vermes, Geza. "Bible and Midrash: Early Old Testament Exegesis." In *The Cambridge History of the Bible, Vol. 1: From the Beginnings to Jerome*, edited by Peter R. Ackroyd and Craig F. Evans, 199–231. Cambridge: Cambridge University Press, 1980.

Vlacos, Sophie. *Ricoeur, Literature, Imagination*. New York: Bloomsbury, 2015.

Volf, Miroslav. "Soft Difference: Theological Reflections on the Relation between Church and Culture in 1 Peter." *Ex Auditu* 10 (1994) 15–30.

Vos, Geerhardus. *Biblical Theology: Old and New Testaments*. Grand Rapids: Eerdmans, 1948.

Waaler, Erik. *The Shema and the First Commandment in First Corinthians: an intertextual approach to Paul's re-reading of Deuteronomy.* WUNT 2.253. Tübingen: Mohr Siebeck, 2008.

Wagner, J. Ross. "The Christ, Servant of Jew and Gentile: A Fresh Approach to Romans 15:8–9." *JBL* 116 (1997) 473–85.

———. *Heralds of the Good News: Isaiah and Paul "In Concert" in the Letter to the Romans.* NovTSup 101. Leiden: Brill, 2002.

Wand, J. W. C., ed. *The General Epistles of St. Peter and St. Jude.* Westminster Commentaries. London: Methuen, 1934.

Watson, Duane F. "Destroyer, The." In *ABD* 2.159–60.

———. *Invention, Arrangement, and Style: Rhetorical Criticism of Jude and 2 Peter.* Society of Biblical Literature Dissertation Series 104. Atlanta: Scholars, 1988.

Watts, Rikki E. *Isaiah's New Exodus and Mark.* Tübingen: Mohr Siebeck, 1997.

Webb, Geoff R. *Mark at the Threshold: Applying Bakhtinian Categories to Markan Characterisation.* Leiden: Brill, 2008.

Weimann, Robert. "Textual Identity and Relationship: A Metacritical Excursion into History." In *Identity of the Literary Text,* edited by Mario J Valdés and Owen Miller, 274–93. Toronto: Toronto University Press, 1985

Weiser, Alfons. *Der zweite Brief an Timotheus.* EKK XVI/1. Zürich: Benzinger, 2003.

White, Eugene E. *The Context of Human Discourse: A Configurational Criticism of Rhetoric.* Columbia, SC: University of South Carolina Press, 1992.

Whitmarsh, Tim. *Greek Literature and the Roman Empire: The Politics of Imitation.* Oxford: Oxford University Press, 2001.

Williams, James. *Understanding Poststructuralism. Understanding Moments in Modern Thought.* New York: Routledge, 2014.

Wilson, Robert R. *Genealogy and History in the Biblical World.* New Haven: Yale University Press, 1977.

Witherington, Ben, III. "The Influence of Galatians on Hebrews." *NTS* 37 (1991) 146–52.

———. *Paul's Letter to the Philippians: A Socio-Rhetorical Commentary.* Grand Rapids: Eerdmans, 2011.

Woan, Sue. "The Psalms in 1 Peter." In *The Psalms in the New Testament,* edited by Steve Moyise and Maarten J. J. Menken, 213–29. London: T. & T. Clark, 2004.

Wolter, Michael. *Die Pastoralbriefe als Paulustradition.* Göttingen: Vandenhoeck & Ruprecht, 1988.

Wright, N.T. *The New Testament and the People of God.* Minnaepolis: Fortress, 1992.

Young, Frances. *Biblical Exegesis and the Formation of Christian Culture.* Grand Rapids: Baker Academic, 2002.

———. "Typology." In *Crossing the Boundaries: Essays in Biblical Interpretation in Honour of Michael D. Goulder,* edited by Stanley E. Porter, Paul Joyce, and David E. Orton, 29–48. Leiden: Brill, 1994.

Zamfir, Korinna. "Review of Craig A. Smith, *Timothy's Task, Paul's Prospect: A New Reading of 2 Timothy.* Sheffield: Sheffield Phoenix, 2006." *Ephemerides theologicae lovenienses* 85.1 (2009) 190–94.

Author Index

Aichele, George, xiv, xviii, 108–9, 127
Albl, Martin C., 79
Albright, William F., 226, 229
Alfaro, Maria J. M., 108, 113, 253
Alkier, Stefan, vii, xiv, xix, 127–30, 146, 208–9
Allen, Graham, xviii, 111, 113, 127
Allison, Dale C., 18, 38, 111, 227
Aloisi, John, 225
Anderson, H., 230
Anderson, R. Dean, 195
Attridge, Harold W., 262
Auerbach, Erich, 83–84
Aune, David, 9

Bacher, Wilhelm, 70
Bak, Samuel, 109–14, 116, 122–26
Bakhtin, Mikhail, xiv, 3–4, 14–15, 108, 110, 112–14, 124, 131, 146
Barnett, Albert E., 258
Barr, David L., 12–14
Barr, James, 223, 241
Barrera, Julio T., 64–65, 72–73, 79
Barrett, C. K., 64, 79
Barthes, Roland, 107, 132, 146, 209, 219
Bauckham, Richard J., 12, 14–15, 27, 36, 183, 208, 216, 218, 267, 269
Bauks, Michaela, xviii, 178, 186
Baum, Armin D., 244
Bazerman, Charles, xviii
Beal, Timothy K., xv
Beale, Gregory K., 12, 155, 241
Beaton, Richard C., 237

Beetham, Christopher A., 155, 159, 255
Bekken, Per J., 172
Ben-Porat, Ziva, xvii
Benveniste, Émile, xvi, 187–89, 193, 206
Berding, Kenneth, 255–56, 258–59
Best, Ernest, 260
Bigg, Charles, 267
Bird, Michael F., 256
Bloom, Harold, 108
Bloome, David, xix
Bock, Darrell L., 81
Borgen, Peder, 85, 91
Boring, M. Eugene, 8, 13, 233
Bormann, Lukas, 186
Bourquin, Yvan, 187
Boxall, Ian, 116
Boyarin, Daniel, xv, 67, 80, 127
Bredin, Mark, 9, 14
Brettler, Marc Z., 64
Brodie, Thomas L., xviii, 28, 253
Broich, Ulrich, xviii
Brooke, George J., 28, 65, 231
Brown, Candy G., 179
Brown, Jeannine, vii, xv, 29, 31–33, 36, 38–41, 70
Brown, Raymond E., 27, 116–20, 124
Brox, Norbert, 244
Brucker, Ralph, 183
Buchanan, George W., 112
Budd, Philip, J. 74, 78
Burnett, Fred, 121
Buttrick, David G., 179

Caird, George B., 8, 11, 13
Campbell, Douglas A., 195
Campbell, Lee, 118
Capes, D. B., 75, 238
Carr, David M., xv, 176
Carter, Warren, 120–21, 236
Carton, Evan, 107
Christensen, Sean M., 37
Clark, Billy, 207
Clayton, Jay, xviii, 186
Cockerill, Gareth L., 81
Collier, Gary D., 72, 76–77
Collins, Raymond F., 70, 245, 247–48,
    251
Colson, F. H., 85
Cook, Johann, xv
Cooper, Craig, 176
Cornell, Drucilla, 107, 115
Coutts, John, 262
Crossan, John D., 117, 262
Culler, Jonathan, xv, 208–9
Cullmann, Oscar, 166
Curtis, Adrian, xix

Daube, David, 261
Davids, Peter H., 262, 267, 269
Davidson, Harriet, 3–4
Davies, W. D., 38, 72, 111, 227
Davis, Barry C., 231
DeMaris, Richard E., 261
Derrida, Jacques, 107–8, 110, 112,
    114–15, 125, 209, 219
Deutscher, Max, 115
Dewey, Arthur J., 200
Dillon, John M., 87
Doane, A. N., 186
Doane, Sébastien, 117
Dodson, Joseph R., 205
Doeve, Jan W., 65, 69, 72
Donaldson, Terence L., 258, 272
Donelson, Lewis R., 244–45
Donker, Gerald J., 257
Draisma, Sipke, xviii
Draper, Jonathan A., 186
Duarte, Alejandro, 116
Duling, Dennis C., 177
Dunn, James D. G., 183, 186

Eaglestone, Robert, 125
Eco, Umberto, 129
Edenburg, Cynthia, xvii, 177–78
Ehrman, Bart D., 243–44, 253
Ellens, J. Harrold, 237
Ellingworth, Paul, 262
Elliott, John H., 35
Elliott, Mark W., 183
Ellis, E. Earle, 74, 79–80
Elman, Yaakov, 65
Emadl, Samuel, xviii
Enns, Peter E., 74, 81
Evans, Craig A., xv, xviii–xix

Fackenheim, Emil, 109, 117
Farmer, Ron, 9, 13
Fee, Gordon D., 155
Fewell, Danna N., xvii, xix, 122
Finnegan, Ruth, 179
Fish, Stanley, 84
Fishbane, Michael, xix, 65, 67
Fisk, Bruce N., 61
Fitzmyer, Joseph A., 18, 225, 231
Foley, John M., 186
Fossum, Jarl, 261
Fowl, Stephen, 183–84
France, R. T., 118–20
French, Patrick, 107
Frenschkowski, Marco, 244
Friedman, Susan S., xv
Fung, Glenn, 257

Gadamer, Hans-G., 84
Gaechter, Paul, 224
Gamble, Harry Y., 51, 62
Gaskin, Richard, 4
Geertz, Clifford, 223
Gennette, Gérard, xiv–xv, 16–28, 107,
    237
Gignac, Alain, vii, xvi, 196, 206
Gillmayr-Bucher, Susanne, xvii
Gilmour, Michael J., 255–56, 258–59,
    262, 267, 272
Gnilka, Joachim, 235
Goodacre, Mark S., 262
Goppelt, Leonhard, 84
Gora, Thomas, 206
Gordley, Matthew E., 155

Green, Barbara, 4, 15
Green, Gene L., 207–8, 216–17, 219, 267
Green, Michael, 267
Greenberg, Irving, 117
Greene, Thomas M., 4–5
Gregory, Andrew F., 255, 272
Greimas, A. J., xvi, 166
Gundry, Robert, 121, 224, 227
Guthrie, George H., 81
Gutt, Ernst-A., 207, 221

Hagner, D. A., 229, 235, 262
Hance, Kenneth G., 45
Harrington, Daniel, 119, 121
Harris, William V., 51, 62
Hartman, D. L., 108, 118, 120–21
Hartman, Geoffrey, 108
Hatina, Thomas R., xv, 222
Havercroft, Barbara, 190, 206
Hauerwas, Stanley, 121
Hay, David M., 85
Hayes, John H., 177
Hays, Richard B., xv, xvii, xix, 5–7, 31, 33, 38, 40–41, 70, 73–74, 82–83, 92, 112, 127, 136, 146, 166–67, 169, 175, 208, 222, 236
Hebel, Udo J., xix
Hellerman, Joseph H., 249
Herzer, Jens, 244
Heubeck, Alfred, 100
Hezser, Catherine, 52, 62
Hill, Charles E., 262
Hill, Leslie, 114
Hirsch, E. D., 223
Hoehner, Harold W., 260
Holladay, Carl R., 177
Hollander, John, xvii, 5, 30–31
Holquist, Michael, 3, 15
Holthuis, Susanne, 131
Holtzmann, Heinrich J., 261
Horsley, Richard A., 186
Horstkotte, Silke, 237
Hübner, Hans, xv, 191
Huizenga, Leroy A., xix, 127, 146, 208
Hultgren, Arland J., 38
Hunter, Richard, 98
Hurst, Lincoln, 89

Hurtado, Larry W., 75

Instone-Brewer, David, 68
Issacharoff, Michael, 186
Iverson, Kelly R., 177

Jakobson, Roman, 83
Janse, Sam, 174
Jeal, Roy R., vii, xiv, xvi, 70, 164
Jervis, L. Ann, 71
Jobes, Karen H., 34, 37, 257, 267
John of Damascus, 250
Johnson, Luke T., 235, 243
Johnson, Mark, 82
Johnson, Marshall D., 27

Kahmann, Johannes, 258, 262, 267
Kaiser, Walter C., 81
Kamesar, Adam, 85, 92
Kasher, Rimon, 64–65, 67–68
Keener, Craig S., 70, 232
Kelly, J. N. D., 262, 267, 269
Kenny, Anthony, 257
Kern, Philip H., 183
Kern-Ulmer, Rivka, 65, 69
Kingsbury, Jack, 121
Kirk, J. R. Daniel, viii, xvi, 20, 168–70, 173, 175
Koch, Dietrich-A., 256
Köhler, Wolf-D., 255
Koutrianou, Elena, 207
Kristeva, Julia, xiv–xv, xix, 3, 107–14, 117, 125, 134, 146, 151, 219, 242–43, 253
Kugel, James L., 66–67
Kümmel, Werner G., 262

Lakoff, George, 82
Lane, William L., 262
Langmuir, Gavin, 116
Larsson, Kristian, xiv
Leitch, Vincent, 108, 115
Leith, Dick, 44
Leithart, Peter J., 239, 241
Lentz, Tony M., 176
Leonard, Jeffery M., 255, 258–59, 262
Levi, Primo, 123
Levinas, Emmanuel, 108, 116–17, 126

Lieberman, Saul, 66, 80
Lightfoot, J. B., 162
Linafelt, Tod, 108
Lincoln, Andrew T., 159, 259–60
Lindemann, Andreas, 255
Linell, Per, 241
Liszka, Jakób J., 147
Litwak, Kenneth D., xv, 30, 40
Longenecker, Bruce W., 167, 175
Longenecker, Richard, 82
Lord, George D., 6
Loriggio, Francesco, 206
Lotringer, Sylvere, 206
Lucas, Alec J., xv, 33, 38
Lust, Johann, 7
Luttenberger, Joram, 252
Luz, Ulrich, 109, 112, 117–21, 124, 227, 239

MacDonald, Dennis R., viii, xv, xviii, 93–94, 98, 105, 253
MacKinnon, Donald, 121
Mai, Hans-Peter, 109, 113, 116, 127
Maier, Harry O., 161
Maier, Johann, 65
Malik, Rachel, 207, 209, 221
Malina, Bruce J., 223
Malkiel, Yakov, 188
Mallen, Peter, 32, 41
Man, Paul de, 108
Mann, C. S., 226, 229
Margolis, Joseph, 115
Marguerat, Daniel, xix, 187
Marmur, Michael, 186
Marshall, I. H., 245, 247, 250–52
Marshall, John W., 243–44
Martin, Dale B., 208
Martin, Ralph P., 177
Martin, Troy W., 261
Masterman, J. H. B., 262
Mayordomo, Moisés, 117
McAfee, Noëlle, xiv
McEwen, Alastair, 72
McGrath, James F., viii, xiv, xvi, 179, 181, 184
McKay, Niall, xix
Meade, David G., 243
Mealand, D. L., 257

Meek, Russell L., xv
Meeks, Wayne A., 72–73, 77
Merkel, Helmut, 249, 251–52
Merz, Annette, xvii, 242–45, 252–53
Michel, Otto, 250
Mieder, Wolfgang, 179
Mihaly, Eugene, 69
Miller, Robert J., 262
Mitton, C. L., 258, 260, 262–63
Mody, Rohintan K., 77
Moffatt, James, 267
Moi, Toril, xiv, xix, 3
Moltmann, Jürgen, 14
Moo, Douglas J., 267, 269
Moore, Stephen D., 108
Morgan, Thaïs E., xix
Moyise, Steve, xiv, xvii, xix, 7, 34, 36, 62, 155, 256
Murphy, Frederick J., 12
Myers, Elizabeth A., viii, xvii, 257, 262, 265, 272
Myerson, George, 44

Nadella, Raj, 4
Neville, David J., 262
Neyrey, Jerome H., 182, 208, 216, 218, 267
Niditch, Susan, 186
Nye, Andrea, 116

O'Brien, P. T., 248–49, 260
O'Day, Gail R., 262
Oberlinner, Lorenz, 245, 251
Olbrechts-Tyteca, Lucie, 44, 46
Orchard, Bernard, 261
Oropeza, B. J., xiii–xv, xix, 72–73, 75, 78, 164
Orr, Mary, xix

Patte, Daniel, 113
Pattemore, Stephen, 207–9, 211, 215, 217, 221
Peirce, Charles S., 129
Perelman, Chaïm, 44, 46
Perrot, Charles, 78
Petöfi, János S., 128–29, 147, 209
Pfister, Manfred, xviii

Phillips, Gary, viii, xv, xviii, 108–9, 111, 116–17, 121–22, 127
Phillips, Gregory Y., 241
Phillips, Peter, 28
Phua, Richard L.-S., 78
Pietersen, Lloyd, 14
Pilkington, Adrian, 207, 214
Piotrowski, Nicholas G., 32, 34
Pizzuto, Vincent A., 155
Plag, Christoph, 70
Plett, Heinrich F., xix, 107–8
Plotnitsky, Arkady, 115
Poetovio, Victorin, 134
Pokorný, Petr, 243
Ponterotto, Joseph G., 223
Porter, Stanley E., xv, xvii, xviii-xix, 33, 62, 241, 243, 253, 256
Powell, Mark A., 33, 38, 40
Prior, Michael. 250–51
Puskas, Charles B., 246

Quinn, Jerome D., 250–51

Rainbow, Paul, 231
Resseguie, James L., 9–10, 13
Rensburg, F. J. van, 241
Reumann, John. 183
Ricard, Alain, 186
Ricoeur, Paul, 83, 108
Riffaterre, Michael, xiv
Riley, Harold, 261
Robbins, Vernon K., xvi, 92, 151–54, 161, 164, 223
Robinson, Robert, 180
Roloff, Jürgen, 243
Rorty, Richard, 114
Rubanovich, Julia, 186

Sanders, E. P., 262
Sanders, James A. xv, xviii
Sandmel, Samuel, 223, 254–55, 272
Saussure, Ferdinand de, 110, 112–14
Schechter, Solomon, 70
Schenck, Kenneth, viii, xv, 82, 85, 88–89
Schmidt, Brian B., 176
Schmidt, Karl L., 158
Schnelle, Udo, 249

Schreiner, Thomas R., 267
Schutter, William L., 255
Seesengood, Robert P., 247
Shimada, Kazuhito, 255
Shroyer, Montgomery J., 85
Shuart-Faris, Nora, xix
Silva, Moisés, 184, 248
Smith, Craig A., 245, 250–51
Sparks, James T., 24
Sperber, Dan, 209–11, 220–21
Speyer, Wolfgang, 244
Spicq, Ceslas, 249–50, 267
Stahlberg, Lesleigh C., 28, 69
Stamps Dennis L., 62
Stanley, Christopher D., ix, xv, xviii-xix, 43, 48, 50, 53–54, 59, 70, 178, 181, 185
Stein, Robert H., 255, 262
Stegner, William R., 69, 72
Stemberger, Günter, 64–66
Stendahl, Krister, 222, 224–25, 230–31
Stern, David, 64
Still, Judith, xix, 112, 127
Stockhausen, Carol K., 70
Stowers, Stanley K., 195
Suggit, John, 32
Sumney, Jerry L., 155, 164
Sweet, John P. M., 8, 13

Thatcher, Tom, 32, 41
Thiessen, Matthew, 75
Thompson, Michael, 255–56, 258, 262
Thurén, Lauri, 267
Tobin, Thomas H., 199
Tolmie, D. Francois, 181
Towner, Philip, 243
Tribble, Phyllis, 109
Trick, Bradley R., 230
Tsagalis, Christos, 186
Tuckett, Christopher M., 255, 272

Van Rooy, Herrie F., 241
Van Tilborg, Sjef, 112
Van Wolde, Ellen, xv, 26, 112
Vanhoozer Kevin, 82
Veit-Wild, Flora, 186
Vermes, Geza, 64, 67, 80
Vlacos, Sophie, 108

Volf, Miroslav, 35
Vos, Geerhardus, 166

Waaler, Erik, ix, xiv, xvi, 225, 236
Wacker, William C., 250–51
Wagner, J. Ross, 167
Wand, J. W. C., 258, 267
Watson, Duane F., 78, 164, 267
Watts, Rikki E., 29
Webb, Geoff R., 3, 15
Weiser, Alfons, 246, 248–49, 251–52
White, Eugene E., 46–48
Whitmarsh, Tim, 94, 105

Williams, James, 107
Wilson, Robert R., 22
Wilson, Deidre, 209–11, 220–21
Witherington, Ben, 258
Woan, Sue, 36–37, 41
Wolter, Michael, 245–46
Worton, Michael, xix, 112, 127
Wright, N.T., 167

Young, Frances, 84, 92

Zamfir, Korinna, ix, xvii, 245

Biblical and Ancient Literature Index

OLD TESTAMENT

Genesis

1–2	31
2:4	141
2:8–10	31
3:1–19	38
4:1–8	38
4:15–16	38
4:17–18	38
4:23–24	38
4:24	34, 38
5:1	141
6:1–4	216
11:1–9	86
15:16	xiv
17:1–27	156
17:4–5	32
17:11	158
17:14, 23, 24, 25	158
18:10	69, 191n12
21:12	69
25:23	69
25:25	69
26:8	77
34:24	158
35:14	249n43
38	26
49:8–11	11
49:9	11

Exodus

3:4	226
3:6	224n12, 228–230
3:6	232
3:15, 16	229
4:5	229
4:22–23	32
4:22	110
4:25	158
9:16	69, 191n12
12:23	78
14–32	32
14–17	72
14:21–22	32
16:13	76n38
17:1–7	74, 74n44
17:5–6	74
17:6	75n36
24	18
25:29	249n43
32	77
32:6	76, 77
32:26–28	77
33:19	69, 191n12
34:34	5

Leviticus

12:3	156, 158
16	89
18:5	198

Leviticus (cont.)

18:34	227
19:3–4	235n38
19:18	227, 234
26:1	157

Numbers

4:7	249n43
9:2–3	66
11	77
11:4–9	76
11:4	76
11:32	76
11:33	77n42
13:26	76
14	76
14:1–5	76
14:6	76
14:16	76
14:22	77n44
14:29–33	76
16:11–14	78
16:11	78
16:30	78
16:41	78
20	72
20:1–13	74
20:1–5	76
20:1	74
20:3–5	76
20:7–11	74
20:15	72
20:22–29	74n33
21:4–6	78
21:6	77
23:24	10
25:1–18	77
25:2	77
25:9	77
25:10–12	73, 77, 78
32:8–13	76
33:37–39	74

Deuteronomy

5:11	238
6:4–5	226, 235
6:5	225, 227, 228, 232, 234

6:8	232
9:4	197, 198
9:7–8	77n44
9:22	77n44
10:16	156
25:5	229
30	xvi
30:6	157
30:11–15	171–172
30:12–14	170, 172, 197, 198, 200
30:12	171
30:14	171
32	74
32:3	73
32:4	73
32:15	73
32:18	73
32:19–21	77n44
32:21	73
32:30–31	73
32:43	202–4

Joshua

2	26
6	26

Judges

13:5, 7	119
14:5	10n25
21:21	77

Ruth

4	22, 23, 26
4:12	26
4:18–22	22
4:18	22

1 Samuel

17:34	10n25

2 Samuel

7:14	173
11	144
23:13–17	250n45

1 Kings

13:24	10n25

1 Chronicles

1–8	22
1–3	22–
2	22
1:27—3:17	23
1:27	23
3:10–14	25
3:17	23
11:18	250n45

Job

10:6	11

Psalms

2	xvi, 173
2:2	224
17:50	203–204
18:49	202
22:22	252
34	xv, 34
34:5	34n29, 36
34:7	34, 36
34:8	35, 36
34:9	34, 36
34:11	34, 36
34:12–16	35
34:13	36
34:15–16	34
34:17–18	36
34:21	34
77:3–5	72n25
77:18–19	77
89:26	173
107:26	171
110:1	228, 230, 231, 236
110:4	235
110:5–6	235
117:1	202–4

Isaiah

1:9	69
2:18	157
7:1	143
7:9	143
7:10	144
7:14	142–43, 145
7:18—8:4	144
8:5–8	144
8:8	143
8:10	144
8:14	191n12
10:22–23	69
11:10	202, 203
16:12	157
19:1	157
21:9	157
28	60
28:7–13	xv, 57–58
28:7	59
28:11–12	56, 59
28:16	37, 191n12, 198
31:4	11
31:7	157
45	xvi
45:23–26	75n35
45:23	177
46:6	157
52:7	231n35
56	xvi
56:2, 4, 6, 8	169
57:9	30
57:14	30
57:19	30

Jeremiah

4:4	157
7	xvi
7:11	169
7:18	249n43
7:25	214
9:25–26	157
31:15	110, 119, 120
31:16–17	119
51:17, 19, 25	249n43
50:44	11

Ezekiel

20:28	249n43
37:10	6
37:21	6

Ezekiel (cont.)

38:2–16	6
38:22	6
39:4	6
40:2	6
40:5	7
43:2	7
44:6–7	157
47:12	7
48:30–34	7

Daniel

5:4	157
5:23	157
6:21	252
9:6	214

Hosea

1:10	69
2:1	191

2:23	69
2:25	191
5:14	11
9:4	249n43
11:1	110, 118

Joel

2:32	75n35, 198

Amos

3:7	214

Micah

5:1	119
5:3	119

Malachi

1:2–3	191n12
1:4	69

APOCRYPHA

Tobit

3:7–9	229n26
5:3	159
9:5	159

Wisdom

18:20–25	78

Sirach

50:15	250n46

1 Maccabees

14:41	235

3 Maccabees

1:3	159n27

4 Maccabees

3:14–16	250n45
4:24	159n27
7:11	78
16:25	230

PSEUDEPIGRAPHA

1 Enoch

6–19	217
60:8	218
89:61–64	159
93:3	218

2 Enoch

53:2–3	159

2 Baruch

56:10–16	217

Apocrypha of Zephaniah

7:1–8	159

Jubilees

1:23	157
5:1–2	217
7:39	218

Pseudo-Philo
Liber Antiquitatum Biblicarum

10.7	74n34

Testament of Abraham

12:7–18	159

Testament of Issachar

5:2	227

Testament of Job

11:11	159

NEW TESTAMENT

Matthew

1	22, 23
1:1	32, 139
1:2–17	139, 146
1:2	22n19, 24, 32
1:3–6	22, 125
1:3	23n19
1:5	23n19
1:6	22n18, 23n19, 141
1:10	38
1:11–12	23n19
1:11	23n19, 24
1:13–17	23
1:16	23n19, 142
1:17	22n18, 23n19, 32n16, 139
1:18–25	139
1:18–21	140–41
1:21	140, 141
1:22–23	140
1:22	119, 140
1:23	141, 142
1:25	141
2:13–23	109, 117, 121, 124
2:13–15	118
2:15	110, 118, 119, 140
2:16–18	118, 121
2:16	117, 126
2:18	111, 119
2:19–23	118
2:23	119
3:9	32n16
3:15	117
4:4–10	224
5:20	126
5:21–24	38
5:38	117
8:11	32n16, 239
13:14–15	143, 144
16:19	126
17	18
18:1	38
18:2–5	38
18:6–9	38
18:6	122, 126
18:10	38, 122
18:12–14	38
18:15–20	38
18:16	38
18:17–18	38
18:21–35	38
18:21–22	37, 38
18:23–24	38
19:14	122
19:19	225
21:45	234
22:15	234
22:22	234
22:29	226, 234
22:31	226, 229, 232
22:32–40	228
22:32	32n16, 224n12, 227, 228, 230
22:33	234

22:34	239
22:36	235
22:37	224
22:38	235
22:41–42	223, 224, 230, 239
22:43–44	226
22:43	223–224
22:44	224–228
22:45	226n21
22:46	234, 239
23:5	232
23:31–46	xvii
23:35	38
27:25	109, 121, 126
27:33	123
28:10	126
28:17	126
28:19–20	126
28:20	139

Mark

1:2–3	135, 136
1:2	135
1:9–45	94
2:1–2	95
3:6	95
3:13–17, 19	95
4:35–41	95
5:1–20	95, 98–101
5:2–5	98
5:2–3	99
5:4, 5	99
5:6–8	99
5:9	100
5:10–13	100–101
5:11	98
5:14–17	101
5:18–20	102
5:18	101
5:21–43	95, 98–101
6:1–56	95
7:24–30	95
8:1–41	95
9:2–13, 30–31	95
10:17	169
10:32–52	95
10:44	213
11:1–14	95

11:15–18	96
11:15–17	xvi, 169
12:1–12	96
12:28–34	234
12:30	224, 225
12:40–44	96
13:1–32	96
13:1–2	170
14:1—15:1	96
14:58	157
15:2–41	96
15:26	160
15:46—16:4	97
16:5–8	97

Luke

10:25–27	225
10:27	225
13:28	239
16:19–31	94n2
16:22–31	239
19:1–10	133
23:26–31	94n2

John

2:19	6
2:21	6
3:16	181
18–20	31
18:1	31
18:26	31
19:41	31
20:15	31

Acts

2:38	73
6:9–15	94n2
10:1–23	94n2
11:24	231
11:25	231
12:1–17	94n2
13:15	87n23
13:16–41	xvi, 173
15:1–35	94n2
16:9–12	94n2
19:13–30	94n2
19:5	73

20:7–12	94n2
28:1–11	94n2

Romans

1:1	208, 212
1:3–4	173
3:9–20	187
3:21	172
4:1–25	49
4:3	xiv
5:1—8:30	43n2
5:12–21	55
6:3–4	158
9:1–3	192
9:6–33	192
9:6–29	69
9:6–13	191
9:7	69
9:9	69, 191n12
9:12	69
9:13	191n12
9:14	191n12
9:15	69
9:17	69, 191n12
9:24–26	191–192
9:24	192
9:25–29	xvi
9:25–26	69, 191, 195
9:25	191n12, 192, 193
9:26	69
9:27–29	191, 194–95
9:27	69
9:29	69
9:33	191n12
10:5–17	187
10:5–13	xvi, 188, 197–98
10:5–11	198
10:5	172, 200
10:6–12	xvi, 172
10:6–10	170, 172
10:6–9	200
10:6–7	200
10:8	201
10:9–10	201
10:10–13	75n35, 200
10:10	201
10:11	188
10:12	172

10:14–17	200
10:15	231n35
11:2–4	43n1
11:22	14
13	13
14:11	43n2, 182
15:7–13	202–203
15:7–9	xvi
15:7	203
15:8–9	205
15:9–12	203
15:9	204
15:10–11	204
15:13	204
16:3–16	55

1 Corinthians

1:11	56
1:13	73
2:9–13	71
2:12–13	70
5:1	56
5:7–8	72
5:9–11	45
6:9–20	72
6:12	137
7:1—8:13	43n2
7:1	56
8:1–6	236
8:1	56
8:10	77
8:13	76
9:9	43n2
10:1–22	73
10:1–12	55
10:1–11	xv, 43n1, 71–79
10:1–4	78
10:1–3	72, 158
10:1	72
10:4	73
10:5–11	75, 78
10:5	76
10:6	78
10:7	77
10:8	77
10:9	77
10:11	78
10:13	73

10:22–23	78
10:22	73
11:17–34	53n16
11:18	56
12:1	56
12:4–11	57
12:8	71
12:12–26	57
12:13	73
12:15–16	57
12:17	57
12:21	57
12:27–28	57
12:28–29	71
12:29–30	57
13:1–13	57
13:1–3	57
14:1–40	53n16
14:1–5	59
14:2, 4, 9	60
14:5	57
14:6–12	57
14:6	57
14:7–8	57
14:11	57
14:13	57
14:15	57, 60
14:18–19	57, 59, 60
14:20–25	xv, 58
14:20	57
14:21	43n2, 56, 57
14:22–25	60
14:23	59
14:24–25	59
14:27–28	60
15:2–27	57
16:1	57

2 Corinthians

2:14	160
3:7–18	55, 72
3:16	5
4:7–18	49
4:13	43n2
5:1—8:30	43n2
5:1	157
9:9	43n2
10:8–11	45

Galatians

1:14	70
3:1–3	45
3:6–9	72
3:6–8	55
3:8	187
3:16	55
3:19—4:7	43n2
3:22	187
3:27–29	72
3:28	55
4:21–31	55

Ephesians

2:1	159
2:3	158
2:5	159
2:12	30
2:17	30
5:19–20	53n16
6:21–22	260

Philippians

1:1	208, 266
1:6	266
1:7	248
1:8	266
1:11	266
1:12–18	249
1:13–14	248
1:15	249, 266
1:17	248, 249, 266
1:19	249
1:21–24	249
1:20–21, 23	249
1:23–24	245
1:23	251
1:25	249, 266
1:26	266
1:30	245, 249
2:3	266
2:6–11	xvi, 177–85
2:9–11	75n35
2:10–11	183n16
2:10	266
2:11	266
2:14	266

2:16–17	245
2:16	249
2:17–18	249
2:17	249–251
2:19–24	245
2:19–23	250
2:23	249
2:24	250
2:25–30	250
3:1–21	43n2
3:3, 4	266
3:5	70
3:8	266
3:12–14	249
3:19	266
4:5, 8, 15	266
4:18	250

Colossians

2:6—3:4	161
2:6–7	162
2:8–10	162
2:8	155, 161
2:9–10	161
2:10	163
2:11–15	xvi, 154–64
2:11	156, 158, 160
2:12	158
2:13	158, 162
2:14–15	162
2:14	159
2:15	158, 160
2:16–21	156
2:16–18	161
2:17	88
4:7–8	260
4:14	248

2 Thessalonians

1:10	247

1 Timothy

1:3	253
3:15	253
3:16	247n28
6:12	252n56
6:14	247n28

2 Timothy

1:2	247
1:8	247, 251
1:10	247n28
1:11–13	247
1:12	246
1:13–14	246
1:13	247
1:15	247
1:16	251
1:17	247
1:18	246
1:30	251
2:1	247
2:2	246, 253
2:3–5	247
2:3	247
2:9–10	247
2:9	251
2:14–15	246
2:16–18	246
2:16	251
2:24–25	246
3:1–9	13, 246
3:10	247
3:11	246, 247, 252
3:14–15	246
3:14	247
4:1–8	xvii, 245–47
4:1–4	246
4:1–2	246, 252
4:1	247n28
4:3–4	246
4:5	247
4:6–8	247, 253
4:6	249–51
4:7–8	251
4:7	247, 251–52
4:8	246, 247n28, 252
4:9	247
4:10–12	248
4:10	247
4:14	247
4:16	247
4:17	252
4:18	252
4:19–21	248
4:21	247

Titus

1:5	253
2:13	247n28

Hebrews

8:2	88, 89
8:5	88
8:6	88
9:7–11	89
9:9–10	81
9:9	89
9:11	88
9:24	88, 157
10:1–4	89
10:1	88, 89
11:28	78
11:32	89n30
12:18–19	5
12:18–25	5
12:22–24	5–6
12:25	6
13:22	87n23

James

1:1, 4, 7, 9, 17, 25, 26	266
2:23	xiv
2:4	266
3:14, 15, 17, 18	266
4:5, 13	266
5:7, 8, 10, 16	266

1 Peter

1:1	34n29, 35
1:15	35
1:17	34, 36
1:18	35
2:1	35
2:2	36
2:3	35, 36
2:4	36
2:6	37
2:11—3:12	35
2:11	34n29, 35
2:12	35
2:15	36
2:18	36

3:1	36
3:10–12	xv, 35
3:14	36
3:15–16	37
3:16	35
4:3–4	35
4:14	35
4:16	37
4:19	37
5:8	10

2 Peter

1:1, 2, 5, 12	268
2:1–3	269
2:4, 6, 10	268
2:10	270
2:11–18	268
3:2, 3	268
3:15–16	xviii
3:17, 18	268

Jude

1–25	268
1	208–15
2	215–16
4	216
6	216
8	270
14–16	218

Revelation

1:12–18	11
1:7	12
2:7	9
2:11	9
2:17	9
4–5	13
5	12, 13
5:5–6	7–8
6:16	8
7	9, 10
9	9
9:8	10–11
12	9
13:2	11
13:11	11n26
14	9, 10

14:10	9	20:15	14
15	9	21	9–10
17:14	9, 11	21:10	6
19	12	21:12–13	7
19:13–16	11–12	21:15	7
19:16	11	21:22	6, 7
19:21	6, 14	21:23	7
20:4	6	21–22	13
20:8	6	22:1–2	7
20:9	6		

DEAD SEA SCROLLS

1QapGen

		11QMelch	
21:2	225	2:6–8	231
22:32	225	2:13	231
		2:18	231

1QS

		11Q13	
1:11b–13a	225	2:15–16	231n35
1: 16–17a	225	2:18	231n35
4:27–5:1	225n18		

1QSb

		CD	
5:29	11	2:17–31	217

4Q523

	7

RABBINIC WRITINGS

b. Niddah

		Leviticus Rabbah	
19b	66	29:11	218
22b	68		

b. Pesaḥim

Tanḥuma
Genesis

66a	66	12:12	11

b. Shabbat

Targum Onqelos
Numbers

13a	68	21:16–20	74n34

Genesis Rabbah

97	11

GRECO-ROMAN WRITINGS, JOSEPHUS, PHILO

Achilles Tatius

Leucippe and Clitophon

2.23   98n9

Apollonius

Argonautica

4.557–752   98n9
4.1638–88   98n8

Apuleius

Metamorphoses

1:7–13   98n9
8.11–13   98n8

Aristotle

Art of Rhetoric

1.15, 2.21, 2.2.3   44n4

Cassius Dio

Roman History

62.26.4   250n48

Euripides

Cyclops

                                            98n8

Bacchae

284–85   250n47

Herodotus

History

2.104   156

Homer

Iliad

6   95–97
22   95–97
24   95–97

Odysseus

1–2   94–105
4–6   94–105
8–12   94–105
14–19   94–105
22   94–105

Josephus

Antiquities

1.3.1.73   217
1.246–48   272–73
2.224   93n1
4.109–10   93n1
6.362–63   93n1
12.241   157
12.424–25   93n1

Contra Apion

2:18, 25, 178   52

Jewish Wars

3.516–19   93n1
4.359–62   93n1

Lucian

Vera Historia

2:46   98n9

Ovid

Metamorphoses

14   98n9
23.749–897   98n8

Philo

Confusion of Tongues

190   86

Decalogue

106–110   227

Giants

52   159n27

Opificio mundi
(Creation of the World)
165   86

Legum allegoriae
(Allegorical Interpretation)
1.55   159n27

Migration of Abraham
89   85
91–92   86
93   85

Quis Rerum Divinarum Heres sit
(Who is the Heir of Divine Things?)
183   250n46

Vita Moses

2.150   250n46

Philodemus
On Poetry
5.30.36–31.2   93

Petronius
Satyricon
97   98n8
127–34   98n9

Plutarch
Aemilius Paullus
32–34   160

De Iside et Osiride
353b   250n47

Quintilian
Institutio Oratoria
5.36–44   44n4

Strabo
Geography
17.2.5   156n19

Tacitus
Annals
16.35   250n48

Vergil(Virgil)
Aeneid
3   102–3
7   102–3

EARLY CHRISTIAN WRITINGS

1 Clement
44.5   251n51

Acts of Pilate
2.3   121

Eusebius
Historia Ecclesiastica
2.22.5   251n51

Gregory of Nazianzus
Funebris (Oration 43)
78.1.2   251n51

Ignatius

Romans

2.2   250n49

John Chrysostom

De laudibus sancti Pauli apostoli

1.3.15   250n49

Severianus

Fragmenta

344:12   250n49

Subject Index

accessibility (criteria), 97, 98, 208n5, 220

Achilles, 95–98

Adam (first, last, & Eve), 23–24, 55, 84, 86, 177, 180–81, 184–85, 218–19, 244

Aeneas, 93, 102–103

a fortiori, See Kal waḤomer

Aggadah, 67, 69, 79, 120

allegory, 4, 60, 81, 84–87

allusion, xiv–xv, xvii–xviii, 4, 6–7, 11n27, 14, 17, 21, 30–40, 42–43, 63, 70, 72n25, 73, 76, 79, 112, 119, 131, 136, 153, 156, 169, 171, 177–82, 185, 215, 222–23, 242–53, 255–56, See Echo, Parallels

Amazing Grace, 179

anachronism, xv, xviii, 52

analogy, 13, 40n48, 53n, 57, 65–68, 84–85, 92, 98, 114, 129, 240

angel, 4, 5, 7, 9, 28, 139, 141, 217, 268

apocalyptic, 8, 12, 120, 158–61, 163, 252–53

application, 19–20, 42, 59, 67, 114, 142, 196–201, 231, 236–37, 241, 250n44, 257, 262, 265–66, 271–72

architextuality, 17

argumentation, 43n2, 46, 48, 50, 60, 152–53, 155–56, 158, 161–64, 190, 200. See rhetoric

audience capabilities, 35, 50–56

authority, 44–45, 48–49, 56–57, 61, 68, 88n26, 126, 135, 161–62, 208, 217–18, 226–27, 238, 240, 243–45, 248, 253

availability (criteria), 33, 38, 53, 208n5

awareness, 34, 55, 134, 176, 207, 209n11, 217–21, 223, 226, 241

Beatles, the, 219

biographical, 165, 253

borrowing (Intertextual) xviii, 97, 99, 105, 108, 151, 194, 205, 222, 254–72

catchwords, 68–70, 76–79

challenge-riposte, 161

chiasm, 75

christology, 36, 120, 175, 178, 181, 183–84, 232–33, 236, 240. See Rock

Circe, 98–104

circumcision, 86, 155–63, 172, 202, 204–5

citation, See quotation

cognitive effects, 211, 213–16, 218, 221

cognitive environment, 210–16, 218, 220–21

cohesion (textual), 233

Collective (Bak artistic work), xvi, 111, 122–24, 126

commandment/decalogue, 171–72, 198, 224–25, 226–28, 232–36, 238, 269

communicative intention, 33, 128, 209. See intent(ion)

conversion, 73, 172

criteria (intertextual)
quote, allusion, echo definitions, xviii, 17, 33, 42–43nn1–3, 153, 255–56
seven/several criteria, xvii, 33, 97, 208n5
cross, crucifixion, 8–10, 14, 18, 83, 96, 120, 123, 160–61, 163, 171–72
cultural intertexture/setting, xvi, 4, 35–36, 68, 82n4, 94, 107, 129, 153–64, 176n1, 223, 226, 228–30, 236, 240–41
Cyclops (Polyphemus), 95, 97–104

deconstruction, 108, 114–16, 242, See poststructuralism
density (criteria), 97–98, 102, 104, 114, 118, 124, 137
diachronic/synchronic, xvi, 129, 228
dialogism/dialogical, xiv, 3–15, 113, 133
différance, 109–114, 125
directness, directionality, 258–64, 266, 268
distinctive trait (criteria), 97, 98, 102

echo, xv, xviii, 30–34, 39–40, 42, 58, 70, 119, 124, 136, 153, 158, 177–85, 204, 208, 214–15, 222–23, 244, 255–56, See Metalepsis
empire, 13–14, 93, 154
encomium, 185
encyclopedic relationships/knowledge, 129–30, 139–41
enthymeme, See argumentation
enunciation, xvi, 187–206
eschatology, 12, 37n38, 65, 165, 172, 184, 217, 248–49, 252
ethics, 12, 82n4, 106–9, 115–17, 125–26, 236
ethos, 132
extratextual, 129–30, 256

feminist (interpretation), 13, 110
fictitious self-exposition, 242, 245, 248, 251–52
figurative/Figural language, 81–91, 210
focalization, 24, 237

foreshadow, See shadow
forgery, 18–19, 244n13, 245n18

Gemara, 72–72
genealogy, xv, 22–28, 108, 125, 139, 141–46, 257–58
generative intertextuality, 131–33, 135, 138, 146
genre, Gattung, 14n37, 17, 22, 137, 165, 233, 244n14, 246
Gezerah shavah, 65–70, 73–79, 227

Haggadah – See Aggadah
Halakah, 63, 67
Heqesh, 68
hermeneutic(s), 29–42, 63, 65n4, 82n4, 83, 117, 141, 168n8, 188, 204, 254
Hey Jude, 219
Hillel (school of Interpretation), xv, 65–68, 70
historical correlation, 261
historical intertexture, 154–55, 158, 160
historical plausibility (criteria), 33, 208n5
history of interpretation (criteria), 33, 208n5
Holocaust, 107–9, 111, 117, 122
hook words, See catchwords, Gezerah shavah
household, 35–36
humor, 26, 239
hymn, xiv, 34, 177–86
hypertextuality, xv, 16–28
hypotext, 18–19, 21, 25, 27

"I-You," 188–90
illiteracy, See literacy
imitation, xv, 4, 5n9, 18–20, 28, 134, 140, 183, 227, See Mimesis
infancy narrative, 108–9, 117–25, 139–45
inspiration, See spiritual inspiration/ illumination
intent(ion), 9, 21, 33, 50, 60, 83, 112–13, 115, 118, 120, 128, 136, 209–10, 219, 221, 223, 226, 231, 236, 240, 243–44, 247n32, 256–57

internal chronology, 261
interpretability (criteria), 97, 102, 105
intertextuality, v–vi, xiii–xix, *See* allusion, criteria, echo, modes of intertextuality, quotation
intratextual, 26, 130, 135–36, 139, 242
irony, 9, 12, 71n21, 143–44, 214, 239

Kal wa⬚omer, 65
kerygma, 64, 70, 195, 199
Kethib/Qere, 8, 119, 124

lamb, xiv, 6–14, 66–67, 180
Law, *See* Torah
lion, xiv, 6–14, 103, 252
literacy, illiteracy, 50–54
literary dependence, xvii, 255–71
logical directness/indirectness. *See* directness
logical relationships, 261–62

metalepsis, xv, 29–41, 70, 136n14, 228, 236
metaphor, 10, 73, 76, 82–84, 87, 90, 120, 151, 160, 162, 229, 247, 249–50, 252–53
metatextuality, 17
Middot (seven rules), 65–66
Midrash, xv, 4, 11, 63–80, 118, 120
militarism, 9–12, 14, 24, 247, 252n55
mimesis, xv, 93–105
Mishnah, 52
modes of intertextuality (writing, reading, composing), 131–37, 141–42, 145
monotheism, 181–85, 233, 236
motive (intertextual), 233, *See* Intent(ion)
multidimensional intertextuality, xvi–vii, 222–41

narrative transformation, xvi, 165–75
new creation, 184
new Jerusalem, 6–7
norms of language, 228

Odysseus, 94–96, 98–103, 105

optimal relevance, 211–21, *See* relevance theory
orality, oral tradition, xvi, 53, 55, 70, 97, 104, 152, 155–56, 158–61, 176–86,
oral-scribal intertexture, 152–53, 155–56, 158–60
order (criteria), 97

parallelomania, 222–23, 254, 272
parallels, xvi–viii, 19, 34, 72n25, 75, 84, 87, 91, 97–98, 103–5, 173, 182, 223–24, 254–71
Passover, 66–67, 78
pathos, 200
perceived response (communal), 234
personification, 57, 187–206
Pesher, 64n3, 118, 231
phenotext, 235, 237, 240
Philo(nic) interpretation, 85–87
Plato(nism), 84, 86–87, 89–90
plot, 18, 26, 31, 95–96, 100, 171, 175, 187, 234, 238, 246
poetic effects, 45, 214, 217, 220–21
poetry, 4–5, 31, 45, 57, 74n31, 130, 132, 138, 214, 217, 220, 221n35
polemic, 239, 246
poststructuralism, xiv–xiv, 106–27
prayer, 35, 96, 169–70, 203–4, 216
prefiguration, 78, *See* shadow
pretext, 226–28, 235, 240
processing effort, xvi, 211–15
production-oriented intertextuality, 130–32, 135, 139, 141, 145–46
prophecy, prophetic fulfillment, 17, 20, 58–59, 64–65, 71, 83, 93, 96, 99, 111, 118, 229, 133, 140, 143–45, 170–72, 174, 204, 218–19, 224n11, 227, 236, 240
Pseudepigraphy, 243n12, 244n13, 245, 270–71

Qal wahomer, *See Kal wa⬚omer*
quotation, xiii–xv, xviii–viii, 6n13, 17, 21, 32, 34n28, 35, 40, 42–62, 69–70, 77, 79, 91, 118–20, 124, 131–33, 136, 140–43, 151–55, 169, 177–83, 185, 187–88,

190–200, 203–5, 214, 218–19,
    222–24, 232, 234, 240, 243–44,
    254–56
  quotation formulae, xviii, 43n3, 118,
    120, 124, 139–40, 223–24
  mixed quotation, 234–35

Rahab, 26–27
reception-oriented intertextuality,
    130–32, 135, 146
recognition (criteria), 97, 103
reconfiguration, xvi, 107, 112, 151–53,
    156, 158–59, 161, 181
re-contextualization, xiv, 71–72,
    152–53, 155–56, 222–27, 230, 32,
    234, 237–40
recurrence (criteria), repetition, 9, 33,
    36, 38, 120, 208n5, 214, 224–26
reference-text-oriented allusions, xvii,
    242–53
Relevance Theory, xvi, 207–221
responsible reading, xvi, 109
resurrection, 31–32, 64, 121, 140, 158–
    59, 161–63, 169, 171, 173–74,
    199, 201, 229–30, 232, 247n28
rhetoric, xv, xvi, 4–5, 30–31, 33n23,
    38n41, 70–71, 88, 93, 114, 130,
    178, 183, 188, 190, 195n16,
    198, 213–14, 223, 34, 239,
    See Argumentation, Pathos,
    Sociorhetorical
rhetoric of quotation, 42–62
rhetorical force, 151, 164
righteous sufferer, 34–37
righteousness, xiv, 55, 126, 169–70,
    172, 188, 197–201, 252, 266
rock, 73–75, 79
Ruth, 22–28

Sabbath, 66–67, 86, 88
sacrifice, sacrificial, xiv, 8, 10, 13, 66,
    72–73, 76–77, 83, 89–90, 160,
    169, 180, 249, 253
salvation, 36–37, 79, 81, 84, 90, 144,
    166, 168–69, 171–72, 183–84,
    199–201, 208, 216, 249, 252
Samaritan Midrash, 73n28
Satan, devil, 9–10, 12

satisfaction (criteria), 33, 208n5
semantics, 83, 113, 129–30
semiotics, xvi, 4, 5n9, 113, 128–46
seventy-seven times, 37–40
shadows, foreshadow, xv, 63, 73, 81–91
slave(ry), 31, 36, 39, 96, 154, 208–14,
    266, 268
social intertexture, xvi, 154, 158–59
social setting/context/background, 35,
    37, 42, 44, 46, 49, 51–52, 106–7,
    113, 121, 130, 161, 163–64
sociorhetorical 51–64, 223
sociological dynamics/models, 223,
    229–30
spiritual inspiration/illumination 67,
    70–71, 224n11, 227
stylometric method, 256–57
symbol/symbolic, 7, 9–10, 14, 85–87,
    90, 111, 132, 153, 250n45

Talmud, 52, 66–67, 73, 79n50
Tel Quel, xiv, 107
temporal mode, 261
tendencies, 261–62
testimonia, 79n50
text (definition), 3–4
thematic coherence (criteria), 33, 38,
    208n5, 256
tongues (other), 56–61
Torah, xv, 52, 55, 57, 63, 65–68, 84–90,
    156, 158, 169–73, 182, 187,
    197–98, 225–26, 232, 236, 238
transfiguration, 18–19, 21, 95
transformation, xiv, xvi, 5, 7, 17–20,
    26, 28, 71, 106, 110, 115, 118,
    139–40, 145, 151n2, 184, 242, See
    narrative transformation
transposition, 18–19
transtextuality, 16–17, 20
transumption, 31–32
triumphal procession, 160–61, 163
typology, 4, 78, 84–85, 88–89, 181,
    222. See shadow

universe of discourse, 129–30, 135,
    140–41, 144

veil(ed), 5, 107, 157n22, 243

verbatimity, 224–26
volume (criteria), xvii, 33n22, 38,
    208n5
Vorlage, 222, 224, 237

wilderness, 132, 72–79, 81

"With–us–God", 140–42
woman, Women, 22–28, 51, 56, 77,
    95–96, 116, 125, 142–43, 145,
    217, 229
worldview, 223, 226, 230–32, 239–40

Made in the USA
Middletown, DE
02 November 2016